Population and Economic Development in Brazil

1800 to the Present

Population and Economic Development in Brazil

1800 to the Present

THOMAS W. MERRICK
and DOUGLAS H. GRAHAM

THE JOHNS HOPKINS UNIVERSITY PRESS
Baltimore and London

Copyright © 1979 by The Johns Hopkins University Press

Manufactured in the United States of America

The Johns Hopkins University Press, Baltimore, Maryland 21218
The Johns Hopkins Press Ltd., London

Library of Congress Catalog Number 78–20523
ISBN 0–8018–2182–7

Library of Congress Cataloging in Publication data
will be found on the last printed page of this book.

Contents

Tables

Figures

Preface

Brazil has emerged in the 1970s as one of the most dynamic and controversial models of economic development in the Third World. While aggregate economic growth has been impressive, stubborn issues such as equity, an increasing debt burden, and dependence on outside energy sources remain. Population—its size, structure, and geographic distribution—touches on almost every aspect of Brazilian economic development. Population increase has slowed somewhat from its peak level of previous decades, but Brazil still ranks among the most rapidly growing countries of the world. Faced with the prospect of feeding, housing, educating, and employing these increased numbers, Brazilian authorities are recognizing more and more the importance of the demographic aspect of development planning.

This is a study of the demographic dimension of Brazilian economic development. It seeks a deeper understanding not only of recent economic and demographic trends but also of the broader historical perspective that is so often lacking in the literature on economic-demographic relations in the developing countries. Brazil offers attractive and at the same time challenging opportunities for such an effort because of its rich but largely untapped store of demographic data, an extensive literature on its economic history, as well as the variety and complexity of economic and demographic patterns revealed by these sources.

Our approach is fundamentally empirical; the objective is to mine census and survey data for clues to questions that have been raised in the theoretical and empirical literature on population and development, and by the data themselves. It is a method that reflects the strong influence of our mentors, Simon Kuznets and Richard A. Easterlin. Indeed, the idea for undertaking the task of putting together a long-term review of population and development in Brazil was inspired by Easterlin's "The American Population" (1972). Both provided valuable comments on an earlier version.

We are indebted to a number of colleagues who generously provided helpful suggestions on the manuscript, including Eduardo Arriaga, Werner Baer, Jorge Balán, Mary Garcia Castro, Bainbridge Cowell, Jr., David Denslow, Peter Eisenberg, Tomas Frejka, Thomas Holloway, Martin Katzman,

Herbert Klein, George Martine, Robert McLaughlin, Jaime Reis, and Wilson Suzigan. Needless to say, the responsibility for errors and omissions remains our own.

We would also like to acknowledge the assistance of Carol Dunham, Jacqueline Hafner, Jacqueline Mulcare, Kathleen Paroby, Nancy Piness, Ronnie Rabin, and Nicoletta Tavares at Georgetown University and Roberta Riddle and Mary Ann Thinnes at Ohio State University in the preparation of the manuscript, especially its many tables and references.

This study draws on earlier versions of work that has been published in the following journals: *Demography, Economic Development and Cultural Change, Estudos Econômicos, The Journal of Developing Areas, Pesquisa e Planejamento Econômico,* and *Population and Development Review.*

The project originated during the authors' tenure as visiting professors at CEDEPLAR, The Center for Regional Development and Planning of the University of Minas Gerais, with the support of the Ford Foundation, and at IPE, The Institute for Economic Research of the University of São Paulo, under the AID/Vanderbilt program for Graduate Economics in Brazil. More recently, partial sources of support for the effort include the Rockefeller Foundation (Grants #72029 and 76102); The Kennedy Institute, Center for Population Research, at Georgetown University; the Institute for Economic Research at the University of São Paulo; and the Department of Agricultural Economics and Rural Sociology at Ohio State University.

The authors' participation in closely related projects on Brazil with the World Bank and Agency for International Development has also contributed. Brazil's Census Bureau, the Fundação IBGE, and its president, Dr. Isaac Kerstenetzky, provided invaluable assistance with numerous documents and special census tabulations. Words are not adequate to describe the value of the support and collaboration of the directors and staff members of our host institutions, Paulo R. Haddad and José Alberto M. de Carvalho at CEDE-PLAR and Affonso C. Pastore and José R. Mendonça de Barros at IPE. We alone are responsible for the statements and interpretations that follow. For their continuing encouragement over the several years that this work has been in progress, we dedicate it to our spouses, Jill Merrick and Jane Graham.

Population and Economic Development in Brazil

1800 to the Present

I   Population and Economic Development in Brazil: Introduction

Brazil, like the United States, is one of the few countries in the world to have experienced comparatively high rates of population growth for a century or more. In contrast to the United States, Brazil's population growth rate has accelerated rather than declined in this century, so that it is rapidly on its way to becoming the most populous nation in the Western Hemisphere. From a total of about 3 million in 1800, Brazil's population expanded to 10 million at the time of the first census in 1872. In the century between 1872 and 1972, there was a tenfold increase to 100 million, implying an average annual rate of growth of 2.3 percent. Though a portion of this growth was concentrated in periods of high immigration (1890–1900) and natural increase (1950–70), growth rates of around 2 percent per annum were sustained over the entire period.

While the rate of population growth in Brazil between 1950 and 1970 was (at 3 percent per annum) among the highest in the world, Brazilian reaction to the notion that this high rate of growth was an impediment to economic development has ranged from skeptical to hostilely negative. The roots of this opposition are varied, but they would certainly include the strong nationalist sentiment of Brazilian political and military philosophy, as well as a sophistication in economic thinking, which recognizes that population factors have had relatively little to do with ups and downs in the recent performance of the Brazilian economy.

Outside observers, even convinced neo-Malthusians, are forced to take a second look at conclusions about the adverse effects of rapid population growth on economic development in view of Brazil's outstanding recent economic growth performance, even with a high rate of population increase. The traditional macroeconomic argument incorporating the double effect of high fertility on per capita income growth (slowing capital formation and product growth through high dependency ratios, while increasing the population denominator of the per capita income equation) is not very convincing in the Brazilian case. Former Finance Minister Delfim Netto relished rebutting this argument by pointing out the much greater impact of fiscal incentive programs

1

on per capita GNP growth compared to what might be accomplished by reducing the population growth rate.

The political economy of Brazil's population size and growth can be traced to colonial times and to the need for population to establish hegemony over territory that was being contested by Spain and other European colonizers. At the same time, the expansion of the plantation system generated a large demand for cheap labor, which led Brazil to become the largest single participant in the slave traffic in the Western Hemisphere. The abolition of slavery and expansion of the coffee trade created further demand for labor and the need to promote European immigration in the nineteenth century. The resulting growth of population, as well as the entrepreneurial spirit of Italian immigrants in São Paulo, made an important contribution to the expansion of industry in Brazil during the later years of the expansion of the coffee trade.

Population size figures strongly in Brazil's current aspirations to become a major world power. It already ranks among the "top ten" in terms of territory, total GNP, and population. It has made striking progress in narrowing the gap in per capita GNP between itself and the major industrial powers (according to the most recent *World Bank Atlas*, the ratio of U.S. to Brazilian GNP per capita dropped from 11.3 to 6.9, i.e., by 39 percent, between 1970 and 1975).[1] A postage stamp was issued to commemorate Brazil's achievement of a 100 million population in 1972 (which also corresponded to the centennial of its first census in 1872), and newspaper accounts of the event speculated hopefully about the amount of time that it would take to reach 200 million, making careful note of the rapidity with which Brazil was closing this gap vis-à-vis the United States.

Brazil's position on the question of population and development was articulated strongly at the 1974 World Population Conference and incorporated in its most recent development plan.[2] It was supported by the majority of the Third World representatives at the conference. Population per se is not an obstacle to development; rather development is the key to demographic modernization. Much attention has been drawn to an apparent break in Brazil's "hard line" on publicly supported family planning in the Brazilian Ambassador's closing statement to the conference that governments should, for welfare objectives, make family planning available to couples whose low income may prove an obstacle in their access to these services. Still, this was prefaced by a strong and emphatic denial of the need to control population growth in order to achieve macroeconomic objectives.

Since the 1974 statements, Brazilians have been cautiously rethinking their position. They are not yet ready to accept the notion that slower population growth might be beneficial, nor have they moved very forcefully to implement

---

[1]See *World Bank Atlas*, Washington: The World Bank, 1978, pp. 4–5.

[2]See Brazil, Secretaria de Planejamento, 1974. A detailed discussion of the population policy articulated in this plan is presented in Chapter XI.

the recommendation to broaden access to family planning for those who cannot afford it. On the other hand, population questions have not been left out of discussions of the path of the Brazilian model under the Figueiredo administration, which takes office in March 1979. President Ernesto Geisel, whose term ends at that time, reflected some of this thinking in an interview given during a visit to Mexico in late 1977. When asked whether Brazil would benefit from a population policy similar to Mexico's (which in 1973 turned from a pronatalist position to adoption of family planning in order to reduce the adverse effects of its rapid population increase[3]), Geisel replied that Brazil still viewed the main task to be provision of employment, schools, and other basic necessities for its increasing population, but admitted that the task was not easy. His closing remarks on family planning capture much of the current thinking in Brazil:

> Another formula, unquestionably, is the limitation of the birth-rate. This is the formula which the developed countries have adopted and which gets implemented as people get more educated. You will see that it is the more favoured classes, the more educated ones, the ones with greater financial resources, who do their own family planning and limit their birth-rate. And it is exactly the poorer classes, the sick, the less educated, those who have the least working capacity, who have the biggest families. And this then means, in the human sense, almost a degeneracy? We believe that birth limitation must not be imposed. It must remain at the discretion, at the will, at the choice of the couple. It is up to the husband and to the wife to resolve their problem. But they must be informed about the issue. And they must receive guidance about how to carry out their own family planning. This is my personal viewpoint. Let me say that this is not yet happening in Brazil. In Brazil, in a general way, there is a decrease in the population growth rate, but this is spontaneous, it is very slow and, if we look forward to this image in the year 2000, the problem may become perhaps extremely serious and very difficult if we do not start now thinking a little bit more about family planning (cited in Rodriques, 1978).

The extent to which these views will be reflected in policies of the Figueiredo administration remains to be seen, but the need and desire for deeper understanding of the relation between population and development in Brazil is clear.

In this study, we seek a critical understanding of the Brazilian viewpoint. On the one hand, we think that a balanced assessment requires understanding of historical Brazilian concerns with labor supply, market size, and settlement of her vast territory, along with the more recent emphasis on the role of population size in achievement of world power status. On the other hand, we agree with critics, many of them Brazilian, who observe that past preoccupation with aggregative growth objectives, not only the demographic but also those touching other facets of the socioeconomic structure, has come at the expense of avoidable social costs on the micro or individual/family level. Indeed, aggregative concerns may have led to the neglect of important demographic

[3]See Ellen M. Brennan (1977), for details of Mexico's population policy.

dimensions of these social issues, particularly those affecting the welfare of lower-income groups on such scores as adequate employment and earnings opportunities, access to adequate housing, health services, and education.

We propose to trace the basic contours of Brazilian demographic history over the last two centuries and, in so doing, establish the role that demographic factors have played in past and current development in Brazil. In part, the historical emphasis has been adopted in order to avoid hinging the discussion of economic-demographic relations in Brazil on the upsurge in population growth that has characterized the post-World War II period. While not denying its significance, we feel that this period in Brazilian economic-demographic history needs to be understood in relation to the socioeconomic structural relations that emerged during the export cycle, which ran from the mid-nineteenth century to the world depression of the 1930s. The regionally diverse and somewhat halting demographic transition process that Brazil now appears to be entering cannot be evaluated without reference to this structural legacy.

The discussion begins with a brief overview of Brazilian economic history from colonial times to the 1970s (Chapter II), which is designed to introduce readers not familiar with the main features of the Brazilian economy to the historical framework in which the study has been undertaken. This is followed by a detailed analysis of major trends in the growth of population since 1800 and of the demographic composition of that growth (Chapter III). This demographic profile of Brazil identifies several major phases underlying the long-term trend, which correspond to related socioeconomic changes and to the varying demographic parameters associated with each. It concludes with a comparison of Brazilian patterns to those of other Latin American countries and to the United States, the only country in the Western Hemisphere whose demographic history shares the scope and extension of the Brazilian experience.

Chapters IV and V focus on the two major socioeconomic-demographic institutions associated with the coffee export phase in Brazilian economic history: slavery and European immigration. Major attention is given to data on the demographic characteristics of the slave population in early Brazilian censuses, to the issue of slave mortality, and to the relative importance of manumission and natural increase in the growth of both the slave and free population in the nineteenth century. Abolition and the problems associated with the transition to wage labor are also discussed, emphasizing contrasts between the Brazilian experience and those of other immigrant-receiving countries in the late nineteenth and early twentieth centuries. Census data are also used to analyze the contribution of foreign-born labor to the economic expansion that Brazil experienced in both the agricultural and industrial sectors in the early decades of this century.

Regional diversity has characterized both economic and demographic trends in Brazil since the colonial period, and Chapter VI examines changes in the spatial distribution of population over the long run (1778–1970), as well as the differential patterns of migration and natural increase that have shaped the regional population structure. Census data are utilized to estimate inter-regional migration flows during a century-long span, and the relation of these flows to major socioeconomic trends is analyzed.

The focus then shifts to long-term trends in the growth and structure of the Brazilian labor force (Chapter VII). Though all but one of the Brazilian censuses taken since 1872 have included information on the economic characteristics of the population, changes in the institutional and statistical meaning of economic activities require that much care be exercised in tracing the path of Brazilian labor force growth. Chapter VII attempts to reconstruct labor force trends in the early censuses and to compare the main patterns of change in the century between Brazil's first national census in 1872 and the most recent one in 1970. Detailed attention is given to changes in occupational structure during the import substitution phase, from 1950 to 1970, including an analysis of shifts in the composition of economic activity by occupation and branch of activity.

Urban population growth trends are reviewed in Chapter VIII. Starting with the export growth period in the nineteenth century, the evolution of Brazil's urban structure is tracked through to the post-World War II industrial expansion. Structural changes in the distribution of the urban population by region and city-size class are described and analyzed. The chapter concludes with a comparison of urban growth to recent trends in the expansion of industrial sector employment and the effects of its high rate of concentration along the Rio de Janeiro-São Paulo axis on problems of its high rate of urban development.

This theme is continued in Chapter IX, which addresses the problem of urban poverty, and seeks to determine the extent to which the imbalance between industrial employment and urban population growth has led to greater unemployment, underemployment, and a worsened urban income distribution. Special attention is given to the effects of this imbalance on the structure of urban labor markets and to the role that employment in the less capitalized, less organized urban informal sector has played in urban labor absorption and the generation of earnings for the low-income population. Since migration has been a major demographic factor in the recent growth of Brazilian cities, comparisons of migrant and native performances on employment and earnings scales have been assembled in a synthesis of the voluminous research that has been produced from special tabulations of the 1970 census and in several recent survey research projects.

Chapters X and XI return to the broader question of population and economic development. A major issue revolves around the applicability to Brazil of demographic transition theory, which has been utilized to explain the relation of industrialization and urbanization to declines in fertility and mortality in Europe. Important doubts have arisen about the use of this theory in predicting a reduction in population growth in developing countries, because exogenous factors (public health and mass inoculation programs) brought mortality declines in an earlier stage of industrialization, while birth rates have remained high. There is major concern that the resulting rapid rate of population growth would stymie the very process of growth in per capita income needed to bring a reduction in fertility. Chapter X attempts to assess the demographic side of the transition paradigm for Brazil by analyzing the relation of fertility and mortality trends to socioeconomic changes that have occurred in the postwar period. Important aspects of both regional and rural-urban differentials are brought into this assessment.

Chapter XI looks at the other side of the coin, the effect of Brazil's rapid population increase on economic growth in this period. Both macro- and microeconomic dimensions of recent economic-demographic relations are reviewed, with attention to possible conflicts between macro growth objectives and social costs incurred at the level of individual welfare. Human resource capacity implications of the changes in population composition deriving from recent growth are also studied. The entire discussion is presented in the context of Brazilian economic planning and the role that demographic factors have been assigned in that process.

Chapter XII looks ahead both to the immediate future of Brazilian population growth in the remaining decades of this century and to the eventual stabilization of population size sometime in the next. It continues the focus on demographic factors in long-term economic planning adopted in Chapter XI and emphasizes the implications of changes in population structure as stability is approached for the design of strategies to provide education, employment, housing, and other services for the two or three "other Brazils" that the momentum of current population growth seems almost certain to bring.

We conclude with a summary of our findings and an attempt to synthesize the lessons that can be learned from the Brazilian experience in the understanding of economic-demographic relations. This synthesis falls short of proposing a "Brazilian model" of population and economic development, in part because the story is still unfolding, but also because we are convinced that the Brazilian experience cannot be forced into the mold of an adapted neo-Malthusian model of the adverse effects of population growth on economic development.

The outcome of present and future interactions between population increase and economic development in Brazil depends, in the last analysis, on the response of Brazilian authorities to the challenges and opportunities represented by her recent experience. While the achievements of recent years have been impressive, the implications of continued growth with unequal distribution of its benefits are serious. We hope that this effort to lay out the demographic evidence will be useful to those responsible for decisions affecting the path of Brazilian growth and to those who are seeking to understand the dynamics of our ambitious neighbor to the South.

II The Brazilian Economy in Historical Perspective

Introduction

Brazil is striking to those who observe it for the first time both in size and in diversity. Its area of 8.5 million square kilometers is surpassed only by the Soviet Union, Canada, China, and the United States. This territory comprises about half of the South American continent and is three times larger than the next largest country in Latin America, Argentina. In this expanse, one encounters important differences in culture, geography, and economic development. Indigenous Indian populations still inhabit the Amazon region, and Afro-Brazilian cultural influences are evident especially in Bahia, Pernambuco, and Minas Gerais, where slavery was once important. Portuguese and Italian immigrant influences are strong in Rio de Janeiro and São Paulo, while communities in which the main language spoken is German or Japanese illustrate the importance of these immigrant groups in the Southern part of the country. Brazil contains some of the poorest as well as some of the wealthiest areas of Latin America. Much of the Northeastern region is still dominated by subsistence agriculture, while the booming industrial South, centered in São Paulo, is often compared to Japan, because of the economic dynamism that it has shown in the last several decades.

This chapter is a general introduction to Brazil and an overview of the important events in Brazilian economic history needed to create a backdrop for the discussions of economic-demographic interrelations in later chapters. For earlier periods, it draws heavily on economic histories by Roberto C. Simonsen (1969), Celso Furtado (1971), and Caio Prado, Jr. (1971), as well as the recent work of Villela and Suzigan (1973). For more recent trends, a number of commentators on industrialization and its consequences in Brazil have been utilized.[1]

[1]See especially Baer (1975), Bergsman (1970), Tavares (1972), Furtado (1972), Ellis (1969), and Suzigan et al. (1972).

Geography

Brazil's geographic position, straddling the equator, has endowed it with both tropical and subtropical climates.[2] Rainfall, latitude, and altitude contribute to the climatic variations that are observed. A high plain (the *planalto*) encompasses much of the central Brazilian land mass, and is ridged by several mountain chains running in a generally southwest to northeast direction. The first of these chains is a coastal escarpment that divides the relatively narrow coastal plain from the interior. Bordering the *planalto* are two large basins that spread out over the territory covered by Brazil's main river systems, the Amazon and its tributaries, which cut a wide path as they flow from West to East just below the equator, and the Paraná system, which flows from North to South through Southwestern Brazil to become the River Plata in Argentina and Uruguay. Temperatures range from very hot most of the year in the tropical rain forests of the Amazon region, to the chilly and damp Southern winters. A wide band of lands, starting on the Northeast coast and then jutting out from the Amazon into the interior in a Southwesterly direction, is known as the *sertão*. This region is a semiarid high plain and has suffered many severe droughts. The São Francisco River, which runs through this area, is an important feature of the area's geography. In contrast, the low plains that follow Brazil's Atlantic coastline are warm and humid, with more rain in the winter months (June–August). Rainfall is more regular and temperature variation is less in the interior *planalto* regions located further to the South and West.

Brazilian geographers have divided the country into five major regions for purposes of social and economic description.[3] Summary data on these regions for around 1970 are presented in Table II–1. The first region is the North, which includes most of the Amazon basin and is the largest, with 42 percent of the land area. It is also the least populated, with 4 percent of the total. Its population density in 1970 was just over one person per square kilometer, and this average is an overstatement because most of the region's population is concentrated in and around the cities of Manaus and Belém. Per capita income was a little more than half of the national average.

The second region, the Northeast, consists of nine states that run along the Atlantic coast from Maranhão to Bahia and accounts for 18 percent of the land area. This region includes most of the *sertão* as well as a narrow coastal plain suitable for tropical agriculture. Most of its population is concentrated along

[2]See Andrade (1973), Smith (1972), and Poppino (1973). These books give detailed data on the geographic and social setting in Brazil. Poppino's overview of Brazilian history is especially useful background.

[3]See Brazil, Fundação IBGE (1971). The regional breakdown employed in the 1970 census differs somewhat from that used in 1960, with the main change involving São Paulo being moved from the Southern to Southeastern region, and Bahia and Sergipe being moved from the Southeast to the Northeast.

Figure II-1. Map of Brazil Showing Macroregions, States, and Main Cities.

the coast. While the Northeast holds 30 percent of the national population, it contributes a little less than 12 percent of national income—thus leaving it with a per capita income level of less than half the national average.

Third comes the Southeastern region, which contains Brazil's urban-industrial heartland, including her three largest cities, São Paulo, Rio de Janeiro, and Belo Horizonte—as well as 43 percent of the national population. This region comprises 11 percent of the national territory. Rich mineral deposits in Minas Gerais and farmlands in São Paulo contribute to its wealth. The region dominates Brazil economically, in all sectors, with 65 percent of total income originating here and a per capita income that is 53 percent greater than the national average. This dominance is even more pronounced in its share of urban population (56 percent) and manufacturing output (80 percent).

The fourth region is the South of Brazil, which starts in Paraná and includes Santa Catarina and Rio Grande do Sul. It is also endowed with good agricultural land, but has less industry than the Southeast. Still it is quite prosperous, especially when compared to the predominantly agricultural but

Table II-1. Characteristics of the Major Regional Subdivisions of Brazil, 1970

Region	Area	Percentage of total Population	Urban population	Output	Industry output	Population density (persons per square kilometer)	Income per capita (Brazil = 100)
North	42.0	3.9	3.1	2.1	1.1	1.03	54
Northeast	18.3	30.2	22.6	11.7	5.6	18.59	39
Southeast	10.8	42.8	55.5	65.5	80.3	43.90	153
South	6.8	17.7	14.1	17.1	12.0	29.68	97
Central-West	22.1	5.4	4.7	3.6	1.0	2.75	72
TOTAL	100.0	100.0	100.0	100.0	100.0	11.18	100

Source: Fundação IBGE, Anuário Estatístico do Brasil, 1971; Fundação Getúlio Vargas, Conjuntura Econômica 31 (July 1977): 90–102.

poor Northeast. Its share of income and population were both about 17 percent and its per capita income just equal to the national average.

The last region is the Central-West, the new frontier of the sixties. It is the second largest in area, with 22 percent of the national total, and next to least populated with 5 percent of the total. This region also is mainly agricultural. Availability of agricultural land in the Central-West has drawn many settlers from rural areas in both the Northeast and the Southeast, where land is now more limited. The new federal capital, Brasília, is located in the region, and this, in combination with its proximity to markets for farm products in the Southeast, has contributed to the agricultural expansion that is occurring there.

The Colonial Heritage

The temporal scope of the material that follows covers a period that starts at the beginning of the nineteenth century and runs to the present. This starting point corresponds roughly with the end of the colonial period in Brazil. It is also significant in that it marks a time of important changes in the world economy. These include the final decline of Spanish and Portuguese influence in the Western Hemisphere (as their homelands were occupied by Napoleon's armies) and further consolidation of British influence in these areas, especially after Napoleon's defeat. Transfer of the Portuguese court to Rio de Janeiro, because of the Napoleonic occupation of Lisbon, led eventually to Brazilian independence, and the rise in British influence led to a new set of trade and financial relationships that dominated the Brazilian economy for most of the nineteenth century (Furtado 1971: 98).

While the colonial era falls outside the scope of this study, it set patterns that are important for the understanding of later trends and events. Thus a brief synopsis of colonial history will be useful. Much of the diversity of Brazil—cultural as well as economic—stems from the colonial period. Most of the acquisition of her vast territory took place during that time. Domination of the economy by a series of export growth cycles, which has only recently begun to change, dates from the very beginning of colonial days.

Almost from the moment of Cabral's landing in 1500, the Portuguese exploited Brazil's natural wealth. Brazilwood, from which the country took its name, was the first of these resources whose value was recognized. It was the basis for her first export boom, which took place in the sixteenth century. That century was also marked by a struggle with France for control of Brazilian territory. The latter part of this century brought another territorial struggle with the Dutch, who succeeded in occupying part of the sugar region around Recife for a period in the seventeenth century.

Though the Treaty of Tordesillas granted Portugal the lands of the Western Hemisphere East of a line at the longitude about 48 degrees west of Greenwich, it soon came to be recognized that sovereignty over the land depended more on occupation than claims. Starting with efforts to establish coastal outposts in the sixteenth century, this realization has evolved over the years as an important characteristic of Brazilian policy. It was later exemplified in expeditions of *bandeirantes* from São Paulo, who extended Portuguese occupation west of the Tordesillas line in the seventeenth century at the same time that they attempted to enslave Indians who lived in Jesuit reductions in Paraguay, (Poppino 1973: 72-84). This viewpoint on "occupational" sovereignty was formalized in the Treaty of Madrid in 1750, after which territorial limits were defined on the basis of possession rather than previous treaty lines.

By 1600, the colonial population had increased to 100,000 (Roberto C. Simonsen 1969: 121). Sugar production, which dominated the economic and social landscape for most of the colonial period, was by then the most important activity. Encouraged by rising European demand and facilitated by Dutch traders (who brought capital and know-how), the sugar economy flourished most in the humid littoral of Northeast Brazil. It was a plantation economy, with offshoots of smaller-scale farm units, which provided staples and draft animals. Efforts to exploit indigenous Indian labor proved unsuccessful, and the planters turned to the African slave trade for their supply of labor.[4] By the turn of the seventeenth century, 70 percent of the colonial population was non-European (Furtado 1971: 46).

The Brazilian sugar economy reached its high point in the middle of that century (Roberto C. Simonsen 1969:382). The Portuguese succeeded in expelling the Dutch from the Northeastern sugar regions, which had been occupied for a quarter of a century. Sugar accounted for 95 percent of the value of exports from the colony (see Table II–2). Furtado (1971:46) estimates that the per capita income of the plantation enclave in 1600 was about 350 dollars (1950 value), a level that exceeded that of many European countries of

---

[4]For a comprehensive review of the evolution of the plantation economy and slave labor, see Beckford (1972).

Table II-2. Brazilian Exports Distributed by Commodity Categories and per Capita, 1650-1950

	1650	1750	1800	1841-50	1891-1900	1921-30	1945-49	1970
A. Percentage share of main export categories in total earnings								
1. Sugar	95	47	31	26.7	6.0	1.4	1.2	4.9
2. Coffee	–	–	–	41.4	64.5	69.6	41.8	35.8
3. Cotton	–	–	6	7.5	2.7	2.4	13.3	6.0
4. Others– including minerals & manufactured goods	5	53	63	25.4	26.8	26.6	43.7	53.3
B. Export earnings per capita in gold pounds								
	23.5	2.9	1.1	0.8	1.7	2.2	a	a
C. Population in millions								
	0.17	1.5	3.3	6.7	16.4	32.0	48.5	93.1

[a]Comparable data not available; Dashes signify negligible.
    Source: 1560-1800, Simonsen (1969: 302) and Buescu (1970: 167, 199); 1841-1929, Fundação IBGE, Anuário Estatístico do Brasil, 1939/40, pp. 1358-81; 1945-49, Baer (1965: 36); 1970, Fundação IBGE, Anuário Estatístico do Brasil, 1971, pp. 305-09.

the time and one that Brazil was not to achieve again until the twentieth century. Of course, the benefits of this high per capita income were very narrowly distributed within the slave economy.

The prosperity was relatively short lived, though the importance of sugar in the economy did not diminish immediately. A combination of political and economic factors contributed to the decline.[5] Early in the seventeenth century, Portugal, while under Spanish domination, had lost some of her colonies in the Orient and also suffered a weakening of her position in the Atlantic. She turned to England for support in an effort to become more independent of Spain. The Methuen Treaty (1703) had important economic repercussions for both Portugal and Brazil. To counter Spanish influence and secure British protection for its Atlantic trade, Portugal conceded a commercial monopoly to English manufactures in her territories, at the same time agreeing not to establish her own competing industries. As a result, much of the gold mined in Brazil in the eighteenth century ended up as payment to English merchants.

A major blow to the sugar economy of the Northeast came with the establishment of competing production in the West Indies by the Dutch, English, and French. Though total demand was not immediately affected, profitability declined. Production was expanded with out-moded technology as slave prices increased. Caribbean countries had a greater comparative advantage in producing sugar. According to Furtado (1971: 69), the sugar economy drifted into stagnation during the eighteenth century. Many of the farmers who supplied food and draft animals to the sugar system fell back into

[5]For a recent analysis of why sugar maintained its regional dominance in the Northeast of Brazil at this time, in spite of the decline of sugar in world markets, see Taylor (1970).

subsistence agriculture during this period, though sugar continued to be an important crop in terms of total output. As profits declined, alternative economic opportunities were not available to absorb resources once needed for sugar production. Thus, stagnation became endemic to the Northeast.

Discovery of gold and diamonds in Minas Gerais around the turn of the eighteenth century began a gradual shift in the economic center of gravity from the Northeast to the South and brought considerable pressure on the limited colonial labor supply in the South. *Bandeirantes* from São Paulo led the penetration into these gold regions, and were soon followed by a wave of Portuguese immigrants. Brazil's population increased from around 300,000 at the beginning of the eighteenth century to over 3 million by the beginning of the nineteenth century (Furtado 1971: 36). This tenfold increase, consisting mainly of the Portuguese immigrants and slave imports, makes the eighteenth century the period of most rapid relative increase in Brazil's population.[6] Of course, the initial base was quite small. Larger absolute increases came later.

Minerals accounted for nearly half of the value of colonial exports during the peak of the boom in the middle decades of the century (Simonsen 1969: 382). Portuguese authorities attempted to control the extraction; they established accounting centers in several *Mineiro* towns, limited access to the region, and attempted to collect the royal *quinto* (or fifth) on all production. The efforts were less than successful. By the final decades of the century the dynamism of the gold expansion was lost and uprisings in protest against harsh colonial policies had occurred. The period also brought disruptive events in Europe, as mentioned at the beginning of this section: the French Revolution, the Napoleonic Wars and occupation of Lisbon, and further consolidation of British power with Napoleon's defeat. Brazilian exports fell by 40 percent in the last quarter of the century, and sugar sales fell to the lowest level in over two centuries.

Brazil in the Nineteenth Century

Furtado (1971: 96) has described the Brazilian economy at the beginning of the nineteenth century as a "series of systems, some of which were mutually connected whereas others remained nearly isolated." The two main nuclei were the sugar and gold economies, which were loosely connected through the cattle-breeding regions that ran along the São Francisco River. A third nucleus was found in the forest extractive system in Maranhão, which was the only part of Brazil to enjoy a relative degree of prosperity at the end of the eighteenth century. A limited boom was brought by the transfer of the Portuguese royal court to Rio de Janeiro in 1808, setting in motion a sequence of events that

[6]Data on African slave imports can be found in Curtin (1971) and Klein (1972). The next chapter provides further discussion of eighteenth-century population growth trends.

resulted in Brazilian independence in 1822, after Pedro I decided to remain in Brazil as Emperor, while his father King João VI returned to Lisbon (Poppino 1973: 178–82).

The nineteenth century brought a renewed expansion in the export economy established during the colonial period, though the start was sluggish. Furtado (1971: 11) is doubtful of any growth in per capita income in the first half of the century and estimates that the level at mid-century did not exceed that of the colonial period.[7] Sugar exports resumed after 1815, and cotton production gained importance. Both were prejudiced by falling prices in the 1820s but from the late 1830s through the 1860s sugar and cotton recorded respectable growth rates. Thereafter, coffee provided the main thrust to Brazil's nineteenth-century exports. Even by the 1830s it was already contributing more than 40 percent of the total value of exports.[8]

Cultivation of coffee started in the eighteenth century in the Paraíba River Valley, which runs through Southern Minas Gerais toward São Paulo. The region enjoyed access to the port of Rio de Janeiro and an available supply of slave labor from the declining mining areas to the north. Expansion of production was not inhibited by the general decline in commodity prices in the 1830s and 1840s, and the third quarter of the century brought a sizable upward trend in coffee prices. On the other hand, sugar prices declined from the 1870s onward, because of competition from Cuba and the surge in beet sugar production in Europe.

Coffee was less capital-intensive than sugar. However, it required about as much labor and was more land-intensive. Because of the abundance of suitable land, its expansion in Brazil was limited only by the supply of manpower. Labor supply became a critical issue when efforts to extend coffee into São Paulo were undertaken in the last quarter of the century. Major attention will be devoted to this question in later chapters. For now, it is sufficient to note that the abolition of the slave trade in 1851, dwindling supplies of slaves and limited employment of ex-slaves in the South, and the declining interregional transfers of slave labor from the Northeast all led Paulista planters to look to Southern Europe for most of the labor that was to establish coffee cultivation in their state.

The combination of available land (with unusual fertility and the proper climate and topography for coffee), immigrant labor, and increasing prices of coffee on the world market stimulated rapid expansion of coffee cultivation. National production doubled from the 1850s to the 1880s and then tripled in the last decade of the century. Coffee grew to account for nearly 70 percent of Brazilian export earnings. This, in combination with uninhibited expansion of coffee plantings and production, left Brazil extremely vulnerable to instability

[7]Furtado's estimates are based on the growth of exports, and thus do not reflect growth in the nonmonetary sectors.

[8]For detailed data on the growth and structure of Brazilian exports from 1821 to 1939, see Fundação IBGE, *Anuário Estatístico do Brasil 1939/40*.

in world markets. The first of a series of crises in export earnings, brought on by serious oversupply and a decline in the world market price for coffee, occurred at the end of the century.

The last quarter of the nineteenth century also brought a series of important political changes in Brazil (Poppino 1973: Chapter 6). A protracted war with Paraguay in the 1860s was very costly and revealed the many weaknesses of the imperial government. During these years, the coffee economy was also providing a basis for establishment of an entrepreneurial class in the state of São Paulo. This group exercised increasing economic and political influence over the country. They represented a contrasting and competing set of political views to the more traditionally oriented Northeastern planters. After more than a decade of debate about ending slavery and the gradual dissolution of the institution through manumission, abolition was formally decreed in 1888. The planters were nonetheless dissatisfied with abolition. This, and the disaffection of the army after the Paraguayan War, led to the overthrow of Emperor Pedro II, in 1889, and the establishment of a republic.

The Early Twentieth Century and Brazilian Industrialization up to 1945

At the beginning of the twentieth century Brazil had a population of nearly eighteen million. International migration, much of it to the coffee regions in São Paulo, had accelerated population growth.[9] In 1900, the country had become an export economy in the fullest sense. Sugar production was still the main economic activity of the Northeast, and there had been few changes in either the social or economic structure of the plantation economy since the colonial period. Cacao had risen to importance in Bahia, and cotton production had enjoyed a brief boom in the Northeast during the American Civil War. The turn of the century also brought a short-lived rubber boom in the Amazon region. At the center was coffee production, the hinge on which the Brazilian economy was to swing for several decades to come.

Up to this time, industrial development had been limited to artisan manufacturing in food-processing and clothing, often in rural areas (Baer and Villela 1973). Commercial privileges granted to the British early in the century and a free-trade policy emphasizing exports during the Imperial period had done little to encourage domestic manufactures. The Baron de Mauá was one of the few to encourage manufacturing before 1890. He was instrumental in the construction of railroads to transport coffee to the coast. The Republican period brought wider support for industrial expansion. The currency was devalued, tariffs were established, and government assistance was given to new industries. Brazilian textile and food-processing industries grew substantially in the period just prior to World War I.

[9]More detailed analysis of immigration appears in Chapter V.

The twentieth century revealed more and more of the inherent weaknesses of the export system. Overproduction and instability of world coffee prices brought severe fluctuations in the country's capacity to purchase manufactured goods. Rubber export earnings rose rapidly to nearly 40 percent of total exports in 1910, produced a brief boom in the import of capital goods, and then fell sharply.

Measures were taken to contain the overproduction of coffee and still maintain coffee earnings. Devaluation and government deficits in the 1890s had caused inflation as well as encouraged overproduction of coffee, so the new government revalued the currency in 1899 in an effort to stabilize the economy. In 1906, the first plan for the "valorization of coffee" was put into effect, with the objective of maintaining the earnings of the coffee-producing sector through limiting supply to the world market in support of higher prices. Defense of coffee came at the expense of other sectors, including the rest of agriculture, as well as industry, and led to increased indebtedness to the foreign banks that financed coffee stockpiling.

Brazilian economic history during the period of coffee expansion—roughly 1850 to 1920—is illustrative of both the possibilities and the problems of a staple model of economic development (Watkins 1963, Lewis 1970). Opinion is mixed about the benefits that accrued to Brazil from this period, though most would agree that a large portion of the economic issues of succeeding decades have roots in it: e.g., the extent to which the coffee-producing sector contributed to later industrialization through the earnings it generated and the immigrant labor force it attracted, as well as the regional inequalities either created or accentuated through the concentration of its benefits in the Southeastern region, especially São Paulo.

World War I further disrupted the flow of manufactured imports to the Brazilian market and brought a moderate decline in export earnings. There is disagreement on the extent to which domestic establishments filled the gap in supply of manufactured goods during the war (Villela and Suzigan 1973: 145–50). The immediate postwar period brought an expansion in the production of both coffee and manufactures, but the latter soon faced growing competition from the United States. Relatively free access to Brazilian markets and lower prices gave U.S. products an edge, while increased earnings of the coffee sector contributed to a new boom in imports financed from their earnings. At the same time, a portion of these earnings was channeled into capital formation in domestic manufacturing. By 1929, Brazilian establishments (especially in the textile industry) found themselves with excess manufacturing capacity (Villela and Suzigan 1973: 172–78, Furtado 1971: Chapter 31).

The situation changed abruptly with the world depression. By 1932, the total value of exports had fallen to 37 percent of their 1927 level, and imports were only 24 percent of what they had been at that date. However, the overcapacity that was built up during the 1920s helped to insulate Brazil from the worst effects of the depression, and the 1930s turned out to be a relatively important decade in the expansion of Brazilian manufacturing (Villela and Suzigan 1973: Chapter 6).

The 1930s were also marked by important political changes. Since the founding of the Republic in 1889, political power had been held by a coalition of land-owning interests in São Paulo and Minas Gerais. As urbanization and redistribution of economic power weakened this alliance, political forces from Rio Grande do Sul backed Getúlio Vargas in an unsuccessful bid for presidential election. This was followed by a successful coup when Getúlio's supporters refused to accept the manipulated 1930 election results. Vargas consolidated control, in his *Estado Novo* in 1937, and ruled dictatorially through World War II (Poppino 1973: 267–69). After being forced to leave the presidency in 1945, he ran for the office successfully in the elections of 1950, but was again faced with forced resignation in 1954 (Skidmore 1967, Schneider 1971). Vargas committed suicide rather than accept an ultimatum from the military, an act that helped Juscelino Kubitschek, a Vargas candidate, win the presidential election in 1955.

Vargas's government took an active interest in industrialization during the 1930s. Commercial and exchange policies were changed to maintain the balance of payments, but with beneficial effects for industry. Continued government cash deficits (in part unplanned) and exchange rate devaluation created the local purchasing power and protection required to make domestic industrial expansion profitable. Declining agricultural exports led to a structural shift in the economy, emphasizing domestic manufacturing. Villela and Suzigan (1973) estimate an 11 percent growth rate of industrial product from 1933 to 1939, in contrast to the stagnant industrial performance in the developed countries at this time. Overall growth was considerably less, because of limited demand for agricultural exports during the depression. Brazil's industrial recovery was highly labor-intensive with traditional industries like textiles and food-processing growing to meet growing domestic demand. Important advances were also made in newer areas like minerals, metal, chemical products, and paper. World War II brought further stimulus to manufacturing, though the pace of growth was slower because of shortages in equipment and fuel with which to maintain the expansion. Despite this, the Vargas administration was able to construct the huge state-owned steel complex at Volta Redonda, which more than doubled domestic capacity and stood as a symbol of the nationalistic economic sentiment of the time.

Postwar Industrialization and Import Substitution

By World War II, Brazil had a population of over 40 million. Participation in the war provided her first sense of involvement in the international arena and sparked recognition of a potential to become a world power. The war also left Brazil with a huge balance-of-payments surplus and considerable pent-up demand for consumer goods that were not yet manufactured domestically. Immediate postwar exchange policy overvalued the *cruzeiro* in an attempt to stem inflation and control coffee earnings.[10]

When the surplus was wiped out, in a little more than a year of unrestricted imports, licensing controls were instituted. But the overvalued currency remained. Export earnings declined until the Korean War boom, when a multiple exchange rate system was introduced in order to control the flow of imports. Both the licensing and multiple exchange rate systems favored capital and intermediate goods and were most restrictive on finished consumer goods, thus encouraging domestic production.

Protection of domestic industry was even more explicit in the commercial policy of the expansionist Kubitschek government (1956–60). A system of protective tariffs was instituted in 1957, with very high rates on consumer durables and other final consumption goods. Foreign direct manufacturing investment was given various subsidies in the automotive and other consumer goods industries. This period saw the first major postwar import-substituting industrial growth cycle build up from the mid 1950s to the early 1960s. Overall growth averaged about 8 percent per year and industrial growth 10 to 12 percent. The Kubitschek administration relaxed the more restrictive monetary policies of the early 1950s, which helped to sustain the boom. But this also led to overcapacity in the new industries and unleashed the massive inflation that was to plague his successors. Price increases rose to nearly 90 percent per annum in the early 1960s.[11]

Industrialization in the period from 1945 to 1964 brought a substantial substitution of domestic for imported manufactures (Bergsman 1970: 29–32). Table II–3 shows that the actual substitution of imports that occurred in this period was mainly in the capital goods and consumer durables categories. The share of imports in total domestic supply of consumer nondurables was less than 4 percent in 1949, and intermediate goods' imports were only 26 percent, suggesting that much of this type of import substitution had occurred earlier. Just 19 percent of all manufactures were imported as early as 1949. The largest change from 1945 to 1964 was in consumer durables, whose import share fell from 65 percent to 2 percent. Capital goods imports dropped from 64 percent to 10 percent, and the contribution of all imports to the total supply of manufactures in 1964 was a little over 4 percent. It should be noted that 1964 marked a trough in the economic downturn of the early 1960s, which had a depressing influence on capital imports. Recovery in the late 1960s and early

---

[10]For a summary of postwar commercial policy, see Bergsman (1970), Chapter 3. Overvaluation of the *cruzeiro* vis-a-vis the dollar kept the price of imported goods down (in terms of local currency) and thus helped contain inflation. However, it also stimulated imports to such an extent that a balance-of-payments deficit appeared. The overvaluation also penalized coffee exporters (who earned less in local currency), but this helped to control oversupply and maintain the world market price. Unfortunately, overvaluation penalized other exports as well, thus aggravating the balance-of-payments problem.

[11]See *Conjuntura Econômica* 25 (#9, 1971): 92.

Table II-3. Ratio of Imports to Domestic Supply of Manufactured Goods, 1949–66

	1949	1955	1959	1964	1966
			(percent)		
1. Consumer goods					
non-durables	3.7	2.2	1.1	1.2	1.6
durables	64.5	10.0	6.3	1.6	1.0
2. Producer goods					
intermediate	25.9	17.9	11.7	6.6	6.8
capital	63.7	43.2	32.9	9.8	13.7
3. All manufactured					
goods	19.0	11.1	9.7	4.2	5.0

Source: 1949–64, Bergsman (1970: 92); 1966, Baer (1975).

1970s brought renewed investment, and a rise of imported capital goods, with the rates of capital goods imports rising to 24 percent in 1970 and 28 percent in 1974 (Malan and Bonelli 1977).

Recent evaluations of postwar industrialization have made several criticisms of these policies (Bergsman 1973, Tavares 1972). Tariffs were placed on items whose import substitution had already been achieved, or were maintained too long after the initial protection was needed. An effect was to insulate domestic producers from foreign competition, which might have encouraged more rapid increase in productivity and a more competitive position for Brazilian manufactured exports in the world market. This was detrimental in traditional industries, where the high level of tariff protection was in fact redundant. On the other hand, the protective policies did make it possible to establish productive capacity in capital goods and in some of the more sophisticated consumer goods, which led in time to a degree of competitiveness in world markets.

Another criticism was that the technology that was imported to create domestic productive capacity was more suited to labor-scarce factor markets (like the United States) rather than Brazil's, which combined a scarcity of skilled labor with an abundance of unskilled workers. Industrial production expanded much more rapidly than industrial employment and absorbed only a fraction of the rapidly growing urban labor force (Baer and Hervé 1966). This was combined with an emphasis on the installation of "modern" industries (especially consumer durables), whose products were consumed by the upper classes, and the neglect of "traditional" sectors (like clothing and food processing), which catered to a broader spectrum of the population. The net effect was a worsening in the purchasing power of lower-class incomes and a general worsening of urban income distribution. Attempts to counteract this by controlling the price of staples consumed by urban workers were detrimental to the agricultural sector, and this, along with a generally low priority given to agriculture, did little to stem the exodus from rural areas, which has been occurring at a rapid pace since the 1940s (Smith 1969). In the early phases of postwar industrialization, little attention was given to the legacy of regional imbalances inherited from the nineteenth century. Efforts to counteract worsening regional inequality, when it was recognized in the efforts creating SUDENE (a development authority specifically oriented to the Northeast) often succeeded only in recreating in Northeastern cities the problems of limited labor absorption already characteristic of Southern industrialization.

A major economic crisis occurred in the early 1960s when the populist government of Goulart attempted to respond to demands of the urban working classes and at the same time cope with the inflationary excesses of the Kubitschek era. Political tensions increased as conflicting measures to achieve stabilization and redistribution failed to meet either objective. Goulart's administration found it increasingly difficult to meet scheduled payments on the foreign debt incurred during the expansion of the 1950s, and withdrawal of aid by the United States in 1963 contributed to the deepening economic crisis. By the end of that year the economic situation in Brazil had reached the point of chaos.

All of these factors precipitated the military intervention that overthrew Goulart, in March 1964, and set in motion a new phase in Brazilian political and economic history (Skidmore 1967: Chapter 8). Since 1964, political power has been held tightly by the military, who entrusted economic policy-making to a group of technocrats (mainly economists and engineers) who have guided the economy for more than a decade in a pattern that can best be characterized as export expansion and diversification with integration in the world economy and international financial markets replacing the former import substitution strategy.

Initial efforts (1964–68) of the military governments were directed primarily to the control of inflation, elimination of the balance-of-payments deficit, and rebuilding of the financial system through the indexing of credit instruments for inflation. Anti-inflation wage policy bore heavily on the earnings of the urban working classes, and the real purchasing power of the minimum wage declined substantially during this period (Furtado 1972: 45). After 1968, economic policy became more expansionist and export-oriented under Finance Minister Delfim Netto. Brazilians learned to live with what they considered to be a moderate amount of inflation (about 20 percent a year). Between 1967 and 1970, manufacturing and construction expanded at a rate of 14 percent per annum. Tax incentives for key investments restored the confidence of domestic investors, who were joined by the wave of private foreign capital that contributed to the booming expansion of industrial production between 1969 and 1974. Overall growth averaged about 10 percent in this period. The auto industry played a key role in the boom, growing by 33 percent per annum in 1967–70. It illustrates the Brazilian pattern of combining foreign capital at the final-product end of the spectrum (especially in consumer durables and equipment) with government investment in more basic sectors (like steel and petroleum) and infrastructure, in this case the highways and freeways to accommodate the population explosion in automobiles (Baer 1973).

The growth of exports in this period contrasts sharply with the earlier postwar expansion period (1955–61). Whereas exports remained relatively stagnant from the mid-fifties at 1.2 to 1.5 billion dollars a year, they expanded from the mid-sixties to roughly 8 billion dollars by 1974. This greatly expanded the capacity to import (export earnings plus foreign loans) to such an extent that imports as a percent of Gross Domestic Product doubled from 7 to 8 percent in the mid-sixties to roughly 15 percent in 1974. Until the oil crisis in 1974, most of these imports were intermediate and capital goods that fueled the growing rate of industrial expansion beyond the limits set by the supply of domestically produced capital goods. Also associated with this high rate of overall and industrial sector growth was a rapid rise in foreign debt to cover the growth-induced deficits in the balance of payments.

The second postwar expansion was thus an export promotion model closely tied in with a restructuring of the local money and capital markets through the vehicle of inflationary indexing of financial instruments. These reforms enhanced the capacity of the state to mobilize foreign and domestic savings and reallocate these resources for growth. Industrial employment grew from 13 percent (in 1960) to roughly 18 percent of the labor force (in 1970). However, fiscal incentives to the holders of capital, the high wages needed to attract skilled manpower, and a tight wage policy for less skilled labor increased further the indices of income concentration during this period.

Conclusion: Brazil in the Late 1970s

Though the early 1970s brought a return of rapid growth driven by vigorous exports and industrial expansion, and in part because of this, the Brazilian economy faces a number of serious problems in the years ahead. These are recognized by the military regime as well as its critics; some, like income distribution, have stirred lively debates in Brazilian academic circles and the press (Tolipan and Tinelli 1975, Langoni 1973). Evidence of government recognition is found in the 1975–79 development plan, the *II Plano Nacional de Desenvolvimento,* which addresses itself to issues like energy, population distribution, and income distribution (Brazil, Secretaria de Planejamento, 1974).

The world petroleum crisis was a great shock to the Brazilian economy, which imports more than two-thirds of its fuel. Added to this was an emphasis given to cars, trucks, and highways in recent transport policy, and the relative neglect of railroads and hydroelectric power for transport. Increased fuel prices ate up much of the exchange reserves that had been built up during the early 1970s. This stimulated Brazilian policy-makers to review energy and natural resource policies, which up to this time had been given low priority vis-à-vis economic expansion.[12] While the recent increase in world coffee prices deriving from the Brazilian frost and wars in Africa have mitigated some of the foreign exchange pressures of petroleum imports, the balance of payments continues to be a major constraint on the continuing capacity of the Brazilian economy to grow at rates comparable to the recent past. A slower growth profile is clearly in view for the future and has forced a return to an inward-looking import substitution strategy similar to the late fifties to reduce the import coefficient that has grown so markedly during the recent years of high growth.

The postwar expansions also brought significant changes in the size and composition of Brazil's population. In size, the total increased from less than 50 million at the end of the war to over 115 million in the late 1970s. Most of the net increase has occurred in urban areas through large-scale rural to urban migration. Important interregional migration flows shifted population from backward rural areas in the Northeast to the industrial Southeast, and further flows took rural migrants to agricultural frontier areas bordering on the Amazon region. Rapid urban growth combined with low labor absorption by the industrial sector has left a large portion of the urban labor force outside of the industrial boom. Services and construction provided the main increases in urban employment. Low wages paid to most of those employed in these sectors made it possible to take in workers who might otherwise have contributed to increased open unemployment. However, this also added to the worsening income distribution that has accompanied overall growth.

A high rate of general population growth plus pressures on the cities has brought renewed awareness of the need to utilize the rural sector's potential to provide for domestic food needs, to employ a larger portion of the rural population increase, and to bring in additional foreign exchange from non-traditional agricultural exports. Unfortunately, the policy measures required to achieve such a wide variety of objectives are not always compatible. For example, credit and land-use policies aimed at increasing production on Brazil's agricultural frontier have favored large-scale rural enterprises. Settlers on small plots, using only the simple techniques they brought with them from the Northeast, are losing out in competition with the larger operators.

Finding answers to these and related questions will be of critical importance in determining the structure of the Brazilian economy in coming decades. Aggregate growth in both the economy and the population has gained a tremendous momentum in the last two decades, so that continued growth of

---

[12]The position on environmental and resource problems taken in Chapter 8 of the *II Plano Nacional de Desenvolvimento* contrasts with statements of Brazilian representatives at the World Conference on the Environment in Stockholm a year earlier, see Sanders (1973).

both is most likely in the years ahead. If economic development were adequately measured in the simple ratio of product to population, the prospect would seem quite good on the basis of present trends. Indeed, the Brazilians are likely to surpass the $1,000 per capita income mark, if they have not done so already. This represents a doubling since 1970. However, these aggregates mask important qualitative and distributional factors that weigh heavily on the final measure of economic welfare that growth brings. The population, its growth, composition, and interaction with economic forces, are an important subset of these factors, and it is to these in both their historic and current setting in Brazil that we now turn.

Appendix: Statistical Summary of Twentieth-Century Growth Trends

As a postscript to this overview of Brazilian economic history, it will be useful to draw on the more quantitative view of recent trends that is afforded by the long-term national product series devised by Haddad (1974) and Suzigan (1976). Their efforts, which are summarized in Table II-4, offer additional insight into economic trends since 1900. For convenience of exposition and explanation, Haddad's series has been used for the earlier decades, whereas

Table II-4. Annual Percentage Rates of Growth for Total and Sectoral Product for Brazil for Selected Periods, 1900-74

	Haddad series			
	Agriculture (1)	Industry (2)	Total product (3)	Product per capita (4)
1900–02 to 1910–12	2.31	6.25	3.96	1.74
1910–12 to 1920–22	3.29	5.65	3.97	1.75
1920–22 to 1930–32	3.30	3.51	4.04	1.95
1930–32 to 1940–42	2.86	7.20	4.71	2.56
1940–42 to 1945–47	2.42	9.18	5.49	3.02
1900–02 to 1945–47	2.88	6.03	4.30	2.15
1945–47 to 1969–71	4.39	8.31	6.45	3.03
1900–02 to 1969–71	3.56	6.82	5.05	2.46

	Suzigan series	
	Industry (5)	Total product (6)
1948–52	8.8	7.0
1953–57	8.1	6.1
1958–62	11.2	7.6
1963–67	2.9	3.4
1968–74	12.2	10.1

Sources: Cláudio Haddad (1974); Suzigan (1976).

Suzigan's total product and industrial product series are presented as complementary evidence for the later decades. Several interesting highlights of twentieth-century Brazilian economic growth are evident in these series. Haddad's data on total product reveal an increasing rate of decadal growth from the early 1900s to the present. This pattern is repeated in the industrial product series from the 1920s onward. Suzigan's series from 1948 to 1974 show that the rise in industrial and total product growth has continued into the recent Brazilian growth cycle, reaching levels of 10 to 12 percent during 1968–74. Column 4 shows that despite rising population growth during this century, the growth of total product has been more than sufficient to offset it and to create a rising decadal product per capita from 1.7 percent in the early century to 3.03 percent in the postwar period (1945–71). Finally, the total product and product per capita grew at 5 percent and 2.5 percent, respectively, for the entire seventy-year period in the twentieth century. These rates compare favorably to those recorded by the currently developed countries during their initial stages of rapid economic growth in either the nineteenth or early twentieth centuries. Table II–5 shows that only Japan and the Soviet Union registered higher rates of growth in per capita product among the nine countries listed. It is pertinent to note that Brazil's relative position (third place) does not change, even when one restricts the comparison to the earlier 1900–45 period.

Table II-5. Annual Percentage Rates of Growth of Product per Capita for Selected Countries for Selected Periods

	Period	Rate of growth of product per capita
1. USSR	1928–58	3.71
2. Japan	1878–82 to 1918–22	3.07
3. Brazil	1900–02 to 1969–71	2.46
Brazil	1900–02 to 1945–47	2.15
4. Sweden	1881–85 to 1921–25	2.01
5. Germany	1871–75 to 1913	1.87
6. France	1871–80 to 1901–10	1.77
7. United States	1880–1920	1.61
8. Imperial Russia	1860–1913	1.35
9. Great Britain	1841–81	1.33

Source: Brazilian data from Table II–4. Data for other countries from Kuznets (1971: 18–19).

III Long-Term Trends in Population Growth, 1800–1970

Introduction

Analysis of the long-term trend in Brazilian population growth is a hazardous exercise at best. The first national census occurred only in 1872. Prior to that time there were a number of ecclesiastical and official headcounts, but these were invariably compromised by incomplete coverage and by misleading or exaggerated "corrections" applied to the original tallies.[1]

National censuses in 1872 and after were affected by political instability as well as administrative inefficiency. The 1880 census was canceled, and the 1890 and 1900 efforts, affected by the lack of proper funding and poor management, were not complete.[2]

Censuses planned for 1910 and 1930 were also canceled because of adverse political conditions, while the 1920 census, though completed in great detail, was compromised in part due to a recognized 12 percent overcount.[3] Starting in 1940, the Brazilian Census Bureau began to plan, carry out, and publish population enumerations meeting international standards of design, collection, and accurate reporting. After reasonably good censuses in 1940 and 1950 there was a relapse in 1960. Due to the political and administrative instability of the early sixties, publication of the 1960 demographic census broke down after only a few state volumes were completed. Not until 1977,

---

[1]For a detailed review of censuses taken prior to 1920, see Oliveira Vianna (1922), and for the colonial and imperial data, see Sousa e Silva (1870) and Brazil, Instituto Histórico e Geográfico Brasileiro (1895). Mortara (1941) also discusses the early census estimates, making his own revisions for the 1770–1870 period. More recent assessments of early population estimates are found in Alden (1963) and Marcilio (1973). For another discussion of ecclesiastical and colonial censuses, see Prado (1963: 29).

[2]See Brazil, Diretoria Geral de Estatística (1922, vol. I: 403–04).

[3]See Mortara (1970: 9–21). Mortara also found undercounts of 3.1 percent and 4.8 percent in the 1890 and 1900 censuses. His revised totals for the three censuses are:

1890	14,791,507
1900	18,184,396
1920	27,294,950

25

after a delay of seventeen years, did the detailed and definitive national data appear. Of necessity, the main sources of information on the Brazilian population are the censuses. Collection of vital statistics at the national level began only in 1974, and it will be several years before the birth and death rates provided by this system will permit analysis of trends. Though registration has been carried out in the larger cities for a longer period, most estimates of fertility and mortality depend on indirect measures from census data. While the censuses are not perfect, they can, if used with care, provide a reasonably comprehensive picture of Brazilian population history. The 1970 census is already being regarded as a landmark in this respect and provides many new opportunities for the analysis of demographic phenomena in Brazil. In addition to the decennial census, each year the Brazilian Census Bureau conducts large-scale sample surveys similar in scope to the current population survey in the United States. These are the Pesquisas Nacionais por Amostra de Domicilios (PNAD), and the most recent of these covers all but the rural population of the Amazon region.

Brazil's Population in 1800

Uncertainty as to the size of the Brazilian population at the beginning of the nineteenth century makes it difficult to establish a benchmark for analysis of trends in the period prior to 1872. Available estimates of population size are based on ecclesiastical records, colonial registers, and provincial censuses. Nothing akin to published census reports based on these population counts exists, though much of the material is available in colonial archives (Alden 1963). Demographers have recently returned to these archives and are reassembling important segments of colonial population history (Marcilio 1973). Oliveira Vianna's (1922) summary of early population censuses refers to contemporary estimates for various dates between 1776 and 1823. Later commentators refer to estimates of total population and its ethnic distribution (Contreiras Rodrigues 1935, R. C. Simonsen 1969).[4] Though these estimates were based on provincial census reports, none represents a national level population census estimate.

Estimates reported in these early synopses constitute the first of three types of population estimates that are available for the period before 1872; second is the work of the historical demographers mentioned above; third come the series covering the period 1770 to 1870 prepared by Mortara (1941). He was a pioneer in the application of demographic analysis to population estimates,

---

[4]The 1798 estimates, which are attributed in most sources to Santa Apolonia, have proved difficult to track down. A number of recent studies refer both to the population totals and break-downs by racial origin provided by Contreiras Rodrigues (1935), who simply mentions Santa Apolonia as a source. But no mention of Santa Apolonia is found in the early reviews mentioned in footnote 1.

seeking consistency between population size and plausible growth rates for particular periods. Mortara's work predates the contributions of the historical demographers, so that he chose his early nineteenth-century benchmarks from among the first group of estimates mentioned above. The "official" estimates, at least insofar as appearance in the *Anuário Estatístico* would indicate, are those of Mortara. The approach here is similar to his, but will take account of more recent evidence in assessing the plausibility of the growth rates implied in available population estimates for the years before 1870.

Table III–1 presents a summary of various estimates of Brazil's population for the period 1776 to 1819. If attention is focused on estimates for 1798, with a view to determining what the total might have been at the turn of the century, it is clear that there is a relatively wide range of estimates to choose from. Alden, who utilized archival data from provincial censuses, arrived at the lowest total of 2.29 million. Three contemporary commentators—Apolonia, Alexander von Humboldt, and Correa da Serra—present higher totals, ranging from 3.25 million to 4 million. Mortara, who based his interpolations on reports of the Portuguese Ministry of War (4.0 million for 1808) and a later estimate by Velloso de Oliveira (4.4 million for 1817–18), arrived at a total of 3.57 million for 1798. Mortara noted that his pre-1808 totals could be too high because of generous rounding that he suspected in his benchmark for 1808 (1941: 42).

One way to narrow the range of estimates is to examine the potential sources of their differences. Estimates based on available data clearly run the risk of incomplete coverage, whereas contemporary observers, for various reasons, are prone to exaggeration. While heeding Alden's caution about inaccuracies and exaggeration in the contemporary estimates, we get additional insight by examining the 1798 estimates attributed to Apolonia, in which the population was broken down by ethnic origin. Table III–2 presents these data, along with population composition as reported in the 1872 census, which provides a forward reference point for testing growth rates implied in the 1798 estimates. In addition to the estimated three million population of European and African origin, this source indicates a 252,000 indigenous population. Estimates for indigenous groups (Indians as well as *caboclos*, or mixed blood) vary widely, depending on whether they included only Indians in settlements or attempted to guess at the entire number. Later estimates run as high as 800,000 (R. C. Simonsen 1969: 271). Roughly 20 percent of the nearly two million population of African origin (406,000) are listed as free, presumably slaves who were manumitted, leaving about 1.5 million slaves at the beginning of the nineteenth century, a figure viewed by students of slavery in Brazil as consistent with data on slave imports during the eighteenth century (Curtin 1969, Conrad 1972).

Alden's 1798 estimates were based on a projection of totals he compiled from provincial censuses for the period 1772–82. In the projection, he employed a rate of natural increase of 1.18 percent per annum, also derived from

Table III-1. Estimates of Brazilian Population for the Period 1770–1820

Date	Author	Estimate (in millions)	Source
1776	Alden (average)	1.79	a
	Correa da Serra	1.90	a
	Mortara	2.70	b
1798	Alden (average)	2.29	a
	Apolonia	3.25	c
	Mortara	3.57	b
	Humboldt	3.65	c
	Correa da Serra	4.00	a
1808	Marcilio	2.43	d
	Balbi	3.62	c
	Mortara	4.00	b
	Portuguese Ministry of War	4.00	a
1817–19	Marcilio	3.60	d
	Velloso de Oliveira	4.40	b
	Mortara	4.51	b

Sources: a) Alden (1963)
         b) Mortara (1941)
         c) Reported in Simonsen (1969)
         d) Marcilio (1973)

contemporary sources. Alden did not indicate whether or how slave imports were included in his projections to 1798.

While Alden's 1798 estimate is considerably lower (30 percent) than the next highest available, his 1776 total of 1.79 million is much closer to Correa da Serra's 1.9 million. Several explanations of the differences between Alden and the other 1798 totals suggest themselves: underestimation of the rate of natural increase, neglect of slave imports, or exclusion of the indigenous population.

The rate of natural increase does not appear to be a problem. Alden's 1.18 percent rate is equivalent to the 1.2 percent per annum rate used by Mortara, whose population estimate for 1798 is almost 1 million higher. Of course, Mortara arrived at this by projecting back from a higher 1808 base. As for slave imports, economic conditions in Brazil in the last quarter of the eighteenth century were not such as to warrant the assumption of a great surge in importation. On the other hand, Curtin's (1969) estimates of the volume of Portuguese slave trade for the eighteenth century (presumably for the Brazilian market) do not indicate any substantial decline in the last three decades of the century.

Estimates of the indigenous population are much more problematic, however, some estimate should be included in a 1798 base to avoid distorting calculation of growth rates in the nineteenth century that include them in later totals. Even if we accept a total such as the 250,000 in the Apolonia estimates, we account for only one-quarter of the difference between Alden and the next highest estimate.

Table III-2. Brazilian Population Growth by Ethnic Origin, 1798 to 1872

Ethnic origin	1798 (1)	1872 (2)	Average annual rate of growth, 1798–1872 (3) A	(4) B
European	1,010,000	3,787,289	1.80	1.66[a]
African (and mixed))				
Free	406,000	4,245,428⎫	1.44	1.08[b]
Slave	1,582,000	1,510,810⎭		
Indigenous	252,000	386,955	0.58	0.58
TOTAL	3,250,000	9,930,478	1.52	1.26[c]

[a]Excludes 383,000 foreign-born reported in 1872 population.
[b]Net of 1,351,600 estimated slave imports. Freed and slave Africans are combined, because it is impossible to separate effects of natural growth, manumission, and importation in their growth.
[c]Excludes populations mentioned in [a] and [b].
Sources: 1798, Apolonia, as reported in Simonsen (1969).
1872, Census data (Brazil, Diretoria Central de Estatística, 1873).

Another explanation is that Alden's 1776 total is low, and that more rapid population increase occurred during the gold boom period of 1720–70. If the whole eighteenth century is taken as a frame of reference, we can get an idea of the kind of population increase required to raise the nonindigenous population from 300,000 to 3,000,000 between 1700 and 1798.

According to Furtado (1971: 46), population of European origin was about 100,000 in 1700. Assuming a rate of natural increase of 1.2 percent per annum, the European population would have increased to about 320,000 in 1798. An additional increase of 680,000 through immigration of Europeans and natural increase of the migrants is required to obtain the 1 million European population total in 1798 reported in Table III–2. Assuming that natural increase of immigrants contributed about one-third of the residual 680,000, the remainder attributable to immigration itself (460,000) is within the limits of Furtado's range estimate of not less than 300,000 and perhaps as many as 500,000 Portuguese immigrants to Brazil during the eighteenth century. Mortara's (1947b) estimates for the direct versus indirect contribution of immigration to growth in a later period yielded a figure closer to 50 percent for each component, so it is not difficult to account for the migration component.

Turning to the increase in the non-European population, Furtado estimated that the 1700 base was about 200,000. He did not discuss the indigenous population, but it is safe to assume that it was not included in his total. Judging from evidence (see below, Chapter IV) on Brazilian slavery, it is unlikely that the slave population reproduced itself directly, though slave imports may well have contributed indirectly to natural population increase through manumissions and the natural increase of the free colored (Klein 1969). Net increases in the slave population itself would have come mostly from slave imports. Estimates for 1798 include a substantial number (over 400,000) of free Africans, presumably including many ex-slaves (but excluding Indians) who had a rate of natural increase that would have fallen somewhere between that of the slaves and that of the European population. Assuming that one-third of this group were children of ex-slaves and the rest had arrived as slaves, we arrive at an implied importation of about 1.65 million slaves over the century (1.58 million slaves in 1798, plus 270,000 who had been imported but freed, less the 200,000 base population in 1700). This too is a plausible figure when compared with evidence on the Portuguese slave trade over the eighteenth century, though it is on the high side of the range (Curtin 1969, Klein 1972).

A final consideration with regard to the choice of a 1798 estimate is what it would imply for population growth rates in the first half of the nineteenth century. The lower the 1800 estimate, the higher the growth rate implied for that interval. For example, choosing Alden's 2.3 million for 1798 and Mortara's 6.2 million for 1840 implies an average annual rate of increase of 2 percent per annum for the period 1798–1840, which is higher than anything recorded until much later in the nineteenth century. Table III–2 (columns 3 and 4) shows the rates of increase of various population groups over the period 1798–1872, implied by the 1798 estimates when they are compared to the 1872 census. Two sets of growth rates are given: "A" gives the recorded rate, while in "B" the foreign-born are excluded from the 1872 data, which should provide a rough approximation of natural increase. This suggests a rate of about 13 per thousand for the total population, with 17 per thousand for the European population, and about 11 per thousand for the African population. It was not possible to separate freed and slave Africans, but it is safe to presume that the slave share was low, if not zero, so that this natural growth should be assigned to the free group. By 1872, they accounted for 74 percent of total Africans. These rates will be discussed in more detail in the next section. We can conclude by saying that such rates are plausible and that the estimate of 3.25 million total population in 1798 appears to be consistent with later population totals and the intervening growth rates they imply.

This is clearly a compromise position between the lower estimates based on colonial censuses and the higher estimates derived in reverse projection of later population totals. Adding two years' growth at 1.2 percent per annum to the 1798 figure gives us an estimate of 3.3 million for 1800, which we will adopt as the base for our discussion of nineteenth-century population trends in Brazil.

Population Growth Trends since 1800

Keeping data limitations in mind, it is possible to trace the long-run contour of the growth of the Brazilian population. Like the United States, one of the most striking features of the population of Brazil is its sustained long-term growth. Since 1870, the average rate of increase was 2.3 percent, a figure that results in a doubling of numbers every thirty years. This rate compares with the

Table III-3. Population Increase in Brazil and the United States, 1800-1970

A. Total population (millions)

Year	Brazil	United States	Ratio U.S./Brazil
1800	3.33	3.93	1.18
1850	7.23	23.19	3.20
1870	9.80	39.82	4.07
1900	17.98	75.99	4.22
1920	27.40	105.71	3.85
1940	41.24	131.67	3.19
1950	51.94	150.70	2.98
1970	92.34	203.21	2.20

B. Average annual rates of growth (percent)

Period	Brazil	United States
1800-50	1.56	3.61
1850-1900	1.85	2.40
1900-50	2.12	1.37
1950-70	2.92	1.52
1800-1970	1.97	2.35
1870-1970	2.27	1.64

Sources: Brazil, 1800, see text; 1850–1920, Mortara (1941); 1920–70, Fundação IBGE (1975a). United States, Department of Commerce (1975).

growth experienced by most other parts of the world only during the surge in population increase after World War II. Few countries other than the United States have experienced such high rates of growth for more than a decade or two.

Table III–3 combines the estimate of Brazilian population in 1800 with data for 1850 and after found in Mortara and Brazilian censuses. Data for the United States are included for purposes of comparison. Several points stand out. We see that Brazil and the United States had roughly the same size population at the end of the eighteenth century—between 3 and 4 million people. The secular growth over the nineteenth century, however, was decidedly different for the two countries. Brazil started the century with moderate growth, while the United States recorded the highest rate of population increase in the world at this time. Column (3) of the table reflects this differential growth in showing how, by 1890, the population of the United States had reached almost 4.5 times the size of Brazil's, even though both started practically equal at the beginning of the nineteenth century.

Patterns in the twentieth century reverse the roles, however, as Brazil recorded a significantly higher population growth rate than the United States. This has lowered the ratio in column 3, Table III–3, from 4.22 in 1900 to a little more than 2.0 in 1970. Such a contrast offers a quick insight into differences in the timing of population growth patterns for the two countries over the last two hundred years.

Understanding of the nature of these differential trends requires examination of the various components of population increase. In the United States, early declines in mortality brought rapid natural increase in the first half of the nineteenth century. This was supplemented by immigration, as fertility declined in the later part of the century.

Very little is known about vital rates in Brazil in the period prior to 1870. The available information is comparable to that on population totals for the period. It consists of scattered evidence from contemporary sources, reconstructions of these sources by historical demographers, and retrospective analyses. Mortara (1941, 1942) suggests that the crude birth rate was about 50 per thousand early in the nineteenth century and that it declined to 47 per thousand after 1850. His estimate of the rate of natural increase at about 14 per thousand implies a crude death rate of over 35 per thousand.

Demographic analysis of vital data for the city of São Paulo in the last part of the eighteenth century by Marcílio (1968) yielded a crude birth rate of 60 per thousand for 1783–98, followed by a decline to 48 per thousand between 1798 and 1836. She cautions that these rates may have been inflated by registration of births and deaths of nonresidents of the city (thus inflating the numerator) and notes that the European population of the period was experiencing birth rates in the upper 30 per thousand range. Lisanti's (1962) data on the entire province of São Paulo for the period 1777–1836 show birth rates in the low- to mid-40 per thousand range and death rates at the mid-20 per thousand level. Also available are vital rates for the province of Minas Gerais in 1815, reported by Klein (1969) in his study of manumission of the slave population, as shown in Table III–4.

Again we are faced with substantial discrepancies among sources, with lower and quite varied estimates from such contemporary sources and higher ones reported by Mortara. Leff and Klein (1974) have questioned the validity of the high birth rates estimated by Mortara for the early nineteenth century. Using Mortara's total population series for 1770–1870, they sought to explain the apparent increase in the rate of population growth from 1.3 percent per annum during 1808–19 to 1.5 percent from 1830 to 1872. Their basic argument is that mortality was still so high in 1870 that mortality decline could not explain the increased rate of growth. Comparing birth rates of less than 40 per thousand for Minas Gerais in 1815 with Mortara's rate of 46 per thousand for Brazil in 1870–1890, they concluded that the only plausible explanation was an increase in birth rates during the middle part of the nineteenth century.[5] Support for the contention that birth rates were lower earlier in the century was drawn from studies of European populations of the period (for example, Livi Bacci 1971), which also report comparatively low birth rates for the late

---

[5]This conclusion is based on the relatively low level for the expectation of life at birth (E_o=25) reported by Arriaga for later in the nineteenth century. As will be seen below, they do not appear to take account of the fact that a low level of life expectancy is consistent with high levels of both fertility and mortality.

Table III-4. Vital Rates for the Province of Minas Gerais, 1815

	Birth rate	Death rate	Natural increase
White	36.6	27.4	9.2
Free-colored	41.7	34.3	7.4
Slave	33.4	32.9	0.5
TOTAL	37.3	32.3	5.0

Source: Klein (1969).

eighteenth and early nineteenth centuries, deriving from later marriage, as well as lower fertility within marriage. The substantial migration of Portuguese to Brazil in the eighteenth century and additional arrivals in the early nineteenth century suggests the influence of Portuguese behavior patterns.

Fragmentary data on Brazilian nuptiality patterns of the period are found in Marcilio's (1968) study of the city of São Paulo. The proportion single among free females ages 20–29 was 61 percent, suggesting a pattern of later marriage. For ages 40–49 the proportion was 36 percent, indicating also that a significant number of women never married. These findings resemble those in Hajnal's (1965) analysis of Western European marriage patterns in the nineteenth century, where later marriage and spinsterhood contributed to the lower birth rates observed for that region, in comparison to those in Eastern Europe and many developing countries. The proportions of single women in the slave population of São Paulo were even higher. At the same time, Marcílio cautioned against the presumption that all births in Brazil at this time occurred within marriage, an important factor in the lower birth rates in Europe. Nearly 40 percent of births registered in São Paulo between 1791 and 1800 were illegitimate or foundlings, suggesting that marriage rates could be misleading evidence on fertility trends in the Brazilian case. The proportion of all free women married in São Paulo in 1789, 31 percent, was only slightly lower than the national level of 1872, 33 percent.

Slavery and manumission also need to be taken into account in dealing with questions about vital rates during the early nineteenth century. Gross estimates of the size of the slave population in 1800 and 1870, combined with the volume of slave imports in the interval, are often taken as proof that the slave population did not naturally reproduce itself. It is true that the unusual age and sex distribution resulting from the slave trade (with a predominance of young adult males), plus inhibitions on slave marriages, were likely to have produced low crude birth rates. Yet the gross data can be misleading. As Klein (1969) has shown, a substantial proportion of the slaves in Brazil were freed prior to formal abolition in 1888. Health and social conditions were generally better for the free African population than for slaves; age, sex, and marital status composition was also more balanced and therefore less likely to produce unusual patterns in crude vital rates. As the free-African population increased its weight in the total (from 12 to 45 percent between 1798 and 1872), it could indeed have created increases in the crude birth rate. However, decreases in the crude death rate, which were also very high in the slave population (Mello 1974), are equally if not more plausible for the same compositional reasons. An additional aspect of composition is that a proportion of the slave population that appears at first glance to have "died out" because of the harsh conditions of Brazilian slavery was really transferred to the free African group through manumission (especially of children of slaves). Even with the higher natural increase of the free African population found in Klein's data, it is impossible to account for the population increase in this group unless such transfers were of substantial magnitude.

In a demographic context like that of early-nineteenth-century Brazil, where immigration and the slave trade left such a substantial mark on the age and sex structure of the population, it is also important to distinguish between crude measures of fertility and mortality and more refined indicators that take account of compositional effect in the interpretation of trends. Eblen (1975) has demonstrated the effects of composition on crude rates for a Latin American slave population in his analysis of population increase among blacks in Cuba between 1775 and 1900. His refined measures showed that fertility and mortality levels were high, even though crude measures indicated lower rates. Slave women had many births, though very few surviving children because of high infant and child mortality.

Leff and Klein's discussion of the question of rising fertility in early-nineteenth-century Brazil does not distinguish between crude and refined measures. Their interpretation of rising fertility as a response to supposed deterioration in the income distribution suggest that they are not concerned with population composition. The evidence on the decline of slavery and increased manumissions just outlined suggest that compositional effects could have been an important factor, and that a rise in births, if it occurred, might well have been concentrated in crude rather than refined measures.

The data on which to base any interpretation are indeed scant. We have Mortara's estimate of an increase in total growth from 1.28 percent to 1.52 percent between 1808–30 and 1830–72 and Leff and Klein's comparison of Minas Gerais crude birth and death data in 1815 with later national estimates. The latter are indeed correct in cautioning against acceptance of retroprojection of vital rates on the assumption that earlier levels could only have been higher. On the other hand, reconstructive analyses like those of Mortara force us to reconcile estimates of population growth trends with the total population at different periods. The very low rate of natural increase reported for Minas Gerais (5 per thousand) is too low to be consistent with even the highest population totals for the beginning of the nineteenth century, even if we allow for slave imports and European migration, as was done in Table III–2. No aggregate estimates of European immigration exist, but suppose that a range estimate of between 100,000 and 400,000 included the 1789–1850 total. With an average total growth rate of 1.56 percent per annum for the interval, these magnitudes imply a rate of natural increase on the order of 12 to 14 per thousand—more than twice Klein's estimate for Minas Gerais, but a little less than Mortara's 14 per thousand.

A further check on the consistency of vital rates for the period can be made by utilizing stable population techniques with available information on age structure and growth rates. Marcílio (1975) applied this method to her data on the free-female population of the state of São Paulo in 1808 and 1818. At that time São Paulo's population had been relatively closed to migration, since most immigrants in the eighteenth century sought destinations in the gold mining regions, principally Minas Gerais. Coale–Demeny "West" model life tables provided a very close approximation to this population at Level 12 (e_0 = 25 years). A growth rate of 1.2 percent per annum at this level implies a birth rate of 54 per thousand and a crude death rate of 42. These estimates suggest that the overall growth rate experienced by Brazil at the time, about 1.2 percent per annum, was possible even with relatively elevated mortality (life expectancy of 25 years), and that the crude birth rate was closer to 50 than to 30 per thousand in the period. Clearly, the free population of São Paulo was not representative of all Brazil at the time, and it is likely that differences in population composition (e.g., age and sex structure, proportion of non-native and slave) would lead to different results elsewhere. Some of the differences between these results for São Paulo and those Klein has reported for Minas Gerais may be due to such differences in population composition. The rest must be ascribed to underreporting in the registers of the period. These comparisons again illustrate how deceptive crude birth and death rates can be in assessing demographic trends in populations that differ even as little as São Paulo and Minas Gerais in the beginning of the nineteenth century.

The preceding discussion also raises questions about Mortara's estimate of the crude death rate at about 35 per thousand for all Brazil between 1800 and 1850. His estimate is probably on the low side, with a range estimate of 35 to 40 per thousand being a safer assumption. In all likelihood, there was considerable variation across regions, with higher rates occurring in urban areas, especially during epidemics. Local data (Cooper 1975) suggest that deaths exceeded births in coastal cities at various times during the nineteenth century, and that expansion of the urban population no doubt had a detrimental effect on the overall death rate trend. The balance of births and deaths in rural areas was probably more steady, though it was affected by the relatively high mortality of the slave population.

Uncertainty about the level of crude birth and death rates makes it difficult to arrive at a definite conclusion about natural increase in the period 1880–50. The summary estimates in Table III–3 indicate that a total rate of population increase of 1.56 percent per annum is probably not far off the mark. Migration may have contributed as much as one-quarter of this, both in the form of European immigration as well as through slave imports. The Napoleonic Wars and later the revival of sugar trade led first to the transfer of the Portuguese court to Rio de Janeiro and then to a flow of Portuguese migrants to coastal cities, like Recife, throughout the first half of the century. In addition to this, there was the limited immigration of German and other colonists in the South.

But the major component of growth in Brazil's population between 1800 and 1850 was natural increase of both the white population and the free-African group. The plausible range for the rate of natural increase falls in the 11 to 14 per thousand range. With crude death rates in the 35 to 40 per thousand range, this implies that crude birth rates were closer to the 50 per thousand level than to the mid-30 level suggested by the data of Klein and Leff. Crude rates in these ranges are consistent with the age structure and growth rates accompanying an expectation of life at birth of twenty-five years in model life tables, just about the level that was derived with more refined demographic techniques from limited subsamples of the population analyzed by historical demographers.

Population Trends during the Coffee Export Boom, 1850–1930

Most of the information available on Brazilian population and its growth in the period *after* 1850 is likewise found in the detailed studies of early Brazilian census material prepared by Giorgio Mortara (1941, 1970). He refined estimates of population in the precensus period, adjusted early censuses for errors of enumeration, and derived estimates of the components of population change from them. Mortara's estimates of birth, death, and migration rates for the period 1840–1940 are shown in Table III–5, along with data for 1940 to 1970 from the Fundação IBGE.

Comparing Mortara's estimate of total population increase for 1840–70 to the estimate for 1800–50 discussed in the previous section, there is very little difference (1.52 percent per annum versus 1.56 percent per annum). Natural increase and its components, the birth and death rates, were probably not much different from the levels indicated earlier, while migration rates in the mid-century interval were lower than those for earlier and later periods. This would be consistent with the relatively sluggish economic conditions of the period.

After 1870, we observe a gradual increase in the rate of population growth—rising from 1.53 percent per year in 1840–70 to 2.42 percent per year in the last decade of the century. Examination of the components of population change suggests that the rate of natural increase rose from 14 to nearly 19 per thousand, principally because of a decline in the crude death rate. Even more important in bringing the rate of total population growth to the relatively high level experienced by Brazil at the end of the nineteenth century was international migration.

Mortara's estimates of the number of immigrants by decade over the interval 1850–1950 are shown in Table III–6. The number of migrants in-

Table III–5. Components of Population Change in Brazil, 1850–1970

	Average annual rates per thousand population				
	Total increase	Migration	Natural increase	Births	Deaths
1840–70	15.2	1.0	14.2	46.5	32.3
1871–90	19.1	2.0	17.1	46.6	29.5
1891–1900	24.2	6.0	18.2	46.0	27.8
1901–20	21.2	2.2	18.6	45.0	26.4
1921–40	20.5	1.8	18.7	43.5	24.8
1941–50	23.8[a]	0.4	23.4	44.4	20.0
1951–60	30.0[a]	0.9	29.1	43.3	14.2
1961–70	27.9	0.1	27.8	40.8	13.0

[a]Adjusted for two-month difference between date of 1950 census and those of 1940 and 1960.
Sources: 1840–90: Mortara (1941*b*: 276, 1970: 16).
   1891–1940: Mortara, in Fundação IBGE (1970).
   1941–60: Fundação IBGE (1969).
   1961–70: Irwin and Spielman (1976).

Table III–6. Migrant Arrivals by Decade, Brazil 1850–1950

Years	Immigrants[a]	Years	Immigrants[a]
1851–60	120	1901–10	670
1861–70	95	1911–20	795
1871–80	215	1921–30	835
1881–90	530	1931–40	285
1891–1900	1,125	1941–50	130

[a]Thousands
Source: Mortara, Fundação IBGE (1970).

creased progressively during the last half of the nineteenth century, reaching more than one million in the last decade, a figure that was nearly 8 percent of the 1890 population. Despite the magnitude of immigration in this period, it was still natural increase that accounted for the major part of Brazil's population increase. Using additional data from Mortara, we can see in Table III–7 the relative contribution of immigration to population growth between 1870 and 1930.

After adjusting the data in Table III–6 for return migration and mortality among immigrants, Mortara arrived at the net increase in the foreign-born population shown in column 3 of Table III–7. This constituted 13.5 percent of total growth in 1872–90 and increased to 30.2 percent in 1890–1900, which was the peak decade in terms of the impact of immigration on Brazilian population growth. In the next four decades, the figure was 7 to 8 percent. These percentages represent the direct contribution of migrants to population growth. Mortara (1947b) also attempted to determine the indirect contribution of migrants to growth through fertility and mortality. He found that migrant mortality was lower, again for compositional reasons. With proportionally more young adults, the age distribution of the migrant population was

Table III-7. Influence of Immigration on Brazilian Population Growth, 1872–1940

Period	Total (1)	Population increase (in thousands)		Percent due to immigration (4)	Growth rate		
		Excess births - deaths (2)	Immigration (net) (3)		Overall (5)	Natural (6)	Immigration (7)
1872–90	4,221	3,651	570	13.5	2.01	1.63	0.38
1891–1900	2,984	2,081	930	30.2	2.42	1.82	0.60
1901–20	13,317	12,377	939	7.0	2.12	1.86	0.22
1921–40	10,617	9,757	859	8.1	2.05	1.87	0.18

Source: Mortara (1947*b*: 1).

less subject to mortality risk. Both age and sex selectivity of migration led also to an initial dampening effect on fertility. If we calculate migrant births and deaths for 1890–1900, the contribution of migrants' natural increase to population growth comes to only 3 percent of total growth. The fertility component increased with time, as migrants became settled and established families. However, their mortality also increased as they aged, and this partially counterbalanced the fertility effect.

This leads to the conclusion that the combined effects of migration on growth never exceeded more than one-third of total population increase. Over the whole period, Mortara estimated that the combined direct and indirect effect of migration to growth was about 19 percent, divided about equally between the direct and indirect contribution. As can be seen in Table III–8, this also implies that the relative impact of migration was lower in Brazil than in the other countries in which migrants settled in the Western Hemisphere between 1840 and 1940. The relative contribution was greatest in Argentina, 58 percent, followed by the United States and Canada, with 41 percent and 22 percent. Though the absolute volume of migration to Brazil between 1870 and 1940 was roughly equal to that of Argentina, the relative contribution to growth was smaller because of Brazil's larger base population. Nevertheless, the increase in the rate of population growth in the last part of the nineteenth century was due to the rising migration flow. Further, the impact of migration in Brazil was concentrated in São Paulo and the Federal District. Later discussions will show that the aggregate demographic effect was not a true indicator of the social and economic impact of immigration.

Turning to components of natural increase, the death rate appears to have declined by the turn of the twentieth century, contributing to the rise in natural increase observed between 1872 and 1900. From a level of nearly 40 prior to 1870, there is a decline to around 30 in 1900. This decline is limited in comparison with later ones, since conditions in Brazil were hardly conducive to substantial mortality reduction. Epidemics in the coastal cities were common after 1850. And post-1870 stagnation of the cotton and sugar economies of the Northeast and the disastrous drought of 1877–80 undoubtedly led to a lower rate of natural increase for this populous region. Conditions in the Northeast

Table III-8. Relative Contribution of Natural Growth, Immigration, and Immigrants'
Children to the Population Increases of Argentina, Brazil, Canada, and the
United States, 1841–1940 (percentages)

	Natural growth	Immigration	Immigrants' children
Argentina	41.9	29.0	29.0
Brazil	81.0	9.4	9.6
Canada	59.1	21.8	19.0
United States	78.4	9.8	11.8

Source: Mortara (1947b).

would also have affected the rate of natural increase for the free-colored population.

On the positive side, it is worth noting three factors that could have contributed to lower mortality as the century came to a close. The gradual elimination of slavery, with its high mortality, was one. A second was the increase in public health activities, which grew out of strong social pressures to reduce the recurrent epidemics in the major urban centers. Real success in this effort came at the turn of the century, when Brazilian public health authorities under the leadership of Dr. Oswaldo Cruz successfully eradicated yellow fever (Cooper 1975). Finally, immigration had a depressing effect on the crude death rate deriving from the introduction of age groups less subject to mortality.

After 1900, the rate of total population growth declined from the level it had attained just prior to the turn of the century. With a declining rate of international migration, total growth fell from 24 to just under 21 per thousand between 1900 and 1930. Natural increase remained relatively steady during this period. The death rate continued the gradual decline that began during the previous period, while the birth rate, which had remained virtually constant in the last half of the nineteenth century, appears to have declined slightly by the 1930s. As a result, natural increase rose by only 0.5 per thousand, which was not enough to offset the decline in total growth due to decreased immigration.

Recent Growth Trends, 1930–70

Mortality

Starting sometime in the 1930s, Brazil's rate of natural increase began to rise again, this time more substantially. Mortality decline was the main factor in this. As seen in Table III–5 there was little if any decline in the birth rate in this period. The crude rate remained near 45 prior to 1950, and may even have increased slightly in the 1950s. In an effort to achieve a more precise measure of the mortality levels underlying these trends, Mortara (1942, Fundação

IBGE 1970) derived estimates of the expectation of life at birth by comparing census age distribution and intercensal population growth rates. Later, Arriaga (1968) applied stable population techniques to Brazilian census data and arrived at an independent set of estimates. Both are presented in Table III–9.

In comparing Mortara and Arriaga for the decades prior to 1930, we find that Mortara's estimates of life expectancy are higher and, more importantly, that the increase from 1872–90 (33.9 years) to 1890–1920 (39.3 years) is much greater than in Arriaga's results. Arriaga's estimates show a rise from 27.5 to 29.9 for the same interval. Mortara shows an increase that is almost twice Arriaga's, in addition to being at a higher initial level. Arriaga concluded that differences between their estimates for the 1870–90 base period derived from age misreporting in the censuses used by Mortara, which was particularly acute at younger ages. He attempted to avoid this in his work by restricting the census data base to ages 10 to 59. It should be noted that Mortara did employ corrected age distributions in his estimates, and that bias, if it exists, would have resulted from errors in his correction process. Testing the consistency between either author's estimates of the expectation of life and other population parameters for the 1872–90 period is complicated by the inaccuracies of these early censuses. The 1890 census is generally regarded as more accurate on age than other early censuses, though it is limited to a combined age distribution for both sexes. Mortara adjusted the age distributions of the native-born for 1872, 1890, and 1920 (he regarded age data in the 1900 census as being too erroneous even to try). His corrected 1890 data are actually quite close to Arriaga's smoothed estimate in the age range (10–59) in which Arriaga worked. Application of age-specific mortality rates derived from the two life tables to the entire smoothed 1890 age distribution of the native-born population yields the following crude death rates: in the Arriaga table ($E_0 = 27.8$) the result is 37.7 per thousand; Mortara's table ($E_0 = 33.9$) yields a rate of 29.5 per thousand. Reconciliation of these mortality rates with other population parameters requires an estimate of the natural growth of the native population at the time. Mortara's estimate (18.9 per thousand) is higher than Arriaga's (16.3 per thousand). The main difference between them appears in the birth rates implied by their respective mortality estimates. Arriaga's data imply a rate of around 54 per thousand, in comparison with Mortara's 48 per thousand. Both are higher than available estimates for the total population (46.5 per thousand), in which the lower rates for immigrants weighed.

Mortara appears to have achieved better internal consistency between his mortality estimates and other population parameters for this period, and his efforts are sufficiently convincing for us not to reject his estimate of the *level* of life expectancy (33.9 years for 1870–90) in favor of Arriaga's lower estimate (27.8 years for 1890). However, Arriaga's calculations also reveal a problem in Mortara's estimate of the *trend* in life expectancy between 1890 and 1920.

Mortara's 1890–1920 estimate of 39.3 years implies an improvement of about 16 percent, whereas, Arriaga's results showed only 9 percent. Mortara's calculations were made before he discovered that the 1920 census included an overcount that became apparent only after the 1940 census was tabulated. The overstatement was about 10 percent and led to a systematic upward bias in the survival rates he used to calculate the 1890–1920 life table. A rough correction of Mortara's calculations brings his 1890–1920 estimate down to around thirty-seven years, so that the estimated increase from 1870–90 to 1890–1920 is about the same as reported by Arriaga, i.e., 9 percent.

The main implication of Arriaga's revision of the life expectancy estimates for Brazil, if they are accepted, is to assign the largest portion of the improvement (mortality decline) to the post-1930 period. In conjunction with this, he has argued (1970) that most of Brazil's mortality decline resulted from the importation of modern medical technology, a process that was independent of the level of economic development. His interpretation does allow that some improvement occurred prior to 1930 (from 27.3 years in 1880 to 34 years in 1930), which could have been associated with improving economic conditions. The amount of improvement (7 years) is about the same as in Mortara's data (34 years in 1870–1890 to 41 years in 1920–40), though Mortara's level of 34 years for the pre-1890 period is attained only in 1930 in the Arriaga results. When account is taken of the 1920 census errors, the two sets of trend estimates are more alike. The basic difference is that when they finally converge at a life expectancy of about 43 years around 1950, Arriaga's results indicate a greater concentration of the improvement in the period after 1930.

Census data for 1940 and after provide additional opportunities for analysis of vital rates in Brazil and shed some light on the latter part of the pre-1940 period, because they allow another approach to 1930–40. Since 1940, Brazilian censuses have included questions on children ever born and surviving to mothers of different ages. These questions make it possible to derive estimates of fertility and child survivorship, using techniques developed by William Brass (United Nations 1967). From survivorship data one can derive life table values for early-age cohorts and calculate the expectation of life at birth by matching these to model life tables. Such estimates are still deficient in one fundamental respect. Though they permit calculation of life table values for younger age groups from available data, it is still necessary to use model life tables for the remaining age categories. Again, there is no sure way of determining whether the model table to be utilized is actually appropriate for the population in question.

Several recent studies have applied the technique to the Brazilian census data and thus provide a better tracking of mortality trends between 1930 and 1970 than was possible for previous decades. Because of differences in dealing with deficiencies in the data and in the choice of the appropriate life table to use in making the estimates, we do not find complete agreement among them. Carvalho (1973, 1977) applied the Brass techniques to 1940, 1950, and 1970

Table III-9. Estimates of the Expectation of Life at Birth for the Brazilian Population, 1870–1970

	Mortara	Arriaga	Carvalho	IBGE
1870		27.3		
1880	33.9 years	27.6		
1890		27.8		
1900		29.4		
1910	39.3 years	30.6		
1920		32.0		
1930		34.0		
1940		36.7	41.2	
1950	43.7 years	43.0	43.6	
1960		55.5	49.6	52.3
1970			53.4	59.3

Reference Periods: Mortara as indicated; Carvalho and IBGE, the decade prior to census; Arriaga, the census date.

Sources: Mortara (1941*a*) and Fundação IBGE (1970); Carvalho (1973, 1977); Arriaga (1968, 1977); IBGE (1960); Lyra Madeira and Cassinelli (1970); Irwin and Lyra Madeira (1972).

census data and made interpolated estimates for 1960 as well. After finding that existing model life tables distorted the relationships between adult and childhood mortality levels, he substituted a Mexican life table for the Coale–Demeny model in computing missing life table values. His estimates of life expectancy for 1930–40 to 1960–70 are shown in Table III-9. The table also shows estimates derived by the Brazilian Census Bureau from Coale–Demeny model tables and the Arriaga and Mortara results for recent decades.

Carvalho's estimate of life expectancy for 1930–40 is 41.2 years, and his 1940–50 estimate of 43.6 years comes very close to both Mortara's 43.7 and Arriaga's 43 years. After 1950 there is less agreement. Carvalho's estimates for 1950–60 and 1960–70 (49.6 and 53.4 years) suggest a more gradual decline in mortality after 1940–50 than does Arriaga. The IBGE tables, on the other hand, show a more substantial increase in life expectancy between 1960–70 and suggest a continuation of the trend identified by Arriaga. Carvalho's results imply that the increase from 44 to 54 years took two decades rather than the one suggested by Arriaga. Further, Carvalho's estimate of 41 years for 1930–40 suggests that the whole 1930–70 trend was much more gradual than suggested by Arriaga. Combining Carvalho and Mortara results, which seem relatively consistent with each other, we find a view of long-term mortality trends in Brazil that contrasts with that of Arriaga with respect to the timing of mortality decline. Both views suggest that the rate of decline improved after 1930, but Mortara/Carvalho indicate that the change was much less abrupt and the post-1930 improvement much less dramatic than does Arriaga.[6]

[6] Results are very sensitive to the family of life tables that are used. Frias and Leite (1976) have compared a set of "Brazilian" model life tables derived from vital statistics available for several urban municipalities with the Coale–Demeny "West" family and found that the same life table

Interpretation of the relation between mortality and socioeconomic development versus the importation of medical innovations depends to some extent on which view is accepted. A more gradual trend implies that generally improving economic conditions after 1870 may have played a more significant and earlier role in mortality decline in Brazil. Unfortunately, research on relations between Brazilian mortality patterns and economic conditions, as well as on the impact of imported medical technology, such as the epidemiological efforts described earlier, has been limited, and adequate interpretation of the trend requires much further study.

Although Brazil's crude death rate is presently low by international standards, the mortality level is still higher than that found in more developed countries. Because of the youthful age distribution of the population, deaths at older ages do not weigh as heavily as they do in a European population. And Brazil's infant mortality rate is still close to 100 per thousand live births, more than five times the Western European standard—where rates range between 10 and 20. Recent evidence suggests that urban poverty has contributed to an increase in infant mortality in cities such as São Paulo. This question, along with that of regional and rural-urban differentials in mortality, will be discussed further in Chapter X.

Recent Fertility Trends

Estimates of the recent trend in fertility are also varied. Irwin and Spielman (1976) have compiled an inventory for the 1940–70 period. All of the estimates are based on census data derived either from information on children ever born or by reverse survival of the population at early ages to obtain the number of births in the years prior to the census. Table III–10 shows a selection of the estimates of crude birth rates available for this period: one prepared by the IBGE (Table III–5), a series by Arretx (1973) of CELADE, estimates by Carvalho (1973) in the study mentioned above, and a series developed by Merrick (1974).

A number of differences can be observed. The series start at 1940 levels ranging from 43.5 per thousand to 46 per thousand. The closer to the higher estimate the 1940 level actually was, the less likely it is that there had been any decline in the crude birth rate prior to 1940. Differences relate to the timing of the decline and to the level of the rate in the later 1960s (which depends on the level in 1940, since most sources show a decline of 8 to 9 percent from that date).

---

values for the 0–4 age groups would yield a differential in the expectation of life at birth of a little over one year, with Coale–Demeny indicating a lower level because adult mortality associated with a given level of child mortality is higher in their tables. Use of inappropriate models may thus lead to misstatement of life expectancy with this method.

Table III-10. Estimates of the Crude Birth Rate from Census Data for Brazil, 1940-70

Census	IBGE	Arretx	Carvalho	Merrick
1940	43.5	n.a.	46.0	44.4
1950	44.4	42.2	45.3	43.9
1960	43.3	41.4	43.7	43.4
1970	40.8	38.8	42.3	40.5

Note: IBGE and Merrick used reverse-survival method; Arretx and Carvalho used children-ever-born data. The reference period is the decade prior to each census.
Sources: See text.

The question of timing depends to a large extent on the 1960 census data and their reliability. The survival ratio estimates suggest that the birth rate declined only after 1960, because the proportion of young children in the population increased from 1950 to 1960. However, estimates derived from questions on children ever born reported in 1960 indicate a more gradual decline over the whole period. Because of questions about the quality of the 1960 data, neither approach rests on a very firm footing.

Since mortality decline was the main factor responsible for the rise in the rate of natural increase that occurred between 1940 and 1960, the main interest in establishing the trend in fertility lies in what it may imply for future reductions in the rate of natural increase.

For this purpose, the crude birth rate is, like the crude death rate, a misleading index of actual fertility trends, since it incorporates the effects of changing age structure associated with declines in both fertility and mortality.

Without vital statistics data and in the absence of questions on current fertility in censuses taken before 1970, age decomposition of fertility trends is difficult. Carvalho (1973) combined information on children ever born in the 1940 and 1950 censuses (which establish the level of fertility) with an age profile derived from 1970 data and concluded that total fertility (the sum of age-specific fertility rates) declined very slightly between 1950 and 1970, from 6.3 to 6.1 births per woman, as shown in Table III-11. Carvalho's results suggest that age composition accounts for about half of the decline in the crude birth rate between 1950 and 1970, so that the actual fertility decline was much less than indicated by the crude birth rate.

Crude rates also mask another underlying demographic dimension of the growth process, which is the interaction between declines in mortality and fertility. By increasing the chances of survival of daughters to the childbearing ages, mortality decline has dampened the effect of declining fertility on the population's growth potential. This can be measured more precisely by the net reproduction rate. This rate is a variant of the total fertility rate and combines age-specific fertility rates with probabilities of surviving to specific child-bearing age cohorts. This gives an index of the relative size of the succeeding generation, which, in Brazil's case, increased from 2 in 1950 to 2.3 in 1970.

Table III-11. Fertility Rates for Brazil and Other Regions

	Total fertility rate	Net reproduction rate
Africa, 1965–70	6.4	2.1
Brazil		
1950	6.3	2.0
1970	6.1	2.3
Latin America, 1965–70	5.5	2.3
South Asia, 1965–70	6.2	2.2
North America, 1965–70	2.9	1.3
Europe, 1965–70	2.7	1.2
Japan	2.1	1.0

Sources: Brazil: Carvalho (1973: Chapter 2).
Other areas: Frejka (1973: 84).

When the index is equal to 1, succeeding generations are equal in size and zero population growth results. The implications of this increase for future population growth will be discussed further in Chapter XII.

Despite the recent decline, the birth rate in Brazil is still high by both international and historical Brazilian standards. Table III–11 also shows comparative data on other countries in 1970. Brazil's total fertility rate is among the highest in the world, even if we take the lower value in the range of estimates available for 1960–70. Since the death rate is already approaching levels at which further substantial declines are unlikely, it is clear that Brazil's population growth has entered into a new phase, in which changes in the fertility will be the main determinant of future growth trends. Age-composition effects, which contributed a part of the recent decline in crude birth rates, are likely to be temporary. Future trends will depend on the social and economic factors that influence reproductive behavior, a topic that will be examined in Chapter X.

Brazilian Population Trends from 1800 to 1970: A Synopsis

In a comparative perspective, Brazil's demographic expansion since 1800 stands between the very rapid increase of the United States, which was fed by both high natural increase and high immigration, and most other countries in Latin America. Table III–12 shows that at the end of the eighteenth century Brazil had slightly more than half the population base of Mexico, about three times the population of Peru, and perhaps four times the population of Colombia and Venezuela. One hundred and seventy years later, however, Brazil had increased its relative status to nearly twice the size of Mexico, seven times the size of Peru, and nine to ten times the size of Venezuela and Chile, respectively. Colombia held approximately the same relative position, and only Argentina has increased vis-à-vis Brazil over this period, since it grew from a

Table III-12. Comparative Population Growth Trends Since 1800, Brazil and Selected
Latin American Countries

A. Total population

	c. 1800	c. 1900	1970
Argentina	551,000	4,743,000	24,352,000
Brazil	3,330,000	18,184,396	92,341,556
Chile	440,000	2,904,000	9,717,000
Colombia	827,000	3,825,000	22,160,000
Mexico	5,837,000	13,607,000	50,718,000
Peru	1,077,000	3,791,000	13,586,000
Venezuela	780,000	2,344,000	10,755,000

B. Rates of population growth (average annual percentage rate)

	1800-1900	1900-70	1960-70
Argentina	2.2	2.4	1.5
Brazil	1.7	2.4	2.8
Chile	1.9	1.7	2.3
Colombia	1.4	2.5	3.3
Mexico	0.9	1.9	3.4
Peru	1.2	1.8	3.0
Venezuela	1.1	2.2	3.2

Source: Sanchez-Albornoz (1974: 169, 184–85). Except Argentina—see Lattes e Lattes (1975, p. 23).

small population of roughly 551,500 in 1800 to nearly 25 million by 1970. This was due exclusively to massive European immigration from 1800 to roughly 1930. Since World War II, Brazil has been growing much more rapidly, because Argentina did not share in the large rates of natural increase recorded in recent years in the rest of Latin America.

Comparatively high population growth rates in all three columns of panel B of Table III-4 help to explain how Brazil substantially increased its relative demographic weight in Latin America between 1800 and 1970. Brazil is the only Latin American country to have participated fully in all three population increasing processes during this period: (1) the importation of slaves (sixteenth to nineteenth centuries), (2) large intercontinental immigration (nineteenth and twentieth centuries), and (3) high rates of natural increase prior to fertility decline (nineteenth and twentieth centuries). Other Latin American countries usually experienced only one of these demographic thrusts and, on rare occasions, two, but never all three. Indeed, the only other country in the hemisphere to have experienced all three of these population phenomena over a prolonged interval was the United States and, significantly enough, this is the only new world country to which Brazil is comparable in population size.

However, the path of Brazilian growth stands in sharp contrast to that of the United States. The United States recorded a 3 percent rate of population growth throughout the first half of the nineteenth century, primarily through a high rate of natural increase, reflecting a continuation of high fertility and declining mortality associated with an early onset of significant economic growth and development. In Brazil, population growth in the early part of the nineteenth century was about half that of the United States, but Brazil's rate increased over the course of the century, while that of the United States declined. A gradual decline in the death rate brought a rise in the rate of natural increase, though an additional factor, immigration, was needed to raise the Brazilian population growth rate above the 2 percent level.

International migration played contrasting roles in the long-term population growth trends of the United States and Brazil. In the United States, the major waves of European immigration came at a time in which they were able to counteract the effect of a decline in fertility on the rate of total increase. In Brazil, immigration came well before rates of natural increase reached levels comparable to those brought by declining mortality combined with high fertility in the United States. The sequence of the immigration versus natural growth components was thus much different. This chapter has examined some of the demographic effects of this process in Brazil, and Chapter V will explore the broader implications vis-à-vis economic changes that were occurring.

In Brazil, as in the United States, the rate of international migration declined after the 1920s, although the absolute volume was still substantial up into the 1950s, except for a fall-off during the war years. However, immigration's relative contribution to growth declined when measured against a growing population base. This is evident in 1950–60, when net immigration was over half a million, but resulted in less than one-tenth of a percentage point rise in the rate of total increase.

Brazil's mortality declined slightly in the late nineteenth century, but the real contribution of mortality decline to its population growth came between 1930 and 1960. As a result of the decline in the immigration rate, total population increase, which was 24 per thousand in 1890–1900, dropped to 20–21 per thousand between 1900 and 1940. In the meantime, the death rate was declining, at first gradually and then more rapidly—resulting in a decrease of about 50 percent between 1920–40 and 1950–60. With no appreciable decline in the birth rate, population increase rose from 20.5 to 30.5 per thousand in 1950–60, which will probably stand as the decade of most rapid population growth in modern Brazilian history.

A new phase in Brazilian population trends appears to have begun around 1960. The 1960s brought Brazil's first marked decline in the crude birth rate, from 43–44 per thousand in 1940–60 to near 40 per thousand in 1960–70. About half of its effect in reducing total population growth was offset by continued mortality decline. Still, the total growth rate has clearly reversed its pre-1960 trend.[7] The total growth in 1960–70 was 27.9 per thousand, down 8.5

[7]A source of confusion in discussion of growth rates since 1940 are the two population totals referred to in census volumes. All growth rates discussed here refer to the *de facto* population (*população presente*), however, population characteristics are reported for the *de jure* population (*população residente*). As can be seen in the table below, the relation of the two totals varies

percent from its level in the previous decade. Since mortality is relatively low, the future trend will depend mainly on fertility. The growth rate will fall more in the 1970s if the decline in fertility continues, though the decline may be sluggish because of the age structure effects mentioned earlier.

The most recently completed phase of Brazilian population growth is strikingly similar to the first phase of the U.S. demographic pattern (1800–50), in which high birth rates combined with low death rates to produce a high rate of natural increase. Since the momentum of this high rate of population growth is built into the future, the gap between the two populations (the United States and Brazil) is narrowing, as can be seen in column 3 of Table III–4. Sometime in the next century, Brazil will probably overtake the United States in population size, if the present trends prevail.

In concluding this summary of the long-term trend in Brazilian population growth, we can divide its experience into five broad phases: (1) 1800–50: moderate, possibly increasing growth associated with slave imports, limited European immigration, and possibly rising natural increase; (2) 1850–90: moderately increasing growth associated with continuation of the rise in natural increase and a gradual rise in the contribution of immigration to growth; (3) 1890–1930: substantial growth associated with immigration, followed by decline as immigration slowed; (4) 1930–60: further increases in growth associated with declining mortality and maintenance of high fertility; (5) 1960 and after: declining growth associated with a decrease in fertility rates.

Each of these periods of demographic change in Brazil was closely interwoven with the changing social and economic structure of the country as outlined in the previous chapter. Succeeding chapters seek to explore in greater depth the interrelations between these demographic processes and the broader socioeconomic changes of which they were both determinants and consequences.

---

between censuses, so that growth rates need to be based on the same concept for consistency. Preliminary census tabulations also report a *população recenseada*, including all individuals enumerated, with no regard to double counting. Readers will find a wide assortment of population growth rates reported in the literature on Brazil, and the differences arise from the authors' choices of a population concept and whether data are derived from preliminary or final census reports. Fortunately, all of the final census reports for the 1940 through 1970 censuses are now available and are utilized here.

Census	População presente	População residente
Sept. 1, 1940	41,236,315	41,165,289
July 1, 1950	51,944,397	51,941,767
Sept. 1, 1960	70,191,370	70,070,457
Sept. 1, 1970	92,341,556	93,139,037

IV   Slaves and Slavery in the Demographic History of Nineteenth-Century Brazil

For most of the nineteenth century, slavery was the dominant feature of the Brazilian socioeconomic structure.[1] In demographic terms two-thirds of Brazil's population was, through slavery, African in origin. This chapter provides a demographic perspective on slavery, which is important for clarification of the role of coerced labor in nineteenth-century Brazil and for understanding the imprint left by slavery on Brazil after the transition to free labor through abolition and immigration at the turn of the century.

As with other facets of her demographic history, Brazil contrasts with the United States and the rest of Latin America with respect to the institution of slavery and the way in which slavery was abolished. African slavery was much less extensive in Spanish-speaking Latin America than in Brazil, the Caribbean Islands, and the Southern United States. The large Indian population in many of the Spanish colonies made recourse to imported African labor less necessary. Their formal enslavement of Africans was abolished shortly after independence early in the nineteenth century. The institution was much more pervasive and longer lasting in Brazil, the Caribbean, and the United States, but important differences are found in these three areas; these contrasts will be examined in greater detail in this chapter.

Responsiveness to changes in economic conditions, crops, and climate gave both durability and national scope to Brazilian slavery. Thus, it is not sur-

---

[1]The references here are extensive. Some of the more pertinent Brazilian references in Portuguese on nineteenth-century slavery in Brazil are as follows: Beiguelman (1968), Calmon (1938), Cardoso (1962), Fernandes (1965), Freyre (1933), Furtado (1956), Gouveia (1955), Ianni (1962 and 1969), Mattoso (1972), Mello (1978), Portocarrero de Castro (1973), and Viotti da Costa (1966 and 1969).

The leading references in English dealing with Brazilian slavery, manumission, and abolition for this period are Conrad (1972), Dean (1976), Degler (1971), Denslow (1975), Eisenberg (1972 and 1974), Galloway (1971), R. Graham (1966 and 1970), Holloway (1978), Karasch (1973 and 1975), Klein (1970), Leff (1974), Mello (1977), Reis (1972, 1974, 1974, 1976), Schwartz (1974), Skidmore (1969 and 1975), Slenes (1976), Stein (1957), Toplin (1969 and 1972).

prising that slaves maintained a high relative weight in the total population throughout the colonial period and the early empire. Slaves were relatively more important in Brazil than in the United States. In 1800, slaves comprised roughly half the total population of Brazil (Chapter III, Table III–2), and the colored population as a whole (including the free colored) probably comprised 60 percent of the total population. Curtin's data in Table IV–1 explain in part why this was so. Brazil was by far the heaviest importer of African slaves in the Atlantic slave trade from the fifteenth century to the end of the nineteenth century, accounting for 38 percent of the total Atlantic slave trade from 1451 to 1870, or 3,600,000 slaves. The next largest importers (the French and English Caribbean areas) each recorded less than half of Brazil's slave imports throughout this period. Table IV–1 also shows that these large Brazilian imports were uniformly higher than those for the other slave societies for every century in the period. The United States, in contrast, accounted for only 4 percent of total Atlantic slave trade imports. Accordingly, the population of African origin came to have a large demographic weight during this period and a pervasive influence on the organization of labor in Brazil.

The first part of this chapter focuses on demographic aspects, emphasizing contrasts with the United States. Particular attention is paid to the issue of manumission and the major determinants of growth in the slave population (fertility, mortality, and slave imports). The second part sets forth evidence drawn principally from the 1872 census on the position of the slaves and colored population in the occupational and regional structure of the Brazilian economy of the nineteenth century, and emphasizes those features that left an important mark in later Brazilian society. The final section reviews some of the unique features of the abolition process in Brazil.

The Major Demographic Features of Brazilian Slavery

Scope and Size in Time and Space

In contrast to the United States, where slavery was associated with one region, Brazilian slavery was national in scope. Beginning in the sixteenth century in the sugar regions of the Northeast, it spread later to the mining region of Minas Gerais in the seventeenth and eighteenth centuries, and finally to the coffee-producing regions of Rio de Janeiro and São Paulo in the nineteenth century. In the process, all regional economies came to depend on slave labor in varying degrees, and slavery became the dominant form of labor organization in the export cycles in colonial and imperial Brazil.

Another distinguishing feature of Brazilian slavery was its relatively large urban component, especially in the early nineteenth century. Slavery in Brazil reached extensively into the urban occupational structure. Karasch (1975) points out that slaves could be found in a wide variety of skilled and unskilled

Table IV-1. Estimated Slave Imports into the Americas by Region, 1451-1870 (in thousands)

Region	1451-1600	1601-1700	%	1701-1810	%	1811-70	%	Total	%
British North America	–	–		348.0	(6)	51.0	(3)	399.0	(4)
Spanish America	75.0	292.5	(22)	578.6	(9)	606.0	(32)	1,552.1	(16)
British Caribbean	–	263.7	(19)	1,401.3	(23)			1,665.0	(17)
French Caribbean	–	155.8	(11)	1,348.4	(22)	96.0	(5)	1,600.2	(17)
Dutch Caribbean	–	40.0	(3)	460.0	(8)			500.0	(5)
Danish Caribbean	–	4.0		24.0				28.0	
Brazil	50.0	560.0	(41)	1,891.4	(31)	1,145.4	(60)	3,646.8	(38)
Old World	149.9	25.1	(3)	–		–		175.0	(2)
TOTAL	274.9	1,341.1	(100)	6,051.7	(100)	1,898.4	(100)	9,566.1	
Annual average	1.8	13.4		55.0		31.6		22.8	

Source: Curtin (1969: 268).

labor activities and that they actually dominated many trades in the city of Rio de Janeiro. This reflected the absence of a large pool of European immigrant labor in the city until the mid-nineteenth century. Salvador, Rio de Janeiro, Recife, São Luis, and Belém, along with other regional cities, had a large number of urban slaves from the mid-eighteenth to the mid-nineteenth century. In some cases, slaves numbered well over half the urban labor force. The absence of a large factory system facilitated the problem of control and supervision of urban slaves, since most of the manpower was located in artisan household activities. It is also true that in Rio de Janeiro slaves were beginning to be incorporated into early factory employment after the middle of the nineteenth century (Lobo 1975). This process undoubtedly depressed salaries and working conditions of indentured European immigrant laborers, who also worked in these establishments.

The growth of urban slavery was closely bound to declines in the regional export economies at the end of the eighteenth century. As the demand for slave labor declined in rural–based activities (sugar, mining, etc.), the growing excess supply of labor released from plantation work or mining was transferred, rented, or sold into urban activities. Urban slavery can be looked upon as an escape valve for further remunerative slave activity in the face of cyclical export stagnation. A further aspect is that when new export cycles occurred, with rising prices and output, there was a significant transfer or sale of urban slaves back into rural cash crop activities. Karasch describes how this process became important in the province of Rio de Janeiro, when the coffee boom that started in the 1840s began to drain slave manpower from the cities to the plantation areas in the state (Karasch 1975).[2] By 1872, slaves accounted for less than 18 percent of the total population of the city of Rio de

[2]It is-interesting to note that Claudia Goldin makes the same argument with respect to the net out-migration of urban slaves to the cotton plantations in the South during the cotton boom of the 1850s in the United States. See Claudia Goldin, "A Model to Explain the Relative Decline of Urban Slavery: Empirical Results," in *Race and Slavery in the Western Hemisphere: Quantitative Studies*, edited by Stanley L. Engerman and Eugene Genovese, Princeton University Press, 1975.

Janeiro, whereas in 1849 they had comprised 33 percent of the city's population and, in 1834, 44 percent. Urban slavery was thus able to grow as extensivel as it did in Brazil due to the relative scarcity of European immigrants and to prolonged periods of export stagnation that released slave manpower from rural occupations. As the rural export economies revived, however, there was a transfer of slaves from urban back to rural activities.

Manumission and Miscegenation

Manumission and miscegenation were much more common in Brazil than in the United States. Chapter III (Table III–2) has highlighted the growing numbers of the free-colored population throughout the nineteenth century in Brazil. In 1800, the free colored numbered less than 12 percent of the total population. By 1872, they comprised 45 percent of the total. Fogel and Engerman (1975) report, in contrast, that on the eve of the Civil War, in 1860, free Negroes in the United States comprised no more than 11 percent of the total non-white population.

In Brazil, the free-colored population comprised 20 percent of the total colored population in 1800 and 74 percent in 1872. These percentages reflect a high rate of manumission and also point to the greater importance of miscegenation in Brazil. By 1872, the mulatto component of the total colored population had reached 66 percent. Brazil had become a racially mixed society with a large free-colored component long before the final abolition of slavery in 1888. These features were also common to the Caribbean societies, but contrast sharply with the United States South. The rapid rise in miscegenation throughout Colonial and Imperial Brazil has been explained largely by the relative scarcity of European women characteristic of Portuguese colonization of Brazil during this period (Degler 1971).

What is less clear, however, are the social and economic reasons for manumission. Why would it have been in the interests of slave owners to have freed so many of their slaves over such a long period of time? This intriguing feature of Brazilian slavery merits further discussion. To gain perspective, it is helpful to set forth the demographic characteristics of the freed slaves. Schwartz (1974) has documented the manumission process in the province of Bahia from 1684 to 1745, using information from the notorial registers that recorded the juridical act of freeing slaves (cartas de alforria). Females gained their freedom at a ratio of 2:1 over males, despite the fact that males outnumbered females in the Atlantic slave trade. Female slaves were thus gaining their freedom at a greater rate than their statistical representation in the population. Brazilian-born slaves made up almost 70 percent of the manumitted slaves in Schwartz's sample, while mulattoes comprised slightly less than half. These percentages highlight the bias of manumission in favor of the Brazilian-born and mulattoes, since African-born slaves made up close to two-thirds of the total slaves in Colonial Brazil versus 10 to 20 percent for mulattoes. Though age reporting was incomplete in these registers, Schwartz's analysis led him to conclude that children constituted between one-quarter to one-third of the total. Older slaves (at the date of manumission) made up only a small proportion of the total.

Approximately one out of every two freed slaves gained their freedom through self-purchase. This proportion grew (and gratis manumission declined) during periods of rising slave prices. Mattoso's data (1972) from the same notorial registers corroborates Schwartz's findings on the strong female and mulatto bias, as do Karasch's (1973) data on early-nineteenth-century Rio de Janeiro. Self-purchase was also important in their findings.

Recent work completed by Robert Slenes (1976: 486–530) offers additional material on the manumission process in the 1870s and 1880s in Brazil. Drawing upon official manumission records during this later period, he reports a manumission rate of 6 per 1,000 during the period of 1873–75, with a high of 21 per 1,000 for the city of Rio de Janeiro and low rates of 3.4 to 5 per 1,000 for the plantation states of Rio de Janeiro, Alagoas, São Paulo, and Pernambuco. These are considerably higher than the manumission rates Slenes reports for the United States in 1850 (less than one-half person per 1,000). He further points out that the number of slaves manumitted between 1873 and 1885 represented 13 percent of the 1873 slave population base in Brazil. Again, relatively high percentages were recorded in the nonplantation provinces and urban areas and lower percentages in the plantation provinces. Other findings from his work indicate a rising trend in the rate of manumission in the 1880s; a much higher rate for slave women (especially in urban areas) and older slaves than for prime-age slaves and, finally, the probability that close to 50 percent of the slaves manumitted from 1873 to 1885 gained their freedom through some form of self-purchase.

The foregoing offers limited insight into possible generalizations concerning the manumission process. First, the motives were mixed and complex. No single factor explains the pattern. Humanitarian concerns and surrogate paternity (in addition to biological paternity) explain part of the process. Mistresses and masters freed both young as well as working-age slaves to whom they felt some attachment. A second explanation, callous abandonment of older slaves (to avoid old age maintenance costs) was evident, but remained a small proportion of the total. Third, female slaves were particularly favored in both gratis and paid manumission. This suggests that female slaves were probably better placed in the urban environment to gain jobs that enabled them to purchase their freedom on an installment plan than were male slaves and were able to benefit from the close contact and relationship as house slaves in the plantation setting. Prime-age male field hands in rural areas were the least likely to receive or earn manumission. A fourth consideration is that the high manumission of Brazilian-born slaves was facilitated by the constant influx of African slaves, which permitted slave owners to replace Brazilian-born slaves through the slave trade. At the same time, locally born slaves were probably better trained to take advantage of self-purchase possibilities than African slaves, many of whom were handicapped by speaking a foreign tongue and ignorant of local customs and skills. Finally, we should not forget that from the slaveowner's perspective positive inducements or rewards also played a role along with negative sanctions in controlling the slave labor force. The possibility of manumission, earned or gratis, would very likely lead to more loyal and productive behavior on the part of slaves than relying on negative sanctions alone.

Another point worth noting is that the change in occupational status for many manumitted slaves may not have been much different from what they had been doing before as slaves. Thus, slave owners frequently became employers of former slaves. This would appear to have been characteristic of the Northeast, where a free-colored rural proletariat was becoming a growing component of the plantation work force (Eisenberg 1974). It was probably less characteristic of the Southeast and of urban areas in general, where broader economic opportunities were available for the free colored. However, future mobility options (for children) were at least potentially more open than they would have been if they had remained in bondage.

While manumission reflected more than merely economic conditions and motives, it is clear that economic factors were important in the process. To begin from the slave master's perspective, a high level of infant and child mortality, combined with a high opportunity cost in using local capital to maintain slave dependents, provided a rationale for freeing locally born slave children (or at least making it less costly to do so) and for relying on African slave imports of prime age rather than slave-rearing to fill adult labor needs (Denslow 1974, Leff 1974). This would have made economic sense if there was an elastic supply of imported slaves and low to moderate slave prices, enabling slave owners to avoid the cost of creating a local supply of slaves from birth. Thus, continuation of the slave trade in Brazil until 1851 undoubtedly facilitated the manumission process. Put in economic terms, the rate of return on rearing domestic slaves was relatively low because of the high risk of infant and child mortality, the high opportunity cost of capital, and the relatively low price of the alternative source of prime field hands through the African slave trade (Denslow 1974).[3] In such circumstances, the costs to owners of manumitting slaves at birth and during childhood was probably very low.

[3]This line of reasoning is becoming more popular among scholars currently engaged in a more formal and quantitative analysis of the economics of slavery made popular by the work of Robert Fogel and Stanley Engerman on American slavery (Fogel and Engerman 1974). Questions of profitability, productivity, and efficiency are discussed in some detail. These authors reflect the spirit of applying economic theory and quantitatively testing various hypotheses about the performance of the slave system in Brazil.

In the Northeastern setting, Denslow (1975) and Reis (1972, 1974, 1976) have made valuable contributions. In the South, Pedro Carvalho de Mello's work (1977, 1978) is a recent ambitious attempt to apply Fogel and Engerman's frame of reference to the slave system on the coffee plantations in Rio de Janeiro. Leff (1974) and Portocarrero (1973) continue this analysis, in a more general way, with a national perspective, while Slenes (1976) has recently completed a comprehensive quantitative analysis of the demography and economics of slavery from 1850 to 1888.

While this kind of economic calculus may not have been the dominant motivation in every Brazilian slave owners' decision to grant or sell freedom to his slaves, the importance of these underlying factors is dramatized if we contrast the Brazilian setting with the Southern United States. Had Brazil, like the United States, enjoyed a relative abundance of capital (and low interest rates), had slave mortality been lower and slave imports prohibited, and had slave prices been rising since 1800, then the pace of manumission would very likely have been considerably less. Indeed, it was much less in the Southern United States, where such conditions did, in fact, prevail.

The protracted periods of decline and stagnation in Brazil's export cycles were a further factor facilitating manumission in Brazil. As export earnings declined or disappeared, the burden of maintaining slaves grew. Alternatives like rental, sale, or earned manumission became more attractive. Again, the Brazilian experience contrasts with the United States South, which did not undergo such prolonged periods of stagnation. These circumstances also facilitated manumission from the point of view of the individual slave. Schwartz (1974) has correctly emphasized that before self-purchase could have become an avenue to freedom, a market economy must have existed, with sufficient opportunities to allow slaves the possibility for earning wages to buy their freedom. Though there has been little research on this point, Karasch's work in Rio de Janeiro strongly suggests that such opportunities did exist, at least in the urban environment of Rio de Janeiro (Karasch 1975).

At the same time, there must have been a strong incentive for slaves to want to incur the burden of extra work in buying their freedom through work on Sundays and holidays. The shift from slave status to a colored freedman status must have represented a sufficient improvement in the quality of life to have made the effort worthwhile. Brazilian society was certainly less progressive and less mobile than American society in the nineteenth century. However, it may not have been so in relative terms with respect to blacks and, more specifically, for manumitted slaves. Although racial discrimination was characteristic of both societies, it is possible that this form of discrimination was more rigid and debilitating in American society at the time than in Brazilian society. This fact, combined with the differing economic conditions in Brazil and the Southern United States, could have made manumission relatively more feasible, on the one hand, and more open for free-colored opportunities on the other, for the Brazilian slave population than for the American slave population.

Slave Mortality and the Rate of Natural Increase

Slave mortality was considerably higher and the rate of natural increase of the slave population lower in Brazil than in the United States. Mainly for this reason, the once accepted humanitarian interpretation of Latin American slavery (as compared to U.S. slavery) by Freyre and Tannenbaum has been

56   DEMOGRAPHIC ASPECTS OF SLAVERY

challenged by more recent historians (Cardoso 1962, Ianni 1962, Genovese 1971, and Conrad 1972). These critics have invariably pointed to the much higher death rates and lower rates of natural increase for Latin American slaves as evidence against significant humanitarian features in Latin American slavery. That the rate of increase of the slave population was considerably lower in Brazil than in the United States is clear. Throughout the entire four-century history of the Atlantic slave trade the United States imported only 400,000 slaves. Yet, by 1860 there were over 4,000,000 slaves in the United States. Brazil, on the other hand, imported close to 3,600,000 slaves over this same period, yet there were only 1,500,000 slaves in Brazil in 1872.

It is important to remember, however, that these numbers refer to increases in the number of slaves and not to the growth of the total colored population. In the United States, where manumission was minor, the order of magnitude of this increase in the number of slaves is a reasonable reflection of a higher rate of natural increase (births minus deaths) among the black population as a whole. However, the decline in the number of slaves in Brazil does not by itself imply that a negative rate of natural increase prevailed. Because of more widespread manumission, part of the "loss" in the African population was due to transfers into free-colored status.

Even so, natural increase in Brazil was much lower. If we add the free-colored population to the number of slaves to correct for manumission, the total colored population in Brazil still amounted to only 5,700,000 persons in 1872. The U.S. slave population (ignoring the small free-colored component) increased tenfold over the number imported through the slave trade, while the total colored population in Brazil (including slaves and the free colored) increased by only 60 percent over the number imported during these centuries. Clearly, there was a different mortality environment in the two countries and for the slave population in particular.

Slave mortality was high in Brazil in part because mortality was also high for the nonslave population. It is of particular interest to learn whether and to what extent the death rate was substantially higher for slaves in Brazil as compared to nonslaves and the possible implications of this for differential rates of natural increase for the slave and nonslave populations. Contemporary reports on mortality provide only a vague notion of the crude death rates for slaves. In general, the estimates were high, but represented a wide range, from as low as 20 per thousand up to a high of 60 per thousand, depending upon the region, period, observer, and the occupational class of slaves under study (Mello 1975). The nature of the data used in these studies and the facile assumptions underlying them seriously compromise their reliability. Life expectancy estimates based on contemporary commentators (planters, travelers, etc.) and attempts to establish some age-specific mortality rates also show a wide variation.

An important contribution to the better understanding of slave mortality in Brazil is the work of Mello (1975), who employed stable population tech-

Table IV-2. Data on Life Expectancy for Male Slaves and Total Population in Brazil and the United States in the Mid-Nineteenth Century

Brazil–1872		United States (ca. 1850)	
Male slave	Total population	Male slave	Total population
(1)	(2)	(3)	(4)
18.26	27.40	35.54	40.40
col. 1/col. 2	col. 3/col. 4	col. 1/col. 3	col. 2/col. 4
(5)	(6)	(7)	(8)
.68	.88	.51	.68

Source: Mello (1974: 30–32), Evans (1962: 213).

niques to estimate life table values for the slave and free-colored population reported in the 1872 census. This census did not provide all of the detailed age-distribution data required by the stable population technique, nor was the population "closed" either to entrants (older slaves born in Africa and imported to Brazil) and exits other than mortality (principally slaves freed through manumission) as required by the techniques. Therefore Mello was forced to make a number of additional estimates in regard to slave imports, manumissions, fertility, and the age distributions in order to arrive at life expectancy.[4] The risk of error is obviously higher because a combination of assumptions was required in order to overcome lack of data for these variables. However, Mello's approach, which included a careful analysis of the possible sources of bias, provides us with what appear to be plausible life expectancy figures for slaves in the decades just prior to abolition. Table IV–2 presents his results for male Brazilian slaves and comparable measures of life expectancy for the slave and nonslave populations of the United States.

The data in the table permit several useful comparisons. The first relates to the slave populations themselves (column 7), where it can be seen that Brazilian male slaves had roughly half the life expectancy of U.S. slaves in the mid-nineteenth century. This is expected, since Brazilian slaves lived in the higher-risk environment of a society where mortality was higher for the general population. As seen in column 8, the life expectancy for the total population in Brazil was only two-thirds the level of the U.S. population. More importantly, the Brazilian slave was much worse off *vis-à-vis* his nonslave counterpart: the ratio of the life expectancy of a Brazilian male slave to that for the total population in Brazil (column 5) was 0.68, while the same ratio for the American male slave was much higher at 0.88 (column 6). One effect of Brazil's generally

[4]The most difficult task facing Mello was estimation of separate age-sex distributions for the native African group and then separating them from their descendants. The manumission problem was handled by first calculating life expectancy for the entire colored population (slave and free) and then using this as an upper bound estimate for the slave population, which experienced more severe mortality conditions.

lower level of overall development at this time appears to be that differential mortality for slaves was greater. The extent to which the narrower differential between slave and nonslave mortality in the United States can be attributed to better conditions in general versus differential harshness in the institution of slavery in the two countries is open to question. An important aspect of this question relates to infant and child mortality, which is a significant component of mortality in any high-mortality regime. This issue will be discussed next in conjunction with conditions affecting family formation and fertility under Brazilian slavery.

Marriage and Fertility Patterns of the Slave Population: Problems of Measurement and Interpretation

As with death rates, evidence on slave birth rates is incomplete and, in part, misleading. Given the lack of vital statistics information in nineteenth-century Brazil, analysts have had to rely on indirect fertility measures such as child/woman ratios for various periods and regions. Such a measure, which relates the number of slave children under age 10 to the number of slave women ages 15 to 49, is less than ideal. The numerator (slave children) can be understated through the manumission of children, while the denominator (slave women) can be inflated by the entrance of slave women without children through the slave trade (or by interregional migration in regional comparisons). Of more importance is the fact that the numerator is affected by infant mortality, which was very high in slave populations. Adequate measurement of fertility trends and differentials requires that account be taken of these factors and of the possible effect of differential age composition between slave women and other women, resulting from differential slave mortality and the slave trade. Limitations of the Brazilian data prevent detailed examination of these effects. Their importance in making an adequate assessment of slave fertility patterns has been demonstrated in a recent study of slave fertility in nineteenth-century Cuba by Eblen (1975), who took account of infant mortality and corrected for the age and sex biases introduced by the slave trade. His findings show that the intrinsic rate of increase of the slave population in Cuba (the rate relevant to a closed population with a quasi-stable age structure) was about the same as that for the nonslave population. Such studies have not been undertaken in Brazil, so that the true fertility rate of the slave population is still open to question.

Despite the biases inherent in crude measures like marriage rates and child/woman ratios, it is still revealing to review those that are available for various population groups in early censuses. Contrasting orders of magnitude offer some suggestive evidence on racial differentials. Table IV–3 shows the percent married by various racial groups in Brazil in 1872. It is curious to note the declining percentage as one moves from whites (where 30 percent are

Table IV-3. Percent Married for Racial and Slave Status in 1872 and Racial Categories in 1890 in Brazil

	Black		Mulatto		White	
	Male	Female	Male	Female	Male	Female
A. Percent married	(1)	(2)	(3)	(4)	(5)	(6)
1872						
Slave	8	8	8	8	–	–
Nonslave	20	21	26	26	30	30
B. Percent married						
1872	14	15	23	24	30	30
1890	24	22	25	24	28	29

Source: Demographic censuses of 1872 and 1890.

married) to nonslave mulattoes (26 percent), nonslave blacks (20 percent), and to slaves, where only 8 percent are recorded as married in 1872. The racial distinction between mulattoes and blacks appears to make a difference for the free-colored population, since the mulatto nonslaves have a higher percent married than nonslave blacks. Within the slave category, however, there is no difference between mulattoes and blacks.

Marriage rates can be a useful index to reflect family stability and cohesion, and the percentages in panel A reflect a distinct racial hierarchy in this regard as one moves from white to slave status. Of particular importance here is the much higher percentage married for the free-colored population than for the slave population, presumably reflecting a much more institutionalized pattern of family life. Within the free-colored class, free mulattoes enjoy a slight advantage over free blacks. The considerably higher marriage rates among the free colored than among the slaves may be an important clue to one of the attractions of manumission; namely, the opportunity for a more stable pattern of family formation and, as will be seen below, greater chance for children's survival.

Table IV-3 also shows that by 1890 black men and women raised their marriage percentages significantly compared to 1872. Apparently, the abolition of slavery in 1888 created the possibility for a more normal family pattern, with a consequent rise in former black slaves registered as married.[5] There is, of course, always some question about the accuracy of these data and, further, with respect to slaves in 1872, a question about the meaning of the census definition of marriage. It is doubtful that cohabitation was considered marriage; more probably marriages recorded in the census refer to formally registered marriages, thereby underestimating the true level of cohabitation, which would have had a higher incidence among the slave population than other population groups. In any event, the sharp differentials evident in Table

[5] Also, this rise in the percent married for the black population in 1890 may also be reflecting society's tendency to classify former slave cohabitations as "married" in the early postabolition period in Brazil.

IV–3, even if only for formally recorded marriages, appear sufficient to suggest that there were greater inhibitions on slave marriages, with a consequent negative impact on family formation and family life as compared to the free-colored population. A contributing factor to this low percent of married slaves would be the slave holders' interest in discouraging formal marriages among slaves, since it would be more economical to sell slaves individually rather than in family units. This, of course, merely underlines the precarious nature of family life for slave unions, especially informal union or cohabitation, which could more easily be broken up by slave owners.[6]

Regional variation in these differentials is also important in the major slave-holding provinces of the Southeast (Rio de Janeiro and São Paulo). In contrast to Rio de Janeiro and to the national pattern just described, marriage rates for the free colored and, to a lesser extent, slaves in São Paulo were closer to rates for the white population.[7] This suggests a different institutional environment for marriage and family formation for the free colored and slaves between these two regions. São Paulo, perhaps due to its frontier milieu and stronger church tradition, created a more hospitable environment for conventionally recorded family unions for these groups. This indirect evidence suggests that Paulista planters may have been more concerned with securing a stable family environment for their slave labor force than planters in the province of Rio de Janeiro. Familiarity with the environment (as reflected in intermarriage and place of birth) may also have been a factor, since blacks and Africans com-

---

[6]Slenes (1976: Chapter IX) points out sharp regional variations in the percent of slave women that were married in the 1872 census and the 1873 slave *matrícula* (i.e., inventory). In general, he concludes that planters were more interested than nonplantation slave owners in creating formally sanctioned marriages to create family stability and facilitate social control within large average-sized slave populations. Nonplantation slave owners, especially in urban areas, had much smaller-sized slave holdings and experienced a more rapid turnover of their slaves. They were, therefore, less interested in promoting formal slave marriages and a stable slave family setting and more likely to be selling and buying slaves on an individual basis, thereby creating a more unstable slave family setting than that characteristic of plantation settings.

[7]Data from the 1872 census shows the following for the percent of women married for these two provinces:

	Nonslave			Slave	
	White	Mulatto	Black	Mulatto	Black
Provinces					
Rio de Janeiro	39	16	13	5	7
São Paulo	30	26	25	12	15

The above data shows a sharply higher marriage percentage for slaves in São Paulo, however, it should be pointed out that the province of Rio de Janeiro still showed a much higher percent married than the city of Rio de Janeiro, where less than one percent of the slave women were recorded as married in the 1872 census. Thus, these results are still consistent with the finding of Slenes (see footnote 6), emphasizing the larger percent married and more stable slave family setting in plantation as contrasted to nonplantation areas. However, within the plantation setting itself, there is clearly a difference between São Paulo and Rio de Janeiro, as Slenes himself also points out (Slenes 1975: Chapter IX).

prised a much larger percent of the total slave labor force in Rio de Janeiro than mulattoes and *crioulos* (Brazilian-born slaves).

Turning to fertility, there is a similar pattern of racial differentials in the national child/woman ratios in the 1872 census. Comparing the ratio of children 6 to 10 years of age to women 16 to 40 years of age, whites recorded the highest ratio (57 children per 100 women), followed by the free colored (50) and then slaves (35).[8] However, the ratio for slaves is probably biased downward for reasons mentioned earlier: manumission, slave infant mortality, and differences in age structure. Correcting for manumissions would narrow the gap between them and the free colored (whose ratio would be lowered as that for slaves increased). The differential favoring whites would remain.

A comparison of differentials in the child/woman ratios, where slaves averaged about two-thirds of whites, to the pattern in marriage ratios, where slave marriages were less than one-third of whites (except São Paulo), suggests that cohabitation and illegitimacy must have been high among the slave population in Brazil. This combination of a higher incidence of cohabitation and illegitimacy with harsh working conditions very likely contributed to a high rate of slave infant mortality. Moreover, this rate must have been considerably higher than that associated with the free-colored population, whose more stable and cohesive family life meant that their marriage and child-bearing practices could have been conducted within the more normally constituted and typical family life of the time.

Evidence from the Northeast indicates that the rate of natural increase of the slave population was negative. Records kept on slave births after 1871 indicate that annual births, on the average, were 2,300 or 30.6 per thousand in an average slave population of 73,679 slaves in Pernambuco between 1873 and 1887. The general mortality rate in Recife was never below 27 per thousand during this period and generally varied between 29 and 35 per thousand for the total population. Since the mortality rate for slaves (especially infant mortality) was clearly higher than for nonslaves, this would strongly suggest that slaves experienced a negative rate of natural increase during this period (Eisenberg 1974: 150–51).[9]

[8]The infants chosen for this ratio are age 6 to 10 years, since one year before the 1872 census the Rio Branco Law freed slave children of slaves born from that time onward. The 1872 census records no "slave" children from zero to roughly three years of age.

[9]The only other attempt to estimate a natural rate of increase for the slave population is by Slenes (1976: Chapter VIII, pp. 363–64). First, he estimated the general fertility rate of 138–167 births per 1,000 women, derived from the average number of births recorded in the matriculas of slaves from 1871 through 1875 to women aged 15 to 44 years. Then, using his estimate of mortality from his sample data on four estates in Campinas, which corresponds closely to Arriaga's estimates on life expectancy derived from the 1872 census, he establishes that slave mortality estimates in Brazil are similar to Coale and Demeny's extreme mortality models West 1 through West 4. With this estimated range of fertility and mortality, he can offer a rough estimate of the intrinsic rate of growth or decline of the slave population, using stable population model tables. The findings for these Brazilian slave data show a rate of decrease between −0.5 and −1.5 percent per year. From this exercise he concludes that the Brazilian slave population was declining in the 1870s even after controlling for manumissions and slave flights.

Table IV-4. Number of Children per Couple by Various Racial Categories in the Federal District (Rio de Janeiro) in Brazil in 1890

Racial couples	Number of live children per couple	Total children ever born per couple	Percent of total couples[a]
White and white	2.53	3.53	73.5
Mulatto and mulatto	2.34	3.30	10.5
Mulatto and white	2.22	3.11	5.1
White and black	2.16	2.80	0.8
Mulatto and black	2.07	2.96	1.4
Black and black	1.99	2.98	5.7
TOTAL (N = 42,309)			97.0

[a]Percentages do not add up to 100, since *caboclo* category (3 percent) is excluded.
Source: Censo Demográfico do Distrito Federal, 1890.

Table IV–4 offers an additional interracial perspective on fertility patterns in the city of Rio de Janeiro in 1890, two years after abolition. Here the total number of children ever born (live children plus children who had died) are recorded for six types (by race) of unions. In principle, infant mortality is controlled in these data. As expected, unions of whites and the colored groups that had been free for a longer time (mulatto-white and mulatto-mulatto marriages) record a higher number of live children at the time of the census than for marriages between individuals who had probably just been freed (black-black and black-mulatto). This also holds for the total number ever born (column 3), suggesting that actual fertility was lower for newly freed slaves. However, the low proportion of colored marriages in the total suggests that consensual unions were not included, again leading to greater bias in the case of colored racial groups than among whites. The total number of children ever born for the black population in these unions might have been higher than for those blacks registered as formally married in Table IV–4. Also, there is no control for age. White women (and probably mulatto women) had a longer life expectancy than black women and thus a longer time span to have had more children. Age-specific fertility for the 20 to 24 year age cohort might indeed have been much closer for the two groups than for all women in child-bearing ages. Until these factors can be controlled, we cannot draw any firm conclusion about true fertility differentials among different races at this time.

In summary, no ideal data base exists to determine differential fertility of slaves in Brazil. Child/woman ratios need to be corrected for infant mortality, manumission, and the peculiar age-sex structure introduced by the slave trade. More satisfactory measures, like children ever born, are available only for "official" marriages in 1890 in Rio de Janeiro, and, in addition, are not reported by age, thereby preventing an estimate of age-specific fertility rates. Nevertheless, the evidence clearly points to limited formal marriages for slaves and high levels of cohabitation and illegitimacy outside the normally constituted family pattern. This lack of a stable family environment and the harsh working conditions of slavery contributed not only to limited child-bearing opportunities but, even more importantly, to the high levels of infant and child mortality that so reduced the survival chances for a child born of a slave mother. Mortality also reduced the chances for slave mothers to survive to the completion of their child-bearing years. Other factors, manumission and the slave trade, contributed to slave births being low in proportion to the slave population, principally because of their effect on the age and sex structure of the slave population. In the end, slavery was not a demographically viable institution in Brazil in that losses through slave mortality and manumission outweighed increases derived from fertility and the slave trade.[10]

The Slave Labor Force: Interregional Transfers and Labor Force Characteristics in Mid- to Late-Nineteenth-Century Brazil

The growth and allocation of slave labor in Brazil was intimately associated with the patterns of regional growth in the Brazilian economy. Changing interregional economic relations conditioned several important sociodemographic features of Brazilian slavery: the racial composition of the various provincial labor forces, the allocation of slaves into rural and urban settings, and sectoral and regional patterns of labor force participation of the slave population. Likewise, widespread use of slave labor affected the growth of the internal market and the possibilities for nonslave labor participation in the economy. The plantation economies of the Northeast and the Southeast created a highly unequal distribution of income and wealth. Their concentrated land ownership led to subsistence-squatter patterns of rural dependency for the nonslave population and restricted their rate of internal migration. Urban and industrial growth were limited. All of this severely reduced the potential for social change in nineteenth-century Brazilian society, creating a milieu that would change, and then only partially, only after the abolition of slavery and the growth of a wage economy built on immigrant manpower.

In this frame of reference, it is instructive to review important aspects of the regional distribution and sectoral allocation of slave labor in the Brazilian economy in the decades prior to abolition. The main features can be summarized as follows:

1) Inter- and intraregional reallocation of the slave population from mid-century onward clearly reflected the derived demand for slave labor associated with the changing patterns of regional growth in the Brazilian economy. The coffee-producing provinces of the Southeast significantly increased their relative proportion of the total slave population, while the Northeastern provinces experienced a decline. Moreover, within Southeastern provinces

---

[10]This does not mean that slavery may not have been profitable or efficient from the point of view of resource allocation in the eyes of the slaveowner.

the coffee municipalities gained at the expense of the noncoffee municipalities and, further, acquired a greater relative number of the prime-age and male slaves available in the declining national stock of slave manpower in the decades preceding abolition.

2) The interregional slave trade within Brazil created a much larger migratory component in the slave labor force of the Southeast than for any other region in the country. Within this region, African-born slaves were relatively more important in the province of Rio de Janeiro than in other regions, while *crioulo* slaves born in the Northeast comprised a more important part of São Paulo's migrant slave population.

3) Free-colored and mulatto populations made up a much larger part of the total population in the Northeast than in the Southeast, reflecting a longer history of manumission and miscegenation. In the Southeast, both the black and the slave population were relatively larger than in the Northeast, reflecting an economic pull on the remaining stock of slaves (which were primarily blacks) exercised by the rapidly growing coffee culture.

4) Although in absolute terms slaves were more numerous in rural areas than in urban areas in all regions of Brazil in 1872, in the Northeast slaves were relatively more important in the major metropolitan areas than in rural areas, suggesting that, in the face of a decline in the regional export economy in the Northeast, slaves were shifted gradually into urban activities. In the Southeast, the opposite occurred, as the coffee booms took hold after the 1840s and slaves were drawn out of such urban areas as Rio de Janeiro.

5) Sectoral labor force data on the slave and nonslave labor force highlight the heavier agricultural participation of the slave as compared to the nonslave and foreign-born labor force. This sectoral bias, however, was much more pronounced in the Southeast than in the Northeast.

6) Although industrial occupations comprised a small part of the total slave labor force distribution, the slave labor force still represented 11 percent of the total number of manual and mechanical industrial workers in Brazil in 1872, and over 25 percent of the total industrial labor force in the province of Rio de Janeiro.

7) Finally, racial occupational groupings in the city of Rio de Janeiro in 1890 show a clear racial hierarchy in occupational rankings. The mulatto labor force worked in more promising occupations than the black labor force. This would suggest that the miscegenation-manumission process was related to social and occupational mobility.

The Growth and Change in the Regional Composition of the Slave Population

Table IV–5 shows comparative growth rates for the white, colored, and slave populations in Brazil during the nineteenth century. As indicated in earlier discussion, the free colored grew twice as rapidly as the white population and

Table IV-5. Rate of Growth of White, Free-Colored, and Slave Populations for Brazil
during the Early and Mid-Nineteenth Century (average annual percentage rate)

Region & period	Rate of growth			
	White (1)	Free-colored (2)	Slave (3)	Total colored (4)
Brazil				
1798 – 1817-18	0.2	1.8	1.4	–
1817-18 – 1872	2.4	3.7	-0.4	–
1798–1872	1.8	3.2	-0.1	1.5
1872-90	2.9	–	–	0.9 (1.5)[a]

[a]The rate of growth in parentheses for total colored includes the *caboclo* category, as well as blacks and mulattoes. The lower rate refers only to the latter. However, many were considered *caboclo* in 1890. See footnote 11.
Sources: Provincial and national censuses.

more than three times faster than the slave population. This was due to the accession of slaves to free-colored status through manumission, as well as their higher natural rate of increase. The slave population (1.5 million) was approximately the same in 1872 as in 1798. There was very likely a slight increase up to 1851 and then a gradual decline to 1872. Termination of the Atlantic slave trade in 1851, manumissions, and high mortality all contributed to this lack of growth. After 1872 the slave population declined even more rapidly as a result of the Free Womb Law of 1871 (freeing slave children), the Sexagenerian Law of 1886 (freeing slaves over 60 years of age), and abolitionist pressures. Between 1883 and 1887 the slave labor force was reduced by roughly half (from 1,240,806 to 723,419 slaves) through increased manumissions and slave flights (Table IV-6). The white population grew at a slightly higher rate than the total colored population from 1800 to 1872 (1.8 vs. 1.5 percent). In the latter part of the century, however, the growth of the white population base was markedly higher, reflecting the influx of European immigration.[11]

Table IV-6 portrays the changing relative distribution of the total number of slaves among the major regions and provinces throughout the nineteenth century. Several features stand out. As late as 1864 the older Northeastern region still claimed approximately half the total number of slaves in the country and more than the Southeastern coffee region. By 1872, these relative positions had changed abruptly, with the Southeast accounting for almost 60 percent of the slave population and the Northeast only 32 percent. Thus, the high point of the interregional transfer of slaves in Brazil took place in the 1860s and early 1870s.[12]

[11]The low rate of growth of the total colored population from 1872–90 (0.9) is probably understated as some mulattoes were classified in the *caboclo* non-white category, especially in the Northeastern states in 1890. The non-white definition is probably more accurate here (1.5 percent). Different model life tables (Coale–Demeny "West" series) were then compared to arrive at a lower life expectancy estimate for the slave population.
[12]For a discussion of the interregional slave trade from the Northeast to the South during this post-1851 period, see Conrad (1971); Viotti da Costa (1966); Klein (1971); and Slenes (1976).

Table IV-6. Percentage Distribution of the Slave Population by Regions and Selected Provinces in Brazil, 1823-87

Region	Percent				
	1823 (1)	1864 (2)	1872 (3)	1883 (4)	1887 (5)
North[a]	4	2	2	2	1
Northeast	53	49	32	28	28
Pernambuco	13	15	6	6	6
Bahia	20	17	11	11	11
Maranhão	8	4	5	4	5
Others	12	13	10	7	6
Southeast	38	44	59	63	67
Espírito Santo	5	1	2	2	2
Minas Gerais	18	15	25	24	26
Rio de Janeiro[b]	13	17	19	21	22
Rio de Janeiro (city)	–	6	3	3	1
São Paulo	2	5	10	13	15
South[a]	2	4	6	6	2
Rio Grande do Sul		2	4	5	1
Others		2	2	1	1
West	3	1	1	1	1
Brazil (%)	100	100	100	100	100
Brazil (no.)	1,163,746	1,715,000	1,510,806	1,240,806	723,419
rate of growth		(0.9)	(-1.1)	(-2.1)	(-16.5)

[a]Data for Amazonas (in North) and Paraná (in South) for 1823 are from 1819 census.
[b]Includes both the city and the province of Rio de Janeiro in 1823.
Sources: Census of 1823 and 1819, J. F. Oliveira Vianna (1922: Vol. 1, pp. 404–05, 414).
Estimates for 1864, Agostinho Marques Perdigão Malheiro, *A Escravidão no Brasil*, vol. 2, 2nd edition, São Paulo, 1944, p. 198.
Census of 1872, Recenseamento da Populacão do Império a que se Procedeu no dia 1 de Agosto de 1872, Rio de Janeiro, 1873–76, 21 volumes.
Matrícula 1884, Relatório do Ministério da Agricultura, 30 April 1885, p. 372.
Matrícula 1887, Relatório do Ministério da Agricultura, 14 May, p. 24.

By 1887, the coffee-producing regions in the Southeast accounted for two-thirds of the declining national stock of slaves. Within the Southeast, São Paulo's relative share of the national slave population rose from 5 to 15 percent from 1864 to 1887. This strong pull of the coffee regions, and São Paulo in particular, shows that the transfer of slaves throughout this period reflected the shifting derived demand for slave manpower from the Northeast to the Southeast, from cotton and sugar to coffee.

Disaggregated municipality-level data in Table IV-7 (panel A) illustrates this even more in showing that the Southeastern slave population share increased in the coffee municipalities, while it declined in the noncoffee municipalities from 1874 to 1883. Moreover, these increases were most substantial in the key coffee-producing provinces of Rio de Janeiro and São Paulo. At the same time that these provinces were increasing their share of the total slave population, they were also improving the human capital content of their slave

Table IV-7. Change in Regional Concentration and Age and Sex Characteristics of the Slave Population within the Major Coffee-producing Provinces of Southeastern Brazil, 1872-74 and 1883-87

A. Regional concentration of slave population between coffee and noncoffee municipalities of São Paulo, Minas Gerais, and Rio de Janeiro in 1874 and 1883

	Percent of total slaves in state	
Province	1874	1883
São Paulo		
a) Coffee municipalities	53	64
b) Noncoffee municipalities	47	36
Total no. slaves	174,622	167,493
Rio de Janeiro		
a) Coffee municipalities	49	58
b) Noncoffee municipalities	51	42
Total no. slaves	301,352	268,831
Minas Gerais		
a) Coffee municipalities	25	29
b) Noncoffee municipalities	75	71
Total no. slaves	311,304	301,125

Source: Derived from data in Conrad (1972: appendix tables 12-14).

B. Percentage distribution of male and prime-age slaves in São Paulo, Rio de Janeiro, and Brazil 1872-87

	Percent of national total	
Province	1872	1887
São Paulo		
a) Male	11	16
b) Prime-age	11	15
Rio de Janeiro		
a) Male	20	23
b) Prime-age	18	21
Rest of Brazil		
a) Male	69	61
b) Prime-age	71	64

Source: 1872 Inventory in *Recenseamento 1872;* 1887 inventory in *Relatório do Ministério da Agricultura,* 14 May 1888, p. 24.

labor force. Panel B of Table IV-7 shows that from 1872 to 1887 (just prior to abolition) Rio de Janeiro and São Paulo increased their share of the total national stock of male and prime-age slaves, while the rest of Brazil registered corresponding declines for these groups.

Within the Southeastern region, a revealing contrast emerges between Rio de Janeiro and São Paulo. While the migratory component was relatively large in both instances, African slaves comprised a much larger absolute and proportional contribution to the slave population in the province of Rio de Janeiro, while *crioulo* or native-born slaves were more important in São Paulo. Data from the 1872 census show that 40 percent of the total number of African slaves in Brazil at the time were located in the province of Rio de Janeiro. They accounted for close to 20 percent of the province's total slave population. The comparable percentages in São Paulo were only 9 and 8 percent, respectively. In contrast, slaves born in other provinces of Brazil made up less than 1 percent of the provincial slave population in Rio de Janeiro, whereas they comprised 14 percent of the slave population in São Paulo. Moreover, a substantial part of these *crioulo* migrants in São Paulo were born in the Northeast.

The strong African component in Rio de Janeiro's slave population implies that the province had an older slave population than one in which *crioulos* predominated (i.e., São Paulo), since the 1872 census came twenty-one years after the termination of the African slave trade. If we assume a conventional prime-age slave import bias (16–30 years) in the late 1840s, then most of these African-born slaves would have been over 40 years of age in 1872. Age cohort data in the 1872 census confirm the older average age of the slave population for Rio de Janeiro vis-à-vis São Paulo. Over 34 percent of the male slave population in Rio de Janeiro was over 40 years of age. The comparable percentage for São Paulo was only 23 percent. There were, clearly, important human capital differentials in their slave labor force, which in turn suggests differential prices affecting the demand for slave manpower. The more profitable Paulista coffee sector was in a stronger relative position to bid for the younger and more economically attractive *crioulo* slave labor from the Northeast and elsewhere, at this time.

In summary, at the same time the total national stock of slaves declined, from 1,715,000 slaves in 1864 to 1,240,806 slaves in 1883, there was an interregional and intraprovincial concentration of the remaining slave population into the major coffee municipalities of the provinces of Minas Gerais, Rio de Janeiro, and São Paulo. From 1874 to 1883, there was an actual increase from 317,147 to 350,085 slaves in their coffee municipalities. Thus, the national decline of the slave population up to 1883 did not compromise the absolute growth of slave manpower in the coffee areas of the Southeast (especially São Paulo). Furthermore, these areas actually improved the human capital characteristics of their plantation labor force during this period, as well as increasing their numbers. These findings help explain the lack of interest on the part of coffee slave owners in importing European manpower for the coffee plantations prior to the mid-1880s. Only after abolitionist pressures increased, in 1883, did these coffee municipalities begin to experience a net decline in their slave-based manpower. And it was only after 1883 that plantation owners in São Paulo seriously began to consider mobilizing provincial support and resources to attract labor from abroad.

In contrast to the relative strengthening of slave labor in the coffee regions of the Southeast during the decades just prior to abolition, important transformations of this institution were occurring in other regions, especially the Northeast, where the economic basis for slavery was eroded. This was in large part related to the decline in the export markets for Brazilian sugar and the growing inefficiency of local production. Eisenberg (1973) and Denslow

(1973) underline how Brazil was gradually driven out of the American market due to superior Cuban production and efficiency and, later, by special preferences given to Hawaiian and Cuban output by the American Congress. At the same time, beet sugar outcompeted cane sugar in the European markets. In addition, the Northeast was unable to take full profitable advantage of the large-scale technology associated with the large sugar mills (*usinas*) that were introduced in the 1880s. Denslow shows that the hilly terrain, combined with less fertile soils in the littoral (low yield per hectare), reduced the growth potential in the supply of cane and compromised the effectiveness of railroads to transport the large supply of cane needed to guarantee full capacity utilization of the *usinas*. More primitive and costly forms of mule transport were frequently used. Cuba, besides having more fertile soil to increase cane output per hectare, had extensive flatlands that lent themselves to more effective use of railroad transport for bulk shipments of cane to the large central mills.

On the demographic side, manumission, miscegenation, and migration of slaves to the Southeast contributed to a relative decline in the importance of slave manpower in the Northeast. Some of the more important features of these shifts are evident in data on the racial composition of the Brazilian population by province in the 1872 census (Table IV–8). While the colored population in 1872 was roughly 58 percent of the total population in Brazil, the colored population (mulatto plus black) made up a considerably larger percent of the total population of the Northeastern provinces than they did in the coffee provinces in the Southeast (panel A, Table IV–8). The mulatto population was roughly twice the black population in Brazil in 1872 (38 versus 20 percent), but relatively more important than the blacks in the Northeastern provinces, where the colored population, on the whole, was a larger part of the total population. In the Southern provinces, mulatto predominance lessens and in the case of the province of Rio de Janeiro nearly disappears. This pattern shows the greater effects of accumulated manumission and, by the same token, miscegenation in the Northeastern provinces over the Southeastern areas. The predominance of mulattoes over blacks in the Northeast also reflects the interregional transfer of the predominantly black slave population into the growing export activities of the coffee culture in Minas Gerais, Rio de Janeiro, and São Paulo.

Panel B of the table permits a rough interregional contrast of urban-rural differentials for selected racial groupings through ratios showing the relative weight of a given racial group in the major urban center of a province vis-à-vis its weight in the province as a whole. Whites are relatively more important in all the major metropolitan areas than they are in the respective provinces, with the exception of Rio Grande do Sul (where European immigration moved into rural colonization programs) and Ceará.

Again North-South differences are important. There are more slaves in Northeastern cities. But in the coffee regions of the Southeast (São Paulo and Rio de Janeiro) we see many more slaves in the provinces (i.e., rural areas). In

Table IV-8. Interregional and Urban-Provincial Demographic Characteristics by Race and Slave Status in Brazil in 1872

A. Racial distribution and slave nonslave status for the colored population for selected provinces in Brazil in 1872

	Total population				Total colored population		
	White %	Mulatto %	Black %	Total[b]	Nonslave %	Slave %	Total[b]
Northeast	(1)	(2)	(3)		(4)	(5)	
Maranhão	28.8	46.7	21.4	359,040	69.4	30.6	244,584
Ceará	37.3	49.5	5.9	721,686	92.0	8.0	400,013
Pernambuco	34.6	49.1	14.9	841,539	83.4	16.6	538,575
Alagoas	25.5	60.6	12.1	348,009	85.9	14.1	252,847
Bahia	24.0	45.7	26.6	1,359,616	83.2	16.8	998,255
Southeast							
Minas Gerais	40.7	34.5	23.1	2,039,735	68.5	31.5	1,176,426
Rio de Janeiro	38.8	25.7	23.1	782,724	37.9	62.0	471,597
São Paulo	51.8	31.4	12.1	837,354	57.0	43.0	364,457
Rio Grande do Sul	59.4	16.4	18.3	434,813	55.0	45.0	150,729
Brazil	38.1	38.2	19.7	9,930,478	73.8	26.2	5,756,234

B. Urban-provincial population differentials by racial and slave status for selected provinces in Brazil in 1872

	Urban-provincial index[a]		
City-province	White	Free colored	Slave
Northeast	(1)	(2)	(3)
São Luis/Maranhao	1.31	0.92	1.18
Fortaleza/Ceará	0.98	0.99	1.06
Recife/Pernambuco	1.18	0.90	1.47
Maceió/Alagoas	1.45	0.87	1.77
Salvador/Bahia	1.24	1.03	0.83
Southeast			
Rio de Janeiro/Rio de Janeiro	1.42	1.58	0.65
São Paulo/São Paulo	1.16	1.18	0.76
Porto Alegre/Rio Grande do Sul	0.88	1.04	0.96

[a]Share of racial group in total metropolitan population divided by share of racial group in total provincial population.
[b]Percentages may not add up to 100, since *caboclo* category is excluded. Residual percentage pertains to *caboclo* (indian plus white).
Source: 1872 Census.

the face of regional export declines, slavery became a relatively more urban phenomenon in the Northeast than in the Southeast, where the coffee expansion increased demand for rural slave labor.

All these findings underscore the contrasting regional features of miscegenation and manumission. Manumission had become clearly more extensive in the Northeast (and in the older mining state of Minas Gerais) than in Rio de Janeiro and São Paulo. Mulattoes were clearly the major beneficiaries of this process. In the key coffee provinces to the South, a much smaller percentage of the colored population was free. The economic drive to expand the slave labor force kept more mulattoes in slavery than was characteristic of the declining regional economies of the Northeast.

This decline in the stock of slave manpower in the Northeast did not create a labor shortage for the plantations, however. The growing number of free mulattoes created a major source of rural manpower (the *moradores*), which became considerably more important than slaves in the rural supply of labor in this region. Reis (1974) reports that in the early 1870s there were 68,861 slaves producing roughly 100,000 tons of sugar per year in the *zona da mata* of Pernambuco. By 1887 (by deaths, manumissions and sales), we see a slave labor force reduced to only 27,854, but a rise in output to 150,000 tons (Reis 1974: 7). He concludes that slaves probably accounted for only 20 to 25 percent of the sugar zone plantation labor force as early as the 1870s. The accumulated momentum of manumission and miscegenation created an elastic supply of free-colored and *caboclo* labor in the Northeast that moved into a squatter situation (*moradores*) on or near the plantation areas (Reis 1972, Eisenberg 1974).

Thus, by the end of the third quarter of the nineteenth century, the racial configuration of Brazil reflected an accumulated process of manumission and miscegenation and, at the same time, the economic forces affecting the interregional and rural-urban location of slavery. Within this scenario there were significant interregional differences between the Northeast and the Southeast. These differences were important not only in highlighting the way in which past patterns of regional growth had altered the racial profiles of Brazil but also in pointing out some important demographic features lying behind the future problem of transition to a free labor force.

Occupational Characteristics of the Slave and Free Labor Force

The impact of slavery on the Brazilian economy in the nineteenth century must be measured not only by its responsiveness to changes in the balance of regional agricultural development but also by its role in other economic sectors and its influence on the supply of free labor. Both are evident in data on the occupational structure of the Brazilian labor force in this period.[13] More detailed discussion of the uses and limitations of labor force data in early Brazilian censuses will be found in Chapter VII. It is sufficient to note here that the relatively unsophisticated nature of the Brazilian economy at mid-century and the large component of household artisan activity in both rural and urban settings make it difficult and, in part, inappropriate to apply modern definitions

[13]The economically active component of the total population (i.e., the labor force) was derived by subtracting those classified as *sem profissões* in the 1872 census.

of sectoral and occupational activity. Nevertheless, the 1872 census does permit limited insight into the pattern of labor force participation for the slave and the nonslave. Unfortunately, the lack of a racial breakdown for the Brazilian-born nonslave labor force in the 1872 census prevents occupational comparisons between the slave and free-colored labor force. Also, there is no distinction between African-born and Brazilian-born slaves in the occupational data for slaves. Thus, no direct analysis can be made of the occupational contrasts among the free-colored, slave, and domestic white labor force on the one hand, or between the African-born or Brazilian-born slave labor on the other.

Table IV–9 confirms what was indicated in the previous section: that by 1872 the slave labor force was relatively more important in the four Southeastern provinces than in the Northeastern provinces, comprising almost one-half the labor force in the province of Rio de Janeiro. Only Maranhão recorded a relatively high slave labor force in the Northeast. As a result, the Brazilian nonslave labor force was relatively more important in the older Northeastern provinces. As mentioned earlier, this area was establishing the base for a nonslave labor force long before the abolition of slavery. Table IV–9 also confirms that in 1872 the foreign-born nonslave labor force (European immigrants) was relatively insignificant in the country as a whole and in all regions, except for Rio Grande do Sul and Rio de Janeiro. This was still well before the large inflow of Italian immigration into São Paulo, starting at the end of the 1880s.

Participation of slaves in the urban economy ranges from 15 to 23 percent for the four major cities shown. This percentage would have been substantially higher earlier, that is, before the drain of slave manpower from urban pursuits to the new rural plantation economies from the 1840s onward in the Southeast. Within this urban framework the relative participation of slave manpower in the cities of Rio de Janeiro and São Paulo (21 and 16 percent) is considerably less than for the respective coffee provinces surrounding them (Rio de Janeiro, São Paulo, and Minas Gerais) reflecting a greater concentration of slave manpower in the rural plantation economy than in the urban economy. In contrast, there is a relatively higher participation of slave manpower in the Northeastern city of Recife than in the provinces surrounding it (Alagoas, Pernambuco), reflecting the less dynamic rural export sector in this region.

There is a larger percentage of foreign-born labor in all four cities (far greater than their participation in the provinces). This reflects the urban orientation of immigrant labor (mainly Portuguese) at this time in the city of Rio de Janeiro and signals the beginning of a substitution of immigrants for previous slave manpower. Finally, Table IV–9 directly confirms the growing rural concentration of slave labor in the Southeast. Column 5 shows that 70 to 90 percent of the total slave labor force in these provinces was involved in agricul-

Table IV-9. Percentage Distribution of Total Labor Force by Selected Population Groups
and Distribution of Slave Labor Force in Agriculture for Selected Regions
in Brazil, 1872

Region	Total	Slave	Foreign nonslave	Brazilian nonslave	Percentage of slave labor force in agriculture
Provinces					
Northeast					
Pará	151,692	12.2	3.6	84.2	59
Maranhão	223,652	24.6	1.4	74.0	67
Ceará	424,547	4.7	0.3	95.0	37
Pernambuco	1,303,268	14.3	2.0	83.7	62
Alagoas	182,391	14.4	0.6	84.9	44
Bahia	852,093	14.9	1.3	83.8	65
Southeast					
Minas Gerais	1,023,867	31.9	1.7	66.4	85
Rio de Janeiro	447,873	45.2	6.9	47.9	70
São Paulo	568,773	21.6	2.5	75.9	69
Rio Grande do Sul	293,525	18.7	12.2	69.1	89
Cities					
Federal District	182,866	21.1	34.7	44.0	–
Porto Alegre	25,787	23.4	13.9	62.7	–
São Paulo	20,667	15.0	9.9	75.1	–
Recife	57,363	16.7	10.1	73.2	–
Brazil	5,758,364a	20.0	3.7	76.3	70

aExcludes *"sem profissões"*
Source: See Table IV-6.

tural activities. The comparable percentages for the Northeastern provinces range from only 37 to 67 percent.[14]

In agriculture, the slave labor force included a large female as well as male component. While 81 percent of the economically active male slaves are found in agricultural occupations, as compared to 72 percent for nonslave male Brazilians, Table IV-10 shows that slave women participated in the agricultural labor force at almost double the percent of nonslave Brazilian-born women (57 versus 32 percent). Among the three groups shown in the table, only slave women show higher rural than urban labor force participation. In part, this may reflect the duality of female roles in agriculture: nonslave women who did some farm work were not considered economically active, whereas slave women would have been considered workers even if they devoted a good part of their time to domestic tasks that were similar to those of

[14]The absolute percentage levels in agriculture should be looked upon as a lower-limit threshold, since other occupational classifications, such as day laborers (*jornaleiros e serventes*) and domestics, could also have been located within a rural setting. However, these data are probably reliable as an indicator of field hands in agricultural work. Also, the interregional differentials that are the most interesting and relevant contrasts discussed in the text would presumably not be affected substantially by a more inclusive classification.

Table IV-10. Percentage Distribution of Slave and Nonslave Labor Force by Sex
in Agricultural and Nonagricultural Activities in Brazil, 1872

Labor force	% in agriculture			% in nonagriculture			% Economically active
	Men	Women	Total	Men	Women	Total	Total
Slaves	81	57	70	19	43	30	76
Brazilian-born nonslaves	72	32	53	28	68	47	87
Foreign-born nonslaves	42	37	41	58	63	59	54

"Sem profissões" subtracted from total labor force.
Source: 1872 Census.

nonslave women. However, this did not alter the traditional female bias in non-agricultural occupations within the declining slave labor force. Forty-three percent of all female slaves in the country still worked in urban areas, compared to only 19 percent of the total male slave population. Finally, data on the economically active component of the three major population groups (slaves, Brazilian nonslaves, and the foreign-born) show that the foreign-born had an unusually high percent economically active (87 percent), in large part because of the high working-age male bias among the foreign-born and the relative absence of children. Next comes the slave labor force (76 percent) and, finally, the nonslave Brazilian-born labor force (54 percent).

The sectoral distribution of workers in 1872 in Table IV–11 shows that slaves made up 25 percent of the agricultural labor force in Brazil. This reached 50 percent in the province of Rio de Janeiro. Although only 2.5 percent of the slave labor force worked in industrial occupations (panel A, Table IV–11), they still comprised 11 percent of the total industrial work force (mechanical and manual workers). In the city of Rio de Janeiro, this participation reached 13 percent, and for the province of Rio de Janeiro 25 percent of the total industrial work force. These same data for this city underscore the growing importance of the foreign-born in the urban industrial work force. Fifty-eight percent of its industrial work force was comprised of immigrants. Thus, in the largest urban industrial setting we find that slaves and the foreign-born together comprised over 70 percent of the total manual labor and mechanical occupations recorded for the industrial sector. It is true that much of this was artisan rather than factory labor and some of the slave occupations may have been segregated from those dominated by European immigrants. Nevertheless, historical accounts from the period reveal a mixture of both slave and immigrant labor in the same establishments, suggesting the prevalence of the poor working and wage conditions for heavily indentured Portuguese immigrant labor in Rio de Janeiro.[15]

[15]Recent work by Eulália de Lobo corroborates this in the artisan factory setting in the city of Rio de Janeiro, "A História do Rio de Janeiro," paper presented at IBMEC, Rio de Janeiro, September 1975.

Table IV-11.Total Slave and Foreign and Brazilian Nonslave Labor Forces Distributed by Occupational Groupings and as Percentages of the Same Occupations, 1872

A. Distribution by occupation	Slave	Nonslave	
		Foreign	Brazilian
	Total %	Total %	Total %
Liberal professions	—	1.0	1.0
Artists	0.0	3.0	0.7
Army	—	0.1	0.6
Navy	0.0	1.5	0.4
Fishermen	0.0	0.3	0.4
Property owners	—	0.9	0.7
Manfacturers	—	1.2	0.4
Commerce & office	—	14.9	1.6
Seamstresses	3.5	3.6	10.4
Industrial workers	2.5	8.8	4.9
Agriculture	70.1	40.8	53.5
Salaried day workers	8.2	13.5	6.5
Domestic servants	15.2	10.4	19.3
	100.0 (1,153,007)	100.0 (211,429)	100.0 (4,398,928)

B. Distribution within occupations	Slave		Foreign	Brazilian
	Total %		Total %	Total %
Liberal professions	100	—	0.0	100.0
Artists	100	4.5	15.6	79.9
Army	100	—	1.1	98.9
Navy	100	8.2	14.3	77.5
Fishermen	100	7.1	4.1	88.8
Property owners	100	—	6.2	93.8
Manufacturers	100	—	13.0	87.0
Commerce & office	100	—	30.8	69.2
Seamstresses	100	8.0	1.5	90.5
Industrial workers	100	11.0	7.1	81.9
Agriculture	100	24.9	2.7	72.4
Salaried day workers	100	23.1	7.0	70.0
Domestic servants	100	16.8	2.1	81.1

Note: 0.0 means less than 0.1; — means none reported.
Source: 1872 census.

A final piece of evidence relates to the hierarchical nature of shifts in the occupational allocation of the labor force by race in the city of Rio de Janeiro between 1872 and 1890. The slave, nonslave, and foreign-born labor force in 1872 are shown in panel A. The 1890 census came two years after the abolition of slavery and was the last census to record information on the labor force by race. Panel B of Table IV–12 shows the occupational distribution in each of four 1890 racial groups. The status patterns among the four groups are clear and consistent. The foreign-born are more heavily represented in the more prestigious occupations than the native-born whites, while the mulattoes are consistently better represented than blacks in these same occupations. The foreign-born recorded a higher degree of relative participation in industrial

Table IV-12. Occupational Distribution by Racial, Slave, and Foreign-born Status
1872-90, Federal District (Rio de Janeiro)

A. 1872

	Brazilian		Foreign-born
	Slaves	Nonslave	
	(1)	(2)	(3)
1) Domestic servants	58.5%	25.9%	17.9%
2) Salaried day workers	14.8	·7.3	22.1
3) Agriculture	14.6	12.4	2.1
4) Industry	9.0	15.8	19.7
5) Commerce	–	7.6	27.4
6) Liberal professions and property owners (including artists)	1.3	6.6	1.8
7) Miscellaneous	1.8	24.4	9.0
TOTAL	100.0%	100.0%	100.0%
(number)	(39,040)	(80,397)	(63,429)

B. 1890

	Native-born			Foreign-born
	Black	Mulatto	White	
	(1)	(2)	(3)	(4)
1) Domestic servants	54.0%	45.9%	27.8%	14.2%
2) Agriculture	8.1	6.9	4.7	1.6
3) Industry	13.0	20.3	19.7	21.9
4) Commerce	4.3	5.8	25.3	28.1
5) Transport	2.5	2.9	3.5	6.6
6) Artists	0.9	2.8	2.3	2.7
TOTAL	100.0%	100.0%	100.0%	100.0%
(number)	(33,327)	(47,375)	(75,902)	(86,972)

Occupations not broken down by race (liberal professions, govt. & military)	Native-born	Foreign-born
	26,801	2,042

Sources: 1872 and 1890 censuses.

occupations, commerce, transport, and artists, followed by the native-born whites, then mulattoes, and finally blacks. In contrast, the clearly unskilled and lower paying jobs (domestic service and agriculture) accounted for 62 percent of the black labor force, 52 percent of the mulatto labor force, 32 percent of the native-born whites, and only 15 percent of the foreign-born.

Unfortunately, 1872 census publications do not provide a breakdown of the Brazilian-born component of the labor force by race, thereby limiting the possibilities of comparison with 1890. However, this indirect picture suggests that miscegenation and manumission were probably viable avenues to occupation mobility, since mulattoes are recorded in more prestigious occupational categories than blacks, but not sufficiently mobile to challenge the occupational status of either the white or the foreign-born groups. The available data do suggest that these latter two groups stood out much more strongly in commerce in comparison to mulattoes, while their relative participation in industrial pursuits were roughly equal. Commercial activities were likely to be more promising avenues to exploit social mobility than manual industrial occupations at this time.

In summary, slave labor was clearly a major source of manpower in 1872, but much more so in the Southeast than the Northeast. In the Southeast, though export-oriented agricultural activities absorbed slaves more than urban occupations, urban-industrial employment was also important, particularly in the Federal District and the province of Rio de Janeiro. But what stands out at the beginning of the final quarter of the nineteenth century is the role of slaves in satisfying plantation labor needs in the coffee areas. This became a factor of major importance in the abolition process and the transition to a free labor force.

Abolition

The abolition experience in Brazil contrasts in several important respects to that of the United States and Caribbean societies.[16] Brazil was the last country to abolish slavery in the new world (in May, 1888). As Mello (1978) points out, this meant that Brazilian planters were in a position to study and learn from the abolition experiences of other slave societies. Problems associated with alternative forms of labor supply and organization resorted to by these other societies were discussed rather extensively in Brazil prior to abolition, a point to which we will return in the next chapter.

Brazilian abolition was a gradual process brought about by four parliamentary acts over a forty-year period, starting with the ending of the Atlantic slave trade, in 1851; this was followed by the passage of the Free Womb Law, freeing the children of slaves, in 1871; the Sexagenarian Act Law, freeing slaves 60 years of age or older, in 1886; and finally abolition of slavery in 1888. Associated with these legal measures were growing pressures from liberal urban constituencies not only to eliminate slavery, but also promote immigration, and develop small-holding agriculture and agrarian reform. The growth of abolitionist pressures did not lead to prolonged violence or a civil war, though a growing number of slave flights and sporadic violence did appear in the mid 1880s.

Brazilian abolition took place without indemnification. The United States also avoided indemnification, but, in contrast to Brazil, this grew out of the

---

[16]The most rigorous analysis of the interaction between political events and the economics of slavery during the abolition can be found in Mello (1978).

abrupt termination of slavery and violent civil war. On the other hand, English and French Caribbean colonies attempted various forms of indemnification after peaceful emancipation was forced upon them by colonial governments. In large part, this indemnification was a bribe paid by the colonial powers to gain quick acceptance of emancipation by planter classes in their Caribbean colonies, in order to assuage the abolition movements in their home countries. Spain also attempted a form of indemnification (a patronage system) in Cuba, after formally abolishing slavery at the end of the Ten Years' War, though the plan was not fully enacted because the take-over of the Cuban sugar industry by American companies hastened the end of the patronage form of slavery (Knight 1970).

Unlike any of the Caribbean slave societies, Brazil constitutes the only example of a former slave society that followed a relatively pacific transition into full emancipation without indemnification. This was facilitated by a rapid decline in the market price of slaves after 1882–83, which was brought about by abolitionist pressure and slave flights, affecting the future economic return on the purchase of slaves as earning assets. Thus, by 1888 the issue of indemnification had been replaced by the issue of an alternative labor supply. Paulista planters, for example, were more than ready to sacrifice any claims to indemnification for confiscated assets of declining value as long as they could be assured of a viable form of labor supply to maintain their profitable cultivation of coffee.

Abolition came during a major upswing in the coffee cycle, starting in the mid 1880s. Growing coffee proceeds were helpful in securing an adequate substitution for slave labor. Tax revenues on the growing proceeds of coffee expansion were used to spread the costs of subsidizing European immigration. This contrasts with the situation in the English Caribbean countries, where there was a downturn in production (in sugar) following emancipation earlier in the century (1830s and 1840s), and Cuba, where capital intensive methods were important in substituting for slave labor. The United States South also experienced a period of relatively slow growth in cotton output in the immediate post-bellum period. In Brazil, however, this coincidence of abolition with a growth in the world demand for coffee not only avoided a decline in output following abolition but, on the contrary, contributed to a sharp rise in output.

Brazil also contrasts with other former slave societies in drawing upon European immigrant manpower as the substitute for slave labor in its most important crop, coffee. While the United States also had large-scale immigration from Europe, it was not utilized in the South as a substitute for former slave manpower, as was the case in Paulista coffee plantations in Brazil. Brinley Thomas has argued (1973: 134) that European immigration into the United States in the post-Civil War period foreclosed a migratory outlet to the North for the former slaves and kept them in post-bellum sharecropping activities in the South. Caribbean societies also relied upon former slaves for their postemancipation labor supply, by restricting alternative opportunities in subsistence farming. This forced emancipated slaves back into low-wage plantation work (Beckford 1972). To the extent that overseas labor was tried (as in British Guiana), it was East Asian indentured coolie labor or non-Europeans from other parts of the region (as in Cuba). Though Cuba attempted to encourage immigration for her sugar regions, the large majority of Spanish immigrants went to Havana instead.

Finally, Brazilian abolition had a different regional impact, depending on the relative importance of the slave labor force in the final decade of slavery, the availability of alternative sources of domestic nonslave labor, and the economic prospects for the regional economies in question. The economics of slave versus free labor and the problem of transition to free labor receive more detailed treatment in the following chapter. The new source of labor, subsidized European immigration, was to have significant economic consequences not only on the expansion of coffee production in the South but also on growing regional disparities, patterns of urban growth, and industrial development in Brazil.

V   Immigration: Its Role and Impact on the Labor Force and Economic Growth

The period from 1880 to 1930 represents a watershed in Brazilian economic history. This was the period in which coffee became the dominant agent of change in the Brazilian economy and São Paulo became the dominant region. During this period, over 4 million immigrants entered the country, with close to 60 percent of this total locating in the province and later the state of São Paulo.[1] This was also the period that saw the abolition of slavery, the growth of a wage economy, and the expansion of the Western frontier in São Paulo.[2] It was a time of rapid urban growth and the beginning of early manufacturing development based on textiles, construction, and food-processing industries.[3] Politically, this period witnessed the demise of the imperial power structure and the creation of a republic, with a constitution creating a decentralized

[1]Several recent works review the quantitative importance and institutional role of immigration during this period in Brazilian history. A standard work is T. Lynn Smith (1972). Extensive analysis of the foreign-born in census and immigration data from 1872 to 1920 can be found in a special appendix prepared by Maria José Santos in the volume by Villela and Suzigan (1973: Appendix B). Another work reviewing this same data-base throughout the last century (1870–1970) is Levy (1974). An examination of the interface between internal migration and foreign immigration during the period 1872–1940 can be found in Graham and Buarque de Hollanda Filho (1971). More detailed analyses of Italian immigration into Brazil during the late nineteenth and early twentieth centuries have been undertaken by Hall (1969) and Holloway (1974). A similar historical analysis of Portuguese immigration into Brazil at this time can be found in Pescatello (1970). Skidmore (1974) evaluates the role of immigration in the evolving racial attitudes and racial ideologies of the period, while Graham (1973) places the pattern of immigration within the context of the international business cycle during the period 1885–1913. Finally, Balán (1973) offers a useful comparative analysis of immigration and internal migration in Brazil, Mexico, and Argentina during this period.

[2]The major works dealing with the issues of the transition from a slave to a wage economy are the various references cited in footnote 1, Chapter IV.

[3]Major monographs on the economic history of Brazil during the late nineteenth and early twentieth centuries are: Dean (1969), Fausto (1975), Fishlow (1972), Furtado (1963), Eisenberg (1974), Graham (1968), Luz (1961), Prado (1971), Stein (1957a, 1957b), Villela and Suzigan (1973), and Viotti da Costa (1966).

federation of states.[4] Within this federation the most powerful states (São Paulo and Minas Gerais) dominated the young republic, largely sharing the succession of presidents and controlling economic policy for the promotion and defense of coffee interests.[5]

Within this alliance, São Paulo was the most dynamic and powerful partner, whose pattern of economic growth was to alter the structural and institutional parameters of Brazilian development as a whole. In this context, European immigration played a crucial role in promoting change and becomes a focus of our analysis in this chapter. The first section discusses the major issues associated with the transition to free labor in the 1880s, such as the profitability of slavery, alternative sources of labor supply, and the changing regional attitudes toward abolition. The second section sets forth the long-run patterns of immigration, the changing ethnic composition, regional concentration, and the important relationship between this immigrant flow into Brazil and the international business cycle from the 1880s up to World War I. The third section investigates in some detail the impact of this immigrant manpower base on the growth and sectoral change of the Brazilian labor force. Of particular interest here is the role of European immigrants in the growth of the industrial and commercial labor force, an interesting development in view of the fact that their initial role was to relieve a shortage of agricultural labor in the postabolition setting. The final section reviews the evidence on the social and occupational mobility of these immigrant groups during this period in an attempt to draw some conclusions on the impact of European immigration on Brazilian society. Here their impact on early industrialization is emphasized, along with their role in changing the agricultural land-holding patterns in São Paulo.

The Transition to Free Labor

The Regional Setting

In addressing the issues associated with the transition from slave to free labor, it is significant to stress again the important changes in the division of regional economic power that were occurring in the decades just prior to abolition. These shifts contributed not only to the changing regional importance of slave labor but also to differential economic conditions for the growing nonslave labor force.

[4]Standard references on the social and political history of this period are Carone (1971, 1972). A more recent major collaborative effort is Fausto (1975) and Love (1973).
[5]The interplay between the defense of coffee interests and economic policy can be found in Delfim Netto (1959), Villela and Suzigan (1973), Versiani and Versiani (1977), Fishlow (1972b), Peláez (1971, 1972), and Silber (1977).

The erosion of Brazil's competitive position in the world market for sugar (and also cotton), combined with exclusionary tariff systems, generated a secular decline in regional income in the Northeast from the 1870s up to World War I.[6] This, in turn, translated itself into lower levels of real wages for plantation workers, since the continuing growth of the nonslave population eliminated any bargaining strength that scarce labor might have created to improve the lot of plantation labor.[7] The adjustment to the decline in the fortunes of the export economy fell much more heavily on the rural proletariat than on the producers. The lack of employment opportunities in urban areas, combined with the lack of any cash crop alternatives or promising frontier subsistence outlets, limited the options for the use of this growing population base. Nonslave manpower thereby became a growing component of the plantation work force from the 1850s onward. By the 1880s this population growth in the face of limited employment opportunities and the absence of free land (for subsistence activity) depressed real wages of nonslave labor sufficiently to permit plantation owners to replace a large number of slaves with this supply of rural-based landless squatters and sharecroppers well before abolition (Eisenberg 1973; Reis 1972, 1974). The traditional patterns of paternalistic labor control and the dominance of the sugar hierarchy remained as strong in the postabolition as in the preabolition period, while the living conditions for the rural population deteriorated significantly (Reis 1972, Eisenberg 1973).

Even with their export potential diminished, Northeastern slave owners still held a valuable source of potential capital gains, their slave manpower. This became particularly apparent with the rise in the market price for slaves, following the termination of the Atlantic slave trade and the rise in demand for slave labor in the coffee culture of Rio de Janeiro and São Paulo. These were the ingredients that led to the rise of an interregional slave trade from the Northeast to the South from the late 1850s through the 1870s.

As slaves were shipped South, free labor was moving North to the new rubber areas in the Amazon. This movement picked up in the 1880s, after the famous drought of 1877–80, and continued into the nineties and the first decade of the twentieth century. Of interest here is that the population base of the Northeast, in the final quarter of the nineteenth century, had grown sufficiently in size to service the manpower needs of the new rubber areas to the North, the demand for slave labor on the expanding coffee plantations in the South, and, at the same time, facilitate the transition from slave to free labor on the sugar plantations in the littoral of the Northeast itself.

Such a pattern was not evident in the South, where the rapid expansion of coffee production was outstripping the local supply of manpower and raising

[6]The relative economic decline of the Northeast during this period has been analyzed in several works. Furtado (1966) is a classic in the field. More recently, Eisenberg (1974) and Reis (1972, 1974a, 1974b, 1975) have contributed to the analysis on the sugar industry and slavery. Finally, Leff (1972b) and Denslow (1973, 1974, 1978) have engaged in a recent debate on the causes and the significance of the decline in the Northeastern economy during this period.

[7]On this, see Eisenberg (1974): Chapter 8.

the cost of labor. Following the abolition of the Atlantic slave trade in 1851, experiments with indentured European immigrants were tried on several Paulista plantations with little success (Viotti da Costa 1966). By the late 1850s the interregional slave trade had satisfied this growing labor demand sufficiently to eliminate the need for higher cost immigrant labor. During the 1880s, however, high import taxes were placed on the interregional traffic of slaves by the Southern provinces themselves, so that the Northeastern provinces would not be drained of all their slaves and thus become more abolitionist in spirit (Conrad 1972, Viotti da Costa 1966). In this setting, intraregional shifts of slave manpower within the South became a more important source of labor to service the growing expansion of coffee production into the Western frontier of São Paulo.

Thus, three domestic sources of slave labor met the growing demand for manpower on the coffee plantations, following the decline and termination of the Atlantic slave trade in 1851: (1) the intersectoral shifts of slave labor from urban areas to rural plantations within the South itself, in the 1840s and 1850s, discussed in earlier sections; (2) the interregional transfer of slave labor from the Northeast to the Southeast, from the late 1850s to the late 1870s; and (3) finally, the intraregional shifts within the Southeastern provinces from the noncoffee and less productive coffee areas of Minas Gerais and Rio de Janeiro to São Paulo, from the late 1870s to abolition. Thus, in contrast to the Northeast, which had a growing labor base sufficiently large in numbers and cheap in wage costs to service its local demand for labor, as well as supply the interregional traffic to the North and permit slave sales to the South, the Southeastern provinces since 1850 were consistently net importers of slave manpower. This was due to the much larger growth of its cash crop agriculture, combined with an apparent inadequate supply of local nonslave labor to meet these demands, as compared to the Northeast.

The Major Issues of Transition

The foregoing raises three related questions regarding the transition from slavery to free labor in the late-nineteenth-century economic growth of Brazil.[8]

[8]Recent works analyzing slavery, manpower problems, and the issues associated with the transition to free labor in the South are many. Cardoso (1962), Fernandes (1965), and Ianni (1962, 1969) led the way with a critical study of slavery in the South. Viotti da Costa (1966) made a substantial contribution in analyzing the evolution of the coffee plantation system and the changing manpower base and organization of labor in this key activity in São Paulo. Conrad (1972), R. Graham (1966, 1970), Toplin (1972), and Holloway (1976) have made contributions to the debate on the role of the abolition movement and political issues associated with the change from slave to free labor. Hall (1969), and later Holloway (1974), have contributed to the controversial debate on the role and assimilation of immigrants in this process. Finally, as pointed out earlier, recent work by Mello (1977, 1978) and Slenes (1976) have made challenging contributions to our understanding of the economics of slavery in Southern Brazil and the transition to wage labor in this area, within the context of the new economic history made popular by the work of Fogel and Engerman (1974) on American slavery.

First, was there really an insufficient supply of nonslave manpower in the South to permit an economically feasible transition to the free labor force from domestic sources? *Second*, to what extent was slavery becoming an unprofitable or moribund institution in post-1850 Brazil, and did this in any way condition the rapid transition to free labor? And *third*, what were the conditions that led the Northeastern and Southeastern slave owners finally to support abolition in the late 1880s or, put differently, is it conceivable that slavery could have lasted longer in Brazil under different circumstances? This last question leads us to consider possible alternative scenarios to better appreciate the importance of the impact of the economic environment on the process of abolition.

The Domestic Supply of Labor. Several considerations are important regarding the issue of the local labor supply in the Southeast. In contrast to the Northeast, there was clearly a large and growing demand for plantation labor in coffee production, because of Brazil's marked comparative advantage over other world producers in meeting the rapidly growing world demand for this product. Again, in contrast to the Northeast, there were competing nonplantation demands for local labor in this region, growing out of the induced demand for labor linked to the expansion of coffee production: Railroads, roads, and port construction were among the more important of these. Urban growth was also beginning to manifest itself more visibly in the 1880s in the Rio de Janeiro-São Paulo areas than in the Northeast, thereby leading to another source of demand for nonslave labor in urban activities. Finally, the existence of a large agricultural frontier, especially in São Paulo, created possibilities for a satisfactory subsistence agricultural livelihood for nonslaves, in contrast to the Northeast, where land for subsistence agriculture was much less available. That which was utilized by squatters in the Northeast was far less satisfactory to insure an adequate livelihood and forced them to seek supplemental earnings in wage labor on the neighboring sugar plantations. This frontier subsistence outlet at satisfactory levels of living in São Paulo in effect raised the implicit cost of local labor.

Domestic planters generally held local nonslave labor in the South in low regard, since free labor proved to be less docile and more costly than slaves. This labor force was used for the clearing and felling of trees and other sporadic part-time plantation labor needs, but rarely as prime field hands. The degree of regimentation and gang labor used on the coffee plantations required a form of discipline that was particularly distasteful to rural laborers, who had the option for subsistence farming and carried bitter memories of previous plantation work (as former slaves). Translated into contemporary economic terminology, the nonslave labor force was trading income for leisure and, on the average, probably worked only seven to nine hours a day in their subsistence activities. Slaves, in contrast, did not have this choice and worked fourteen to sixteen hours a day. With this large differential in participation rates, it is not surprising that slavery (in the Southeast) was considered far more productive than free labor. To procure the same work effort from free labor, plantation owners would have been forced to offer real wages far higher than they felt economically feasible. Their profit margins would have been drastically reduced.

This was the major fear of the planters over abolition. The rapid decline in the labor participation rates of the former slave labor force was considered inevitable, in view of the almost universal experience of other former slave societies in this regard. Women and children would drop out of the labor pool altogether, and the former male slaves would clearly work less than before at the wage level that planters felt they could offer.

Owner's expectations regarding wage costs were thus a central considera- tion in the issue of labor scarcity in the Southeast. Clearly, the planters felt there was a shortage of labor, in the sense that they could not hire nonslave labor to work fourteen to sixteen-hour days as prime field hands at the implicit wage currently paid to slaves. Planters feared they could in no way procure the same level of labor services from an emancipated labor force, having satisfac- tory frontier subsistence alternatives along with noncoffee employment possibilities, at anywhere near the low cost they had incurred with slave labor. Wage data on coffee plantations at this time are scarce, however, contem- porary observers and reporters frequently commented on the high cost of nonslave labor in the coffee areas (Van Delden Laerne 1885: 147, 227; Taunay 1945: vol. 8, pp. 44, 179; *South American Journal* [August 18, 1888]: 524). Hence, in contrast to the Northeast, the Southeastern planters were costantly driven to seek an expanded labor supply from external sources, at first from within the country and eventually from overseas.

In summing up reasons why Paulista planters did not recruit labor from the Northeast instead of drawing on foreign immigrants, several points stand out. First, it was not so obvious that a substantial labor surplus existed in the Northeast, especially given the institutional importance of low-wage labor in that region. From 1885 to 1900, as will be seen, approximately 1.5 million foreign immigrants came into the Center-South of Brazil, primarily to São Paulo. It is difficult to imagine an interregional labor transfer of this magni- tude coming out of the Northeast without causing serious economic and politi- cal repercussions and interregional hostility, since activities in the Northeast depended so heavily upon the exploitation of cheap and abundant labor (Furtado 1959: 21, 24; Balán 1973). Second, intercontinental maritime transport costs were lowered substantially by the end of the century, making Southern European sources of labor more available. Third, push factors were intense in an overpopulated, stagnant Italy at the time, creating a ready reserve of manpower free from any internal political complications within Brazil. Finally, there was an implicit bias among Southern planters, favoring peasant labor from Italy over *caboclo* labor from the Northeast based on an assumption that the latter were less productive. All these factors promoted the use of foreign rather than domestic sources of labor supply for the Paulista coffee expansion and delayed large internal labor transfers until a later period.

The Profitability of Slavery. This leads to our second concern. The extent to which slavery became unprofitable from 1850 to 1888 and, as a result, led to the natural transition to free labor and abolition. Here a distinction should be made between unprofitability due to essentially economic reasons and unprofitability due to political factors. Until recently, little work had been undertaken to establish an empirical basis for discussion of the profitability of slavery in Brazil.[9] Earlier it was seen that slavery had always been demographically unviable (i.e., the slave population was incapable of reproducing itself domestically to offset deaths and manumissions). However, this does not imply that slavery may not have been productive and profitable for slave-owners as a form of labor organization.

Denslow and Reis have established that, even with declining economic conditions, slavery was profitable in the Northeast during most of this period. Denslow (1972) shows that in the 1850s the rate of return on slave investments was around 10 percent per year, while the return on alternative investments in prime commercial paper earned less. Reis (1974) continues the analysis into the late 1870s, when slave prices were at their highest. Drawing upon the analytical framework of Conrad and Meyer's work on the profitability of U.S. slavery, Reis estimated the investment costs, life expectancy, and, finally, their productivity at this time. He concludes from these data that slaves generated an internal rate of return of roughly 10.5 percent per year during the late 1870s, while alternative investments in public utilities and industrial activities generally earned less (Reis 1974: 13). Although Northeastern sugar production was inefficient by international standards, as discussed earlier, this did not mean that it could not and did not compare favorably to alternative economic activities within the region.

At least until the 1880s slave labor was probably cheaper than free labor. Without slavery, Northeastern sugar production would have been even more inefficient (with lower rates of return). But by the mid-1880s the profitability of slavery declined, as the growing supply of nonslave labor eliminated the cost differential between slave and free labor in this region.[10] At the same time, abolitionist pressures had created sufficient doubts about the future of slavery that the age-price profiles for slaves flattened out from the early 1880s onward (Denslow 1974, Reis 1977). Prime-age slaves no longer commanded high prices, because potential buyers anticipated a short working life for this capital asset. Future returns were discounted heavily, due to the expected demise of the institution. In summary, we can say that the growing availability of

[9] The recent works that have added to our knowledge in this area are Reis (1974, 1977), Denslow (1974), Leff (1974), Mello (1977, 1978), and Slenes (1976).
[10] See Eisenberg (1974), Denslow (1974), and Reis (1974).

nonslave labor in the Northeast at low real wages was an economic factor tending to make slavery less profitable, while abolitionist pressures, a political factor, were reinforcing this tendency and eliminating the value of slaves as capital assets from the early 1880s onward.

Pedro Carvalho de Mello (1978) has undertaken a similar analysis of the economics of slave labor on the coffee plantations in the Paraiba Valley of Rio de Janeiro. Drawing upon a sample of plantations in the early 1870s, Mello arrived at an estimate of profitability through estimating the rate of return on slave capital and comparing this to alternative rates of return on other capital assets. The return on slave capital was higher. Planters in this region (which was relatively backward compared to São Paulo) were making profits and their demand for slave labor continued through the decade. Mello has questioned the interpretation that slavery in Brazil had become economically unviable (holding the political variables as constant) and that it lacked flexibility and efficiency as a precapitalistic institution under changing conditions. In fact, he argues that slavery was profitable even in relatively backward regions like the Paraiba Valley in Rio de Janeiro.

After 1881–82, profitability declined. The demand for slaves in the Paraiba Valley declined from 1882 to 1888. The market price of prime field hands tended to fall below the costs of rearing and maintenance. Associated with this was a flattening out of the age-price profile in Rio de Janeiro similar to what Denslow and Reis discovered in the Northeast.[11] Political and ideological forces for abolition in the 1880s weakened political support for the institution, and organized abolition groups provoked slave flights and large-scale disobedience. Police and army units frequently refused to play the role of the enforcer in these situations and so indirectly encouraged them. Thus, there was a gradual erosion of the wealth invested in the ownership of slaves. Slavery as an economic institution was experiencing a political death. Concern over indemnification was replaced now by concern with labor scarcity.

An important exception to the general decline in slave prices was the hire price for slave "rentals," a further indication that expectations played a major role in the overall decline. According to Mello, the short-term rental market held up until early 1888, when the pressures for total emancipation became pervasive. In the meantime, the world market conditions for coffee, the comparative advantage Brazil enjoyed in the crop, and the derived demand for slave manpower maintained these short-term hire rates at a high level. If slavery had become unproductive and unprofitable for essentially economic

---

[11] Slenes (1976) also analyzes the economic rationality of planters in the Campinas region in the 1870s and 1880s and concludes that they acted as cautious rational investors in their purchases of slaves. However, he feels that in the 1880s they did not discount sufficiently the likelihood of abolition. Their investment behavior then represented an oversanguine estimate on the prospects for the continuation of the institution (Slenes, 1976: Chapter V).

(as distinct from political) reasons, this trend of the hire rate would not have been positive during this period. On the contrary, it would have declined along with the price (i.e., asset value) of slaves. Abolitionist pressures, in affecting the expectations for indemnification, clearly depressed the asset value of slaves (as reflected in the age-price profiles) from 1881 onward, but not the annual hire rates. Only when abolition was practically a *fait accompli* did these rates decline.

The Planters and Abolition. This leads to a final question. What were the conditions that led Northeastern and Southeastern planters to accept abolition by late 1887 and early 1888? Was it the force of political pressures alone or were economic factors also important?[12] In the Northeast, it is clear that the growing supply of nonslave labor at low real wages satisfied the sugar planters that an adequate substitute for slave labor had emerged. Thus, by the early 1880s, their intransigence to abolition had waned considerably.

In the Southeast, Paulista planters remained intransigent on the abolition issue until the mid-1880s. But faced with the lack of a domestic substitute for slave manpower, these planters did form an immigration society in 1886 (Sociedade Promotora da Immigração) to promote the inflow of European immigrants (essentially Italian). As Holloway (1976) has shown, earlier attempts to promote immigrant manpower had failed because of the continuing profitability of slavery. By 1886, however, the time had arrived for the immigrant strategy to succeed. Immigration expenses in São Paulo represented only 2 to 3 percent of total provincial revenue in the early 1880s. By 1886–87, they grew to 20 percent of these revenues, testifying to the determination of the planters and provincial officials to harness the machinery of state and provide resources to alleviate the anticipated shortage of labor in case of abolition (Holloway 1974: 144). From 1880 to 1885, subsidized immigrants to São Paulo numbered only 4 to 5 thousand per year. In 1887 and 1888, there was an abrupt rise in the number of immigrants into the province, reaching 92,086 immigrants in 1888 alone. Holloway (1976) points out that about 104,000 subsidized immigrants of working age entered São Paulo from 1882 through 1888, with most of this inflow occurring in the last two years. This compares to a count of 71,338 slaves in the Santos coffee zone in 1886–87. Thus, by the time of abolition, immigrant manpower had gone a long way toward resolving the labor supply problem in Paulista agriculture. In view of this, it is not surprising to see Paulista Planters finally converting to abolition

---

[12]The works of Toplin (1972), Conrad (1972), and Dean (1975) essentially support R. Graham's earlier thesis (1966) that abolitionist political forces from the urban areas generated the climate that promoted massive slave flights in 1886–87. This, in turn, forced the planters to accept the inevitability of abolition. Holloway (1977), while agreeing on the role and significance of the abolition movement, also emphasizes the adept response of the Paulista planter ruling class at this time. To protect their interests they stalled and bought time to create a substitute labor force through measures promoting subsidized immigration from 1885 onward.

so as to minimize social unrest and get on with the business of restocking the plantation with immigrant labor.[13]

In contrast, the planters from the older Paraiba Valley in Rio de Janeiro enjoyed neither an abundant supply of local nonslave labor (as in the Northeast) nor a growing supply of immigrant labor (as in São Paulo). It is among them that we find the most militant defenders of slavery down to the bitter end. They stood to lose the most, since they would be able to draw upon only the stock of former slaves in clearly less advantageous labor market conditions following abolition. Indeed, a rapid decline and stagnation of coffee production within the region followed shortly after abolition (Stein 1957).

In summary, three economic parameters conditioned the successful transition from slave to free labor in Brazil: (1) rising coffee prices from 1885 onward; (2) the marked international comparative advantage Brazil enjoyed in coffee production in São Paulo; and (3) the availability of nonslave labor through domestic sources (in the Northeast) and external sources (in São Paulo). Two out of the three major slave holding regions were able to resolve their labor supply problem. This facilitated the success of the abolition movement. This analysis is not meant to deny the predominant importance of political forces in promoting abolition. The absence of a satisfactory substitute for slave labor probably would not have postponed abolition for long, but the emergence of domestic and foreign sources of nonslave labor clearly minimized the cost of transition for the planter classes and, in the process, reinforced the oligarchical control of the traditional sugar barons of the Northeast and permitted the rapid growth of a new, more dynamic class of planters in São Paulo.

This raises the interesting question of whether Brazil might not have been better off if there had not been an elastic supply of European immigrants available for the coffee plantations during and after abolition. Leff (1970) argues that in such a situation Paulista planters would have been forced to offer considerably higher wages to draw the nonslave and former slave labor force out of their subsistence and other nonplantation activities in the Southeast. This would have led to a greater distribution of coffee income to wages rather than profits and, as a result, have stimulated a broader-based local consumption market and more labor-saving innovations in coffee production. At the same time, more modern agricultural practices might have appeared in tradi-

---

[13]In summary, the costs of subsidization were easily absorbed by the rise in coffee prices and the increased income generated by the expansion of coffee output with the elastic supply of labor. Other factors contributing to this favorable climate for the use of foreign immigrants in the 1880s and 1890s in São Paulo were the economic stagnation in Italy, creating an available supply of immigrants at a relatively low supply price, and the decline in intercontinental maritime transport costs. In contrast, the economic return from slave labor was declining (in comparison to the 1860s and 1870s) in the face of the pressures growing out of the abolition movement. In this context, the shift from domestic slave labor to immigrant wage labor made economic sense to the Paulista planter class.

tional agriculture, as this sector would have lost much of its labor supply to a higher-wage and modern coffee sector. In short, Brazil would have become a more labor-scarce, high-wage economy with a more equitable distribution of income, a weakened plantation oligarchy, and a more diversified and modern agricultural sector through time.

Such a scenario presumes a high degree of institutional and technological responsiveness to a shortage of labor, rather than a relapse into a slow growth milieu. Ignored in this counterfactual reasoning is the real possibility that the much higher cost of labor implicit in this pattern of growth could have cut so deeply into the profit margins of coffee producers as to reduce or eliminate the comparative advantage Brazil experienced over other world producers at the time. A high cost of production would have limited the capacity for extensive frontier expansion of coffee throughout the state. It also would have reduced capital formation and limited the range of external economies, facilitating industrial growth that did in fact grow out of the coffee cycle. One would have to argue that the level and the pattern of demand and investment derived from the hypothetical income distribution generated through a higher-wage economy would have substituted as effectively as an engine of growth as the profit-led pattern of coffee expansion that actually did occur. Also ignored in this scenario is the socioeconomic impact of European immigration on Brazilian society and industrialization, which deserves to be considered in some detail.

Immigration and Economic Growth, 1880–1930

The Patterns of Immigration: Magnitudes and Composition

This section reviews the major patterns of international immigration into Brazil from 1872 to 1972, with particular emphasis on the period 1885–1930, the period when Brazil's economic growth was dominated by its agro-export growth cycle in coffee.[14] Table V–1 shows that approximately four million immigrants entered Brazil from 1880 to 1930. The decade of the 1890s registered the largest gross immigration in Brazilian history, with over one million immigrants. The abrupt change this represented from previous decades can be appreciated by noting that the total number of immigrants entering Brazil in the 1890s was roughly seven times larger than the number that entered in the 1870s and three times larger than those that arrived in the 1880s. Four major cyclical patterns emerge from this data, with large inflows in the 1890s, the period 1910–13 (when 70 percent of the inflow for the decade 1910–19 occurred), the 1920s, and the 1950s. Sharp declines are apparent during the early years of the twentieth century, World War I, the thirties and World War II.

[14] For the principal works analyzing the changing patterns, magnitude, and role of immigration in Brazil during the period, see the references cited in footnote 1 of this chapter.

Table V-1. Immigrants into Brazil by Decade and Nationality, 1872–1972

A. Absolute number

Decades	Portuguese	Italians	Spanish	Germans	Japanese	Others	Total
	(1)	(2)	(3)	(4)	(5)	(6)	(7)
1872–79	55,027	45,467	3,392	14,325	–	58,126	176,337
1880–89	104,690	277,124	30,066	18,901	–	17,841	448,622
1890–99	219,353	690,365	164,293	17,084	–	107,232	1,198,327
1900–09	195,586	221,394	113,232	13,848	861	77,486	622,407
1910–19	318,481	138,168	181,651	25,902	27,432	123,819	815,453
1920–29	301,915	106,835	81,931	75,801	58,284	221,881	846,647
1930–39	102,743	22,170	12,746	27,497	99,222	68,390	332,768
1940–49	45,604	15,819	4,702	6,807	2,828	38,325	114,085
1950–59	241,579	91,931	94,693	16,643	33,593	104,629	583,068
1960–69	74,129	12,414	28,397	5,659	25,092	51,896	197,587
1872–1972	1,662,180	1,622,491	716,052	223,517	248,007	878,642	5,350,889

B. Percentage distribution

	(1)	(2)	(3)	(4)	(5)	(6)	(7)
1872–79	31.2	25.8	1.9	8.1	–	33.0	100
1880–89	23.3	61.8	6.7	4.2	–	4.0	100
1890–99	18.3	57.6	13.7	1.4	–	8.9	100
1900–09	31.4	35.6	18.2	2.2	0.1	12.4	100
1910–19	39.1	16.7	22.3	3.2	3.4	15.1	100
1920–29	35.7	12.6	9.7	2.9	6.9	26.2	100
1930–39	30.9	6.7	3.8	8.3	29.8	20.5	100
1940–49	40.0	13.9	4.5	6.0	2.5	33.6	100
1950–59	41.4	15.8	16.2	2.9	5.8	17.9	100
1960–69	37.5	6.3	14.4	2.9	12.7	26.3	100
1872–1972	31.1	30.3	13.4	4.2	4.6	16.4	100

Sources: 1) Data on immigrants from 1872 to 1883 from *Boletim Comemorativo da Exposição Nacional de 1908*, pp. 82–85.
2) Data on immigrants from 1884 to 1953 drawn from *Anuário Estatistico do Brasil de 1954*, p. 49.
3) Data for 1954–67 drawn from various issues of *Anuário Estatistico do Brasil* 1955–1967.
4) Data from 1968 to 1972 from Divisão Nacional de Migração, DNMO, Ministério do Trabalho e Previdência Social and reproduced along with data for the earlier periods in Levy (1974: Table 1).

The ethnic composition is also distinct for various decades (panel B, Table V–1). The 1870s show the traditional dominance of the Portuguese in the early pattern of Brazilian immigration, accounting for approximately one-third of all immigrants during that period. However, this pattern changed significantly in the following two decades (the 1880s and 1890s), as Italians came to dominate Brazilian immigration. This predominance reached approximately 60 percent of the rapid growth of immigration into Brazil in the last two decades of the nineteenth century. Following this period Italian immigration declined in both absolute and relative terms. Portuguese immigration generally held steady between 30–40 percent throughout the twentieth century. Only in the 1930s did a new ethnic group, the Japanese, challenge this relative dominance of the Portuguese. Throughout the entire century, however, three Southern European nationalities (Portuguese, Italian, and Spanish) accounted for close to three-fourths of the total immigration into Brazil. Northern European immigration, while important in certain regions (Santa Catarina and Rio Grande do Sul), never reached a large proportion of the total.

Regional concentration is another major feature of Brazilian immigration, with São Paulo the dominant state in the national pattern. Throughout this

Table V-2. Selected Data on Total and Subsidized Immigration into São Paulo for Selected Periods, 1882-1929

	Immigration into Brazil	Immigration into São Paulo	
		% of Brazil	% subsidized
	(1)	(2)	(3)
1882-84	87,178	14	n.a.
1885-89	319,541	53	n.a.
1890-94	600,735	70	91
1895-99	597,592	69	73
1900-04	249,042	52	51
1905-09	373,365	54	39
1910-14	667,778	58	41
1915-19	147,675	56	45
1920-24	373,126	53	34
1925-29	473,521	61	39
1889-1929	3,547,999	57	45
1872-1972	5,350,889	57	n.a.

Sources: 1) For the period 1882 to 1884, data on São Paulo immigrants drawn from *Relatório* apresentado ao Exmo. Sr. Presidente da Província de São Paulo pela Comissão Central de Estatística, São Paulo, Typografia King, 1887.

2) Immigration data from São Paulo from 1885 to 1972 from Departamento de Imigração e Colonização, Estado de São Paulo and reproduced in Levy (1974: Table 8).

period, São Paulo accounted for 57 percent of the total recorded immigration (Table V-2). During the high-water mark of the 1890s this concentration reached 70 percent. In no period after 1884 does it fall below 50 percent. A second feature of this regional concentration is the rising share of São Paulo during the periods of cyclically rising national immigration (1890-99, 1910-14, 1925-29) and its declining share during periods of aggregate decline on the national scene (the early 1900s, World War I, and the early 1920s). This pattern emphasizes the catalytic role of regional growth in São Paulo as the major impulse behind the growth of total immigration in the country. Each of these three cyclical upswings coincide with the upswings in coffee expansion, with its associated need for additional immigrant labor.

Column 3 of Table V-2 also underscores the importance of São Paulo's state subsidies in the early years of the republic. Over 90 percent of the immigrants into São Paulo during the peak years of immigration in the 1890s were subsidized. This number declined in succeeding periods, leveling out to roughly 40 percent until the end of subsidized immigration in the 1930s. Thus, subsidized immigration was an essential factor promoting the early rise of mass immigration from Europe at the end of the nineteenth century. Without it immigration would have been considerably less. However, by the period 1905-14 nonsubsidized immigration had become an important source of total immigration. Given the fact that subsidized immigration was associated exclusively with the coffee sector in São Paulo, the rising rate of nonsubsidized immigration reflects the growing demand for nonagricultural labor in the Paulista economy after 1905.

Table V–3 summarizes the relative impact of immigration on Brazil from 1872 to 1940. At the national level, the foreign-born increased from roughly 4 percent in 1872 to a peak of 7 percent of the country's population in 1900. By 1920 its relative weight had declined to 5 percent. Rio de Janeiro (both province and city) recorded the highest relative concentration of foreign immigrants in the 1872 census, reflecting the traditional regional focus of earlier Portuguese immigration. By 1900, São Paulo had become the state with the highest foreign-born percentage, followed by Rio Grande do Sul. Both states reflected the new wave of Italian immigration at the turn of the century. After 1900, the relative role of the foreign-born declined in all states. Table V–3 clearly reinforces our earlier conclusions as to the selected regional impact of foreign immigration throughout this period. This impact was largely centered on three states, Rio de Janeiro, São Paulo, and Rio Grande do Sul (and their respective capital cities), with São Paulo predominating from 1890 onward.

The importance of ethnic composition in these regional differentials is also seen clearly in Table V–3, which presents data on the distribution of the four largest immigrant groups (accounting for four-fifths of the foreign-born) in the major immigrant states in the 1920 census. The contrast between the two largest groups is particularly revealing. Italians, closely associated with the coffee culture, dominated in the major coffee-producing states of São Paulo, Espírito Santo, and Minas Gerais. In addition, they were the most important nationality in the Southern state of Rio Grande do Sul, where the presence of German immigrants was also significant. Portuguese immigrants, on the other hand, accounted for only a minor proportion of immigrants in states where Italians predominated and, in contrast, stood out clearly in those states and regions where the Italian presence was minor or insignificant (the North and Northeastern states and Rio de Janeiro). The contrasting regional location of these two major immigrant groups is largely a result of timing and sectoral distribution. Portuguese immigration reflected a longer historical tradition of settling in the older commercial centers on the coast, while Italians were recruited specifically for agricultural undertakings in the coffee areas and colonization programs in the South.[15]

Additional insights into the pattern of immigration to Brazil can be gained by looking at the regional origin in Italy of Italian immigration to Brazil and the magnitude of return migration. Table V–4 underscores the important role of immigrants from Northern Italy for both Argentina and Brazil, while Southern Italians predominated in the United States. Subsidization and selective recruiting clearly played an important role in drawing a large number of

---

[15]For the most detailed studies of Italian immigration, see Hall (1969) and Holloway (1974); for Portuguese immigrants, see Pescatello (1970). Although only important after World War I, and particularly in the 1930s, the impressive role of Japanese immigrants in Brazil also stands out in Brazilian history. The most thorough analysis of this is Suzuki (1969). For a comparative analysis of Brazil and Argentina, see Balán (1973).

Table V-3. Percent of Foreign-born Population in Selected Regions in Brazil (1872–1920), and Distribution of Selected Nationalities within Selected States in 1920

Region	Foreign-born in total population			Selected nationalities of total foreign-born within selected states, 1920				Total no. Foreign-born
	(1) 1872 %	(2) 1900 %	(3) 1920 %	(4) Portuguese %	(5) Italian %	(6) Spanish %	(7) German %	(8)
North and Northeast								
Amazon	3.8	0.8	4.7	45	4	6	—	16,936
Pará	2.4	0.5	2.3	64	5	15	1	22,083
Pernambuco	1.6	0.4	0.5	41	6	9	13	11,698
Bahia	1.6	0.4	0.3	31	14	23	4	10,600
Southeast								
Espírito Santo	5.1	10.2	4.2	9	67	6	7	18,751
Minas Gerais	2.2	2.6	1.5	21	50	8	2	85,705
Rio de Janeiro (city)	31.0	24.1	20.7	72	9	8	1	239,129
Rio de Janeiro (state)	12.2	5.5	3.3	54	20	10	2	50,831
São Paulo	3.5	21.0	18.1	20	48	21	1	829,851
South								
Paraná	2.9	12.2	9.2	3	14	3	8	62,753
Santa Catarina	10.0	9.2	4.7	2	26	3	34	31,243
Rio Grande do Sul	9.3	11.8	6.9	6	32	3	11	151,025
Brazil	3.8	7.0	5.2	28	36	14	3	1,565,961

Sources: Demographic censuses of 1872, 1900, and 1920

Table V-4. Regional Origin of Italian Migrants to Selected Countries, 1876–1930

	A. Countries of destination, 1876–1900			
Regional origin	Europe	United States	Argentina	Brazil
	(1)	(2)	(3)	(4)
Northern Italy	2,445,949	99,023	519,034	561,756
Southern Italy	182,257	673,769	282,328	252,632
	B. 1901–1913			
Northern Italy	3,050,590	678,361	445,780	137,961
Southern Italy	353,657	2,486,590	505,190	255,201
	C. 1876–1930 (percent of total in parentheses)			
Northern Italy	7,556,808 (91)	1,024,572 (20)	1,269,812 (53)	755,526 (57)
Southern Italy	764,634 (9)	4,034,204 (80)	1,116,369 (47)	564,157 (43)

Source: Sommario de Statistiche Storiche Italiane 1861–1955, Rome: Instituto Centrale di Statistica, 1958, tav. 109, pp. 117–18.

Northern Italians to Brazil. The large flow of Southern Italians to the United States, in contrast, were unsubsidized and unrecruited. Further, it is clear that this Northern bias in the origin of Italian immigration to Brazil was particularly strong (column 4) in the earlier period (1876–1900) when Brazilian subsidization policies covered the vast majority of Italians emigrating to São Paulo. In contrast, the later period (1901–13) reflects a larger inflow of immigrants from the Southern provinces. This was the period when resources for immigrant subsidies declined, to cover only 35 to 40 percent of the emigrants to Brazil.

Students of Italian history frequently comment on the contrast between Northern and Southern Italy, with the North standing out as the most developed area in the country. Further, the peasant culture of the Po River Valley in the North was a more promising agricultural milieu from which to draw ambitious and adept agricultural laborers and cultivators than were the secularly depressed areas to the South and in Sicily. The selective recruitment policies by the Paulista planter organizations reflected their belief that there was a more promising human capital content in these Northern Italian agriculturalists. These organizations had no recruiting offices in the South of Italy.[16]

A final feature meriting discussion is the evidence on return migration to Italy from Brazil during this period. Table V–5 presents material from Italian sources on return migration from selected countries from 1902 to 1913. Column 4 shows Brazil registering the highest percent of return migration among the three countries, when one places the return flow over the inflow for the same time period (1902–13). However, this is not an appropriate index of return migration. Clearly, many of those returning during this period were immigrants that had arrived during earlier periods. In the Brazilian case, it is

---

[16]On this, see Hall (1966) and Holloway (1974).

Table V-5. Out-Migration and Return-Migration of Italian Immigrants for Selected Countries and Selected Periods, 1891–1913

Countries	Out-migration from Italy		Return-migration to Italy	Return-migration as % of out-migration	
	1891–1913	1902–13	1902–13	col. 3/col. 2	col. 3/col. 1
	(1)	(2)	(3)	(4)	(5)
Unites States	3,679,278	3,043,812	1,466,537	48%	40%
Argentina	1,318,190	891,089	438,546	49	33
Brazil	973,386	311,003	202,061	65	21

Sources: Sommario de Statistiche Storiche Italiane 1861–1955, Rome: Istituto Centrale di Statistica, 1958. Tav. 21, p. 66.

clear that a substantial number of the return flow recorded from 1902 to 1913 came from immigrants who arrived during the height of Italian immigration into Brazil in the decade of the 1890s. Using this longer time period, from 1891–1913, as a frame of reference, the return flow from Brazil was substantially less than for Argentina and the United States (Table V–5, column 5). Furthermore, if one were to take into account the rate of natural increase of the Italian immigrant population in Brazil during the period, which was substantial, the return percentage falls to very low levels. In summary, despite the rise in return migration during the early years of the twentieth century, the return flow was relatively inconsequential by international standards and in terms of the total foreign-born population base available in the country, including its cumulative growth through natural increase as well as inflows from abroad.

Immigration and the International Business Cycle, 1880–1930

Important in any discussion of Brazilian immigration from the 1880s to 1930 is an understanding of the various factors that permitted Brazil to attract the volume of immigrants recorded during the period. Coffee was the largest and the most rapidly growing tropical export in the world from 1880 to 1930.[17] Brazil produced over one-half of the world's coffee output during this period, with 90 percent of this output coming from São Paulo. Thus, the rise in coffee prices and coffee output were clearly crucial determinants of the inflow of immigrants during this period. This was particularly pronounced in the early period (1885–95), as the aggregate demand for labor in this sector outstripped the local supply at the wage levels coffee planters were prepared to pay at the time. Subsidies covering transport and settlement costs were another important feature permitting Brazil to compete for European immigrant labor during

---

[17] Coffee was the most rapidly growing tropical export crop during this period and, as a result, external demand created a promising base for some of the more growth-inducing impacts of export growth on the domestic economy in Brazil. On this point, see Arthur Lewis (1970).

this early period. In large part, the resources for these subsidies from the province of São Paulo were forthcoming because of the growth of the coffee sector itself, since tax revenues on exports (i.e., coffee) made up a large portion of the resources used for subsidies. Thus, one must look upon the growth of coffee exports and subsidies as a joint effect. The former created the necessary condition, while the latter was the instrument that translated this into both a necessary and a sufficient condition for the initial success of the immigration policy in Brazil at this time.

Still the story is not complete. A third factor generated an inflow of immigrants larger than that which could be attributed to the joint effect of the rise in labor demand cum subsidy. This was the fortuitous way in which the growth of the coffee cycle in Brazil at the end of the ninetenth century corresponded with economic stagnation in Italy, on the one hand, and with an economic down-swing in the main immigrant-competing rivals in the Western Hemisphere, Argentina and the United States, on the other.[18] From the perspective of the United States, the notion of competition for immigrants was unimportant since the aggregate inflow of immigrants to the United States was so large compared to Argentina and Brazil. From the perspective of Brazil, however, the United States was an important competitor for European immigrants. Any decline in immigration to the United States and Argentina could and, in fact, did permit a detour in the flow of European immigrants toward Brazil, as long as coffee output maintained its growth.

Figure V–1, using five-year moving averages to smooth out irregularities, shows three cyclical upswings in gross immigration for Brazil, Argentina, and the United States, between 1880 and 1930. The final two upswings for Brazil (pre-World War I and the middle to late twenties) coincide with similar upswings in both the United States and Argentina (in pre-World War I) or with Argentina alone (in the 1920s). The contrast in the 1890s, however, is sharp and clear. Brazil experienced a significant inflow of immigrants at the very time that both the United States and Argentina were experiencing sharp declines. The decline in both countries was particularly precipitous in the early 1890s. This was the only period in Brazil's history when it recorded a larger inflow of immigrants than Argentina.[19]

Immigration to Argentina largely drew from the same Southern European source (i.e., Italy) as Brazil. Thus, the competitive attraction of Argentina and the importance of the "detour effect" is clear in this case. In contrast, immigration to the United States contained an overwhelming Northern European component. One could argue that the decline in American immigration in the

[18]For an earlier treatment of this peculiar sequence of events, see D. Graham (1973).
[19]For an analysis of the performance of the Argentine economy during this period, see Diaz-Alejandro (1970), di Tella and Zymelman (1967), and Ford (1971). A recent and thorough analysis of the role of immigration into Argentina during this period is Vásquez-Presedo (1971a, 1971b). The impact of immigration on Argentine society is set forth in succinct summary by Germani (1966).

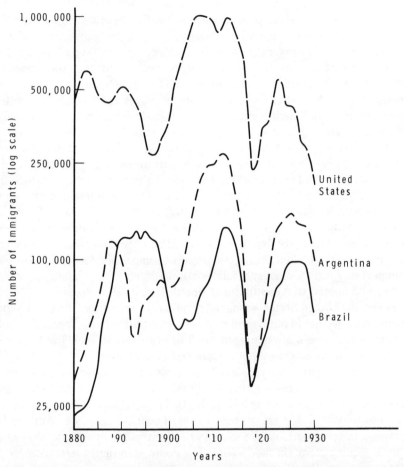

Figure V–1. Gross Annual Immigration into the United States, Argentina, and Brazil, 1880–1930 (Five-Year Moving Averages). *Sources:* (1) U.S. Department of Commerce, *Historical Statistics of the United States, Colonial Times to 1970* (Washington, D.C.: Government Printing Office, 1975, pp. 105–06); (2) *Revista de Imigração e Colonização* 1,4 (1940); (3) Dirección Nacional de Migraciones, *Memorias Anuales,* Buenos Aires, various years.

1890s did not release significant numbers of immigrants to be detoured to Brazil, since they drew from different sources in Europe and should thus be considered noncompetitive. However, Table V–6 shows that in the 1880s the United States already attracted substantially more Italian immigrants than Brazil, over 30 percent of total Italian emigration to the three countries as a whole during this period came to the United States, as compared to 19 percent for Brazil. Thus, despite the recognized predominance of Northern European immigration to the United States, Italian immigration in absolute numbers was still larger to the United States than to Brazil in the early and middle 1880s. Clearly, a competitive relationship was emerging here as well, though weaker

Table V–6. Italian Immigration into the United States, Brazil, and Argentina
for Selected Periods, 1880–1914

Period	Total	United States		Brazil		Argentina	
		No.	%	No.	%	No.	%
1880–87	468,956	144,610 (31)		90,766 (19)		233,580 (50)	
1888–98	1,514,878	469,788 (31)		657,128 (43)		387,962 (26)	
1899–1914	5,014,846	3,483,302 (69)		461,191 (9)		1,070,353 (22)	

Source: Commissariato Generale dell'Emigrazione–*Annuario Statistico della Emigrazione Italiana dal 1876 al 1925,* Rome, 1926.

than that between Brazil and Argentina. In the latter case, Argentina drew almost three times the number of Italian immigrants (from 1880 to 1887) than entered Brazil.

Against this background, Brazil's emergence as the major new-world destination for Italian immigrants in the 1890s stands out in sharp relief. Brazil accounted for 43 percent of total Italian emigration to these three countries during this period. If the American and Argentinian economies had been growing rapidly, many of these immigrants would not have gone to Brazil. This is precisely what occurred during the period 1900–14, as can be seen in Table V–6, as Brazil's relative participation declines sharply.

It is useful to conclude this analysis by contrasting the selected growth indices of the four economies during the period 1885–1902. These are shown in Figure V–2. Although the price of coffee started to decline after 1893 (panel E), frequent devaluations protected the earnings of coffee exporters and prolonged the expansion of coffee earnings and output until 1897 (panel F). At the same time this growth was occurring in Brazil, Italy was experiencing the worst stagnation in its recent economic history. Agricultural output of the five leading crops in Italy declined steadily in the 1890s (panel D). Gerschenkron (1962: 76) reports that Italian industrial output was stagnant from 1888 to 1896, in contrast to relatively high growth prior to and following this period. Bearing in mind that industry was located in the North of Italy (Brazil's main source of immigrants), this meant there was no local urban-industrial employment growth in Northern Italy to relieve the agrarian decline in output and employment. The major indices of economic activity in the export sector in Argentina also registered sharp declines in the early and middle nineties (panels B and C), while unemployment in the 1890s in the United States ranked among the highest rates ever recorded between the Civil War and World War I (panel A).[20]

Considering that Brazil was historically the weakest pole of attraction for European immigrants among these three countries, this fortuitous combination of economic circumstances in the 1890s gave Brazil an unusual opportunity to compete effectively for the growing pool of underemployed Italian labor

[20] For the major sources setting forth the economic data on these four countries, see the sources to Figure V–2.

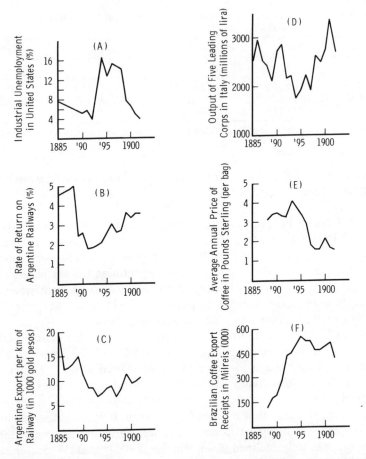

Figure V–2. Selected Indices of Economic Activity for Brazil, Italy, Argentina, and the United States (1885–1902). *Sources:* Panel A—Paul Douglas, *Real Wages in the United States, 1890–1926*, p. 445, for 1889–1902; 1885 figure reported in Stanley Lebergott, *Manpower in Economic Growth* (New York: McGraw-Hill, 1964), pp. 179–80; Panels B and C—A. G. Ford, "British Investments in Argentina and Long Swings 1880–1914," *Journal of Economic History*, 31, 3 (September 1971): 660; Panel D—Harry Jerome, *Migration and Business Cycles*, NBER, New York, 1926, p. 200; Panels E and F—*Annuario Estatistico do Brasil 1939–40*, pp. 1375–78.

against her otherwise more formidable rivals, Argentina and the United States. In summary, Brazil enjoyed the maximum advantage in the 1890s, attracting migrants through its own demand-induced coffee expansion and subsidization policies, as well as through supply-induced push factors in Northern Italy and the detour effect of declining growth in Argentina and the United States, its main rivals for European immigrants. Never again would such a set of circumstances interact so strongly in Brazil's favor, and never again would it experience such a sustained period of high immigration. The later two major cyclical upswings of immigration in Brazil (1905–14 and 1920–29), though important, would never reach the average annual decadal rate achieved in the 1890s.

Immigration and the Labor Force, 1872–1920

With the major parameters established concerning the origin, causes, and changing magnitude of foreign immigration to Brazil, this section investigates evidence on the importance of the foreign-born in the evolution of the Brazilian labor force from 1872 to 1920. First, a cautionary note is raised on the difficulties of assessing this evidence. Then material on the participation rates and sex composition of the foreign-born are set forth. This is followed by an analysis of the changing sectoral participation of the foreign-born labor force, and a conclusion is drawn concerning the labor-intensive nature of industrial growth at this time.

Many problems surface in assessing the changing pattern of the foreign-born labor force in Brazil, all dealing with the difficulties of quantifying this role. Inconsistent census definitions and classifications of sectoral and occupational groupings are the main issues here, along with the associated problem of what distinguishes the economically active from the inactive population. The root of the problem lies in the fact that the Brazilian economy underwent significant socioeconomic change from 1872 to 1920. Occupational and sectoral activities had different meanings in 1920 from those used in 1872, as a plantation-based slave economy with household artisan activity was transformed into an immigrant-oriented early industrial urban society by the 1920s. This created an economic environment in which urban and rural occupations were more sharply defined, urban industrial activity more widely located in establishments rather than households, and the definitions of the active labor force made more strict than before.

The problems of inconsistent census definitions and changing sectoral and occupational groupings in these early censuses will be discussed at length in a later chapter dealing with the growth of the Brazilian labor force. To gain reasonable consistency here, we have dealt with four basic problems. First, the 1872 category of salaried day workers (*criados e jornaleiros*), which was not repeated in later censuses, was considered nonagricultural and nonmanufacturing for purposes of later comparisons. Second, the category of essentially artisan workers in the 1900 census (*artes e oficios*) included a loosely defined industrial occupational group, since the occupations classified explicitly as manufacturing in this census were unreasonably low. Third, we consider the category of unknown occupations in 1900 (*ignoradas*) as economically active. Finally, in view of the inconsistent treatment of domestic servants by these three censuses, we have chosen to concentrate the major part of our analysis on the growth of the male labor force alone.

Table V–7. Participation Rates (% Economically Active) by Sex and for Native-born and Foreign-born Populations in Brazil, 1872, 1900, 1920

| | % economically active | | | | | |
| | 1872[a] | | 1900[b] | | 1920[c] | |
Nationality	Men	Women	Men	Women	Men	Women
	(1)	(2)	(3)	(4)	(5)	(6)
Native-born	60	54	64 (60)	53 (51)	50	9
Foreign-born[d]	91	74	87 (73)	61 (51)	89	17
TOTAL	61	54	66 (61)	54 (51)	53	10

[a]Economically active for 1872 is derived by subtracting those labeled without occupations (*sem profissões*) from total population.

[b]Economically active for 1900 includes results from the 1906 census for the Federal District (Rio de Janeiro). Two estimates are offered for 1900. One subtracts only the explicitly inactive category (*improdutivos*) from the total population (for Brazil), as well as those without occupations (for Rio de Janeiro), while the second estimate (in parentheses) is a narrower definition of the economically active, which also subtracts out those in the unknown status category (*ignoradas*) in the 1900 Brazilian census and those with undeclared occupations in Rio de Janeiro in 1906.

[c]Economically active for 1920 is derived by subtracting those labeled with undeclared occupations (*profissão não declarada*) from the total labor force.

[d]Those with "unknown nationality" in the 1900 and 1920 censuses (and 1906 for Rio de Janeiro) were considered foreign-born.

Sources: 1872, 1900, and 1920 national censuses and 1906 census for Rio de Janeiro.

Labor Force Participation and Sex Composition of Immigrant Labor

Table V–7 presents the participation rates (percent economically active) by sex for the native and foreign-born population from 1872 to 1920. As expected, there is a higher proportion of men participating in the work force than women, and the foreign-born record much higher participation rates than the native-born, reflecting their strong prime working age bias. Two sets of estimates are offered for 1900. The first set considers those in the unknown status category (*ignoradas*) as economically active, while the second set (in parentheses) considers them as inactive. This category was not explicit in either the 1872 or 1920 censuses. Using the first set of estimates for 1900, the results are reasonable and uniform between 1872 and 1900, with the native-born showing no drastic change by either sex, similarly, for the foreign-born men. The participation rate for foreign-born women does show a significant decline over this period (from 74 to 61 percent), but this is consistent with the large rise in the immigration of whole family units associated with the influx of *colono* Italian family labor after 1885. Using the second set of estimates still maintains these uniform results, except for the sharp decline in the percent active among foreign-born males. There was a disproportionately larger number of foreign-born males in this unknown status category.

The sharp discrepancy in these data really appear between 1900 and 1920, where the participation rates drop dramatically, particularly for women, but also visibly for men. Only the foreign-born male labor force experienced no decline between these censuses (using the first set of estimates for the economically active in 1900). Clearly, there was a much stricter and more exclusive definition of what constituted the economically active labor force in 1920 than there was in the two earlier censuses. Moreover, this appears to have affected women much more than men. Additional evidence from the 1920 census shows a decline in the number of domestic servants between these two census years, strongly suggesting a much more restricted definition of domestic servants in 1920. The participation rate for native-born men declined, while that for foreign-born men rose, suggesting that the redefinition of the economically active affected the young part-time workers in the ten to nineteen age male cohort, since there is proportionately a larger number of native-born males than foreign-born males (and workers) in this cohort. Unfortunately, the lack of any age breakdowns distinguishing between the foreign- and native-born population in 1872 or 1900 prevents us from creating more refined participation rates for these separate groups over time.

Table V–8 presents the percent of males in the total population and in the total labor force. The strong predominance of men among the foreign-born population is clear throughout, but it is particularly marked in 1872, whether we look at Brazil as a whole or the major in-migrant regions of Rio de Janeiro or São Paulo. Second, this strong male predominance sharply declines both in the total population and in the labor force between 1872 and 1900. This is consistent with the fact that the large influx of Italian immigrants after 1885 consisted of whole families rather than single men. The fact that this decline in male dominance among the foreign-born stands out more in São Paulo than in the Federal District of Rio de Janeiro in Table V–8 reinforces this explanation, since São Paulo was the locale for this Italian immigration. Thus, we can characterize foreign immigration into Brazil just prior to 1872 as strongly male dominated, which implies a large number of single men and, very likely, a transient pattern of return migration (in this case to Portugal). The history of indentured Portuguese immigrant labor in the early growth of factories and shops in Rio de Janeiro reinforces this conclusion (de Lobo 1975).

Once we move from the "Portuguese" to the "Italian" phase of immigration (circa 1885) the nature of this inflow changes abruptly, as most immigrants were directly recruited to work on the expanding coffee plantations in Western São Paulo. To guarantee some degree of labor discipline and minimize turnover, whole family units were strongly encouraged, indeed, almost a requirement, to gain the government subsidies available for immigration. Wives and children were also commonly utilized as an important part of the work force on these coffee farms (Holloway 1974). The net result was that women began to form a larger part of the foreign-born work force. This pattern generally remains stable between 1900 and 1920 for the population as a whole. No data are offered on the percent of males in the labor force in 1920 due to the distortions introduced by treatment of female labor discussed above.

Table V-8. Percent Male in the Native-born and Foreign-born Populations and Labor Force
in Brazil, São Paulo and Rio de Janeiro, in 1872–1900 and 1920

Region	Population (% Male)			Labor Force (% Male)	
	1872	1900	1920	1872	1900
1) Brazil					
a) Native-born	51	50	50	54	55
b) Foreign-born	74	57	59	77	65
2) São Paulo (state)					
a) Native-born	52	51	51	52	56
b) Foreign-born	71	56	56	74	65
3) Rio de Janeiro (city)					
a) Native-born	51	52[a]	48	58	59[a]
b) Foreign-born	76	72[a]	65	81	79[a]

[a]1906.

Sectoral Participation of Foreign-born Labor

With the participation rates and the changing patterns of sex composition
established, it is useful now to study the growth patterns of the native and
foreign-born labor force over time in Table V–9. We have focused our attention on the male labor force alone to avoid the more serious problems of inter-
temporal comparisons associated with the changing definitions of the female
labor force. Throughout the 48-year period (1872–1920) the foreign-born
male labor force increased on the average at 3.5 percent per year, while the
native-born male labor force grew at slightly more than half that rate, or 1.9
percent per year. This rapid increase more than doubled the relative weight of
the male immigrant labor force, from 5 to 11 percent, for the country as a whole
by 1900. At the same time, its contribution rose to between one-quarter and
one-fifth of the growing industrial labor force during this period, recording, on
the average, a growth of 4.7 percent per year.

A second major finding of Table V–9 is that this growth was much more
pronounced in the earlier period (1872–1900) than in the latter period (1900–
20), regardless of which set of estimates we use for the total labor force. Since
none of the substantive conclusions are affected by use of either estimate, we
shall use the broader definition of the labor force for 1900, which is built into
the growth rates in 1–A of Table V–9 and succeeding tables. In this earlier
period, the growth of the total foreign-born male labor force was more than
double that of the male native-born labor force (5 vs. 2 percent). In the later
period, there is a sharp drop in this rate, and the differential favoring the growth
of immigrant labor disappears. This pattern is essentially repeated in all the
sectoral subdivisions in the table, with the exception of commerce. The more
restricted definition of the economically active in 1920 undoubtedly contributed to the lower 1900–20 rates for native-born male workers; however, as
we saw in Table V–7, this definition does not seem to have affected the participation rate of foreign-born male workers. Thus, the low growth rate recorded

Table V-9. Change in the Native-born and Foreign-born Male Labor Force in Selected
Sectors for Brazil, from 1872 to 1920

		Percent			Rates of growth		
Sectors		1872	1900	1920	1872–1900	1900–20	1872–1920
1-A)	Total male labor force	(1)	(2)	(3)	(4)	(5)	(6)
	a) Native-born	95	89	90	2.0	1.7	1.9
	b) Foreign-born	5	11	10	5.0	1.3	3.5
1-B)	Total male labor force[a]						
	a) Native-born	95	90	90	1.8	2.0	1.9
	b) Foreign-born	5	10	10	4.4	2.1	3.5
2)	Agriculture						
	a) Native-born	97	94	94	1.9	1.9	1.9
	b) Foreign-born	3	6	6	4.6	1.9	3.5
3)	Nonagriculture						
	a) Native-born	89	79	79	2.5	1.0	1.9
	b) Foreign-born	11	21	21	5.3	0.9	3.5
4)	Industry						
	a) Native-born	86	76	79	3.9	3.0	3.5
	b) Foreign-born	14	24	21	6.4	2.3	4.7
5)	Commerce						
	a) Native-born	68	76	70	5.1	1.3	3.5
	b) Foreign-born	32	26	30	4.0	2.2	3.3

[a]These alternative estimates for the total labor force exclude those of unknown status
(*ignoradas*) from the active work force in 1900.
Sources: Demographic censuses of 1872, 1900, and 1920.

for immigrant working men from 1900 to 1920 (1.3 percent for the total labor
force) is probably an accurate measure, and the differential favoring the
growth of the native-born male labor force is wider than that evident in Table
V-9.

This decline in the rate of growth of the foreign-born male labor force can be
explained in part by the decline in immigration during World War I. Also, as
seen earlier, there was a larger element of return migration during this period
than during the earlier period. This was particularly true during the years of
recession in the coffee sector (i.e., 1900–07). Work done by Mortara corroborates this idea in showing that the estimated rates of return migration after
1900 were quite high (35 percent), in comparison to the lower estimates for the
pre-1900 period (20 percent) (Villela and Suzigan 1973: 306). This return, or
out-migration, is the single most plausible explanation for the slower rates of
labor force growth for the foreign-born in this latter period.

With this national pattern in mind, it is appropriate now to look at the
results in Rio de Janeiro and São Paulo, the two major centers of economic
growth during this period in Brazil and, not by accident, the two major centers
of immigrant manpower in Brazilian society. Table V–10 illustrates the
sharply contrasting pattern of these two centers with foreign-born labor. In
1872, the state of São Paulo recorded an insignificant number of foreign-born

Table V-10. Change in the Native-born and Foreign-born Male Labor Force in Selected Sectors for São Paulo State and the Federal District, 1872-1920

A. São Paulo (state)

	Percent			Rates of growth		
	1872	1900	1920	1872–1900	1900–20	1872–1920
1) Total male labor force	(1)	(2)	(3)	(4)	(5)	(6)
a) Native-born	96	69	68	2.3	2.3	2.3
b) Foreign-born	4	31	32	11.8	2.7	7.9
2) Agriculture						
a) Native-born	98	78	73	2.1	1.8	2.0
b) Foreign-born	2	22	27	12.1	3.1	8.3
3) Nonagricultural						
a) Native-born	92	53	59	2.8	3.6	3.1
b) Foreign-born	8	47	47	11.5	2.2	7.6
4) Industry						
a) Native-born	89	43	56	2.1	6.4	3.9
b) Foreign-born	11	57	44	11.1	3.7	8.0
5) Commerce						
a) Native-born	79	50	48	5.4	2.4	4.2
b) Foreign-born	21	50	52	10.5	2.8	7.3

B. Federal District (Rio de Janeiro)

	Percent			Rates of growth		
	1872	1906	1920	1872–1906	1906–20	1872–1920
1) Total male labor force	(1)	(2)	(3)	(4)	(5)	(6)
a) Native-born	57	57	63	3.0	2.1	2.7
b) Foreign-born	43	43	37	3.0	0.3	2.2
2) Industry						
a) Native-born	47	51	60	5.1	2.5	4.4
b) Foreign-born	53	49	40	4.6	-0.0	3.2
3) Commerce						
a) Native-born	26	42	45	4.4	2.9	4.0
b) Foreign-born	74	58	55	2.2	1.9	2.1

Source: Same as Table V-9.

(4 percent of the labor force). In contrast, the city of Rio de Janeiro registered as much as 43 percent of its labor force as foreign-born. In the industrial and commercial sectors, this reached over one-half and three-fourths, respectively (panel B, Table V-10). This profile characterizes the old and the new immigration. The old immigration was essentially from Portugal, directed toward the coastal cities like Recife and Rio de Janeiro, and invariably consisted of single men. For example, in 1872, two-thirds of the 84,279 immigrants in Rio de Janeiro were Portuguese and three-fourths of the foreign-born labor force were male.

The new immigration emerged from 1885 onward with the Paulista program of subsidizing Italian family "*colono*" labor to service the labor needs

of coffee plantations along the expanding Western front
abrupt increase in the weight of the foreign-born in São P
this change. The average rate of growth of the foreign-born
almost 12 percent per year, increasing its relative role to
the supply of labor in the state (panel A, Table V–10)
contained an important component of nonagricultural la
half of the growing industrial and commercial labor force in the state were
foreign-born in 1900. In sharp contrast to this performance, the foreign-born
labor force grew much more slowly in the older urban center of Rio de Janeiro
between 1872 and 1906 (around 3 percent per year) and, in the industrial and
commercial occupations, the native-born labor force grew much more rapidly,
leading to a relative decline in the weight of the foreign-born in these occupations.

The final period under review (1900–20) reveals the same pattern of
declining labor force growth for the foreign-born, already the subject of earlier
discussion with the national data. In the case of Rio de Janeiro, no growth was
recorded, with the consequent decline in the relative weight of foreign-born
labor in the total labor supply by 1920. In São Paulo, the foreign-born still
registered positive rates of growth, but much lower than those recorded for the
native-born labor force, except in the agricultural sector. Throughout the
entire period, however, from 1872 to 1920, the growth of the foreign-born
labor supply in São Paulo far outstripped the growth of the native-born overall
and in all sectors. This differential ranged from two to four times the growth of
the domestic labor force, depending on the sector in question.

If data on the children of the foreign-born or from mixed foreign parentage
had been collected in 1900 and 1920, it would have been possible to record the
impact of both the first and the second generation foreign-born on the total
population and the labor force. This would have weighed more heavily in 1920
than in 1900, as the foreign-born would have had more time to raise native-
born children to working age. In all likelihood, this would have more than
doubled the labor force percentages registered for the foreign-born alone in
1920, thereby showing a continuing growth of the direct and indirect (second-
generation) effects of the foreign-born on the population and the labor force.
Only after 1920 would this combined contribution decline substantially with
the sharp decline in immigration to post-1929 Brazil.

Conclusions: Immigration and the Labor Supply

The empirical benchmarks presented above establish the important role of the
foreign-born in the growth of the labor force for selected regions in Brazil,
particularly São Paulo, from 1872 to 1920. This impact was particularly
strong in its direct (first-generation) effect from 1872 to 1900. Immigrant
manpower accounted for 46 percent of the additions to the total labor force in

province of São Paulo during this period, 48 percent of the incremental increase of the agricultural labor force and 45 percent of the nonagricultural labor force. The definition of agricultural activity in 1872 and 1900 was probably restricted in coverage. No doubt some of the nonagricultural occupations are closely related to agriculture. This latter finding underscores the importance of the broadly defined nonagricultural labor market as an outlet for immigrant manpower during this period and shows the error of focusing exclusively on the importance of the plantation sector alone as an absorber of labor. The important role of female immigrant labor is also corroborated here, especially in the agricultural sector, as the total incremental participation of the foreign-born in the agricultural sector in São Paulo was higher (48 percent) than that recorded for males alone (38 percent).

The second major finding alluded to above (the importance of immigrant labor in the nonagricultural sectors) is also relevant on a national scale in that Rio de Janeiro and São Paulo were the most important and fastest growing industrial labor markets in the country at this time. Moreover, we saw that immigrant manpower not only contributed heavily to the rate of growth of these nonagricultural occupations but, in these two centers, accounted for a substantial percentage of the total nonagricultural labor force.

The success of these two centers in absorbing immigrant labor was due in large part to the strong labor absorptive nature of coffee cultivation and to the labor-intensive techniques common to early industrialization in Brazil, which emphasized textiles, food-processing, clothing, and construction. The national rate of growth of the total male industrial labor force from 1872 to 1920 (3.7 percent) was higher than the rate of urban growth of the city of Rio de Janeiro at this time (3 percent). Even for such a rapidly growing city as São Paulo, the rate of growth of male industrial employment was higher than the rate of growth of the city itself (8.7 vs. 6.3 percent). Today, in contrast, industrial labor absorption barely reaches one-third of the rate of urban growth in a major metropolitan center such as São Paulo.

Table V–11 shows that by international standards the rate of growth of immigrant manpower in Brazil at this time was substantial. In comparison to the United States, Brazil registered higher growth rates for the foreign-born labor force overall and in the industrial sector. The fact that Brazil started from a much lower foreign-born base population in 1872 than the United States accounts, in part, for the higher rate for the ensuing period of almost fifty years. Still the time span covered is sufficiently long that we cannot discount the Brazilian performance.

In summary, evidence shows that the role of immigrant manpower was important in the economic growth of Brazil in the late nineteenth and early twentieth centuries. Its quantitative impact was striking in the two major growth centers of Brazil at this time and decisive in conditioning the pace and pattern of labor force growth not only in the major export sector of the country but also in the development of the industrial and commercial labor force in Rio

Table V–11. Average Annual Percentage Rate of Growth of Total and Industrial Male Labor
Force for the Native- and Foreign-born in the United States (1880–1920) and
Brazil (1872–1920)

	Rate of growth	
	U.S.[a]	Brazil[b]
1) Total labor force	1.6	2.0
a) Native-born	1.5	1.9
b) Foreign-born	2.0	3.5
2) Industry	3.4	3.7
a) Native-born	3.5	3.5
b) Foreign-born	3.1	4.7

[a]For the United States, 1880 data base Hutchinson (1956: 98); 1920 data base from 1920
U.S. Census *Population, vol. IV, Occupations,* Washington, D.C.: Government Printing
Office, 1923, p. 341.
[b]For Brazil, data derived from 1872 and 1920 censuses.

de Janeiro and São Paulo. It is now appropriate to analyze the status and
mobility features of this unusual component of the Brazilian labor force and
draw some conclusions concerning its impact on Brazilian society.

Status and Mobility of the Foreign-Born

Earlier we discussed the hypothesis that immigrant labor preempted opportunities for Brazilian-born workers in the postabolition expansion of coffee
production in São Paulo. Closer examination of factors affecting labor supply
in this period reveal a number of reasons why immigrant rather than native
workers played a more prominent role, as just indicated. To carry the consideration of this hypothesis further, it is instructive to turn now to evidence on the
comparative occupational characteristics of the native- and foreign-born labor
force. As with other aspects of labor force data in the early censuses, occupational data need to be handled with caution, because of changes and
ambiguities in their definition. However, they provide additional insight into
the role of immigrants in the Brazilian economy of the late nineteenth and early
twentieth centuries.[21]

Evidence from Census Data

Table V–12 offers evidence on the sectoral distribution of the foreign-born
labor force from 1872 to 1920. Here the sectoral share of the foreign-born is
divided by their share in the total labor force for Brazil, the state of São Paulo,

[21]Among the several studies establishing the important role of immigrants in the economic
growth of Brazil, see Cardoso (1961), Dean (1967), and Holloway (1974).

Table V-12. Ratio of Sectoral Participation of the Foreign-born Labor Force to Their Share in the Total Labor Force, for Selected Sectors and Regions in Brazil, 1872–1920

Sector	1872	1900	1920
	A. Brazil		
Agriculture	0.6	0.5	0.6
Industry	2.8	2.2	2.1
Commerce	6.4	2.4	3.0
	B. São Paulo		
Agriculture	0.5	0.7	0.8
Industry	2.8	1.8	1.4
Commerce	5.3	1.6	1.2
	C. Federal District (Rio de Janeiro)		
Industry	1.2	1.1	1.1
Commerce	1.7	1.3	1.5

Source: Derived from labor force data (Economically Active Population by Sectors) in demographic censuses of 1872, 1900, 1920.

and the Federal District (city of Rio de Janeiro). Nationally, the foreign-born were most dominant in commercial activities in 1872 and, to a lesser extent, in industrial occupations. Their share in total commercial employment was 32 percent, even though they only comprised 5 percent of the national labor force (creating a ratio of relative specialization of 6.4). This relative concentration in commercial and industrial occupations vis-à-vis the native-born labor force generally declines as we move from 1872 to 1920. Changing our perspective from the national level to the comparatively developed regions of São Paulo and Rio de Janeiro, the dominance lessens but still does not disappear. From 1900 onward, the foreign-born are more specialized in industrial occupations in São Paulo than in commerce, while the opposite holds in the city of Rio de Janeiro, reflecting the different focus of growth in these two settings.

Table V-13, on comparative literacy, strongly suggests that the foreign-born also drew upon a stronger human resource base than the native-born. In 1900, the foreign-born registered about double the literacy rate (percent) of the native-born (43 vs. 23 percent). By 1920 this differential had widened further (52 vs. 23 percent). Looking at the city of Rio de Janeiro in 1920, where one would expect to find the most qualified and literate native-born, we see that the foreign-born still held an advantage in literacy (68 vs. 59 percent, with literacy for males even more outstanding, 76 vs. 63 percent). Brazilian censuses did not record educational data in 1900 and 1920. For 1940, comparative indices on education showed the foreign-born to have had substantially higher educational qualifications (panel B, Table V-13). These findings on literacy and education contrast to those in the United States, where the native-born registered higher levels of literacy and educational status than the foreign-born (Easterlin 1972: 150). The host culture in Brazil was much

Table V–13. Literacy Rates for Native- and Foreign-born for Brazil and the Federal District, 1900–20, and Educational Indices for 1940 for Brazil

A. Percent literate

	Brazil		Federal District (Rio de Janeiro)	
	1900	1920	1906	1920
Native-born				
Men	27.9	26.8	54.7	63.2
Women	17.9	19.1	47.6	56.1
Both sexes	23.0	22.9	51.3	59.5
Foreign-born				
Men	49.9	61.7	59.6	76.2
Women	34.1	37.8	38.1	53.7
Both sexes	43.1	51.9	53.5	68.3

Source: Derived from data in 1900 and 1920 demographic censuses.

B. Percent of foreign-born and native-born age 10 or more, with completed education at indicated levels, 1940

Level	Native-born	Foreign-born
1) University	0.3	1.1
2) Secondary	1.1	3.0
3) Primary	5.4	10.1
4) No school or primary incomplete	93.4	85.8

Source: Derived from data in *Censo Demográfico 1940,* Série Nacional, Rio de Janeiro, 1950, vol. 2, p. 31.

less developed than the Anglo-Saxon, native-born culture in the United States. Consequently, foreign immigrants had a more promising opportunity to compete and succeed in the Brazilian setting than in the American environment, where the native-born were more formidable economic competitors.

Additional evidence supports the thesis that the foreign-born experienced some upward social and economic mobility. Table V–14 documents the rise of the foreign-born to landowner status in the rural sector of São Paulo from 1905 to 1934. Twenty years after the first major inflow of Italian *colonos*, 1905 data show that the foreign-born had obtained some share of the land in São Paulo. These aggregate data mask the degree to which immigrants became property owners in selected rural areas. Holloway reports that in 37 of the 97 *municípios* in the Santos coffee zone immigrants owned 30 percent or more of the rural property registered in 1905 (Holloway 1974: 379). By 1920, statewide data show immigrants owning 27 percent of all rural properties worth 19 percent of the total registered value. Although the property percentage remained unchanged by 1934, the increase in absolute numbers was more than threefold, while the relative proportion in area and value increased substantially.

Table V-14. Selected Data on Rural Landownership by Foreign-born in São Paulo,
1905-34

	Properties		Area		Value	
Census year	No.	% of S.P. total	1000's of hectares	% of S.P. total	Millions of milreis	% of S.P. total
1905	7,336	13	804	7	84	8
1920	20,381	27	1,562	13	437	19
1934	73,746	27	4,270	20	1,586	28

Sources: Secretaria da Agricultura, *Estatística Agrícola e Zootécnica 1904-05,* 4 volumes (São Paulo, 1906-10), passim; Diretoria Geral de Estatística, *Recenseamento Realizado em 1º de Setembro de 1920,* vol. 3, part 2 (Rio de Janeiro, 1924), p. xxxv; São Paulo Secretaria da Agricultura, *Recenseamento Agrícola-Zootécnico Realizado em 1934* (São Paulo, 1936), p. 29. Above data reproduced in Holloway (1974).

Table V-15 summarizes data on the ownership of the major cash crop itself, coffee, for 1923 and 1932. By 1932, immigrant owners accounted for almost 40 percent of all the producing coffee trees in the state, with Italians accounting for 22 percent. Panel B shows that the various immigrant nationalities had smaller-sized average holdings than Brazilian coffee owners. Of interest here is that from 1923 to 1932 the increase in the relative role of immigrants as owners of coffee farms (panel A) was associated with a decline in the average-sized holding overall (panel B). In short, immigrants were at least partially responsible for reducing the larger oligarchic land holdings in the Paulista coffee sector as small and medium-sized farms grew in relative importance. When one bears in mind that the sons of earlier immigrants must have represented a relevant portion of the native-born owners by the 1930s, the impact of immigrants on the structure of rural property ownership in São Paulo becomes even more significant.

Institutional Factors

Institutional factors were extremely important in these mobility patterns for the foreign-born in Brazil during the early twentieth century. A major question is how and why immigrants were as successful as they were, when many of them arrived in less than ideal circumstances, i.e., replacing slaves as *colono* agricultural laborers. It is true that not all arrived in such humble straits, as evidenced by the increasing number of nonsubsidized immigrants into São Paulo after the turn of the century. Still, a sufficiently large number did arrive under unpromising conditions and succeeded in surmounting that early stigma of poverty. There are three important points that should be considered.

First, the arrival of the immigrants during a sharp upswing in Brazilian growth after 1885 facilitated their chance for success. At the same time, they were important catalysts in extending this growth into broader multisectoral paths than would have occurred without their presence as laborers and entre-

Table V-15. Selected Data by Nationality on Ownership of Coffee Trees in Western
        São Paulo in 1923 and 1932

A. Producing coffee trees in the Western plateau of São Paulo in 1923
   and 1932, by national origin of owner

Percent

Year	Brazilian	Total Foreign-born	Italian	Portuguese	Spanish	Others
1923	69.5	31.5	18.3	3.7	2.7	6.8
1932	60.5	39.1	22.0	4.6	6.1	6.4

Source: Boletim do Departamento Estadual do Trabalho (São Paulo), no. 50–51 (1st and 2nd quarters 1924); and São Paulo Secretaria da Agricultura, *Lavoura Cafeeira Paulista e Sua Distribuição por Nacionalidade 1932–33* (São Paulo, no date), pp. 8–23, reproduced in Holloway (1974: 410, 413, 420–21).

B. Average coffee trees per farm in the Western plateau of São Paulo
   in 1923, 1932, by national origin of owner

No. coffee trees per farm (thousands of trees)

Year	Total	Brazilian	Italian	Portuguese	Spanish
1923	25	31	15	22	18
1932	18	22	14	16	13

Source: Same as panel A above.

preneurs. Relevant here is that much of their success was in terms of "structural" rather than "exchange" mobility, i.e., their economic participation helped to create new jobs through expansion of the economy (which they then filled in the industrial and commercial sectors) rather than displacing natives from established occupations. [22] Still, their active and successful competition for these new jobs probably did preempt some employment opportunities for native-born workers.

Second, the host culture in Brazil was already Mediterranean in origin, so that problems of cultural adaptation were minimized. This contrasts with the more alien and discriminatory Anglo-Saxon environment that Southern Europeans confronted in the United States. Brazil was not as well developed economically or educationally, and immigrants consequently were faced with a less competitive native-born labor force than in more developed immigrant-receiving societies such as the United States.[23] The net result was an attractive environment for ambitious immigrants, since a growth potential was apparent and local competition to exploit this potential was limited.

A final and important institutional consideration is the role of the *colono* labor system in the Paulista coffee sector in creating opportunities for savings,

[22] On the successful performance for immigrants and the distinction between structural and exchange mobility in this performance, see Bertram Hutchinson (1958).
[23] For an evaluation of the relative competitive success of immigrants in the United States, see Easterlin (1972).

investment, and spatial and upward mobility for immigrant workers.[24] Several features of the *colono* system account for its success in promoting the immigrants' long-run possibilities for economic improvement. A diversified source of income payments freed it of many of the negative features of traditional tenant, sharecropping, and fixed-wage systems. The *colono* received a wage for the weeding and care of a given number of trees throughout the year. This did not depend on what the planter himself got for the crop. Harvest wages were a second source of money income. They were based on a piece-rate arrangement whereby each *colono* received a payment for as many *alqueires* as he and his family could pick. This income fluctuated from year to year, depending on the variation in yield per tree. A third monetary source came from day labor around the plantation, and a fourth (nonmonetary) source of income was rent-free housing and land upon which the *colono* could grow crops and raise livestock to meet his own subsistence needs and sell in local or regional markets.

It was very important that the *colono* paid no rent, either in money or in kind, for the use of housing, food plot, and pasture. Given the relative abundance of land in the coffee areas, this was a way whereby the plantation owner could offer incentives (i.e., use of land for food cropping and livestock) and keep his wage bill down. Food and rent frequently represented close to 60 percent of a typical working class family's consumption expenditures in the region at this time. Thus, rent-free housing and near self-sufficiency in food production allowed *colonos* the opportunity to ecnomize on the use of their money income. This money income (and proceeds from some marketing of food and livestock products) could be used to generate savings and eventually buy small parcels of land or migrate to urban areas with enough to get started in a new setting.

These features of the *colono* system, in conjunction with the other reinforcing influences mentioned earlier, contributed to the immigrants' success in rising above their earlier poverty and becoming, in time, small- to medium-sized landowners in the very rural milieu that no doubt had set out to exploit them as convenient substitutes for slave labor. Alternative employment opportunities in urban areas, the rapid rise in coffee demand, and the competition among plantation owners for *colono* labor generally gave the *colonos* a degree of bargaining power to secure these work and income arrangements that were generally absent in other postabolition settings. In short, the Paulista *colono* arrangement did not turn out to be a debilitating debt-peonage or wage-slavery system as occurred in most other former slave societies through more traditional tenancy, sharecropping, or fixed-wage systems. It was an unusual combination of an annual wage, piece-work payments, daily wage, and nonmonetary perquisites that gave reasonable assurance of a minimum annual income, the reduction of living costs and the possibility of accumulating

---

[24]The best and most complete treatment of this can be found in Holloway (1974).

savings through money income and a low cost of living (Holloway 1974: 92–105).

Migrants and Early Industrialization in Brazil: A Synopsis

No discussion of the mobility patterns of immigrants would be complete without reference to their entrepreneurial role in the growing urban-industrial sector during this period.[25] Willems has catalogued the impressive record of German immigrant entrepreneurs as pioneers in industrial activity in Santa Catarina, Rio Grande do Sul, and São Paulo (Willems 1955). Dean and Cardoso also mention the role of the immigrant in the industrialization of São Paulo (Dean 1969, Cardoso 1960). Finally, in a recent survey of industrial firms in the city of São Paulo, Pereira underscores the role of the immigrant entrepreneurs and, within this group, Italian entrepreneurs. This study canvassed a random sample (i.e., one that represented 36 percent of the universe) of all domestic, nonforeign industrial firms with 100 or more employees in greater São Paulo in 1962. Among other findings the author discovered that approximately 50 percent of the firms in the sample were currently owned and directed by first-generation immigrants. If one includes second-generation immigrants (those whose fathers were foreign-born), this percentage rises to 73 percent (Bresser Pereira 1974: 198–99). Moreover, director-owners who were first- or second-generation Italians constituted the largest single ethnic group in the sample, even in comparison to Brazilians (those whose grandfathers were born in Brazil).

Our own data have underscored the importance of migrants not only as the manpower base for the expansion of the coffee frontier in São Paulo but also for their entrepreneurial and labor force contribution to commercial and industrial growth at the beginning of this century. Their role in fragmenting the large oligarchic land holdings in Paulista agriculture changed important ownership patterns of wealth and land holding in rural São Paulo.

Such a scenario strongly suggests that both the coffee and the immigrant culture interacted to create many positive feedbacks out of the Brazilian export or staple pattern of growth at this time. In the framework of Hirschman's linkage concepts, one would have to conclude that the more conventional production linkages (either backward or forward) were of less importance in this story, except for some forward linkage effects of railroad and port construction for the shipment of coffee (Hirschman 1977). Similarly, the fiscal linkage of government taxation and later reinvestment in new undertakings was minimal, since the coffee culture was not a foreign enclave in the Brazilian economy.

[25]Important studies on the entrepreneurial role of immigrants and their successful social and occupational mobility in the urban-industrial sector at this time are Dean (1969), Pereira (1974), and Willems (1951, 1955).

The essential growth impulse emanating from the coffee culture was what Hirschman has labeled the consumption linkage, namely, the income-induced expansion of early import-substituting industries, growing out of the surplus generated from export earnings. For this to happen, control of the factors of production and the export process must be largely domestic rather than foreign, and this was the case in the coffee culture. In addition, the growth of an internal market requires that an important part of the benefits of this export growth filter down to socioeconomic groups other than the principal oligarchic landowners. The significant labor absorptive features of coffee cultivation and the opportunities for the growth of immigrant family income and savings associated with the *colono* form of labor organization on the coffee plantation contributed in no small way to the growth of the internal market in Brazil at this time, as well as promoting intraregional and intersectoral mobility of the immigrant labor force in São Paulo.

Certain negative features were a part of this scene. Regional income disparities between the Northeast and Southern Brazil clearly widened during this period.[26] This was an inevitable consequence of the regional-specific focus of the coffee immigrant growth impulse located in the Paulista area to the South. The Northeast remained locked into its regional poverty syndrome, with its sugar staple pattern of growth generating negative rather than positive feedback over time. Another possible negative feature in the eyes of some is the possible deterioration in the distribution of income within the South during this period, brought about through the presumed pressure of an elastic supply of immigrant labor on the level of domestic wages (Leff 1970). The data are presently unavailable or unsuitable to draw any firm conclusions on the change in regional income distribution within São Paulo from 1885 to 1930, and it is highly questionable whether real earnings of the immigrant labor force declined over time.[27] Despite the fact that immigrants may have preempted or tempered the rise of some native-born groups (i.e., former slaves or local artisan workers), it would be difficult to argue that the patriarchal, slave-holding, agrarian society that characterized São Paulo in the early 1880s was, in any meaningful sense, more egalitarian than the immigrant-influenced social structure of the 1920s. Sharp inequalities still existed at this later time, however, these inequalities were more dynamic and less static in character, with many elements of growth and structural change now built into the system that were absent in the earlier period. Thus, the flow through the system in the form of increased opportunities for social and occupational mobility has to be

[26]On the controversy and debate concerning the extent and the causes of the regional disparities between the Northeast and the South at the end of the nineteenth century, see Leff (1972) and Denslow (1973, 1978).

[27]Hall (1969) does argue that there was a decline in real wages for Italian *colono* labor in the coffee sector from 1885 to 1913, however, his wage data pick up only a part of their total income package and ignore income earned (and expenses avoided) through the sale and consumption of their own foodcrops and livestock.

set off against traditional static inequality. On this score, the immigrant-influenced socioeconomic structure of the post-1885 period does not come off badly, though wealth and income inequality was still an important feature of Brazilian society at this time.

VI   Population Redistribution, Migration, and Regional Economic Growth

Spatial Distribution: Long-Run Changes, 1778–1970

Since colonial times, Brazil's population distribution has been characterized by a high degree of concentration of settlement in a two hundred mile wide band stretching along the Atlantic coast from the Northeast to the Southern region. The vast interior, considering only the Central-West and Northern (Amazon) regions, holds 65 percent of the land area, but only 10 percent of the population (1970 data). Prior to the initiation of settlement in that region, around 1950, the figure was only 7 percent. Table VI–1 shows that historically the Northeast and the Southeast have been Brazil's most populated regions. They accounted for more than 89 percent of the population late in the colonial period (1772–77) and more than 70 percent in 1970. The historical trend in Brazil contrasts sharply with the United States. In 1790 the U.S. population was also highly concentrated along the Atlantic coast (97 percent), but westward settlement reduced this share to 45 percent by 1870 and 39 percent in 1970.

Geography and colonial policy contributed to the continued dominance of coastal regions in Brazil. Mountainous terrain and lack of rivers flowing from the interior inhibited establishment of transportation links. Portuguese administrators discouraged settlement along the São Francisco River, the main internal link between the Northeastern and Southeastern provinces, in order to keep transport flowing along the coast where it was easier to police. Smuggling of gold and diamonds was a major problem, especially in the eighteenth century. Plantation agriculture was concentrated along the Northeastern littoral, and transport costs were a major factor in the location of Southeastern coffee culture as near as possible to the coast in the nineteenth century. Despite a desire to guarantee sovereignty over the vast territory through settlement, incursion into the interior was limited to military outposts, subsistence agriculture providing fuel and draft animals to the plantations, and

Table VI-1. Distribution of the Brazilian Population[a] by Major Regions, 1772–1970

	1772–82[b]	1872		1900		1940		1970	
North	(4.1)	333	(3.4)	695	(4.0)	1,462	(3.6)	3,603	(3.9)
Northeast	(47.4)	4,639	(46.7)	6,750	(38.7)	14,434	(35.0)	28,111	(30.3)
Southeast	(41.8)	4,017	(40.5)	7,824	(44.9)	18,345	(44.5)	39,851	(42.7)
South	(1.9)	721	(7.3)	1,796	(10.3)	5,735	(13.9)	16,496	(17.7)
Central-West	(4.8)	221	(2.2)	373	(2.1)	1,258	(3.1)	5,072	(5.5)
TOTAL		9,931	(100.0)	17,434	(100.0)	41,236	(100.0)	93,135	(100.0)

[a]Population in thousands; percentages in parentheses; totals may not add to 100 because of rounding.
[b]Percentage distribution.
Source: 1772–82, Alden (1963); 1872–1970, Brazil, Fundação IBGE (1971) and (1973a).

mining settlements. Even in the most populated "interior" state, Minas Gerais, settlement was concentrated in the Southern portion closest to Rio de Janeiro, and colonial authorities limited access to the mining regions in the Northern part of the state (Boxer 1962).

Population redistribution has reduced the share of the Northeast from 47 to 30 percent over the two-century period, with the South and Central-West regions gaining. Migration, both international and internal, as well as differential natural increase have contributed to this redistribution. It is also of interest to note differences in the timing of these changes. During the first century in our comparison (1770–1870), regional population shares hardly changed at all. Only the South gained in relation to other regions. This was due primarily to the colonization policy of the empire, which allocated practically all of the limited amount of foreign immigrants during this period to the South (mainly the state of Rio Grande do Sul). Higher natural increase may have been a secondary factor, as the South has traditionally enjoyed a lower mortality level than the rest of Brazil, because of the higher percentage of foreign-born. Economic progress was generally slow in Brazil during the middle decades of the nineteenth century, and the limited evidence that we have on population growth in this period (Chapter III) suggests that the overall rate of increase was sluggish, if not lower than it had been earlier.

Redistribution picks up substantially as we move to the period 1870–1900. During this period, we observe the sharpest short-run change in population distribution during the entire two-century period. The Northeast's share dropped precipitously from 47 to 39 percent, while that of the Southeast increased from 40 to 45 percent and the South from 7 to 10 percent. The data in Table VI–2 highlight the fact that these major shifts in population shares were concentrated in four states during the period: Ceará and Pernambuco losing relatively to São Paulo and Rio Grande do Sul. As was demonstrated in the two preceding chapters, large-scale immigration was primarily responsible, with internal migration and differential natural increase adding to the process. The most important economic factor was, as we have seen, the opening up of the Brazilian economy to the world export market in coffee (W.

Table VI–2. Distribution of the Brazilian Population by Selected States, 1772–1970 (percentages)

	1772–82	1872	1900	1940	1960	1970
Ceará	3.9	7.27	4.87	5.07	4.70	4.36
Pernambuco	15.4	8.47	6.76	6.52	5.83	5.16
Bahia	18.5	13.99	12.15	9.50	8.44	7.49
Minas Gerais	20.5	20.54	20.61	16.34	13.80	11.49
Rio de Janeiro (with Guanabara)	13.8	10.65	9.96	8.76	9.50	8.99
São Paulo	7.5	8.43	13.10	17.41	18.30	17.77
Paraná	–	1.28	1.87	3.00	6.03	6.93
Rio Grande do Sul	1.3	4.38	6.59	8.05	7.68	6.66
Goiás (with Distrito Federal)	3.5	1.61	1.46	2.00	3.00	3.48
Mato Grosso	1.3	0.60	0.68	1.05	1.28	1.60

Source: Population censuses for 1940, 1950, 1960, and 1970.

Arthur Lewis 1970: Chapters 1, 2, 4). This expansion led to important structural changes in the growth and development of the economy of São Paulo and its relation to the rest of the Brazilian economy (Villela and Suzigan 1973).

During this period, the Northeast of Brazil was suffering from severe droughts, extremely high mortality rates, and prolonged economic stagnation in its traditional exports: cotton in Ceará and sugar in Pernambuco. The net effect of this interregional shift in economic fortunes was to promote a marked regional redistribution of population through the weight of international immigration into São Paulo, growing disparities in interregional death rates because of conditions in the drought-stricken and poverty-ridden Northeast, and, finally, interregional transfers of slaves to the South and, to a lesser extent, the migration of free labor from the Northeast to the South and to the rubber boom in the North.

In contrast, the forty-year period 1900–40 brought only slight changes in the relative regional shares. Again, these shifts stand out more noticeably among states (Table VI–2) than among regions (Table VI–1), indicating that many of the changes by states were offsetting each other within regional categories. São Paulo still gained considerably (from 13 to 17 percent), but this time at the expense of the Southeastern states, especially Minas Gerais, rather than more distant Northeastern states. Indeed, both Ceará and Pernambuco, the major losers in the last thirty years of the nineteenth century, more or less maintained their relative positions throughout the early twentieth century. The Northeast had already reached the lower limit of its relative decline by the end of the last century.

In the last thirty years (1940–70), both Minas Gerais and Bahia continued to be the areas that suffered the sharpest negative declines in their population shares. This time the Central-West region more than doubled its relative participation (from 2 to 5 percent) along with Paraná. São Paulo did not increase its relative share significantly during this period. The main thrust of interregional migration had shifted to the frontier regions. High rates of natural increase on the frontier, due principally to high fertility (Chapter X), have contributed further to their increased population shares.

In summary, over a two-century period Brazil experienced significant spatial redistribution of its population. Moreover, this spatial redistribution was clearly associated with the overall rate of national population growth and the economic development of the country. The first century of this experience, for example, brought little change, not surprising in view of the moderate population growth and lack of marked economic progress. Disequilibrating factors were limited or absent. After 1870, however, marked changes began to occur in the economy and, consequently, in the geographic distribution of the population. The first thirty years (1870–1900) were stamped by expansion of coffee exports and significant international migration. This contributed to regional population shifts, along with continued declines in the economy of the Northeast, its droughts and high mortality, and by internal migration to meet the new regional demand for labor. Similarly, the last thirty-year period had been characterized by a sharp rise in the rate of natural increase, growth in the industrial sector of the economy, and substantial interregional migration. The most recent upsurge in redistribution was caused by substantial migration to cities and migration to new settlement areas on the agricultural frontier. The latter shifts had also been accompanied by higher rates of natural increase among migrants, further accentuating the growth in their relative share of total population.

The demographic components of redistribution are migration and differential natural increase, as well as the interaction between migration and vital rates. As will be seen in Chapter X, there have been regional differentials in birth and death rates in Brazil, and it is possible that these differences have widened in recent decades. Information on natural increase at the state and regional levels is limited to more recent censuses, and most of what can be said about earlier periods must be inferred from what is known about the regional impact of factors that could have created them, e.g., the predominance of international migration in Southern states and the severe droughts in the Northeast. International and internal migration flows are the major direct determinants of population redistribution. The remainder of this chapter is devoted mainly to regional flows and their relation to economic trends.

Internal Migration

Long-Term Trends, 1890–1971

Direct measurements of long-term trends in interregional migration in Brazil do not exist, and applications of techniques that are available for indirect measurement are severely restricted by data limitations. The two most commonly used indirect methods are the vital statistics (or balancing-equation) approach, which derives migration as a residual between each state or region's total and natural rate of population increase, and the survival ratio approach, which determines the number of migrants in an intercensal period by comparing survivors by region (those who have not died in the intercensal period) in each cohort from a previous census with the actual population of the cohort in a succeeding one. Survivorship rates are determined either from life tables (the life-table approach) or by comparison of age distributions at the national level in two censuses (the census-survival approach). The lack of reliable data on vital rates at the state and regional levels in Brazil, except those derived from recent censuses, limits the applicability of the vital-statistics approach. Most of what can be done with the Brazilian data until very recently has been based on the survival-ratio method.

The basic data requirements for estimating migration flows with the survival method are accurate age distribution data at the state/regional level and absence of significant state/regional differentials in mortality and international migration flows. These requirements are necessary because the survival method utilizes ratios that have been determined for the national population (whether from life tables or from comparison of two censuses) to calculate "survivors" from the age distribution of an earlier census for comparison with the actual numbers reported in a subsequent census as the estimate of net internal migration for the intercensal period.[1] International migration can be controlled if these differences can be calculated separately for the native-born population. Mortality differences are a more serious limitation; application of regional life table estimates is the only way to control for this.

Graham and Hollanda (1971) and Carvalho (1973) have prepared estimates of Brazilian internal migration using the survival-ratio approach. Each method has had to make different adaptations of the technique to deal with data limitations. Graham and Hollanda worked with the 1890–1940 data, and have had to cope with the problem of region-specific age distributions for the foreign-born.[2] As was seen in the previous chapter, the differential regional

---

[1] For an analysis of the various census survival techniques, their strengths and shortcomings, see Everett S. Lee et al., *Population Redistribution and Economic Growth, United States 1870–1950*, vol. 1, prepared under the direction of Simon Kuznets and Dorothy Swaine Thomas, The American Philosophical Society, Philadelphia, 1957.

[2] The appropriate age and sex cohorts for both the native-born and foreign-born in Brazil were only available from the 1920 census onward. Earlier censuses merely recorded the total number of foreign-born and native-born and, in addition, age and sex cohorts only for the total population. However, there was a close correspondence in the relative distribution of the foreign-born by age and sex cohorts between the 1920 U.S. and Brazilian censuses. Thus, the earlier relative cohort distributions of the foreign-born from the 1900 and 1890 U.S. censuses were applied (with minor alterations) to the total number of foreign-born in the comparable Brazilian censuses. These estimated cohorts were then subtracted from the total age and sex cohorts reported in the Brazilian censuses, to arrive at the native-born age and sex cohorts required by the survival method. For a more detailed treatment see Graham and Hollanda (1971, vol. 1: Appendix A).

impact of international migration was quite important between 1890 and 1920. For the 1940–70 period, mortality differentials are important. But the most serious problem was the large gap in state/regional age distribution data resulting from the incomplete publication of the 1960 census.

Graham and Hollanda (1971) estimated migration rates for 1890–1950, using census survival ratios. To bridge the data gap for 1960, they used a simplified adaptation of the survival-ratio technique, which is the global survival ratio. Instead of estimating survivors for each ten-year age cohort, as in the full life table survival estimates, they "survived" the entire base population over the ten- or twenty-year interval between censuses and used the difference between the actual and survived population aged ten and over (twenty when the interval was twenty years) as the migration estimate. After comparing the more disaggregated survival results with the simpler global survival estimates for comparable periods, they concluded that the latter provided an adequate approximation for descriptive comparisons of the long-term interregional migration pattern. Before turning to the more detailed attempts at measuring migration in the 1940–70 period, it will be useful to review the longer-term patterns that are indicated by this approach.

The main features of the 1890–1970 trend in interregional migration in Brazil are shown in Table VI–3. Migration rates have been calculated for Brazil and for major sending and receiving regions; the rates express in percentages the number of migrants in the intercensal period divided by the total population at the beginning of the period. Several points stand out. Taking equivalent time periods we see that: (1) the rate of net internal migration has increased from the end of the last century to the present, as can be seen in the data for the ten-year census intervals; (2) if we accept the assumption that the rate for a twenty-year period would be higher than for either ten-year period making up this twenty-year period, then the high rates of net internal interstate migration registered in the post-World War II decades are truly high when compared to earlier twenty-year periods; (3) the slight negative internal migration for the South in the period 1890–1900 was associated with substantial international migration, suggesting that the levels of "internal" migration remained relatively low in the South and the East until after international migration declined in the early 1930s; (4) the regional focus of net internal emigration has shifted from first the Eastern states (primarily Bahia and Minas Gerais) to an equal role for the Northeastern states, while the regions of destination have shifted from the South to the Central-West frontier regions.

The data in Table VI–3 show that from 1890 to 1960 the number migrating as a percentage of the initial population base increases. However, it would appear that the fifties represents a high point, with the sixties showing a slight decline in the rate of migration. While this may be true of "interstate" migration, it may not be true of intrastate or intraregional movements. These "shorter" moves may have continued at an increasing pace in the sixties (DaMata et al. 1973). Four related patterns emerge from this secular trend of

Table VI-3. National and Regional Rates of Net Internal Migration of the Native-born,
Expressed as a Percent of Population in Initial Census Years, Brazil, 1890–1970

A. National Rates

Ten-year intercensal periods	Rate	Twenty-year intercensal periods	Rate
1890–1900	2.97	1900–20	3.79
1940–50	2.94	1920–40	4.99
1950–60	5.51		
1960–70	4.49		

B. Regional Rates

	1890–1900	1900–20	1920–40	1940–50	1950–60	1960–70
North	24.38	16.66	–13.72	– 3.38	0.39	2.78
Northeast	– 1.42	– 1.68	– 0.84	– 2.67	– 9.78	– 5.08
East	– 0.64	– 4.81	– 5.37	– 3.26	– 3.10	– 5.57
South	– 0.97	5.24	11.73	6.07	8.25	5.61
Sao Paulo	5.43	1.13	11.54	5.70	7.80	7.66
Paraná	– 7.47	13.43	19.58	29.28	43.58	18.39
Central-West	2.64	11.88	13.37	7.27	22.52	23.22
Goiás	2.17	10.33	9.92	11.15	21.34	21.42
Mato Grosso	3.81	15.60	21.30	– 0.55	23.59	27.38

Source: Graham and Hollanda (1971, vol. 1: 21–22).

increasing interregional internal migration: (1) the competitive and preemptive role of foreign immigration from 1890 to 1930 and its eventual substitution in the 1930s by internal migrants; (2) the unfolding of four distinct patterns of frontier migration throughout this period; (3) a distinct pattern of urban and rural components within the interregional population transfers of the last decade and; (4) an alternating role of regional divergence and convergence of income per capita associated with the migratory patterns of post-1940 Brazil.

As discussed earlier, the large inflow of foreign immigrants from 1890 to 1930 largely preempted any important labor supply role for internal migrants in the South. Table VI–4 shows this pattern for São Paulo, the most important region for both internal and foreign migration in the twentieth century. Foreign immigration dominated in both the nineties and the first two decades of the twentieth century. Indeed, from 1900 to 1920 there was actually a slight net negative internal migration at the same time there was a heavy foreign in-migration.[3] Only from 1920 to 1940 did internal migrants finally register higher numbers than foreign migrants.

[3] The census survival estimate for the net migration of the foreign-born here is derived from the difference between the net migration estimates for the total population age and sex cohorts and the net migration for the native-born age and sex cohorts. Table VI–3 shows an insignificant net positive inflow of "internal" migrants (from 1900 to 1920) that represented 1.13 percent of the base population of São Paulo in 1900. The negative result for the same period in Table V–4 is derived from a more disaggregated age cohort breakdown with the census-survival technique. The former, more aggregate technique in Table V–3, was used to gain a consistent measure over the

Table VI-4. Forward Census Survival Estimates of Net Internal and Net Foreign Migration for the State of São Paulo, 1890–1940

	A. 1890–1900		B. 1900–20		C. 1920-40	
	Internal	Foreign	Internal	Foreign	Internal	Foreign
São Paulo	70,292	412,297	-19,933	374,250	355,588	341,688

Source: Graham and Hollanda (1971, vol. 1).

Earlier (Chapter V) we examined the hypothesis that the "local" labor force (former slaves and the free colored) in and around São Paulo may have been pushed into marginal employment patterns because of the inflow of foreign-born labor during the coffee expansion of 1890–1920, with much of the potential "national" labor supply (largely in the East and Northeast) having been locked into regional stagnation through the preemptive role of foreign migrants satisfying the immediate demand for labor in the South. Closer examination of this hypothesis revealed that regional factors (demand for labor in rubber regions of the North and the expansion of subsistence agriculture in the Northeast) and the distaste of local labor for working under plantation conditions in the postabolition South were also important. Whatever the causes, the net effect was a very limited contribution of internal migration of native-born Brazilians to population redistribution that occurred in São Paulo between 1890 and 1920.

The first heavy influx of "internal" migrants in the 1920–40 period (Table VI-4, panel C) largely arrived in the 1930s. Data from the São Paulo Immigration Service confirm the broad regional origin of these migrants as coming from the East and Northeast (in particular Minas Gerais, Bahia, and the southern tier of Northeastern sugar states, such as Alagoas and Pernambuco —Camargo 1952). This pattern generally held until the 1950s, when the Northeast rose to prominence as a major supplier of manpower to the South (Table VI–3, panel B).

This internal migration was stimulated by the sharp decline of international immigrants in the thirties, the growing push factors of increased capital-intensive labor displacement in the sugar areas of the Northeast, and the need to replace departing *colonos* and others migrating from the Paulista plantations to the cities. Table VI–5 underscores the rural destination of much of this internal migration as the frontier in Western São Paulo, serviced largely by foreign *colonos* up to the twenties, continued a remarkable demographic expansion from 1920 to 1940. This area increased its population by one and a half times its 1920 base and practically doubled in its relative importance from 12 to 23 percent of the state's population. Thus, the thirties can be char-

long run. The second measure was used in the estimates separating internal and foreign migrants during the period 1890–1940. For a discussion of the small differences in these two different estimates, see Graham and Hollanda (1971, vol. 1: Chapter II).

Table VI-5. Distribution of Population in New and Old Frontier Areas of São Paulo, 1900–40

	1900	%	1920	%	1940	%
Old frontier areas	1,638,065	72	2,713,681	59	2,928,100	41
New frontier areas	275,120	12	1,061,979	23	2,512,414	35
Cities of São Paulo & environs (incl. Santos)	366,423	16	816,528	18	1,739,802	24
		100		100		100

Source: Camargo (1952, vol. 2: Table 22)

acterized as the transition period when local migrants replaced much of the foreign *colono* labor as the major source of Paulista rural manpower, while the first- and second-generation *colonos* became small and medium-sized landowners (hiring internal migrant labor) or continued to migrate to urban occupations.

Frontier Patterns of Rural Settlement

Available evidence on the secular trends on interregional migration in Table VI–3 underscores four distinct patterns of frontier settlement. Our use of the term "frontier" here does not exclude the possibility that some of these areas experienced sporadic settlement for extractive activities in earlier periods. For our purposes, the crucial distinction is the more widespread occupation and settlement of these areas. The first important period of rural expansion, from 1885 to 1930, can be labeled the Paulista-plantation-immigrant pattern. Characteristic here were the initial large landholdings of the rural Paulista oligarchy; significant private sector initiative by this oligarchy in establishing railroads; the large foreign supply of immigrants; the changing tenancy status of foreign labor from tenant to small landowner; and large rural-urban out-migration during periods of economic decline. The most important result of this pattern was that, contrary to earlier periods, it generated a more sustained economic expansion, which eventually spilled over into early industrial development.

A second pattern emerges in the 1940s and 1950s with the rise of Paraná as the new coffee frontier. Among the important features of the expansion into Paraná are a large number of small- to medium-sized holdings and the relative absence of an established rural oligarchy; the successful use of private, foreign entrepreneurship in the infrastructure and colonization efforts (Nicholls 1969, Willems 1972). The success of this pattern was highly conditioned by the nearness to the consuming markets of Rio de Janeiro and São Paulo and the relatively high soil quality, thus also opening up the possibility for many food crops and pork production. This pattern emerged during the apogee of interstate migration mentioned earlier. During the 1950s in-migrants to

Paraná represented almost half the base population of the state (Table VI–3). It changed abruptly in the sixties as a shift from coffee to other crops less vulnerable to Paraná's periodic frosts was undertaken. Most of these were less labor-intensive crops such as soybeans and wheat. As a result, the labor absorptive capacity of the Paraná frontier declined.

The third frontier pattern appears in the fifties and the sixties in the Central-Western region (Goiás and Mato Grosso). Intercensal rates of net in-migration in Table VI–3 reached 23 percent of the base population during these two decades. Moreover, it is interesting to note that the rise in migration into Mato Grosso from the fifties to the sixties (from 23 to 27 percent) is associated with a marked decline in the migration into neighboring Paraná (from 43 to 18 percent). Here we can see the frontier moving West. This move to Goiás and Mato Grosso is the first frontier settlement in Brazilian history that was not oriented to an "international" export cash crop, at least in its initial stages.[4] Instead, the "interregional" export phenomenon moved to the forefront, with frontier staples servicing the rapidly growing demand in the urban centers in the Center-South. Public sector investments in expensive infrastructure (roads) and urban centers (Brasília) replaced the predominant private sector initiative of the São Paulo and Paraná patterns. Large land-holdings (characteristic of the livestock sector) and less labor-absorptive crops (than coffee) also stand out: however, this has been offset by the extensive area involved to promote significant in-migration.

Another important contrast between São Paulo, Paraná, and the Central-West relates to the selectivity of migrants by region of previous residence. Whereas São Paulo's frontier was settled by European immigrants and Paraná by rural migrants from São Paulo and other Southern states (including many second-generation immigrants), the Central-West has drawn a much larger share from lower-income regions like the Northeast and Minas Gerais.

The most recent frontier pattern is the Amazon initiative begun in the 1970s (Katzman 1976). Here massive public investments dominate, through the PIN (National Integration Program) and the Transamazon Highway. Initial colonization schemes proved very expensive and incapable of providing an escape valve for the overpopulated Northeast. Many government-sponsored colonists came from distant São Paulo or even Rio Grande do Sul, since agricultural skills were an important criterion for subsidies. Food crops for the major consuming centers in the South have proved impractical, given the poor soil and long distance transport costs. As a result, the strategy has changed from settlement to mere occupation and exploitation. Large corporate capital-intensive projects in livestock, mining, and extractive agriculture predominate, using the tax credit mechanisms for exports. To date, large interregional labor transfers have been minimal.

---

[4] Recent attempts have been undertaken in the 1970s to promote exportable cash crops to take advantage of the high world prices for selected agricultural products.

Several common themes emerge from these distinct frontier patterns. Three involved large interregional (or intercontinental) transfers of labor (the exception being the recent Amazon experience). None was associated with any significant public sector agrarian reforms, though the Paulista and Paraná patterns did undertake important tenancy changes (São Paulo) and private sector small holding settlements (Paraná). As will be seen below, the continual frontier outlet also prevented national fertility rates from declining as rapidly as they would have otherwise.

All four frontier expansions have followed the classic Brazilian practice of increasing agricultural output by extensive increases in cultivation on the margin rather than intensive increases in productivity. Abundant land resources and improved transport made this a logical and economical strategy, at least until the rise in fuel costs. In more recent decades, the pattern of increased output has become associated with larger average units of operation and more capital-intensive and mechanized forms of production. More public sector involvement is emerging, emphasizing extensive use of fiscal subsidies and infrastructure support for highways and marketing facilities. However, public policy on colonization strategies has been confused and hesitant. Recent public sector initiatives have not been successful in this area. While past frontier settlements have acted as an escape valve, alleviating population pressures and promoting least-cost agricultural expansion on the extensive margin, present costs of continuing mechanization and expensive colonizations suggest more effort is needed on basic biological research to promote increased land yields and a redirection of official colonization and settlement efforts from the Amazon to the more promising areas of Goiás and Mato Grosso.

Detailed Estimates of Internal Migration for 1940–1970

Data from recent censuses allow a somewhat more varied approach to the measurement of internal migration since 1940, though there is still a large gap because of the lack of detailed 1960 census data. Recent censuses provide tabulations of the population by place of birth and present residence and by duration of present residence (1970), which permits an alternative estimate of interregional migration flows. Time reference is a difficult problem with these data, because of the possibility of memory errors and of return or continued step migration. Still they are useful as a complement to and check on survival-ratio estimates.

A problem that was mentioned earlier regarding survival-ratio estimates for recent decades is the likelihood of mortality differentials influencing measurement of migration. Although the main interregional mortality differentials are concentrated in rates for early childhood, which would not affect survivors age 10 and over, the problem warrants further consideration. Carvalho (1973) has developed a set of life tables for each of ten major regions in Brazil from census data on child survival. He calculated age- and sex-specific migration rates for the population ages 10 to 59 years in each of these regions, using the region-specific life tables to correct for the mortality effect. In doing so, he had to deal with the problem of age misreporting and the lack of data for more than half of the regions in 1960. It is useful to compare his results with Graham and Hollanda's global survival-ratio estimates for the population age 10 and over, and with the net flow estimates that can be computed from 1950 and 1970 census data on place of birth and residence.

Table VI–6 presents estimates of net migration by decade between 1940 and 1970 for each of the ten regions, using these different approaches. Columns (1) and (2) show rates for the population age 10 to 59, by sex, calculated by Carvalho. Column (3) gives global survival-ratio estimates, recalculated as rates with the population age 10 and over in the second census as a base, in order to make them comparable to Carvalho. Column (4) shows the net flow of migrants as a percentage of the populations of 1950 and 1970 derived from place of birth data. Also shown (column 5) is an index of regional mortality differentials, e.g., the ratio of regional to national mortality levels. Above average mortality in a sending region such as the Northeast would lead to an overstatement of net migration loss in a sending region such as the South and an overstatement of gains in receiving regions, e.g., São Paulo and Rio de Janeiro.

Comparison of the life-table and global survival-ratio estimates of migration for the three decadal intervals reveals very few basic differences in the magnitude and direction of migration in the two approaches. Even though the rates are not fully comparable (the life-table data refer to the population ages 10 to 59 and the global estimates to ages 10 and over), and different approaches have been taken to fill in the missing 1960 age data, the biases introduced by the assumption of equal mortality in the global survival estimates appear to be slight. The only region in which there are inconsistencies is the first one, the Amazon states. It has already been noted that estimates for this region are problematic, because of changes in the direction of migration and uncertainties about the quality of census data.

It should also be noted that Carvalho's life tables, which are derived from child-survival data in the census, could easily be overstating regional differences in adult mortality, since the adult life-table survival rates were obtained by matching the childhood life-table values to model life tables. As was mentioned earlier, mortality differentials in early childhood are generally greater than among adults. A final point on the comparisons is that age misreporting and differential assumptions about the 1960 data may be responsible for as much, or even more, of the differences between the two sets of estimates as mortality. Carvalho was very skeptical about the quality of the 1940 base data, and with the gaps in 1960 there are only two censuses (1950 and 1970) that we can rely upon.

Table VI-6. Estimates of Net Interregional Migration Rates in Brazil by Alternative Methods of Estimation, 1940-70 (percentages)

Region[a]	From life-table ratios[b]		From global Survival ratios[b]	From net flow: place of birth data[b]	Mortality differentials
	Male	Female			
1940-50	(1)	(2)	(3)	(4)	(5)
Pará-Amazonas	3.6	1.0	- 1.5	4.1	1.02
Northeast I	- 0.1	- 0.2	- 0.8	0.1	1.00
Northeast II	- 4.7	- 3.4	- 3.9	- 5.9	1.22
Northeast III	- 4.2	- 2.1	- 4.9	- 6.6	1.10
Minas Gerais and Espírito Santo	- 7.9	- 7.9	-13.1	-12.5	0.94
Rio de Janeiro and Guanabara	10.8	10.0	10.6	14.0	0.88
São Paulo	1.6	1.4	5.2	6.1	0.87
Paraná	27.8	23.8	28.9	27.9	0.95
Rio Grande do Sul, Santa Catarina	- 2.9	- 2.6	- 0.4	- 2.2	0.73
Central-West	12.1	8.7	8.4	16.3	0.86
Brazil	3.1	2.4	3.5	4.1	1.00
1950-60					
Pará-Amazonas	0.1	- 1.6	4.7		
Northeast I	2.5	0.9	1.2		
Northeast II	-10.6	- 8.5	-15.7		
Northeast III	- 6.0	- 3.3	-10.7		
Minas Gerais and Espírito Santo	-10.9	-11.1	- 9.8		
Rio de Janeiro and Guanabara	9.5	9.8	9.2		
São Paulo	7.9	6.2	9.2		
Paraná	27.4	26.9	28.7		
Rio Grande do Sul, Santa Catarina	- 8.4	- 6.1	- 4.1		
Central-West	17.5	14.0	22.5		
Brazil	5.4	4.4	5.5		
1960-70					
Pará-Amazonas	- 1.2	- 0.5	0.7	2.9	1.02
Northeast I	-13.2	-10.9	-10.5	- 2.6	1.04
Northeast II	- 5.4	- 4.0	- 8.5	-14.4	1.21
Northeast III	-15.0	-16.1	-15.1	-14.7	1.07
Minas Gerais and Espírito Santo	-14.3	-16.1	-16.9	-22.7	0.93
Rio de Janeiro and Guanabara	8.7	12.2	10.4	18.6	0.88
São Paulo	7.2	9.1	10.2	10.5	0.87
Paraná	17.6	14.6	16.7	31.4	0.89
Rio Grande do Sul, Santa Catarina	- 2.0	- 2.9	- 2.4	- 7.8	0.78
Central-West	22.6	17.9	23.1	28.1	1.02
Brazil	5.2	5.1	5.7	7.8	1.00

[a]Northeast I consists of Piauí and Maranhão; Northeast II consists of Ceará, Rio Grande do Norte, Paraíba, Pernambuco, and Alagoas; Northeast III consists of Bahia and Sergipe; Central-West consists of Mato Grosso and Goiás (including the Federal District of Brasília).
[b]Percentages of population at end of period.
Sources: Carvalho (1973), Graham and Hollanda (1971, volume 1), Merrick (1974).

Further confirmation of the magnitude and direction of interregional migration patterns is found in the place-of-birth/place-of-residence data in the 1950 and 1970 censuses. Because of the open time reference in these data, the rates (net gain or loss of a region as a percent of total end period population) tend to be higher than the decadal survival-ratio estimates. However, the direction and relative magnitudes of the rates are quite similar to the survival-ratio results. Except for suggesting extra caution with regard to the Amazon region, these comparisons do not indicate that any of the main points drawn from the global survival-ratio data about long-term internal migration patterns in the previous section need to be modified.

Rural and Urban Components of Interregional Migration, 1970

Tabulations of questions in the 1970 census on the place of previous residence of the population permit us to distinguish between the rural and urban components of interregional migration among the ten major regions of Brazil. Care is required in the interpretation of these data, because of the many possible definitions of "migrant" that can be derived from them. In this instance, we wish to consider as rural and urban interregional migrants those individuals who reside at the time of the census in a rural or urban area of a region other than the one in which they resided previously. This definition excludes intraregional flows, which are a further dimension of the internal migration that is occurring in Brazil. Table VI–7 shows net interregional migration rates for the rural and urban areas of each of the ten regions. The rates are calculated as the net interregional flow (previous residents of other regions residing in the region less previous residents of the region residing in other regions) divided, as a percentage, by the rural or urban population in 1970. Column 1 shows the rates for rural areas and column 2 the rates for urban areas.

In the rural interregional migration column, the frontier regions of Paraná and the Central-West stand out as the only areas in Brazil to experience a significant net interregional migration gain. Both show net inflows of about 20 percent of their 1970 rural population. Comparison of the rates of interregional migration for urban areas of these two regions reveals a contrast between them. The Central-West has also experienced a significant rate of urban migration (22 percent of its urban population), while Paraná shows a much lower rate (9 percent). The rapid growth of Brasilia, along with regional centers such as Goiânia, Campo Grande, and Cuiabá, have contributed to this. Another factor is that Paraná is located closer to the network of cities that has developed in São Paulo. This may have reduced, at least temporarily, the potential for development of Paraná's own urban system. Finally, the coffee culture, with more small to medium-sized holdings characteristic of Paraná, may have provided a more labor-absorptive rural environment in comparison with the Central-West. The differential is only relative, however, and Paraná still ranks fourth in urban migration gains among the regions.

Table VI-7. Rural and Urban Components of Net Interregional Migration by Region in Brazil, 1970

Regions	Net interregional rural migration as % of total rural population of region	Net interregional urban migration as % of total urban population of region
1. Pará-Amazonas	3.6	0.8
2. Northeast I	0.1	- 6,8
3. Northeast II	- 8.4	-12.3
4. Northeast III	- 6.9	-12.2
5. Minas Gerais and Espírito Santo	-16.3	-16.1
6. Rio de Janeiro and Guanabara	3.6	16.9
7. Sao Paulo	- 9.5	12.3
8. Parana	19.9	8.8
9. Rio Grande do Sul and Santa Catarina	- 7.7	- 4.5
10. Central-West	21.5	22.1
Brazil	2.9	2.3

Note: Northeast I consists of Paiui and Maranhão; Northeast II consists of Ceará, Rio Grande do Norte, Paraíba, Pernambuco, and Alagoas; Northeast III consists of Bahia and Sergipe; Central-West consists of Mato Grosso and Goiás (including Federal District of Brasília).

Source: Special tabulations of Censo Demográfico do Brasil—1970—FIBGE/IBI. Reproduced in Milton da Mata et al. (1972: 78).

The Northeastern region registers a net outflow of interregional migrants from both its rural and urban sectors. In contrast to other regions with net losses, such as Minas Gerais, urban out-migration weighs more heavily than rural out-migration in interregional terms. Da Mata (1973: 74–78) has shown that this urban interregional migration deficit has been offset partially through intraregional rural-urban migration, thus forming a stage pattern in which intraregional rural-urban migration within the Northeast eventually translates itself into interregional urban-urban flows to the South.

Finally, the data on São Paulo suggest an additional pattern that is of interest. Here a significant interregional urban inflow of 12.3 percent is associated with an equally significant net interregional outflow from its rural areas. Thus, the net in-migration to São Paulo seen earlier in Table VI–6 is decisively urban and not rural in nature. The net outflow from São Paulo's rural areas has increased greatly in the sixties due to the rapid mechanization of Paulista agriculture and the substitution of less labor-absorptive crops for coffee. It is clear that practically all of the rural interregional outflow from São Paulo is one of the prime sources of frontier in-migrants for Paraná and Mato Grosso and, to a lesser extent, Goiás.

Regional Growth Trends

Regional Patterns in Income per Capita Differentials

Regional disparities in income per capita have been a perennial dilemma in Brazil. The present differentials have historical roots, particularly the

Northeast-Southern syndrome.[5] This differential grew with particular force during the period 1870–1900, as the cotton and sugar economies declined in the Northeast and the coffee economy rose in São Paulo. If Northeastern manpower could have migrated South, this growing regional disparity might have been less severe. As it turned out, foreign immigration supplied the manpower for São Paulo and thus this possible interregional equilibrating mechanism (of mobile labor) was never tested until the third decade of the twentieth century.

In more recent times, available data permit us to measure the regional patterns of relative income per capita differentials and the major sectoral components of these differentials over time. Convergent or divergent regional income per capita can be determined by looking at a simple measure of weighted relative inequality calculated from the percentage share of total income (or product) and total population. The sum of the differences between the income and population shares for the regions, ignoring signs, is a measure of relative income inequality per capita among the regions, weighted by their share of total population. The results are presented for the period 1940–70 in panel D of Table VI–8.[6]

For purposes of analysis in this section, we have adopted a modified regional breakdown from that used earlier: The Northern (Amazonas and Pará), Northeastern, Southern (comprising Paraná, Santa Catarina, and Rio Grande do Sul), and Central-West (Mato Grosso and Goiás) regions have been maintained. However, the three regional growth centers in the Southeast are broken into separate divisions for São Paulo, Rio de Janeiro (city and state), and the combination of Minas Gerais and Espirito Santo (which will be referred to as Minas). Panels A and B of Table VI-8 show the regional shares of total income and population, panel C presents the relative income per capita differentials by region for the census years in question, and panel D presents the aggregate index of weighted relative inequality discussed above.

The aggregate measure of inequality rises from 1940 to 1950 and then declines in 1960 and 1970, reflecting a divergent growth of regional income per capita in the 1940s and a convergent pattern in the 1950s and 1960s. In general, the divergent growth of the forties and convergence of the fifties are more clearly established patterns than the weaker convergence of the sixties.

The more ambiguous findings for the sixties are in large part a reflection of a decade with a mixed growth record, the first half of which experienced decline

[5] A large literature exists on the historical evolution of these regional disparities in Brazil. Some of the more useful recent discussions of this are in Furtado (1963), Leff (1972), Denslow (1973), Hirschman (1963). For pertinent readings on the contemporary patterns of this North-South disparity in Brazil see Baer (1964), Graham (1970), Gauthier and Semple (1972), Goodman and Cavalcanti de Albuqueraue (1974), Haddad and Andrade (1974), Redwood (1974), and Katzman (1977).

[6] For example, if a given state's share of total national income is 15 percent, and its share of total population is 20 percent, the difference (5 percent) is the difference between the relative per capita income of the state in question and the countrywide average (in our example, $0.75-1.0 = -0.25$) weighted by the share of the state in the total population (i.e., 20 percent), Kuznets (1957: 45).

Table VI-8. Income and Labor Force Shares, Relative Income per Capita Differentials, and Aggregate Measures of Regional Inequality in Brazil, 1940–70

	Years			
	1940	1950	1960	1970[a]
A. *Percentage of total income*	(1)	(2)	(3)	(4)
North	2.7	1.7	2.2	2.1
Northeast	16.7	14.6	14.8	13.8
Minas	11.5	11.8	11.1	10.9
Rio de Janeiro	20.3	19.0	17.0	16.2
São Paulo	31.1	34.8	34.7	35.7
South	15.6	16.3	17.8	18.2
Central-West	2.1	1.8	2.5	3.1
B. *Percentage of total population*				
North	3.6	3.6	3.7	3.9
Northeast	35.0	34.6	31.5	30.2
Minas	18.3	16.8	16.2	14.0
Rio de Janeiro	8.8	9.0	9.5	9.7
São Paulo	17.4	17.6	18.3	19.1
South	13.9	15.2	16.7	17.7
Central-West	3.1	3.3	4.1	5.4
C. *Relative income per capita differentials (average = 1.00)*				
North	0.75	0.47	0.59	0.54
Northeast	0.48	0.42	0.47	0.46
Minas	0.63	0.70	0.69	0.78
Rio de Janeiro	2.31	2.11	1.79	1.67
São Paulo	1.79	1.98	1.90	1.87
South	1.12	1.07	1.06	1.03
Central-West	0.68	0.54	0.61	0.57
D. *Aggregate measure of regional inequality[b]*	53.9	56.7	49.9	47.2

[a]Regional income data are for 1969.

[b]Relative income per capita differentials derived by dividing the regional share of income (panel A) by the regional share of population (panel B). Aggregate measure of regional inequality explained in text.

Source: Regional income data come from national account data in *Conjuntura Econômica* (October 1969 and July 1974); regional population data come from population censuses for 1940, 1950, 1960, and 1970.

and stagnant growth and the last half of which generated rapid economic recovery. Thus, the results for the decade as a whole are more mixed and less clear-cut than the accumulated evidence for earlier decades. The decline in Brazilian economic growth from 1961 to 1966 was more pronounced in the major growth centers, such as São Paulo and Rio de Janeiro, than in the less-developed regions, thereby promoting a recession-induced convergence in regional per capita incomes. The ensuing recovery in the last three to four years of the decade, while more divergent in its regional effect than the preceding decline, was not of sufficient duration to erase the predominant convergent pattern established in the first half of the decade. If we had a bench

Table VI-9. Patterns of Regional Growth in Relative Income per Capita and Relative
Sectoral Income per Worker in Brazil, 1940-70

A. Aggregate measure of inequality[a] of relative income per capita and
relative sectoral income per worker by region[b]

Sector[c,d]	1940	1950	1960	1970
	(1)	(2)	(3)	(4)
1. Total	53.9	56.7	49.9	47.2
2. Industry	37.8	32.3	n.a.	40.8
3. Agriculture	39.2	45.6	n.a.	42.6
4. Services	33.0	28.3	n.a.	19.0

B. Summary description of regional growth patterns

Sector	1940-50	1950-70
1. Total	divergent	convergent
2. Industry	convergent	divergent
3. Agriculture	divergent	convergent
4. Services	convergent	convergent

[a]Sum of differences between regional income and labor force shares, ignoring signs.
[b]The seven regions are the same as those in Table VI-8.
[c]Industrial, agricultural, and service sector income data by region from national accounts data
in various issues of Conjuntura Econômica (esp. October 1969 and July 1974); 1970 income
data are for 1969.
[d]Sectoral labor force data by region derived from population censuses in 1940, 1950, and
1970 with 1940 labor force classifications in 1940 population census corrected for comparison
with later censuses as set forth in Chapter VII.

mark year of 1973 or 1974, conveniently coming at the end of the high point of
the Brazilian economic "miracle," the entire intervening period (1960–74)
might possibly show a divergent rather than a convergent trend in regional
growth.

The role of migration in this process of regional growth merits comment.
The modest interregional migration of the forties, large interregional flows in
the fifties, and migratory decline in the sixties were clearly contributing factors
in causing this pattern of regional growth in income per capita to emerge from
1940 to 1970. Of interest here is to note that the small migratory flows of the
1940s were insufficient to offset the stronger disequilibrating pattern of
regional growth of income at that time. This changed sharply in the 1950s
when the large interregional flows of migration reflected a substantial transfer
of population from the lower-income states of Minas and the Northeast to the
higher-income states of São Paulo, Rio de Janeiro, Paraná, and the Central-
West. An earlier study by one of the authors established that the states
recording the highest migratory inflows in the 1950s (São Paulo, Guanabara,
Paraná and the frontier states of Goiás and Mato Grosso) registered the lowest
improvement in relative income per capita throughout the decade.[7] The
growth in population more than offset the rapid growth in output and income to

[7]See Graham (1970).

produce the sharp convergent pattern in regional income per capita evident in Table VI–8. This strong equilibrating function of population transfers was weaker (though still evident) in the sixties.[8]

Regional Patterns in Sectoral Income per Worker and Related Indices.

The overall trends in regional growth discussed above are largely the net result of specific sectoral growth trends of output and income per worker. Table VI–9 summarizes the convergent and divergent regional patterns of growth for the agricultural, industrial, and service sector income per worker during this period. Here we draw upon the same aggregate measure of weighted regional inequality used earlier, except that the sectoral income and labor force data by region are used in place of the total income and population data used in Table VI–8.[9]

The most striking feature of Table VI–9 is the preponderant economic role of the service sector in causing the overall pattern of convergent regional growth during the period 1940 to 1970. The weighted relative inequality of service sector income per worker (for the seven regions) declined substantially from 33 (in 1940) to 19 (in 1970). In contrast, both the agricultural and industrial sector income per worker measures of relative inequality rose from 1940 to 1970. However, the slightly increased divergent growth in these two sectors was more than offset by the sharply convergent behavior of service sector income per worker. Also, the fact that the service sector consistently accounts for over half of national income reinforces the structural impact of this sector upon the behavior of total income per capita.

This raises interesting and important questions about the reliability of the overall results, since the empirical basis for service sector income estimates in the national accounts is notoriously weak in Brazil, as in most less developed countries. Many labor force components of the service sector are imputed a minimum or other arbitrary wage in the national accounting procedure in Brazil. Commerce and personal services are particularly subject to these imputations. Their basis is more ad hoc than reporting or solid field studies.

---

[8]Additional work by Gauthier and Semple and by Haddad and Andrade, using different measures, confirms this convergent growth of regional income per capita during the fifties and early sixties. The first authors used an entropy model derived from information statistics, the latter authors used regional analysis of variance (Gauthier and Semple 1972, Haddad and Andrade 1974).

[9]Thus, the measure of weighted relative sectoral inequality by region is estimated by taking the difference between the percentage share of regional sectoral income (or output) and regional sectoral labor force shares for the regions. The sum of these differences for all regions, ignoring signs, is a global or aggregate measure of relative sectoral income inequality per worker among all the regions, weighted by their share of the total labor force. See footnote 6 and the source cited therein.

This contrasts with actual output estimates used in the agricultural sector and the even more accurate output and remuneration data used for the industrial sector. One would feel more secure about the conclusions of overall convergent regional growth in Brazil from 1940 to 1970 if this pattern had been generated by sectors other than the most data-deficient sector in the national accounts system.

With this caveat in mind, it is still revealing to look at the results for the 1940s and the period 1950–70. Deficiencies in the labor force data by states in the 1960 population census limited our ability to estimate regional income per worker by sectors for 1960. Thus, Table VI–9 presents data only for the period 1940–50 and 1950–70. At the end of this chapter we will attempt to surmount this problem and break down the period 1950–70 into its two separate decades. The overall divergent trend in regional income per capita in the 1940s was associated with a strong divergent pattern in agricultural income per worker by region, a convergent trend in industrial output per worker, and a convergent trend in service sector income per worker. The divergent pattern of growth in the agricultural sector, however, was sufficiently strong to offset the weaker regionally convergent growth pattern within the industrial and service sectors. This reflects the regionally skewed improvement in Brazil's international terms of trade that favored the coffee sector of São Paulo in the immediate postwar period at the same time that immigration into this sector (and state) was relatively limited.

The results for the period 1950–70 show two major shifts. First, an overall and significant pattern of convergent growth appears. Second, the agricultural sector registers a slight convergent growth pattern, while the industrial sector records a sharply divergent trend. These sectoral shifts (in comparison to the earlier decade), combined with the highly convergent pattern of service sector growth, produced the overall pattern of convergence for the period. The overall results in line 1 highlight that convergence was more pronounced in the fifties than in the sixties, however the unavailability of labor force data in 1960 prevented us from directly establishing the separate sectoral patterns for the fifties and sixties.

It is now useful to complement these aggregate measures of regional inequality with rough measures of regional specialization and productivity. Table VI–10 presents the relative distribution of national income by region and by sector. Three general conclusions stand out. First, the service sector presents the most regionally balanced distribution, followed by the agricultural sector, and finally the industrial sector. The latter, as we would expect, presents the most extreme regional imbalance, reflecting the contrasting comparative advantage for industrial activity by region, with more than half of industrial income originating in São Paulo in 1970.

Second, service sector income presents no marked shifts in its regional allocation over this thirty-year period; however, the regional shares of the commodity-producing sectors, agriculture and industry, shift significantly.

São Paulo first gains then loses a substantial share of total agricultural activity as the South and the Central-West gain. In contrast, São Paulo is the only region that gains considerably in its share of industrial activity during this period, with the Northeast and Rio de Janeiro declining substantially. Third, it is clear that most of these shifts occurred before 1960 for both sectors. Thus, the forties and the fifties represent the decades of major structural shifts in the regional allocation of agricultural and industrial income. The decade of the sixties shows only minor changes in these allocations.

Table VI–11 presents the interregional profile of sectoral income per worker (a rough measure of regional sectoral productivity relative to the national average of 1.0). Consistent with our earlier findings of convergent behavior, the service income per worker narrows among the regions from 1940 to 1970. In summary, the regional shares of sectoral income changed relatively little or not at all over this period (Table VI–10). At the same time, however, the sectoral income per worker measure narrowed among regions (Table VI–11). This means there was a proportionately greater absorption of labor in the service sectors of the developed regions (like São Paulo and Rio de Janeiro) than in the lesser-developed regions. The industrial sector, however, after a slight narrowing between 1940 and 1950, presents a widening regional profile of income per worker. Of particular interest here is the widening differential between São Paulo and the other two areas in the South (Rio de Janeiro and the South) between 1950 and 1970. There is also a slight widening in the differential between São Paulo and the Northeast. Thus, São Paulo has not only been the only region to increase its relative domination of total industrial output in the country (Table VI–10), but, at the same time, was the only region increasing its relative productivity in this sector (Table VI–11). Rival regions in the Center-South, such as Rio de Janeiro and the South, and also the Northeast, experienced declining regional shares and also declining relative productivity in the industrial sector over this period. Thus, in contrast to the service sector, there was not a relative increase in the absorption of industrial sector labor in the developed regions from 1940 to 1970 comparable to the increase in their shares of industrial output.

The agricultural sector presents yet another interesting profile of regional change in output and labor force. For the Northeast there was no change in the share of output nor in the agricultural sectoral income per worker. Thus, there was no significant change in its regional share of the labor force from 1940 to 1970. The interesting contrast, however, emerges between São Paulo and the other two major agricultural areas of importance in the Center-South, namely, the South and the Central-West. From 1950 to 1970, São Paulo's share of agricultural output declines (Table VI–10), while its sectoral income per worker rises. Just the opposite occurs in the South and in the frontier regions of the Center-West, thereby highlighting the significant decline in the use of agricultural labor in São Paulo and growth in the use of rural labor in the South and the Central-West. This confirms our earlier results showing the large inter-

REGIONAL POPULATION REDISTRIBUTION

Table VI-10. Percentage Distribution of National Income by Sectors and Regions in Brazil, 1940–70

Region	Industry				Agriculture				Services			
	1940	1950	1960	1970	1940	1950	1960	1970	1940	1950	1960	1970
North	2.3	0.9	1.9	1.3	3.3	1.7	2.0	2.1	2.4	2.1	2.5	2.4
Northeast	12.1	8.9	8.0	6.2	23.0	20.3	22.1	23.0	15.0	13.5	13.6	13.8
Minas	8.5	7.3	6.2	8.1	17.5	18.5	15.5	13.4	9.3	9.6	10.6	11.4
Rio de Janeiro	26.5	21.4	17.0	16.3	4.8	4.7	4.6	3.8	26.4	26.9	23.8	21.2
São Paulo	36.4	47.0	54.3	56.0	24.7	29.2	23.0	20.5	32.7	33.0	32.8	32.1
South	12.9	13.7	11.9	11.3	22.2	22.3	28.1	31.3	12.9	13.6	14.6	16.1
Central-West	1.0	0.6	0.7	0.8	4.5	3.3	4.7	5.9	1.3	1.4	2.0	3.1

Table VI-11. The Change in Interregional Sectoral Income per Worker Relative to Countrywide Average (=1.0) for the Three Major Sectors in Brazil, 1940–70

	Agriculture			Industry			Services		
	1940	1950	1970	1940	1950	1970	1940	1950	1970
North	0.9	0.4	0.5	1.0	0.5	0.6	0.7	0.7	0.8
Northeast	0.6	0.5	0.6	0.5	0.5	0.4	0.6	0.6	0.7
Minas	0.9	1.0	0.9	0.7	0.7	0.7	0.7	0.8	0.9
Rio de Janeiro	1.2	1.5	1.9	1.6	1.2	1.1	1.3	1.3	1.2
Sao Paulo	1.6	2.0	2.1	1.3	1.4	1.5	1.4	1.3	1.2
South	1.6	1.4	1.4	1.1	1.0	0.8	1.0	1.0	1.1
Central-West	1.3	0.8	0.9	0.3	0.3	0.2	0.6	0.8	0.6
Brazil	1.0	1.0	1.0	1.0	1.0	1.0	1.0	1.0	1.0

Source: Same as Table VI-9; 1970 income data refer to 1969.

regional migration into the South (especially Paraná) and the Central-West regions, which, in large part, was migration attracted to the expanding agricultural frontier in these regions. At the same time, these results underscore the rapid rise in agricultural productivity in São Paulo and decline in the other two regions. Significant modernization occurred in Paulista agriculture, emphasizing labor-saving technology, while the frontier regions relied more on traditional practices that emphasized the continued use of labor over capital.

The final set of tables presents the intraregional measures of sectoral specialization in relation to the national sectoral distribution (Table VI–12) and the degree of sectoral inequality per worker within the regions in question from 1940 to 1970 (Table VI–13). The results in Table VI–12, although portraying the intraregional shifts in sectoral activity, are similar to the interregional shifts discussed earlier, with São Paulo showing increasing specialization in industry within its regional economy and, again in comparison to the national sectoral distribution, a declining share or specialization in agricultural activity. The other regions, in contrast, show greater relative specialization in agricultural activities, with relative rises in the Northeast, the South, and the Central-West, particularly since 1950. At the same time, one notes the relative decline of industrial sector income in these very regions. Service sector activity (with the exception of Rio de Janeiro) is much more uniformly distributed within these regions, regardless of degree of development.

Table VI–13 shows that there has been a significant decline in the intersectoral inequality of income per worker among the three major sectors for the nation as a whole. This pattern is even more marked among the developed regions such as Rio de Janeiro and São Paulo. The behavior is more mixed among the remaining regions. If, however, we take the more recent period (1950–70), there was a decline in the degree of intersectoral inequality within every region with the exception of the Northeast and Minas, the two poorest regions in the country. In short, the convergent pattern of national regional development from 1950 to 1970 discussed earlier is associated with an even more notable convergence in sectoral income per worker within the more developed regions of the country (especially Rio de Janeiro, São Paulo, and the South); however, this pattern of intraregional convergence is much less significant within the other regions and actually divergent within the lowest income per capita areas.

Conclusions

In closing this chapter, two questions come to mind concerning the patterns of regional growth discussed above. First, to what extent does the overall convergent trend of regional growth since 1950 represent a turning point toward a secular pattern of convergent national growth similar to what Williamson has discovered in the regional growth history of the currently developed countries

Table VI-12. The Change in Intraregional Specialization of Sectoral Income in Brazil Relative to Countrywide Average (=1.0) for the Three Major Sectors in Brazil, 1940–70

	Agriculture			Industry			Services		
	1940	1950	1970	1940	1950	1970	1940	1950	1970
North	1.3	1.1	1.2	0.8	0.5	0.6	0.9	1.2	1.1
Northeast	1.5	1.6	2.1	0.7	0.5	0.4	0.9	0.9	1.0
Minas	1.3	1.7	1.5	0.5	0.5	0.7	1.0	0.9	1.0
Rio de Janeiro	0.3	0.3	0.3	1.3	1.0	0.9	1.3	1.4	1.3
São Paulo	0.9	1.0	0.7	1.1	1.2	1.4	1.0	0.9	0.9
South	1.6	1.6	2.2	0.8	0.7	0.6	0.8	0.8	0.9
Central-West	2.3	2.1	2.4	0.4	0.3	0.2	0.6	0.7	1.0
Brazil	1.0	1.0	1.0	1.0	1.0	1.0	1.0	1.0	1.0

Table VI-13. Measure of Intersectoral Inequality[a] in Sectoral Income per Worker among the Three Major Sectors within Selected Regions in Brazil, 1940-70

Region	1940	1950	1970
North	68	76	72
Northeast	70	60	66
East	78	46	48
Rio de Janeiro	40	26	8
São Paulo	62	34	18
South	48	40	34
Central-West	26	42	38
Brazil	76	66	54

[a]Sum of differences between sectoral income and labor force shares, ignoring signs.
Source: Same as Table VI-9. Regional income data for 1970 refer to 1969.

(Williamson 1965); and second, to what extent have the last two decades of Brazilian growth (1950–70) presented uniform results or diverse and contrasting patterns?

In answering the first question, we must recognize that the regional differentials in income per capita in Brazil are still wide, and that the current pattern of convergent growth has been relatively small in the face of the tremendous disparities that remain. In reference to the convergent behavior itself, a note of caution is appropriate for two reasons. First, the degree of convergence was clearly less strong in the sixties that it was in the fifties, thereby casting some doubt on the secular strength of the forces behind this behavior. Second, there is no evidence that convergence has occurred in the most dynamic sector of structural change in the Brazilian economy, i.e., the industrial sector. The convergence that has occurred is largely due to the behavior of the most data-deficient sector in the economy, namely the service sector. More time is needed before one can draw secular or long-run conclusions from the patterns of regional and structural change in the postwar era that are, at best, cyclical results. The post-1950 evidence to date could just as well be interpreted as representing a false or premature turning point in which a temporary and short-lived shift toward regional convergence occurred, which could just as easily turn back into a divergent pattern growing out of a resurgence of regionally disequilibrating cyclical forces in the economy.

This brings us to the second question. To what extent are the results for the entire period 1950–70 uniform or diverse for the two separate decades that comprise this period? The answer to this question can offer an insight into the turning point issue raised above. To accomplish this, an estimate was made of the regional distribution of the labor force by sectors for 1960, the missing link in our earlier tables compromising attempts to sort out separate decadal analysis during this period. The labor force estimates were derived by taking the average sectoral percentage distribution between 1950 and 1970 for each region and applying this for 1960. This procedure appeared acceptable in view of the fact that there was only a slight difference between the 1950 and 1970

Table VI-14. Estimates of Aggregate Regional Inequality in Total Income per Capita and Sectoral Income per Worker and the São Paulo/Northeast per Capita and per Worker Differentials for 1950, 1960, and 1970

A. Aggregate regional inequality of total income per capita and sectoral income per worker[a]

Sectors	Years		
	1950	1960	1970[b]
1. Total	56.7	49.9	47.2
2. Industry	32.3	37.7	40.8
3. Agriculture	45.6	43.7	42.6
4. Services	28.3	22.8	19.0

B. São Paulo/Northeast differentials in total income per capita and sectoral income per worker measures[c]

Sectors	Years		
	1950	1960	1970
1. Total	4.7	4.0	4.1
2. Industry	2.9	3.3	4.0
3. Agriculture	4.0	3.4	3.6
4. Services	2.2	1.9	1.7

[a]Sum of differences between regional income and labor force shares, ignoring signs.
[b]Regional income for 1969.
[c]Ratio of São Paulo to Northeast.
Sources: Same as Tables VI-8, VI-9.

sectoral shares in the labor force. The 1960 sectoral income share data by region were, of course, available from the national accounts. The results are presented in Table VI-14 (panel A).

The aggregate total and sectoral measures of regional inequality for these two decades show that the combined convergent growth patterns of the agricultural and service sector income per worker were instrumental in generating the sharply convergent regional growth in income per capita in the 1960s. The industrial sector, in contrast, reflected a strong divergent regional growth record during this decade of import-substitution industrialization, largely located in São Paulo. The abrupt reversal of the regional growth pattern in the agricultural sector, from divergent growth in the forties to convergent growth in the fifties, was due to the sharp deterioration in the international terms of trade for this sector, particularly coffee, which slowed down the income growth of the agricultural sector in São Paulo and the South. This result underlines an important unstable feature in Brazil's regional growth record, namely, the vulnerability of its agriculture (and the regions associated with agricultural performance) to changing world prices. This suggests that the turning points in the regional growth patterns of Brazilian agriculture are much less associated with any secular trends toward sustained convergent growth derived from the domestic setting, but rather reflect cyclical trends in the volatile milieu of world prices for agricultural products. In this setting, the agricultural sector could experience a succession of turning points or reversals rather than a threshold change from divergent to permanent convergent growth.

The decade of the sixties saw a marked lessening of the convergent regional growth trend in income per capita set in the 1950s. The industrial sector maintained its divergent path, but the agricultural sector reflected, at best, only a slight convergent trend. The service sector continued its convergent pattern and maintained an influence on the overall convergent growth path. The lessened convergent growth path in the 1960s in the agricultural sector's income per worker again reflects the improved world prices for agricultural crops. If 1974 had been available as a reference point, it is very likely that a divergent trend would have emerged for this sector, since the world prices for both traditional and new agricultural exports from the South had risen significantly by this time. This fact, combined with the increasingly concentrated industrial growth in São Paulo from 1968 to 1974, strongly suggests that the combined effect would have more than offset the convergent pattern of the service sector and produced an overall divergent pattern of regional growth from 1960 to 1974. Results from the recent 1975 economic census will soon be available to test this hypothesis.

The findings in panel B highlight the most sensitive regional dichotomy in Brazil, that between São Paulo and the Northeast. Here we see a convergent pattern for the fifties and a slightly divergent pattern in the sixties. What is of importance here is to note that the marked convergent patterns of the fifties did not continue into the sixties. Not only did divergence continue in the industrial sector, but it also surfaced in the agricultural sector in the sixties. This was a regionally differentiated reflection of the changing world prices for Brazil's primary exports discussed earlier, which favored the developed South and São Paulo regions. The federal efforts promoting SUDENE, the Northeast regional development institution, with its tax-credit-induced industrial growth strategy, apparently was insufficient to offset the forces of regional divergence between the North and the South, both in industry and in total income per capita in the sixties. Curiously, in the decade in which official federal initiative to correct regional disequilibria was at a minimum (i.e., the fifties), a convergent pattern of regional growth appeared. On the other hand, the decade in which this official concern and corrective policies were most visible (i.e., the sixties) was the decade in which the forces for divergent growth were relatively stronger between these two regions. Two conclusions can be drawn. First, the second major postwar growth cycle in Brazil (i.e., the "economic miracle") from 1967 onward, was apparently more regionally divergent in its impact on the economy than the earlier import-substitution growth cycle of the fifties. Second, despite the large battery of institutional and policy inducements to deal with regional inequality in the sixties, more general economic policies apparently had a pronounced divergent regional impact to counteract the explicit regional policies in question. This is particularly evident in the regional growth patterns between São Paulo and the Northeast.

To summarize, the convergent regional growth trend of the fifties appears to be primarily a result of significant interregional migration and a relative worsening of coffee prices for the exports of the developed regions. In short, the lesser developed regions benefited more through the passive gains of losing population (i.e., migrants) and the decline in the economies of the more developed regions (especially agriculture) than by any active gains generated through their local economies. The decline of the convergent growth in the sixties was also associated with declining migration and gains to the growth of the Center-South. Thus, the main determinants of interregional growth differentials were occurrences in the Center-South and migration, rather than major changes in the economies of the poorer regions themselves.

The sectoral results in the post-1950 period show the most dynamic sector, industry, consistently divergent in its regional growth trend, with the service sector consistently convergent. The agricultural sector shifts in its pattern, largely due to the regional impact of fluctuations in international prices for Brazil's agricultural exports. Given the arbitrary nature of service sector income estimates and that the overall post-1950 regional convergent growth trend depends so much on the performance of this sector, there is some doubt about the reliability of these findings. Furthermore, the volatile nature of the agricultural sector's regional growth path raises equal doubt about its secular tendencies and the degree to which turning points are merely transitory phenomena. In short, the data base needs to be improved considerably and the time span lengthened before one can conclude with any certainty that Brazil is following a secular sequence of first divergent and then permanent convergent growth in regional income per capita similar to the path traced out by the currently developed countries. Nevertheless, the important role of internal migration stands out in this brief analysis and underscores the need for more detailed analysis of the role and impact of this phenomenon in the process of industrialization, the absorption of labor in urban labor markets, and the growth or deterioration of urban welfare in the destination regions. This will be a focus of analysis in succeeding chapters, which are concerned with trends in the growth of the labor force, urbanization, and the problem of urban poverty.

VII   Growth and Structure of the Brazilian Labor Force, 1872–1970

Introduction

The supply and demand for labor represent a major linkage between population dynamics and economic growth in Brazil. The economically active population is one of the most difficult demographic variables to define and measure, because of the complexity of interactions between work status and other aspects of social and economic change. Unlike demographic events like birth and death, the very meaning of labor force participation can change with modifications of the socioeconomic structure of society. This chapter attempts to reconstruct major trends in the growth and structural change of the Brazilian labor force between 1872 and 1970. Previous chapters on slavery and immigration have laid the groundwork for this attempt at a more comprehensive review of labor force trends, while at the same time revealing the difficulties of long-term comparisons in Brazil, which has experienced major shifts from a slave to a wage economy and from an agricultural to an urban and industrial economic base since 1870.

   Application of modern analytical techniques to labor force growth and composition requires a clear and consistent definition of the economically active population. According to recent United Nations' recommendations, the active population (or labor force) is defined as those individuals who furnish the supply of labor for production of goods and services (United Nations 1968 and 1970, Durand 1975). In practical terms, this means that we must be able to determine who is and who is not in the labor force by the same criterion over a number of successive censuses. Normally, the labor force includes paid employees, employers, the self-employed, and unpaid family workers. The armed forces are generally included, and unemployed workers should also be considered, since they represent a part of the labor supply. Not included are housewives, students, retired and disabled workers, young children, and institutionalized individuals, even though they may be receiving income in the form of pensions and returns from assets. In working with the Brazilian data, we must recognize that data collected a century ago reflect not only the structure of society as it existed then but also the understanding of society brought to the measurement process by those who collected the data. Their attitudes and conceptions of society evolved along with the actual social structural changes that occurred.

Durand (1975) has reviewed the main sources of divergence in definitions of the economically active population. A major problem is the classification of individuals with dual roles, the most common example being women who combine housework with production of goods or services for the market. Current international standard definitions of the labor force recognize as active *anyone who is working* during the reference period of the census or survey, though this concept is often difficult to apply in the case of unpaid workers and individuals who engage in artisan manufacture at home (United Nations 1968). This definition contrasts with the earlier "gainfully employed" concept, which was more restrictive in that it excluded individuals with dual roles and who were not "usually" engaged in economic activity. Other points of divergence in definitions relate to the time reference of questions on activity, on the age groups to be included, and in the definition of unemployment. Problems of comparability generally affect the female labor force more than males, because of the higher likelihood of finding dual roles. The same is true of younger and older workers and of the population engaged in agricultural work, where the proportion of unpaid family workers is generally higher.

National data on the working population are found in all Brazilian censuses except that taken in 1890.[1] Earlier censuses (1872, 1900, and 1920) defined and measured activity status in terms of professions (*profissões*). This early Brazilian concept of economic activity is a precursor of what today would be considered as an occupation. The *profissão* concept is broader in that it includes both individuals who were not working (children and housewives, pensioners, etc.) and groups of workers classified by categories of economic activity. *Profissão* in these early censuses combines notions that in more recent censuses are treated as separate classifications: employment by occupation and employment by branch of economic activity. In addition, the earlier classification included a category for unpaid family workers, now regarded as a category in yet a third labor force variable, "status," which also embraces employers, employees, and the self-employed. Over time, Brazilian censuses have become more precise in defining the labor force. Introductions to the 1872 and 1900 censuses provide limited descriptions of professions, but no mention of the problem of delimiting an economically active group (Brazil, Directoria Geral de Estatistica, 1922). Starting with the 1906 census of the Federal District (Rio de Janeiro), census authorities adopted standards recommended by the International Statistical Institute (Brazil, Directoria Geral de Estatistica, 1923: 117). The 1920 census defined the active population for the first time in terms of a person's *principal* activity. This is akin to

[1]Published tables on occupation are available in 1890 for Rio de Janeiro.

the "gainful employment" approach above. It was more restrictive than the definition in earlier Brazilian censuses and also more restrictive than the current International Standard definition. In it a person with two roles, one of which is an economic activity, would still be classified as inactive if the economic activity were not the principal activity. All Brazilian censuses since 1920 have followed some variant of this approach. The 1920 census was also the first to tabulate the active population by age, with separate tabulations for ages above and below age twenty. More detailed age breakdowns for the active population appear only in 1940 and after. Specific attention to individuals who were unemployed and looking for work began in 1960 and was extended to individuals seeking work for the first time in 1970. The principal activity concept adopted in 1920 was continued in 1940 and 1950, though no time reference was used in determining it. The 1960 census definition of activities refers to the habitual occupation in the year prior to the census, while 1970 data return to the principal-activity concept but maintain the 1960 time reference. Recent census publications provide separate tabulations by occupation, major economic sector, and status. Vestiges of the earlier profession concept still remain. Occupations are classed according to a scheme that follows closely on the economic sector of the worker (i.e., occupations in textile, glass, paper, manufacturing) rather than the International Standard Occupational Classification (Instituto Interamericano de Estatística 1971).

Even with the improvements after 1940, discrepancies remain. This is especially true of agriculture, where important discrepancies arise in comparisons between 1940 and 1950 census data. The problem is serious because of the importance of agriculture in total employment. In addition to the guidance that the published census volumes provide on this and related definitional questions, there are a number of useful secondary sources on Brazilian labor force data that will be helpful in determining the long-term trend. Villela and Suzigan (1973) prepared a short appendix on the data for 1870–1940, and Singer (1971), Madeira and Singer (1973), and Borges and Loeb (1957) have dealt with the 1920–60 period. The Instituto de Planejamento Econômico e Social (IPEA 1969) and Kahil (1965) have discussed definitional problems in comparisons of the data for 1940–60.

The comparative neglect of attention in most studies to Brazilian labor force trends prior to 1940 reflects the tenuousness of the data for the earlier period. In addition to the definitional difficulties mentioned above, efforts are hampered further by the low overall quality of censuses. As mentioned in Chapter II, neither the 1900 nor the 1920 censuses are considered to be good enumerations on the whole. The 1900 census was subject to large age-reporting errors and an undercount, and the 1920 census had a substantial overcount. Thus, the three earlier censuses, though useful in providing a baseline for analysis of later trends, require much caution and some adjustment for even the roughest comparisons. For this purpose, it will be useful to begin with a separate examination of the earlier censuses and then proceed to the materials that are available for the period between 1940 and 1970.

The Growth of the Active Population, 1872–1920

Table VII–1 presents data on economic activity from the 1872, 1900, and 1920 population censuses. In these censuses, activities are recorded in household interviews, in contrast to reports taken from establishments in economic censuses, which were not taken until after 1907. Since early population censuses classified individuals according to a concept of occupation that evolved from census to census, comparisons are difficult. Estimation of a consistent labor force series requires evaluation of each occupational class in each of the censuses to determine who qualifies as active.

We can begin by eliminating some classes that do not belong in the labor force. Those living on pensions (line 8, Table VII–1) and those classed as inactive (line 7) should be excluded. "Occupation unknown" (line 6) and "poorly defined" occupations (line 4) are more difficult to deal with. The 1872 census did not provide an "unknown" category; 1900 did provide one, and the 1920 census combined it with "inactive." Occupations classed as poorly defined in 1872 and 1920 may overlap with the "occupation unknown" group. Villela and Suzigan excluded both of these groups from the active list. We have classed all "unknown" occupations as inactive, since when they appear they are either distinguished from "poorly defined" or are grouped with "inactives." We created a separate "poorly defined" category, which is included with the active population.

The remaining occupation categories have been grouped according to major economic sectors or branches of activity. These sectors follow a breakdown suggested by Villela and Suzigan, who distributed the active population reported in the early censuses between agriculture, manufacturing industry, and services. We have departed slightly from their scheme by treating domestic service as a separate subgroup and putting all occupations that were doubtful in the separate "poorly defined" category. This further subdivision also allows us to evaluate these occupations individually and identify some of the potential sources of exaggeration deriving from dual roles and very loose definition of economic activity in the 1872 and 1900 censuses.

In the "poorly defined" category, we have included individuals in apparels manufacture in 1872 and 1920, as well as groups that were defined as a separate occupation in only one census. In 1872, there was an occupation consisting of servants and day workers (*criados e jornaleiros*), who were paid in kind (room and board) or by the day. Quite a number of these were slaves or ex-slaves. In 1900, we find another group, which we call artisans (*artes e oficios*), that consisted of artisans, apprentices, and occupations that did not fit well in other classes. The remaining "poorly defined" are found in the "other" subgroup. In 1900, this included apparels, which was not given separately as in 1872 and 1920.

Domestic service is the occupation in which exaggeration of the size of the active population in the early censuses is most severe and affects mainly females. The 1900 total of 2.3 million domestic servants stands out. It is nearly

Table VII-1. Economically Active Population by Major Sector and Sex, Censuses of 1872, 1900, and 1920 (data in thousands)

Census categories	Total			Male			Female		
	1872	1900a	1920	1872	1900a	1920	1872	1900a	1920
1. Agriculture	3,761	5,071	6,377	2,296	4,001	5,769	965	1,070	608
2. Manufacturingb	282	321	814	144	121	690	138	200	99
3. Services									
a) Domestic, unadj.	1,046	2,477	364	197	158	70	840	2,319	294
b) Domestic, adj.c	(290)	(323)					(93)	(165)	
c) Other	221	640	1,145	204	566	1,059	17	74	86
4. Poorly defined									
a) Clothing mfg.d	506	n.d.	450	n.d.	n.d.	144	506	n.d.	331
b) Defined one timee	410	994	n.d.	275	393	n.d.	135	601	n.d.
c) Other poorly defined	182	233	417	101	151	370	81	82	47
5. Total									
a) Unadjusted	5,908	9,736	9,567	3,217	5,390	8,102	2,691	4,346	1,465
b) Adjustedc	(5,152)	(7,582)					(1,935)	(2,192)	
6. Status unknown	n.d.	733	n.d.	n.d.	488	n.d.	n.d.	245	n.d.
7. Not active	4,172	6,944	21,028	1,984	3,006	7,314	2,188	3,938	13,714
8. Pensioners	32	27	41	23	17	27	9	10	14
9. Total population	10,112	17,438	30,636	5,225	8,900	15,444	4,888	8,538	15,192
10. Population 10+	7,870	11,791	21,447	4,159	5,994	10,788	3,811	5,797	10,659

Note: n.d., category not specified in census.
a Including data for Federal District in 1906.
b Includes construction and mining.
c Adjustment of domestic servants to equal their proportion in 1920 population, females only.
d Includes seamstresses (costureiras), and individuals in vestuário e toucador.
e In 1900, the artes e ofícios class, in 1872 the jornaleiros e criados.
Source: Population Censuses of 1872, 1900, and 1920 as reported in Brazil, Diretoria Geral de Estatística, Vol. IV, 5a parte, pp. VIII–XIII.

three times the number shown for 1872 and close to ten times what is reported in 1920. The total female population increased by 75 percent between 1872 and 1900, against which a 173 percent increase in domestic service must be an overstatement. Comparing the 90 percent decrease reported for domestic service between 1900 and 1920 with the 78 percent total female population increase leads to the same conclusion regarding the 1900 figure.

This change is basically a result of the shift from very loose treatment of the dual roles of females in 1872 and 1900 to the stricter "principal activity" definition of the 1920 census. It is also a clear illustration of the difficulty of adapting the definition of economic activity to changes in the structure of the economy. Slavery contributed to the high rate of economic activity reported for females in 1872. The 1872 census provides data for the slave and free population, and the crude unadjusted female activity rate was 75 percent for slaves and 50 percent for free. About 20 percent of active females in 1872 were slaves, as compared with the 15 percent share in the total population. Slavery was abolished in 1888, but the transition from slave to wage labor was, in fact, a gradual process, and adaptation of measurement concepts to these changes must also have taken time. The high proportion of domestic servants reported in 1900 may be a reflection of the ambiguity regarding economic roles that was inherent in this transition process. Neither the 1900 nor 1920 census made breakdowns by color, which would have permitted further elucidation of this point.

However, the problem of meaningful delineation of economic activity was not limited to the slave population. Female participation was also high for the nonslave population in 1872 (51 percent), as compared to 1920 (10 percent). Economic activity was defined more loosely for the female population as a whole in both 1872 and 1900, and especially in the "domestic service" category. A large number of housewives were included in the active group and, while they may have been engaged in some artisan manufacturing activities, the numbers reported exaggerate the female active population total, especially for 1900.

An alternative is to adjust the earlier domestic service totals downward to bring them more into line with the 1920 level. This can be done by applying the 1920 domestic service share in total female population to 1872 and 1900 data. Since domestic service may have declined some with the early stages of industrialization occurring during this period, this is probably an overstatement. However, it is useful in providing a more plausible range for female employment trends in this period. The resulting adjusted domestic service estimates for 1872 and 1900 are shown in line 3b of Table VII-1.

Nor is the looseness of 1872 and 1900 census definitions restricted to domestic services and females. The "poorly defined" categories (lines 4a, b, and c) include occupations that are subject to overstatement. Seamstresses were a predominantly domestic activity and included an unknown proportion of individuals who combined this work with other domestic activity. The 1900 census presents special problems with both the "artisan" and "other" categories, which encompassed seamstresses as well as artisans and apprentices—all of whom fall into the grey area between active and inactive—as do nonsalaried workers (*criados e jornaleiros*) in the 1872 data.

Because of these limitations, comparison of activity rates for 1872, 1900, and 1920 should be made with great caution. Table VII–2 (Part A) presents crude and refined activity rates for the total, male, and female populations derived from data in Table VII–1. The crude rate uses total population as its base, whereas, the refined rate calculated for the population age ten and over. For the total population, the crude activity rate (Table VII–2, line 1a) declines from 58 to 56 percent from 1872 to 1900 and then to 31 percent in 1920. The male pattern is similar, except that the decline is more gradual (61 to 53 percent). The decline from 1900 to 1920 is much more dramatic for females, from 51 percent to 10 percent. Most of this decline reflects a shift to the stricter (principal occupation) definition of activities in the 1920 census, especially for domestic services. If we adopt the adjusted domestic service totals (Table VII–1, line 3b), the crude 1872 and 1900 female activity rates in Table VII–2 (line 1b) drop to 39.6 and 25.7 percent. These are still high in comparison with 1920 and show the added effect of including members of farm households and individuals other than servants working at or near the home among the active in the first two censuses.

For males, the refined activity rate is shown (Table VII–2, line 2a) to have increased from 77 percent in 1872 to 90 percent in 1900, and then to have declined to 75 percent in 1920. The 1900 figure immediately stands out. There are a number of possible reasons for it being high in comparison to the other two censuses. One is that the foreign-born, whose share in the total population in 1900 was higher than in 1872 and 1920, had a higher proportion active and therefore inflated the aggregate rate. Examination of refined activity rates for native-and foreign-born separately suggests that this could have been a factor, since the rate for foreign-born males was 90 percent. However, the rate for the native-born was also 90 percent, nearly fifteen percentage points higher than in 1872 or 1920.

Another source of inconsistency is age misreporting. According to Mortara (1941) both the 1872 and 1900 censuses had poor age enumeration. Published 1900 age data are a corrected version of original tallies. It is possible that overly generous adjustment of the population under ten years of age might have led to upward bias in the refined activity rate for 1900. However, these data show the proportion of population under age ten in 1900 as 33 percent, compared to 22 percent in 1872 and 30 percent in 1920. The 1872 data were the more likely source of error, in that 22 percent is low for known levels of fertility and mortality at that time. To the extent that the 22 percent represents overstatement of age (and not omission of children from the census entirely), this would have led to overstatement of the number of adults and understatement of the refined activity rate.

Table VII-2. Activity Rates and Sectoral Shares of Active Population, Census Data of 1872, 1900, and 1920 (percentages)

	Total			Male			Female		
	1872	1900	1920	1872	1900	1920	1872	1900	1920
A. Activity rates									
1. Crude rate[a]									
a. (5a)/(9)	58.4	55.8	31.2	61.6	60.6	52.6	55.0	50.9	9.7
b. (5b)/(9)[b]	(50.9)	(43.5)[b]					(39.6)	(25.7)	
2. Refined rate									
a. (5a)/(10)	75.1	82.6	44.6	77.4	89.9	75.4	70.6	75.0	13.9
b. (5b)/(10)	(65.5)	(64.3)					(50.8)	(37.8)	
B. Sectoral shares									
3. Agriculture									
a. (1a)/(5a)	55.2	52.1	66.7	71.4	74.2	71.2	35.9	24.6	41.5
b. (1b)/(5b)	(63.3)	(66.9)					(49.9)	(48.8)	
4. Industry									
a. (2)/(5a)	4.8	3.3	8.5	4.5	2.3	8.6	5.1	4.6	8.5
b. (2)/(5b)	(5.5)	(4.2)					(7.1)	(9.1)	
5. Services									
a. (3a,c)/(5a)	21.4	32.0	15.8	12.4	13.4	13.9	32.1	55.1	25.9
b. (3b,c)/(5b)	(9.9)	(13.1)					(5.7)	(10.9)	
6. Poorly defined									
a. (4a,b,c)/(5a)	18.6	12.6	7.5	11.7	10.1	6.3	26.8	15.7	24.1
b. (4a,b,c)/(5b)	(21.3)	(15.8)					(37.3)	(31.2)	

[a]Refers to lines in Table 1.

[b]Figures in parentheses are the adjusted rates for females after revising domestic service totals in accordance with 1920 shares, as in Table VII-1.

Source: Derived from census data presented in Table VII-1.

A third source of inconsistency is the definition of economic activity. Because of the principal activity concept adopted in 1920, it is likely that both earlier censuses would have counted a larger number of active males than in 1920, so that activity rates in 1920 would have been low in comparison with 1900 because of the changing definition, whereas, 1872 would have been lower because of the age-reporting problem.

Attention should also be drawn to problems deriving from the poor quality of the 1920 census data. A further possible explanation for the sharp drop in the activity rate is that the 1920s overcount of total population led to an understatement of active population. We know little about how the 12 percent overcount reported by Mortara might have affected the data on economic activity. It is conceivable that the exaggerated population base for 1920 has led to downward bias in the calculation of activity rates. An additional test will be to compare 1920 rates to those of 1940 and after, since these censuses were also more restrictive in the definition of economic activity than those prior to 1920. This will be done after we have summarized the distribution of the active population by major economic sectors for the earlier period.

Changing Structure of the Labor Force, 1872–1920

The percentage distribution of the labor force by major branch of economic activity for the 1872–1920 period is shown in Part B of Table VII–2. Methodological issues include how to allocate workers to specific branches, since the "profession" concept refers both to occupation and branch of activity. Workers assigned to the "poorly defined" category present special problems for sectoral allocations, as do day workers (*criados e jornaleiros*) in the 1872 census, who could be placed in "agriculture," as was done by Villela and Suzigan, or treated as a separate "poorly defined" group as was done in Table VII–1. As we have seen, this group consisted mainly of household workers and day laborers (usually males in the latter case) and is, in part, a status category rather than a separate occupational group. In cities, female *criados e jornaleiros* belong with domestic servants. Males are difficult to place. No data exist on which to base a distribution of these workers between agriculture and other sectors. Shifting them all to agriculture would not result in great bias, because of the large share of employment in agriculture to begin with. For males, including them in agriculture raises its share from 71 percent shown in Table VII–2 (line 3a) to 80 percent. The rise for females is about seven percentage points. The average for both sexes would increase by eight percentage points. Leaving domestic servants in the distribution as reported results in an apparent increase in the share of agriculture in total employment from 1872–1900 to 1920 when the more rigid standard on domestic service was adopted. Adjusting for overstatement in the earlier domestic service totals results in a much more plausible trend in the agricultural share, as can be seen by comparing lines 3a and 3b of Table VII–2. There is a slight rise in the agricultural share from 1872 to 1900 and virtually no change between 1900 and 1920. Part of the increase from 1872 to 1900 is due to the exclusion of the nonsalaried group, and including them in agriculture in 1872 would change the trend to a decline in the agricultural share for 1872 to 1900 (from about 71 percent to 67 percent).

Trends within the nonagricultural sector are also distorted by definitional differences. Overstatement of domestic servants in 1872 and 1900 is the most obvious problem. Adjusting for this immediately yields a more plausible pattern in the nonagricultural employment structure. Total adjusted service employment increases from 10 to 16 percent of the active population, with most of the increase being for females. In this case, it reflects an increase in employment in service activities *other* than domestic service.

The trend in manufacturing is likewise difficult to determine. Part, and in some instances, all of the employment in the three poorly defined occupations (lines 4a, 4b, and 4c of Table VII–1) could be assigned to manufacturing. However, there is no consistent way in which to assign these groups to a single branch for all three censuses. The aggregation of artisans and apparel groups in a single class in 1900 includes many individuals classed in manufacturing in 1872 and 1920, and the shifting definition probably explains most of the erratic behavior of the manufacturing industry proportion between 1872 and 1920 (line 4b). At the same time, many poorly defined occupations were household activities and could have been assigned either to agriculture or services. The declining share of poorly defined activities from 1872 to 1900 would be expected as a larger share of manufacture was carried on outside of the home.

Viewing the combined share of manufacturing and poorly defined occupation, we observe a fairly stable level of about 15 percent of active males between 1872 and 1920. At the same time, the balance within this has shifted from the "poorly defined" (more likely to be artisan) to "manufacturing" (more likely to be factory) categories. For females, there is a declining trend in the combined shares and a more steady (around 8 percent) share in the "manufacturing" component. If the "poorly defined" group does represent predominantly artisan activities, then the trend from 1872 to 1920 indicates that the shift toward more organized forms of manufacturing industry came at the expense of female employment in these activities, something which would be expected if this shift also meant a move of employment from home to factory. However, since the former activities were ones in which individuals were likely to have played a more dual role as income producers and housewives, it is impossible to tell the extent to which this trend represents a true decline in artisan activities versus the effect of adopting the stricter definition of economic activity in 1920. This issue will be discussed further in the longer-term setting of Brazilian employment trends, after we have examined the data available for 1940–70.

Growth of the Economically Active Population, 1920–1970

Starting with the 1920 data, Brazilian censuses provide a clearer picture of the growth and structure of the economically active population. Though discrepancies remain in the published data, adjustment of the earlier results by Brazilian statisticians permits reasonably consistent comparisons for the 1940–70 period, and with some caution we can also include 1920 (IPEA 1969). Most ambiguities in the 1940 and 1950 data (especially 1940) are similar to, though not as acute as, those shown in the previous section for 1872–1920. The distinction between "active" and "inactive" was, and remains, a difficult one in sectors where a substantial portion of production is carried on at or near the home. As in earlier censuses, this problem is more substantial for females than males, though it affects both sexes at younger and older ages.

Detailed analysis of these problems and attempts to correct them are found in *Aspectos Econômicos e Demográficos da Mão Obra no Brasil* (IPEA 1969). This document describes differences between the 1940, 1950, and 1960 censuses in the definition and classification of economic activities. The main problem of comparability is for females in the agricultural sector. Published population census data for 1940 and 1950 showed a decline of about 42 percent in the number of active females in agriculture between the two censuses. The agricultural censuses for these two dates, which adopted a much looser definition of economic activity than the population census, but are still a useful check on the trend, also showed a decline, but only 15 percent. The IPEA study has suggested adjusting the 1940 results downward by excluding females whose earnings were reported as "indirect" in that census, which we have followed.[2] The other major definitional differences between 1940, 1950, and 1960 relate to the sectoral distribution of the active population rather than to the definition of economic activity itself. The 1950 and 1960 data are more closely comparable, but 1940 requires regrouping of some subsectors to fit the 1950–60 categories. We have also adopted IPEA's sectoral breakdown for 1940–60.[3]

[2]An alternative approach is to substitute the larger total female employment reported in the agricultural census for both the 1940 and 1950 demographic census data. This results in a considerable upward adjustment for both dates and has been adopted by Borges and Loeb (1956) and, later, Madeira and Singer (1973). While it is the most straightforward approach, it leaves us with the loosest and all-inclusive definition of economic activity in agriculture, and with the problem of comparing data for these two dates to those for later years. The alternative of adjusting 1940 downward by excluding females with "indirect remuneration" is not entirely satisfactory either. This category closely approximates that for unpaid family workers, and the share of female unpaid family workers in agriculture reported for 1940 is only two percentage points higher than for 1950, which makes the adjustment somewhat suspicious. We have accepted it because, as Mortara (1970) suggested, the "indirect remuneration" criterion left the 1940 census open to greater overstatement of economic activity that might result from dual roles than the 1950 census.

[3]The composition of major industrial sectors in the IPEA framework is as follows:
PRIMARY: Agriculture, forestry, and fishing
            Organic extractive industries

Recently published 1970 data follow 1960 in most respects, except that the category "seeking work for the first time" has been added to the list of possible categories of economic activity. This has been removed for comparison with the earlier census data. The only other major changes in 1970 relate to reclassification of extractive activities and a shift of self-employed workers in construction from the "service" to "industry" category. Detailed breakdowns for 1970 permitted us to adjust the 1970 data for the extractive industries, but not in the case of construction workers. The effect of this inconsistency on trends in employment by branch of activity will be discussed below.

Table VII–3 is a compilation of population census data on the active population for 1920 through 1970, as well as its composition by sex and major economic sectors. These sectors are broken into three major categories: agriculture, industry (including construction and utilities), and services—with subgroups shown for industry and services. Because of changes in sectoral definitions over time, care must be taken in interpreting trends in the sectoral breakdowns. We have tried as far as was possible to adopt the 1950 categories as a standard, in order to facilitate a longer-term comparison. Adjustments of the other censuses to conform to 1950 are especially problematic with regard to services, which include many poorly defined activities.

SECONDARY: Nonorganic extraction
                Manufacturing
                Construction
                Production and distrubution of power (gas and electricity)
TERTIARY: Commerce
                Transport, communication, and storage
                Financial intermediaries
                Government
                Personal and domestic services
                Others

The following adjustments were made in the 1940 data to bring them into line with the 1950 and later censuses:

i. The 1940 subcategory "storage of merchandise" in commerce was divided between commerce and services, using the 1950 shares.

ii. Workers engaged in the repair and maintenance of vehicles, who were included in manufacturing in 1940, were shifted to services, again according to their proportional shares in the sector in 1950.

iii. The 1940 subcategory "sale of real estate, insurance, credit, and capital" was shifted into "financial intermediaries," expect for stockbrokers.

iv. Government included national defense and public safety, public administration, justice, and teachers in public schools, except for the subcategories administrators and others in public schools, diplomats, and consular representatives.

v. In addition to the changes above, the following were also included in "services": liberal professions, religous, teachers in private schools, administrators in the private sector, domestic services, of various types. In the "other" class came athletes, urban services, medical assistance, unions and other welfare activities.

vi. All others were grouped in the "other" class.

For the exact title of these categories, see Brazil, Instituto de Pesquisas Econômicas Aplicadas, 1969. No changes were needed in the 1950 and 1960 data. We have regrouped some subcategories in the 1970 results to conform to the 1950 aggregation plan.

Table VII-3. Economically Active Population by Industrial Sector and Sex, 1920–70
(data in thousands)

	1920	1940	1950	1960	1970
A) Males					
Agriculture, forestry, fishing	5,769	8,415	9,496	11,052	11,832
Industry, total	834	1,117	1,955	2,444	4,660
1) Mining	75	113	113	128	172
2) Manufacturing	474	706	1,224	1,471	2,633
3) Construction	264	261	581	774	1,705
4) Utilities	21	37	37	71	150
Services, total	1,499	2,428	3,159	5,177	6,726
1) Commerce and finance	475	740	972	1,494	2,249
2) Transportation and communication	250	465	668	1,014	1,183
3) Government and defense	183	382	468	632	992
4) Personal and domestic services	70	578	747	1,267	1,237
5) Liberal professions and social activities	151	172	266	480	692
6) Other/poorly defined	370	91	38	290	373
TOTAL	8,102	11,960	14,610	18,673	23,218
Total population	15,444	20,614	25,885	35,055	46,331
Population age 10 and over	10,788	14,435	18,089	24,193	32,561
Crude activity rate	52.5	58.0	56.4	53.3	50.1
Refined activity rate	75.1	82.9	80.8	77.2	71.3
Age standardized activity rate	n.a.	82.8	80.2	76.8	71.8
B) Females					
Agriculture, forestry, fishing	608	553	758	1,225	1,258
Industry, total	430	297	392	497	635
1) Mining	–	5	3	3	3
2) Manufacturing	430	289	384	484	609
3) Construction	–	2	4	7	15
4) Utilities	–	1	1	3	8
Services, total	427	1,192	1,357	2,355	4,227
1) Commerce and finance	23	53	102	197	448
2) Transportation and communication	4	14	29	42	62
3) Government and defense	3	24	44	81	160
4) Personal and domestic services	294	963	926	1,497	2,390
5) Liberal professions and social activities	56	127	247	510	1,095
6) Other/poorly defined	47	11	9	46	72
TOTAL	1,465	2,042	2,507	4,077	6,120
Total population	15,192	20,622	26,059	35,015	46,808
Population age 10 and over	10,659	14,603	18,470	24,636	33,306
Crude activity rate	9.6	9.9	9.6	11.6	13.1
Refined activity rate	13.7	14.0	13.6	16.5	18.4
Age standardized activity rate	n.a.	13.9	13.5	16.4	17.5
C) Total					
Agriculture, forestry, fishing	6,377	8,968	10,254	12,277	13,090
Industry, total	1,264	1,414	2,347	2,941	5,295
1) Mining	75	118	116	131	175
2) Manufacturing	904	995	1,608	1,955	3,242
3) Construction	264	263	585	781	1,720
4) Utilities	21	38	38	74	158

Table VII-3. (continued)

	1920	1940	1950	1960	1970
Services, total	1,926	3,620	4,516	7,532	10,953
1) Commerce and finance	498	793	1,074	1,691	2,698
2) Transportation and communication	254	479	697	1,056	1,245
3) Government and defense	186	406	512	713	1,152
4) Personal and domestic services	364	1,541	1,673	2,746	3,627
5) Liberal professions and social activities	207	299	513	990	1,787
6) Other/poorly defined	417	102	47	336	445
TOTAL	9,567	14,002	17,117	22,750	29,338
Total population	30,636	41,236	51,944	70,070	93,139
Population age 10 and over	21,447	29,038	36,559	48,829	65,868
Crude activity rate	31.2	34.0	33.0	32.5	31.5
Refined activity rate	44.6	48.2	46.8	46.6	44.5
Age standardized activity rate	n.a.	48.2	46.5	46.4	44.8

Sources: Population censuses for each decade with adjustments as reported in text.

We have relied on Borges and Loeb (1957) as well as IPEA (1969) in adapting 1920 data to later censuses. Special care is required in 1920, because of the large number in the poorly defined groups (especially males) who were assigned to specific categories in services or industry in later censuses. Several authors, including Borges and Loeb, delete this category from labor force trends, but this leads to an underestimate of the 1920 labor force total, and we prefer to list the poorly defined as a separate category.

Minor adjustments in the distribution of employment by sector were required to achieve consistency in the 1950, 1960, and 1970 data. In most instances (extractive industries, public services, etc.), detailed tables in the census volumes permitted a simple regrouping of the affected categories. A shifting of self-employed construction workers from the service industry category in 1970 proved to be more difficult to handle, since the needed cross-tabulations were not available. Comparison of the 1960 and 1970 distributions of construction workers should have been affected by this shift.[4] Table VII-3 presents the totals for construction reported in the census. Later, the 1950 and 1960 distributions are adjusted on a pro-rata basis for analysis of shifts of employment by occupation and sectoral branch of activity (section F).

[4]It is impossible to determine directly the extent to which the 1970 reclassification of construction workers has inflated the broad "industry" branch results, since the 1970 data do not show the self-employed as a separate subsector and no national tables for 1960 have been published. An order of magnitude is suggested by comparison of 1960 and 1970 data for Guanabara (the only large metropolitan area for which data are available) relating to *all* construction workers in services (employees as well as self-employed). In Guanabara, this group represented 19 percent of the total construction sector in 1960 and 3 percent in 1970. Applying this sixteen percentage point differential to the 1970 national construction total yields a "service" component of 275,000. This estimate is probably on the high side, because it includes all service sector construction.

Turning to Table VII–3 and the overall trend for males (panel A), we observe steady growth in the active population, 8.1 million in 1920 to 23.2 million in 1970, an average annual growth of 2.1 percent per year. This compares with a total population increase for males of 2.2 percent (adjusting the base for the 1920 census overcount, this rises to 2.4 percent). In terms of participation ratios, there is an increase in the crude activity rate (labor force/total population) from 52.5 percent in 1920 to 58 percent in 1940, followed by a decline to 50.1 percent in 1970. A similar trend is observable in the refined rate (labor force/population age 10 and over).

For females (panel B), the active population increased from 1.5 million to 6.1 million between 1920 and 1970. The average annual labor force growth rate of 2.9 percent per annum was 16 percent higher than the rate of total female population growth (after adjustment for the 1920 overcount), in contrast to the lower relative labor force growth rate for males. This reflects a trend toward increased female participation after 1950, with the crude activity rate rising from 9.6 to 13.1 percent in two decades.

As will be seen below, these contrasting trends in male and female participation rates after 1950 resulted from a combination of changes in age-specific rates for both sexes. Increases in the participation rates for both sexes between 1920 and 1940 should be viewed with caution, because of the overcount in the 1920 population total and the possibility that the 1920 overcount did not affect the active population in equal proportion. While it is impossible to determine the extent to which this actually occurred, deflating the 1920 population base by 10 percent yields a more plausible set of activity rates for 1920. For males the crude rate is then 58.3 percent and the refined rate 83.4 percent, and we should revise our characterization of the trend for males to show a fairly level pattern up to 1940, followed by a steady decline thereafter. For females this revision results in a crude rate of 10.7 percent and a refined rate of 15.3 percent, suggesting even more strongly that the trend up to 1950 was downward, followed by an increase in 1960 and 1970.

The total labor force (panel C, Table VII–3) grew from 9.6 million in 1920 to 29.3 million in 1970. The labor force growth rate was 2.3 percent per annum, compared to population growth of 2.2 percent (2.5 percent after adjusting 1920). If we use the upwardly adjusted 1920 activity rates, we observe declines in both the crude and refined activity rates between 1920 and 1970: a decline in the crude rate from 34.7 percent in 1920 to 31.5 percent in 1970 and in the refined rate from 49.6 percent to 44.5 percent over the same period. The declines in the refined rate are larger after 1950. Rising female rates after 1950 have partially offset the effects of the decline in the male rates. Age structure effects in the population as a whole, in the form of a rise in the proportion of the population under age 10 between 1950 and 1960, followed by a decline in 1970, account for the different pace in which the changes in the crude and refined rates occurred between 1950–60 and 1960–70. However, age structure effects within the working-age population had limited effect on the refined activity rate. Age-standardized rates (see the last line of Table VII–3: standardization is based on the average age distribution for 1940–70) differ little from the unstandardized rates, except for females in 1970. The 1960–70 increase in female participation resulted from a combination of increased age-specific participation at younger ages (15 to 29) and increased representation of these age groups in the population, since they represent birth cohorts of the late 1940s and early 1950s, when Brazilian birth rates were at their peak. More detailed discussion of age patterns of participation is found in the next section.

Trends in the sectoral distribution of the labor force can be compared more easily by utilizing the percentage breakdown by sex and branch of economic activity shown in Table VII–4. The most striking change in the sectoral pattern of employment is the shift from agricultural to nonagricultural activities. For males the agricultural share dropped from 71.2 percent in 1920 to 51.0 percent in 1970, while females fell from 41.5 percent to 20.5 percent. The share of total labor in agriculture was 67 percent in 1920, compared to 45 percent in 1970. While this decline is an indication of significant structural change in the Brazilian economy, especially since 1950, the data also highlight the continuing importance of the agricultural sector in Brazilian employment.

Closer examination of these shifts reveals some important differences in timing. The industry share increased from about 10 percent to a little over 13 percent in 1940–50, but showed virtually no change in the next decade. Then, in 1960–70, it increased dramatically from 13 percent to 20 percent. As we recall from the introductory overview of the Brazilian economy in Chapter II, the 1950s were the years of Brazil's conscious efforts in import substitution, during which industrial output grew much more than employment. Following the crisis of the early 1960s, the industrial boom of the later part of the decade appears to have had a more substantial impact on employment creation. However, most of the increase in industry, broadly defined, actually occurred in construction, part of whose increase can be attributed to the statistical reclassification discussed above. The share of manufacturing increased by only three percentage points between 1960 and 1970, in comparison with the seven for industry broadly defined. Almost all of the increase in the nonagricultural share for males between 1950 and 1960 occurred in services; there was little change in the service share in preceding and succeeding periods.

The pattern of change in the female distribution is less clear, in part reflecting difficulties discussed earlier in defining and classifying female activities. In contrast with the male pattern, the industry share for females has declined. For the large decline from 29 percent in 1920 to 14.5 percent in 1940, it is difficult to determine the extent to which this reflects definitional problems vis-à-vis a true shift that may have resulted from the substitution of factory for household production in activities like clothing, textiles, and food-processing. The 1940 figures in Table VII–3 (B), which employ IPEA's

Table VII–4. Percentage Distribution of the Active Population by Industrial Sector and Sex, 1920–70

	1920	1940	1950	1960	1970	1980
Agriculture						
Males	71.2	70.4	65.0	59.2	51.0	?
Females	41.5	27.1	30.2	30.0	20.5	
Both sexes	66.7	64.0	59.9	54.0	44.6	30,1
Industry						
Males	10.3	9.3	13.4	13.1	20.1	
Females	29.4	14.5	15.7	12.2	10.4	
Both sexes	13.2	10.1	13.7	12.9	18.1	29,
Services						
Males	18.5	20.3	21.6	26.2	28.9	
Females	29.1	58.4	54.1	56.6	69.1	
Both sexes	20.1	25.9	26.4	31.6	37.3	
Poorly Defined						
Males	4.6	0.8	0.3	1.5	1.6	
Females	3.2	0.5	0.4	1.2	1.9	
Both sexes	4.4	0.7	0.3	1.5	1.7	

Note: Percentages for each sex sum vertically to 100.

revised (downward) estimate of females in agriculture, may understate female employment in agriculture for that date, in which case it is possible that the increase in services from 29 percent to 58 percent between 1920 and 1940 is exaggerated.

Despite the choppiness of the long-term trend for females, there is a clear indication that the main shift in female activities, and therefore the main factor responsible for recent increases in female employment, has been the increase in services, which rose from 29 percent in 1920 to 69 percent in 1970. Reviewing subcategories of services in Table VII–3, we see that two groups— personal/domestic services and public services/liberal professions—account for most of the gains. Changes in occupational structure within sectors will be examined in more detail later on in this chapter.

Age Patterns in Employment Growth

Underlying the trends in participation for both sexes are major changes in patterns of participation by age. Neither the recent decline in male participation nor the rise in female rates are the result of uniform changes in all age groups. Profiles of the age patterns of economic activity from the 1940 through 1970 censuses are plotted in Figures VII–1 and VII–2, and age-specific activity rates (economically active/total population in age category) for major working-age subgroups are shown in Table VII–5.

The decline in the ratio of economically active males to total population age 10 and over, between 1940 and 1970, has been concentrated mainly in the "entry" (10 to 19) and "exit" (60 and over) age categories (Figure VII–1a). Very little decrease is found in "prime" working ages (30 to 49), and inter-

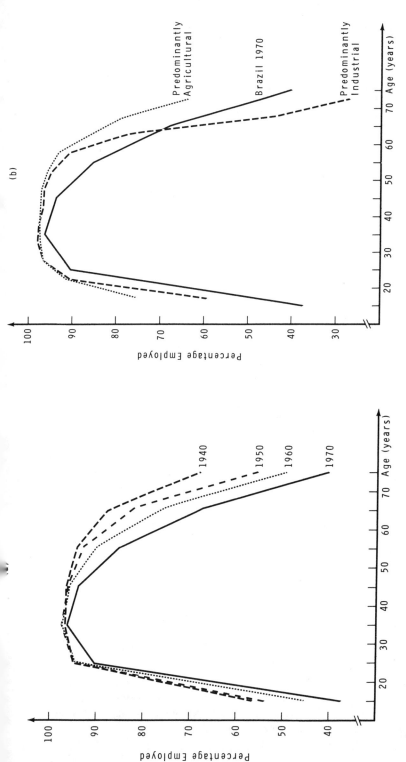

Figure VII–1. Male Age-Specific Activity Rate (ASAR) for Brazil, 1940–70, and Comparison of Brazil in 1970 to Averages for Predominantly Agricultural and Predominantly Industrial Countries. (a) Brazil, 1940–70. (b) Comparison. Brazil 1940–70 from Table VII–5; comparative data, Durand (1975: 97).

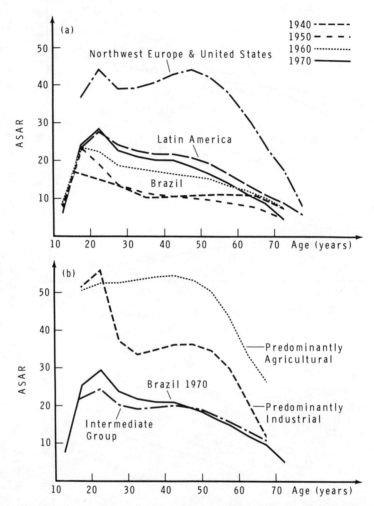

Figure VII–2. Female Age-Specific Activity Rate (ASAR) for Brazil, 1940–70, and Comparison of Brazil in 1970 to Averages for Three Levels of Economic Development. *Sources:* Brazil, from Table VII-5; comparative data, Durand (1975: 133).

mediate declines are observed in age categories on either side of the prime-age group.

Decreased participation in the younger-age groups has resulted mainly from a rise in the proportion of younger males attending school. A detailed discussion of the changing activity patterns of the younger working-age population and the relation between them and other demographic and economic changes in Brazil will be found in Chapter XI, which analyzes a number of economic effects of population change in recent decades.

Durand (1975) has assembled data on labor force participation by age and sex for eighty-four countries around the world. His classification of data by

Table VII-5. Age-Specific Activity Rates by Sex, 1940-70 (percentages)

Age Group	Males				Females			
	1940	1950	1960	1970	1940[a]	1950	1960	1970
10-19	56.4	53.6	45.2	37.6	18.1	15.6	15.0	14.5
20-29	94.6	94.8	94.4	90.2	14.9	16.6	20.8	25.9
30-39	96.7	97.1	97.3	96.2	10.0	11.4	17.0	21.0
40-49	96.5	96.3	96.0	93.9	10.1	10.7	16.6	19.8
50-59	94.3	92.8	90.3	85.2	10.5	9.5	14.5	15.4
60-69	87.7	82.6	76.5	68.1	10.5	7.7	11.5	10.1
70 and over	68.4	56.6	49.3	40.4	7.3	4.6	6.3	4.7
TOTAL (10 and over)	81.6	80.8	77.2	71.3	14.0	13.6	16.5	18.4

[a]Employs IPEA correction of female activity schedule.
Source: Derived from census data.

regions and levels of economic development provides some very useful bench-marks against which to compare recent trends in the Brazilian data. Figure VII-1b contrasts Brazilian male age-specific participation rates from the 1970 census with averages of rates for groups of countries at the lowest and highest ends of Durand's development scale. The declines in Brazilian participation ratios at both extremes of the working-age distribution are seen to be typical of shifts that occur as industrialization and urbanization proceed. The pattern typical of predominantly agricultural economies consists of early labor force entry and late exit, resulting in a high, flat age/employment profile. With urbanization, increased educational opportunities for younger persons, and earlier retirement, the profile shifts to a later entry/early exit pattern characteristic of predominantly industrial areas. The shape of the Brazilian profile falls between these two types. What is striking is that the general level of the participation profile is lower than either the agricultural or industrial economy averages. This is true even for the prime working ages, but especially in ages 40 to 65, where a marked decline from the typical averages is observed.

Published census data provide relatively little information on the nature of the reduced level of participation in the older age groups. It could reflect earlier retirement associated with urbanization and possibly with increased competition by younger "entry-age" workers for jobs once held by older people. Greater disability, resulting from a higher risk of accidental injuries in industrial activities, could also be a cause of earlier exit from the labor force. The effect of declining mortality on participation rates for older age groups is difficult to determine, because both the numerator and the denominator of the participation rate equation are affected. An increase in the expectation of life is likely to benefit both the active and inactive population, but would depress the activity rate for the exit age category to the extent that retiree survival beyond retirement age is increased.

Nation sample surveys (Pesquisa Nacional por Amostra de Domicilios, PNAD; see Brazil, Fundação IBGE 1973) provide additional information on the activities of older males. These surveys have been conducted since 1967, and their coverage has increased to the point that the most recently published

Table VII-6a. Distribution of Adult Males by Age and Activity Status, Survey Data[a], 1973 (percentages)

Ages	Labor Force		Inactive			
	1. Employed	2. Unemployed	1. At home	2. School	3. Disabled	4. Other[b]
10–19	48.0	2.3	2.8	36.3	0.6	10.0
20–29	91.5	2.7	0.2	2.5	0.7	2.4
30–39	95.9	1.0	0.1	0.0	1.0	1.8
40–49	94.0	0.7	0.3	0.0	1.4	3.6
50–59	85.2	0.6	1.0	0.0	2.2	11.0
60–69	69.0	0.4	2.1	0.0	4.3	24.2
70 and over	40.1	0.0	3.6	0.0	8.6	47.3
Total (10 and over)	75.0	1.7	1.3	12.8	1.3	7.9

[a]Represents approximately 95 percent of national population.
[b]Includes retired.

Source: Fundação IBGE, Pesquisa Nacional por Amostra de Domicílios (PNAD), 4° Trimestre de 1973 (Rio de Janeiro: Fundação IBGE, 1975), Table 2.1.

Table VII-6b. Distribution of Adult Females by Age and Activity Status, Survey Data, 1973 (percentages)

Ages	Labor Force		Inactive			
	1. Employed	2. Unemployed	1. At home	2. School	3. Disabled	4. Other
10–19	26.3	1.5	24.5	42.8	0.4	4.5
20–29	41.3	1.7	51.5	3.8	0.5	1.2
30–39	38.0	0.8	59.3	0.6	0.5	0.8
40–49	36.0	0.4	61.3	0.2	0.7	1.4
50–59	28.6	0.2	67.9	0.0	1.2	2.1
60–69	19.7	0.1	74.0	0.1	2.3	3.8
70 and over	8.6	0.0	67.6	0.1	9.2	1.5
Total (10 and over)	32.2	1.1	47.7	15.4	0.8	2.9

(1973) volume represents all but the rural population of the Amazon and Central-West regions (about 5 percent of the 1970 census population).[5] Table VII-6a shows the percentage distribution of male activities by age in 1973. One advantage of the PNAD data is their greater detail on the activities of those reported as not economically active. However, caution is required in comparing census and PNAD results, because of differences in the definition of economic activity. While the census uses a definition of economic activity that approximates the habitual activity concept described above, the survey follows more current standards and considers as active anyone who was working or looking for work in the reference week.

Comparing 1970 census results for males (Table VII–5) with 1973 PNAD results in Table VII-6a, one is struck immediately by the substantial difference between the proportion of all males reported active by the census (71.3 percent, and the PNAD survey (76.7 percent). Comparison of Brazil's age-activity profile in Figure VII–1b to either of the standards shown there suggests that this difference might be related to underreporting of older age

[5]The PNAD surveys (Pesquisa Nacional por Amostra de Domicílios) have been conducted since 1967 to determine levels of employment and unemployment. The survey began with coverage of selected regions in Brazil, and coverage in the most recent rounds has been extended to include all but rural regions of the Northern and Central-Western macroregions (Brazil, Fundação IBGE 1973).

categories in the census. However, comparison of age-specific rates in Tables VII–5 and VII–6a reveals that differences between the census and PNAD do not derive from the older age groups. In fact, the results for ages 30 and over are nearly identical. The main differences are principally in the 10 to 19 group, for whom the census results show 30 percent fewer working than the PNAD survey. These differences are spread through all economic sectors of activity, thus making it unlikely that they have resulted from different treatment of a group like unpaid family workers in agriculture. The differentials clearly derive from variation in definitions of the economically active population. It is possible that the individuals in question were working *and* going to school. PNAD considered them active, since they were working in the reference week, while the census considered them inactive, since they spent most of their time going to school.[6]

Since the lower activity levels at older ages appear in both census and PNAD data, we are inclined to accept them as being genuine. Moreover, the PNAD data permit further analysis of patterns of inactivity, as seen in the breakdown of the inactive population in Table VII–6a. Disability accounts for about one-quarter of reported inactivity for ages 40 to 49 and 50 to 59.[7] The remainder are in either the "at home" or "other" (including "retired") categories. It is impossible to determine the extent to which early retirement masks difficulties older workers face in securing employment (a "discouraged worker" effect). However, since relatively few workers were sufficiently covered by social security, and since those who were had to be disabled or 65 years old to qualify, it is probable that discouraged workers represent an important part of this group.

Age patterns of recent trends in female activity rates offer several contrasts with males. Female activity rates in the entry and exit age categories were relatively low in 1940, and declines from 1940 to 1970 were relatively modest (Figure VII–2a). In 1940, the highest age-specific activity rate was for the entry category, ages 15 to 19. By 1970 the peak had shifted to the 20 to 29 age

---

[6]This basic difference in approach is reflected in the way in which the census and PNAD determine whether an individual is active. On the census schedule, questions relating to economic activity start with a query about respondents' reasons for being inactive and are then followed by questions on the type of activity, if the individual was not disqualified on the previous question. In PNAD, the order is reversed, with the reasons for inactivity coming after the employment questions. As a screening process, the PNAD approach is likely to yield more workers in cases in which dual roles are an issue. The census approach, while more conservative with respect to dual roles, clearly deviates from the international standard approach that recognizes as active a person who exercises *any* economic activity. The census and PNAD also differ with respect to their reference periods, with the census considering the habitual occupation in the year prior to the census and PNAD specifying a specific reference week. Timing, a third possibility, does not seem a likely source of the difference, since the census occurred in early September and PNAD in October to December, both periods in which individuals who were studying would have been in school. Paulo Paiva made some helpful suggestions on this point.

[7]There is some doubt as to the validity of the percentage of workers reported as "disabled," because of variation from survey to survey. The 1972 results for São Paulo report 43 percent of inactive males age 40 to 49 as disabled and a year later report 31 percent.

group, as a result of a ten percentage point increase for this group. Marked increases are also observable in the 30 to 39 and 50 to 59 age groups. Thus, the major part of the increase in the overall female economic activity ratio resulted from increased participation of ages 20 to 29, contrasting with the male pattern of overall decline accentuated by decreases at the entry and exit age categories.

Interestingly, the PNAD data in Table VII–6b show even more substantial increases for females than is indicated in the 1970 census data. However, an increase in the overall (refined) female activity rate from 18 to 32 percent in such a short time is improbable, and it is more likely that differences between the census and PNAD in interpretation of dual roles account for a good part of the increase that appears in the PNAD results.

International comparisons are also provided in Figures VII–2a and VII–2b. Female participation rates in Latin America have generally been low in comparison with the world average. Brazil follows closely on the Latin American average derived by Durand, and the Brazilian age profile is low in comparison with both the predominantly agricultural and the industrialized regional models provided by Durand. At the same time, Brazil's age/activity profile is beginning to take on the shape of those found in more industrialized regions, though still at a lower level. This is occurring mainly in the younger age groups. Brazilian female participation rates have not yet begun to show the second "peak" in activity after age forty, a characteristic of the pattern that has evolved in the United States and Northwestern Europe with the return of older married women to economic activity.

Another feature of the international comparisons provided by Durand that may be relevant to interpretation of trends in participation for Brazilian females is the U-shaped relation between overall activity rates and the level of development found in his recent cross-section. Participation is high at early stages, then declines and rises again with time. As seen in Figure VII–2b, the activity profile is lower for the countries grouped at the middle developmental level than for either the most industrialized group or the predominantly agricultural one. Shifts out of agriculture might account for declines as countries shift toward the middle group, and increased participation of women in the United States and Northwestern Europe explains the higher level of the more industrialized group in comparison with the middle one. Caution is required in interpreting the U-shaped pattern in the international cross-section, because of statistical bias and measurement. Durand adds that the U-shaped behavior of female activity rates was not a universal characteristic of the evolution of female employment in the presently industrialized countries. The hypothesis is of interest in the Brazilian case, however. As will be seen in the concluding summary to this chapter, such a pattern does emerge in the long-term trend for Brazil.

Growth in Employment by Occupation and Branch of Activity, 1950 to 1970

Census data on labor force growth and structure also reveal important changes in the occupational and sectoral composition of employment in the post-World War II period. Concern has been expressed that relative declines in agricultural employment have not been matched by an increase in productive employment elsewhere. Because of the relatively low labor absorptive capacity of technologies utilized in import-substituting industrialization, it appeared to many observers that the only outlets for labor released from agriculture were the low productivity urban services.[8] The failure of any appreciable gain in the share of industrial employment to occur between 1950 and 1960, despite industrial expansion, seemed to confirm these fears. Then the 1970 census results appeared and showed a reversal of these trends. Employment of males in the industrial sector increased from 13 to 20 percent.

Additional insight into the composition of recent Brazilian employment growth can be obtained from tabulations of the working population by occupation and major economic sector. Tables presenting very detailed breakdowns of occupations (about 200 categories) by branch of economic activity can be found in the 1950, 1960, and 1970 census volumes. The breakdown by branch of activity is less detailed, combining such categories as manufacturing, mining, construction, and utilities in a single "industry" grouping. Besides "industry," the list of sectors includes agriculture, commerce, transport and communication, social services, public services, personal services, and an "other" category. To facilitate discussion, the 200 occupational categories were regrouped in 20 summary classes, as shown in Table VII–7. Account was taken of several definitional changes in both occupational and sectoral categories between censuses; an appendix lists the categories that comprise the 20 summary occupational classes to be discussed here. All eight categories of the IBGE's branch of activity breakdown are utilized.

It is immediately apparent that the Brazilian Census Bureau's occupational coding mixes conventional occupational classes, such as the ones recommended by the Inter-American Statistical Institute (1971), with its own classification of occupations according to branch of activity. As a result, the occupational breakdown reflects as much the branch of activity as the differences of skill, status, and function found in conventional occupational classifications. The tabulations by occupation and branch of activity are nearly redundant in categories in which the occupational category refers almost exclusively to employment in a single industrial branch, such as commerce. The detailed occu-

[8]Detailed discussion of the trend for 1950–60 can be found in Baer and Hervé (1966) and Kahil (1965).

pational classification found in the census lends itself only very partially to a regrouping according to status and skill levels. As far as possible, occupations were so grouped in setting up the 20 summary categories. It was nearly impossible to adjust occupational classes that included the full range of unskilled to skilled workers in a particular economic sector. This kind of occupational classification is a holdover from earlier censuses in which the differentiation of activities by skill and status within the different branches of activity was limited and when it was sufficient to know where a person was employed in order to ascertain the qualification required by that employment.

Table VII–7 presents the distribution of total employment by occupation and sex in 1950, 1960, and 1970, as well as the share of each occupational category in the growth of overall employment. Agricultural workers accounted for 62 percent of male employment in 1950 and remained the major category, with 50 percent in 1970. The decline in the share of agriculture between 1950 and 1970 was matched by increases in a wide range of male occupations outside of agriculture. Among the more important gaining occupational categories were clerical and technical workers, metal and machinery workers, construction, commerce, transport and communications, the public sector, and the "other" occupations. The rising share of the latter shows the growing inadequacy of Brazil's mixed sectoral/occupational classification system to incorporate the new types of activity that are emerging as the economy becomes more complex.

Female occupational patterns contrast with those of males in a number of ways. Agricultural workers accounted for only 29 percent of employment in 1950. Domestic services led the nonagricultural occupations, with 25 percent, and were followed by the "mass consumption" manufacturing category (food and beverages, leather goods, clothing and textiles). The remaining jobs are clustered among commerce, teaching, social services, and clerical workers. Most of the increases in nonagricultural employment between 1950 and 1970 occurred in the services categories. The share of manufacturing in female employment declined, even though the overall nonagricultural share increased as a consequence of declines in agriculture. The "other" category also increased for females.

Further insight into the timing and composition of these changes is gained by decomposition of the difference between each occupational group's initial share in employment and its contribution to overall employment growth in the two intercensal periods. As can be seen from columns (4) and (5) of Table VII-7, occupational categories whose shares increased made a larger proportional contribution to employment growth than their share in employment at the beginning of each decade. Those whose shares decreased contributed less.

These differences could arise either from changes in employment in the branches of activity in which particular occupations are found (a "sectoral shift") or from shifts in the composition *within* each industry group (a "compositional shift"). The former are more likely to reflect the impact of changes

Table VII-7. Distribution of Employment and Employment Growth by Sex and Occupation, 1950–70

Occupational category	Percentage share in total employment			Percentage share in employment growth	
	1950	1960	1970	1950–60	1960–70
	(1)	(2)	(3)	(4)	(5)
A. Males					
1. Proprietors	5.13	4.36	4.72	1.60	6.22
2. Managers and administrators	0.86	0.50	1.46	-0.78	5.38
3. Clerical workers	2.28	3.30	4.00	6.98	6.84
4. Teachers	0.26	0.39	0.56	0.84	1.27
5. Professional and technical workers	1.13	1.50	1.84	2.82	3.23
6. Farm and fishery workers	62.26	57.65	50.05	41.06	18.86
7. Miners	0.50	0.47	0.45	0.37	0.38
8. Metal and machinery workers	2.46	3.52	4.17	7.32	6.82
9. Workers in wood, ceramics, graphics	2.90	2.96	2.94	3.19	2.86
10. Workers in food, clothing, leather, etc.	2.47	2.63	1.96	3.23	-0.80
11. Construction workers	3.45	4.27	5.98	7.23	12.99
12. Other industry (utilities, etc.)	0.53	0.47	1.11	0.27	3.72
13. Street vendors	0.74	1.17	1.22	2.70	1.43
14. Remainder of commerce and finance	2.90	2.80	3.62	2.43	6.99
15. Bus, taxi, and truck transport workers	2.43	3.14	3.79	5.69	6.44
16. Remainder of transportation and communication	1.15	1.58	1.00	3.14	-1.38
17. Domestic service workers	0.57	0.54	0.59	0.42	0.83
18. Remainder of personal services	0.52	0.62	0.45	1.01	-0.24
19. Public service, defense, etc.	1.33	1.47	1.93	1.98	3.79
20. Workers in the census's "other" category	6.13	6.65	8.16	8.49	14.38
TOTAL	100.00	100.00	100.00	100.00	100.00

Table VII-7. (continued)

	Percentage share in total employment			Percentage share in employment growth	
	1950	1960	1970	1950-60	1960-70
	(1)	(2)	(3)	(4)	(5)
B. Females					
1. Proprietors	1.21	1.13	1.54	0.98	2.35
2. Managers and administrators	0.64	0.24	0.82	0.39	1.96
3. Clerical workers	4.96	5.89	8.00	7.37	12.19
4. Teachers	5.84	7.15	10.72	9.23	17.86
5. Professional and technical workers	1.88	2.08	2.83	2.40	4.33
6. Farm and fishing workers	29.03	29.80	20.43	31.03	1.64
7. Miners	0.03	0.04	0.02	0.07	-0.02
8. Metal and machinery workers	0.10	0.20	0.24	0.38	0.30
9. Workers in wood, ceramics, graphics	0.68	0.57	0.45	0.38	0.21
10. Workers in food, clothing, leather, etc.	15.91	14.37	9.21	11.92	-1.10
11. Construction workers	0.06	0.11	0.07	0.20	-0.01
12. Other industry (utilities, etc.)	0.61	0.70	1.05	0.84	1.75
13. Street vendors	0.20	0.41	0.63	0.75	1.08
14. Remainder of commerce and finance	3.23	2.46	3.45	1.22	5.43
15. Bus, taxi, and truck transport workers	0.04	0.07	0.06	0.10	0.04
16. Remainder of transportation & communication	0.53	0.53	0.68	0.52	0.98
17. Domestic service workers	25.15	22.68	28.38	18.75	39.76
18. Remainder of personal services	4.55	5.58	4.90	7.23	3.52
19. Public service, defense, etc.	0.00	0.03	0.03	0.06	0.03
20. Workers in the census's "other" category	5.37	5.96	6.51	6.90	7.60
TOTAL	100.00	100.00	100.00	100.00	100.00

in demand and investment patterns on employment growth, while the latter would more typically result from changes in the technology and organizational structure within industries. Of interest also are differences in the timing of these shifts between the two decades for which data are available.

Techniques for decomposition of shifts in the composition of employment by occupational and industrial sector between two censuses are outlined in the United Nations' *Methods of Analysing Census Data on Economic Activities of the Population* (United Nations 1968: 110–19). The term "industrial sector" is used here in the broader sense of branches of economic activity, rather than the specific "industry" category of manufacturing, construction, mining, and utilities found in the Brazilian census. Computational aspects of the decomposition analysis are described in a footnote.[9]

[9]To express the decomposition analysis in mathematical form, let P_{ij} be the number of workers in occupation (i) and sector (j) in 1950 and Q_{ij} be the corresponding number for 1970. At the same time P and Q represent the total labor force and $\overset{\bullet}{P}_j$, Q_j (P_i, Q_i) the total number of workers in each sector (occupation if the subscript is i). The percentage distribution of workers is represented by lower-case notation, with p_{ij}, q_{ij} representing the share of each occupation/sector cell in the total labor force; p_j, q_j the sector marginals; and $p_{i \cdot}$, $q_{i \cdot}$, the percentage distribution of occupations in each particular sector. Using this notation, the absolute growth of the labor force between 1950 and 1970 appears as $Q - P$, and the share of each occupational class in this growth by:

I. $(Q_i - P_i) \ / \ (Q - P)$,
which is shown in column (3) of Table VII–7. In decomposition analysis, growth is broken down into three effects: labor force growth, sector growth, and occupational shifts. To accomplish this the 1970 labor force share of each occupation is recalculated in two ways: first, by utilizing the 1950 occupation/sector distribution for the 1970 labor force total, as in

II. $U_i = \underset{j}{\Sigma} \ p_{ij} \ Q$.
and then by applying 1950 occupation weights to the 1970 sector shares, as in

III. $V_i = p_i \cdot \overset{\Sigma}{q_j}$
The employment growth effect is then represented as

IV. $E_i = U_i - P_i$
The sector growth effect is represented by

V. $SG_i = V_i - U_i$
and the occupation shift by

VI. $OS_i = Q_i - V_i$
In Table VII–7 we express these components as percentages of overall growth $(Q - P)$ of the labor force between 1950 and 1970. The employment growth effect (E_i) is then expressed as $\underset{j}{\Sigma} \ (p_{ij} Q - P_i) \ / \ (Q - P)$, which reduces to p_i, because $P_i = \underset{j}{\Sigma} \ p_{ij} P$ and $\Sigma \ p_{ij} = p_i$ after canceling out $(Q - P) \ / \ (Q - P)$.
Column (1) of Table VII–7 shows p_i, which is simply the distribution of occupations in 1950. To complete the decomposition, we subtract the employment growth effect (p_i) from total growth and break down the residual into the remaining two effects. The residual is column (3) of the table, minus column (1), as in

VII. $\text{Residual} = \dfrac{Q_i - P_i}{Q - P} - \dfrac{E_i}{Q - P} = \dfrac{Q_i - P_i - E_i}{Q - P}$, shown in column (4).
(continued on next page)

Several difficulties limit the usefulness of decomposition analysis for Brazilian data. In all decompositional techniques, there is the problem of interaction between the variables whose effects are being analyzed. The problem is compounded in the Brazilian case by the mixed definition of occupation, which would lead us to *expect* industrial sector shifts to show up as an important factor in decomposition of occupational change. When breaking down employment growth by sector, the compositional effect on sector growth will be almost indistinguishable from "true" sectoral shift to the extent that occupational categories are really sectoral in content.

Table VII–8 summarizes the decomposition of changes in occupational structure over intercensal periods, 1950–60 and 1960–70. Columns (1) and (4) show the percentage point difference between each occupational category's contribution to employment growth in the decade and its base period share in total employment. Columns (2) and (5) show the industrial sector shift effect (e.g., the differences in (1) and (4) attributable to the growth or decline of employment in the branches of activity in which particular occupations are found). Columns (3) and (6) show the shifts in occupational composition within branches, e.g., the percentage points in the differences in columns (1) and (4) attributable to changes in occupational composition within various branches. To illustrate, consider changes in employment in the male agricultural worker category between 1960 and 1970. These workers constituted 57.65 percent of 1960 employment, but contributed only 18.86 percent of 1960–70 employment growth, a difference of 38.79 percentage points. All of this difference (in fact, 39.60 percentage points) can be attributed to decline in overall employment in the agricultural sector. As the illustration demonstrates, sectoral and compositional shifts can offset each other. In this case, compositional effects within agriculture favored farm workers at the expense of other farm occupations (managers and proprietors) and so offset a small part of the large negative sectoral shift. A contrasting situation is observable in the transport sector, which draws heavily from two occupational categories: urban and highway transport workers (bus, taxicab, and truck drivers) and other transport workers (rail, water and air transport, and communication occupations). Employment shares in the transport and communications sector did not change much between 1960 and 1970, but the occupational composition shifted heavily in favor of the road transport group.

Outside of agriculture, shifts in occupational composition within various branches of activity are the main feature. In manufacturing, metal and machinery workers and other manufacturing gained over textile, food and beverages, wood, graphics, and ceramic workers. In 1950–60, the industry sector shift effect was limited, which is to be expected, since industry sector

---

The reader can easily verify that the percentage expression of the sectoral growth effect (V: $SG_i/Q - P$) and occupation shift effect (VI: $OS_i/Q - P$) sum to the residual in VII, since $U_i = E_i + P_i$ and V_i cancels out. The percentage sectoral growth effect is given in column (5) of Table VII–7 and the occupation shift effect in column (6).

Table VII-8. Decomposition of Employment Growth into Sectoral Shift and Occupational Composition Effects by Sex, 1950–70

Occupational category	I. 1950–60 Distribution of difference between 1950–60 growth share and 1950 employment share			II. 1960–70 Distribution of difference between 1960–70 growth share and 1960 employment share		
	Total (1)	Sectoral Shift (2)	Occupational Composition (3)	Total (4)	Sectoral Shift (5)	Occupational Composition (6)
A. Males						
1. Proprietors	-3.53	1.43	-4.96	1.86	1.78	0.08
2. Managers and administrators	-1.64	0.59	-2.23	4.88	0.49	4.39
3. Clerical workers	4.70	3.97	0.73	3.54	3.29	0.25
4. Teachers	0.60	0.05	0.55	0.88	0.91	-0.03
5. Professional and technical workers	1.69	2.89	-1.20	1.73	1.56	0.17
6. Farm and fishery workers	-21.20	-24.67	3.47	-38.79	-39.60	0.81
7. Miners	-0.13	0.06	-0.19	-0.09	1.00	-1.09
8. Metal and machinery workers	4.86	1.32	3.54	3.30	1.86	1.44
9. Workers in wood, ceramic, graphics	0.29	0.66	-0.37	-0.10	4.48	-4.58
10. Workers in food, clothing, leather, etc.	0.76	1.03	-0.27	-3.43	3.28	-6.71
11. Construction workers	3.78	0.56	3.22	8.72	8.57	0.15
12. Other industry (utilities, etc.)	-0.26	0.66	0.40	3.25	0.70	2.55
13. Street vendors	1.96	0.73	1.23	0.26	0.93	-0.67
14. Remainder of commerce and financial	-0.47	3.13	-3.60	4.19	2.42	1.77
15. Bus, taxi, and truck transport workers	3.26	1.46	1.80	3.30	-0.18	3.48
16. Remainder of transportation and communication	1.99	0.96	1.03	-2.96	0.22	-3.18
17. Domestic service workers	-0.15	0.46	-0.61	0.29	0.21	0.50
18. Remainder of personal services	0.49	0.43	0.06	-0.86	-0.27	-0.59
19. Public service, defense, etc.	0.65	0.36	0.29	2.32	1.96	0.36
20. Workers in the census's "other" category	2.36	0.20	2.16	7.73	6.69	1.04

Table VII-8. (continued)

Occupational category	I. 1950-60 Distribution of difference between 1950-60 growth share and 1950 employment share			II. 1960-70 Distribution of difference between 1960-70 growth share and 1960 employment share		
	Total (1)	Sectoral Shift (2)	Occupational Composition (3)	Total (4)	Sectoral Shift (5)	Occupational Composition (6)
B. Females						
1. Proprietors	-0.23	0.14	-0.37	1.22	0.57	0.65
2. Managers and administrators	-1.03	0.16	-1.19	1.72	0.23	1.49
3. Clerical workers	2.41	3.20	-0.79	6.30	3.59	2.71
4. Teachers	3.39	1.77	1.62	10.71	11.80	-1.09
5. Professional and technical workers	0.52	1.91	-1.39	2.25	2.22	0.03
6. Farm and fishery workers	2.00	1.32	0.68	-28.16	-28.24	0.08
7. Miners	0.04	-0.02	0.06	-0.06	-0.10	-0.04
8. Metal and machinery workers	0.28	-0.04	0.32	0.10	-0.04	0.14
9. Workers in wood, ceramic, graphics	-0.30	-0.37	0.07	-0.36	-0.42	0.06
10. Workers in food, clothing, leather, etc.	-3.99	-5.40	1.41	-15.47	-2.96	-12.51
11. Construction workers	0.14	-0.03	0.17	-0.12	-0.03	-0.09
12. Other industry (utilities, etc.)	0.23	-0.33	0.56	1.05	-0.35	1.40
13. Street vendors	0.55	0.10	0.45	0.67	0.55	0.12
14. Remainder of commerce and financial	-2.01	0.12	-2.13	2.97	2.60	0.37
15. Bus, taxi, and truck transport workers	0.06	-0.01	0.07	-0.03	-0.01	-0.02
16. Remainder of transportation and communication	-0.01	-0.10	0.09	0.45	0.02	0.43
17. Domestic service workers	-6.40	-10.69	4.29	17.08	6.67	10.41
18. Remainder of personal services	2.68	-0.38	3.06	-2.06	1.68	-3.74
19. Public service, defense, etc.	0.06	0.00	0.06	0.00	0.02	-0.02
20. Workers in the census's "other" category	1.53	-0.02	1.55	1.64	1.91	-0.27

employment increased little from 1950 to 1960. The industry effect was larger in 1960–70, when relative employment in the sector did increase. Occupational shifts away from more traditional occupations in manufacturing continued—though the overall growth of employment offset much of the impact of this shift on these categories' employment shares.

In service related occupations, the main contrast between the 1950s and the 1960s is that sectoral shift effects contributed a larger share in occupations that gained in the first decade (e.g., the professional and technical group), whereas shifts in occupational composition within sectors figure more importantly in the second period. Clerical workers are the exception, since the sectoral effect is larger in both decades. This change from sectoral to compositional increases in service occupations indicates a growing importance of the more skilled service occupations (e.g., managers, professional and technical workers) in *both* the service *and* industrial branches of activity, which corroborates the similar finding of Ozório de Almeida (1976) in her analysis of changes in service employment between 1950 and 1970. In neither decade do the less skilled service activities, such as street vendors or domestic servants, account for an appreciable share of employment growth among males. Among the low-skill occupations, construction was the main source of employment growth in both decades.

For females, the patterns are quite different. The most striking feature is an increasing polarization of employment between more and less skilled occupations, especially in 1960–70. Agricultural occupations contributed the largest share (31 percent) of employment growth in 1950–60, but only 1.6 percent in 1960–70. Domestic service contributed a less than proportional share of employment growth in 1950–60 (18.55 percent of growth, compared to its 25.15 percent share of employment in 1950), but accounted for nearly 40 percent of employment growth in 1960–70. A similar interdecadal contrast is found in manufacturing, where female employment contributed 12 percent of employment growth in 1950–60, but suffered an absolute decline in 1960–70.

In decomposing these changes, we find that in 1950–60 sectoral shifts were negative in almost all of the nonagricultural female occupations except teachers, clerical workers, and professional and technical workers. Negative sectoral effects continued in 1960–70 for manufacturing (especially in the mass-consumption group), but were further reinforced by compositional shifts toward white-collar occupations (managerial and clerical workers). Sectoral shifts and compositional changes reinforced each other in 1960–70 to produce a concentration of female employment gains in the comparatively high-skill managerial, clerical, teaching, and professional occupations, on one hand, and in low-skill domestic service, on the other.

Summing up the interaction between changes in occupational structure and employment growth in Brazil, we arrive at different conclusions for males and females. For males the principal source of employment in both 1950 and 1970 was agriculture, however, there was a reduction by twelve percentage points of that sector's employment share in the interim. Construction led the list of occupational categories gaining in this shift. At the same time, male occupational redistribution was broadly directed and included several occupational groups in addition to construction. Nor was there any indication that redistribution was concentrated entirely in low productivity jobs. It is true that street vendors and domestic services grew, but their contribution was substantially less than for managerial, clerical, technical, and transport jobs for a large number of industrial occupation categories.

For females, domestic services supplanted agricultural occupations as the chief source of employment. Despite its increased weight, growth of domestic service employment was not far out of proportion with its share in total female employment. In contrast to the relative diversity of male employment growth, structural changes that contributed to female employment growth were limited to teachers and clerical workers. Other occupations that were major employers of females grew roughly in proportion to their initial share (e.g., commerce) or in declining proportion (e.g., industry sector categories, especially mass-consumption goods). The latter reflect technological changes that have occurred in those industries, as well as further decline in artisan and household manufacture. The depressing effect of this on female employment has been outweighed by growth in such professional service occupations as teachers and clerical workers, as well as in domestic services, but with possibly detrimental effects on both the female and overall income distribution because of earnings differentials between these two major employment categories.

Summary and Interpretations

To conclude this chapter it will be useful to review employment trends in a longer-term perspective. This can be done by linking data for 1872–1920 to the 1920–70 series. Figures VII–3 and VII–4 plot total population and employment, with the latter broken down by major sector and by sex, against time from 1872 to 1970. A logarithmic scale is used, so that comparison of the slopes of the population and employment lines will reveal changes in the rate of labor force participation, and differences in the slopes of sectoral trends will indicate changing sectoral shares.

For males, the trends in employment and its composition are comparatively smooth. Interestingly, the bulge in the population growth trend at 1920, which reflects the overcount in that census, does not appear in the labor force trend. This lends support to the view expressed earlier that the error consisted in additions to population totals, but not to subgroups such as the labor force. Most of the sectoral shift to nonagricultural activities, as indicated by changes in slopes of sectoral trend lines, appears to have occurred in recent decades,

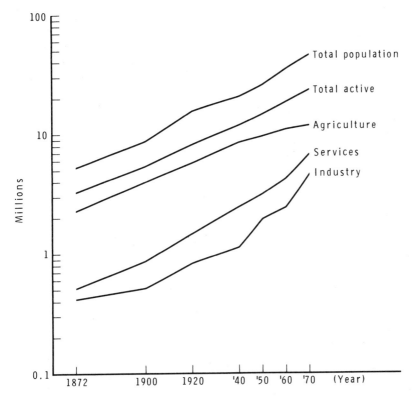

Figure VII–3. Long-Term Trend in the Growth and Sectoral Distribution of the Male Labor Force in Brazil, 1872–1970. *Sources:* Tables VII–1 and VII–3.

that is, since 1940. The rising industry trend was broken in 1960, but has picked up considerably in 1960–70.

In contrast, female trends are more complex, in part due to uncertainties about 1872–1920 data. Over the long run, employment in both agriculture and industry show a U-shaped pattern, with absolute declines in the early period and increases that are less than proportional to population growth in recent decades. Services are the major question mark. If we adopt the lower adjusted estimates of female service employment for the period 1872–1920, as shown in Figure VII–4, then over the long run it is service employment that eventually offsets the effects of declines in industry and agriculture and leads to a relative rise in female employment in later decades. The combination of declines in female employment in industry and agriculture during early decades, with increases in services in later ones, create the U-shaped pattern that is observed in both absolute and relative female employment trends.

Caution is required with regard to the U-shaped pattern, because it is impossible to distinguish definitional deficiencies from a real shift in the mode of

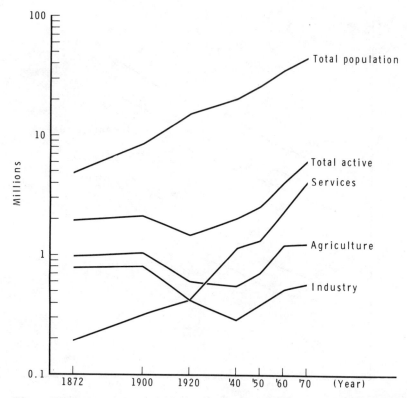

Figure VII-4. Long-Term Trend in the Growth and Sectoral Distribution of the Female Labor Force in Brazil, 1872–1970. *Sources:* Brazil, Tables VII–1 and VII–3.

female participation, that is, from domestic production to work outside the home. To the extent that the latter was occurring, it contributed to a decline in female employment. Definitional and substantive issues are interrelated and reflect changing attitudes on what is "properly female" activity. The introduction to the 1920 census, which outlines the definition of economic activity and the more stringent criteria adopted in that census, is illustrative of this: "She (a Brazilian woman) benefits in addition from the privilege of living for the most part under the protection of a head of the family to whom falls almost exclusively the responsibility of maintaining the household" (Brazil, Directoria Geral de Estatistica 1923: 19).

To the extent that the U-shaped pattern is valid, the longer-term data support the interpretation of Madeira and Singer (1973) in their discussion of trends in female employment in Brazil from 1920 to 1970. They suggest a three-stage model that corresponds closely to the 1872–1970 trend outlined above. Prior to industrialization, a relatively large proportion of females were occupied in agriculture as well as manufacturing and commercial activities in the home; as industrialization progressed, female participation declined, with the elimination of artisan activities and home production. Concomitant with rural-urban migration, the demand for female employment shifted to service activities, but remained small, so that it did not outweigh decreases in manufacturing and agriculture; participation finally increases again as service employment expands enough to outweigh decreases in the other sectors, creating an overall U-shape in the long-term female employment trend.

As mentioned earlier, a U-shaped pattern of female employment growth is not unique to Brazil. Lattes and Lattes (1975) observed a similar pattern in Argentina, and Sinha (1965) found one in analyzing the time trend in India from 1901 to 1961, as well as in cross-sectional data for Indian states in 1961. Both Sinha and the United Nations' *Demographic Aspects of Manpower* (United Nations 1961: 6) found this pattern in international cross sections of countries grouped by level of industrialization and per capita income around 1960, and Durand pointed to a similar pattern in the cross-sectional data for 84 countries in the period 1946–66.

Sinha also explains the U-shaped pattern in participation rates as a process of readjustment in female employment behavior during the shift from rural-based household production to urban industry, and he emphasizes economic factors. Both supply and demand factors contribute to the decline in female employment during this transition. On the labor demand side, replacement of household industry by factory production is biased against women. Factory jobs are less flexible, in comparison with home industry, and create obstacles to female employment as long as women also have household and child-bearing responsibilities. On the labor supply side, a combination of forces is at work. Labor supply analysts have employed microeconomic decision theory to distinguish two main effects: the subsitution effect and the income effect. Substitution effects derive from the trade-off between female earnings (and their cost in time) applied to purchase of goods and services in the market in place of production of these goods and services in the home. Substitution effects have a positive impact on female labor force participation as long as home production is more costly than market production, though the costs are often difficult to measure. The income effect is the incentive to work deriving from the additional earnings of a secondary worker; as husband's earnings increase and thereby raise household income, the need for supplemental earnings is reduced. This theory has been used extensively in analyzing the recent rise in the participation of married women in the labor market in the United States and other industrialized countries, and empirical tests have shown that substitution effects have outweighed income effects, thus explaining the increased rate of participation.[10]

Less attention has been given to changes in female participation patterns in earlier stages of the industrialization process, particularly to the declines in participation that appear to have occurred at this stage. The interpretation of the Brazilian experience given above suggests that substitution effects may have been negative or weakly positive during the transition from home to fac-

---

[10]Evidence and interpretations on the U.S. experience are given in Mincer (1962).

tory production, and therefore incapable of offsetting the negative income effects of rising overall household income on the participation rate. Though production of many goods and services shifted from households to factories and the labor market during this transition, other tasks continued to be done more efficiently in the domestic setting, (and some, like raising children, were done only in that setting). Conflicting demands tended to homogenize female roles, and their activities became more specifically "domestic." This is certainly the interpretation of the excerpt from the 1920 census introduction cited above, and is a further reminder that the basic notions underlying measurement of female activities evolved along with the actual trend, making it even more difficult to know the extent to which there was a true change in the level of participation rather than modifications in the way in which succeeding censuses measured it.

Increases in the female labor force that have occurred in Brazil during the last two decades suggest that a turning point is occurring in the role of women in the Brazilian economy. Since the increase is spread across several age categories, it includes both single and married women. The former, whose impact on participation is most evident in the rate for ages 20 to 29, is related to migration and urbanization, as well as increased education of females. It may also be contributing to delays in marriage, though this hypothesis has not yet been subjected to detailed examination. Increases in participation for women age 30 and over suggests that married women have also shared in the increase, though not yet to the extent that married women have returned to the labor market in more industrialized economies. Both income and substitution effects may be at work in the increases. Increased education levels have raised the opportunity cost of producing goods and services in the home, a consideration that is more applicable to women in higher-income groups. For the low-income population, it is possible that the recent worsening in the personal income distribution may have increased the need for households to supplement the income of the principal earner, in which case the income effect on participation would be positive rather than negative (Sant'Anna, Merrick, and Mazumdar 1976). Both the substitution and income effect hypotheses require further testing.

Whatever its causes, the rising female participation trend has important implications for both economic and demographic change in Brazil in the future. Increased female participation taps a previously underutilized source of productive capacity. The shift of female productive activity from the household to the market affects related areas of household decision, like reproduction and migration. Subsequent chapters will examine these and other economic-demographic interrelations from both the economic and demographic side.[11]

---

[11]Special mention should be made of the many useful comments and suggestions made by Paulo Paiva on early drafts on this chapter. We look forward to the publication of his study of cohort specific labor force participation patterns in Brazil.

Appendix Table VII–A. Occupational Categories for Decomposition Analysis in Table VII–7

Occupational category	Main heading in 1960 and 1970 censuses,[a] Table 16	Subcategory in 1960 and 1970 censuses, Table 16	Corresponding occupational group in 1950 census, line references to Table 26
1. Proprietors	Ocupações administrativas	Proprietários	2 to 7
2. Managers	Ocupações administrativas	Administradores	8
3. Clerical	Ocupações administrativas	Funções burocráticas ou de estritório	9 to 15, 195, 197
4. Teachers	Ocupações técnicas, científicas, artísticas	Professores e funções auxiliares, religiosos, etc.	32, 191
5. Technicians	Ocupações técnicas, científicas, artísticas	All others	16 to 31, 33 to 42
6. Farm Workers	Ocupações de agropecuária	Entire category	49 to 53
7. Miners	Ocupações da produção extrativa mineral	Entire category	54 to 58
8. Metal and machinery	Ocupações das indústrias de transformação e da construção civil	Metalúrgica, mecânica, elétrica	60 to 75, 131
9. Wood, ceramics, graphic	"	Gráfica, madeira e móveis, cerâmica e vidro	78, 79, 81 to 85, 90 to 94, 110, 111
10. Mass consumption: food, clothing, textiles	"	Têxtil, couro, vestuário, alimentação, bebidas	88, 89, 95 to 109, 112 to 121
11. Construction	Ocupações das indústrias de transformação e da construção civil	Construção[b]	122 to 130, 132, 133

Appendix Table VII-A. (Continued)

Occupational category	Main heading in 1960 and 1970 censuses,[a] Table 16	Subcategory in 1960 and 1970 censuses, Table 16	Corresponding occupational group in 1950 census, line references to Table 26
12. Other industry	"	Outros	59, 76, 77, 80, 86, 87, 134 to 137
13. Street vendors	Ocupações do comércio	Vendedores ambulantes	139
14. Other commerce	"	All others	138, 140 to 145
15. Road transport	Ocupações dos transportes e comunicações	Transportes urbanos e rodoviários.	162 to 167
16. Other transport	"	All others	146 to 161, 168 to 173
17. Domestic service	Ocupações de prestação de serviços	Ocupações domésticas remuneradas e de alimentação	168 to 180
18. Other service	"	All others[c]	174 to 177, 194
19. Public sector	Ocupações da defesa nacional e segurança pública	Entire category	185 to 190
20. Other occupations	Outras ocupações, mal definidas, não declaradas	Entire category	192, 193, 196, 198 to 204

[a]The occupational categories of the 1960 and 1970 censuses are virtually identical in terms of the groupings of occupations used here. When a difference occurred, the 1960 occupation was regrouped as indicated below.

[b]As indicated in the text, construction workers who were included in the service sector in the 1960 census tabulations have been shifted to industry on a pro rata basis for this comparison.

[c]Item 270 (*porteiros*, etc.) has been shifted to "other" and items 278–82 (*músicos*, . . . *operadores cinematográficos*) have been shifted to "Technicians."

VIII   Rural-Urban Migration and Urban Population Growth

One of the most striking characteristics of postwar industrialization in Brazil is the rapid growth of urban population that accompanied it. While overall population growth was at its peak level in 1950–60, one-half of it was being absorbed by cities of 20,000 or more inhabitants. These cities accounted for only one-quarter of the population in 1950. Indeed, on the eve of the recent industrialization period, Brazil's urban population proportion (as measured by an international standard definition of an urban area as one having 20,000 or more inhabitants) was low relative to both the world and Latin American average (Table VIII-1). From a 1940 level of only 16 percent, it had increased to nearly 40 percent in 1970. According to the official administrative definition, the urban population passed the 50 percent mark in the 1960s (reaching 56 percent in 1970), and authorities predict that it will reach two-thirds of the total population by 1980. The recent urban population growth rate (5.5 percent for cities of 20,000 and over) was 80 percent higher than the already high rate of overall population increase.

This chapter and the one that follows it are a summary of urban growth trends and an analysis of problems that have resulted from them. The discussion begins with a review of Brazilian urban growth in longer-run perspective (1870–1970), followed by a more detailed analysis of the patterns that have emerged between 1950 and 1970. Special attention is given to regional and city-size differentials in these patterns, to the question of balance between industrial employment and urban growth, and to the problem of creating urban infrastructure to match the increase in urban population. This will lead to a discussion in the chapter that follows on the relation between migration, urban labor markets, and the problem of urban poverty.

Table VIII-1. Comparative Data on Percentages of Population Living in Cities of 20,000 or More in Latin America and Other Regions, 1900-70

	1900	1920	1940	1950	1960	1970
Latin America:						
Argentina	24	37	41	52	58	65
Brazil	10	13	16	21	29	39
Chile	19	28	37	38	50	55
Colombia	8	7	14	21	30	43
Cuba	25	25	30	35	42	48
Mexico	9	11	18	25	32	41
Peru	6	6	13	18	26	33
Venezuela	8	11	19	31	42	56
Regional averages:						
Latin America	n.a.	14	20	25	33	n.a.
North America	n.a.	41	46	51	58	n.a.
Europe	n.a.	35	40	41	44	n.a.
World	9	14	19	21	25	n.a.

Sources: 1900, Latin American Countries, Sanchez-Albornoz (1974: 178). Regional Averages, United Nations (1973, vol. 1: 188); all 1920-40 figures, and regional averages for 1950-60, United Nations (1969): 106; Latin America, 1950-70, Herrera, Gatica, and Jordan (1975: 32-34).

Urban Growth in Historical Perspective

Urban Growth Prior to 1870

The historical roots of Brazil's urban system contrast with those of Spanish-speaking Latin America (Morse 1975). In the early colonial period, most of the population resided in a string of isolated coastal setlements, military outposts, and their environs, which had closer links to Portugal than with each other. There was no preexisting Indian civilization, such as the Aztec and Inca cultures, whose networks of cities and roads were taken over by the Spanish. Not until the gold and diamond boom of the eighteenth century did Portuguese settlement push into the vast interior regions, and the growth of Brazilian cities of this period was patterned on the rise and decline of the extraction of precious minerals for export.

As indicated in Chapter II, the mining boom slackened toward the close of the eighteenth century. Early-nineteenth-century urban growth dropped to insignificant levels, except for Rio de Janeiro and Recife (Conniff 1971). Rio de Janeiro gained stature through the transfer of the Portuguese royal court to Brazil during the Napoleonic Wars and the opening of world trade to Brazil. Rio de Janeiro then supplanted Salvador, which had been the major city and capital during most of the colonial period. Recife gained through the revival of sugar exports from 1830 to the mid-1850s, which attracted both internal and European migrants. From 1850 to 1880, however, urban growth declined, even in these centers, and was low (generally below 2 percent per year) in the remaining cities of the country, a trend consistent with the relatively low pace of economic activity in this period.

The Export Boom, 1870–1920

Only in the last quarter of the nineteenth century, when Brazil was abruptly changed by export specialization (in rubber and coffee) and immigration, did urban growth clearly affect the dominant rural landscape of the country. Table VIII–2 shows selected measures of the urban population in Brazil from 1872 through 1970. Official estimates (based on an administrative definition of an urban place, as in column 1) are available only for 1940 and after, so that the 1870–1920 data must be reconstructed from existing census data. This has been done for *municipios* (municipalities) of various size classes. As can be seen in column 2, only 8 percent of the 1872 population resided in localities having 20,000 or more inhabitants, which consisted of the coastal state capitals and São Paulo. Only three (Rio de Janeiro, Salvador, and Recife) had populations of over 100,000 and none exceeded 500,000. The city that emerged in this period was São Paulo. It grew from 65 thousand in 1890 to 240 thousand in 1900, a growth rate of over 14 percent per annum that nearly quadrupled its population in the decade. In the same period, the rubber port of Belém, in the north, doubled its population. Migrants to the rubber area were attracted almost exclusively from the Northeast. Cities in the Northeastern region, in contrast, declined in relative importance in the period, because of stagnation in the area's sugar and cotton economy.

This period was one in which many Latin American countries experienced a strong increase in the "primacy" of their urban system, i.e., a rapid increase in the growth of the main (usually the capital) city relative to the remaining cities (Browning 1972).[1] Comparative analysis of this feature in the Brazilian system is complicated by the extraordinary growth of the city of São Paulo.

One of the ironies of the immigrant-subsidization policies of the imperial and republican governments, which were shown in Chapter V to be aimed at building up the agricultural labor force needed in the production of coffee for export, is that they contributed as much or more to the growth of the country's burgeoning urban labor force as to the rural labor force. Intraregional migration streams at the turn of the century in the Southeast were directed to the city of São Paulo. Both the foreign-born and many natives who had been displaced

[1] Primacy is ordinarily measured as the ratio of the population of the largest city of the country to the sum of the populations of the next two or three ranking cities. The so called "rank-size" rule, which is used to describe the structure of urban systems in terms of population size, says that the ratio the population in each city after the largest should be inversely proportional to its rank (Berry 1961).

Table VIII-2. Long-Run Trends of Urban Growth through Selected Measures of Urban Population, Brazil, 1872–1970

| | Official definition of Urban | Percent of total population | | | | Percent of city (20,000+) population | |
| | | Municipalities | | | | Rio and São Paulo | |
Date		of 20,000+	of 100,000+	of 500,000+	of Rio and São Paulo	Center	Metro area
	(1)	(2)	(3)	(4)	(5)	(6)	(7)
1872	n.a.	7.9	5.1	0.0	3.0	38.4	n.a.
1900	n.a.	10.0	8.1	4.0	6.0	60.6	n.a.
1920	n.a.	13.0	9.7	6.3	6.3	52.8	64.1
1940	31.2	16.0	12.8	7.7	7.5	47.1	57.3
1950	36.2	21.1	15.6	11.1	8.8	41.8	53.0
1960	45.1	28.8	21.6	16.2	10.2	34.9	47.1
1970	56.1	38.8	29.5	23.6	11.0	28.1	41.0

Source: Data from 1872 through 1920 derived from census tabulations in Morse (1971b: 37). Data for 1940 through 1970 available through official census tabulations reproduced in "Urbanization Trends in Brazil, 1940–70," by George Martine and Cesar Peláez (mimeo. 1971), Rio de Janeiro. Data for Rio de Janeiro and São Paulo from Anuário Estatístico, various years.

in other areas by the foreign-born made up these flows. Thus, the main characteristic of urban growth in this period of Brazilian history is that it originated in the export boom and was fed both directly and indirectly by international immigration.

The regional alignment of Brazil's export economy introduced a modest primacy into its urban growth pattern. Throughout most of the nineteenth century, the population living in the five largest cities (Rio de Janeiro, Salvador, Recife, Belém, and São Paulo) stayed very close to 6 percent of the national population total. By 1900, this increased to 8 percent, with São Paulo and Belém contributing to the increase.

From 1872 through 1890, Rio de Janeiro was approximately eight times the size of São Paulo. In 1872, there were, in fact, seven cities in Brazil larger than São Paulo. By 1900, however, São Paulo shot up to second place and closed the gap to the point that Rio de Janeiro was only three times as large. By the mid-twentieth century, they were roughly equal, and since 1960 São Paulo has pulled ahead. To deal with this, most urban analysts of Brazil have used a bipolar or two-city primacy concept as a focus of their studies.[2] The peculiarities of the Brazilian primacy pattern are seen more clearly when the long-run trends of urban growth are presented for various alternative measures of urban population throughout the last century. Thus, if we look at Rio de Janeiro and São Paulo in Table VIII–2 (column 5), we observe that together they double their relative share in the total population from 1872 to 1900.

From this it would appear reasonable to characterize the pattern of urban growth that predominated in the last thirty years of the nineteenth century as one with features of growth in primacy, in that the two or three largest cities (which were major export centers) grew much more rapidly than the remaining urban localities in Brazil. Brazil's primacy pattern, never very substantial, probably reached its peak in this period. In contrast to countries like Argentina, Chile, and Cuba, Brazil's urban growth pattern since that time has been considerably less characterized by primacy.

The Industrialization Phase, 1920–1970

Though coffee exports continued to be fundamental to the Brazilian economy until well into the post-World War II era, the export boom also laid the foundation for Brazilian industrialization and the urban growth that was associated with it. The tendency toward primacy that had characterized the export growth phase did not persist—at least in terms of population size. Table VIII–2 shows that from 1900 to 1970 Rio de Janeiro and São Paulo increased their percentage share of total population by a multiple of 1.8, while the smaller city-size thresholds (which by definition also include Rio de Janeiro and São

[2]For example, see Browning (1972: 73).

Paulo) increased their shares by multiples of 3.6 (for the measure 100,000 or more) and 3.9 (for 20,000 or more). A more satisfactory measure of declining primacy can be seen in column 6, Table VIII-2. Rio de Janeiro and São Paulo represented approximately 38 percent of the total urban population in 1872. This increased to 61 percent in 1900. By 1940 it dropped to 47 percent, and in 1970 it had fallen to 28 percent. The more recent observation overstates the decline, however, because these percentages omit the rapidly growing suburbs of these two metropolitan regions. Such an omission is really important only after 1950, when suburban growth started to overtake that of the central cities. Prior to that, the central municipalities were dominant. As column 7 shows, the declining primacy trend is evident even if account is taken of suburban growth.

A further way of characterizing the longer-run evaluation of the Brazilian urban system is in terms of its stability. Rank correlations of positions in the urban hierarchy over time provide a measure of this. From 1872 to 1920, the (Spearman) rank correlation coefficient of the top nineteen state capitals was 0.77, suggesting some destabilization of the city system growing out of the impact of expanded foreign trade. The major change was São Paulo moving from tenth to second place. Looking at the top twenty state capitals in 1920 and 1970, and ignoring for the moment the entrance of new cities into the group, the Spearman rank correlation rises to 0.85. The major changes are Natal, which moved from eighteenth to thirteenth place, and Belo Horizonte, which jumped from thirteenth to third place during this fifty-year period. At first glance, this high correlation coefficient would suggest a rather stable city system through time. Within the North and Northeast the correlation coefficient is 0.81 for the top eleven cities from 1920 to 1970 and 0.84 for the nine cities in the Southeast, suggesting a relatively stable pattern within regions as well as nationwide. These findings are very similar to those reported by McGreevey (1974) for Colombia, where the coefficient of correlation for the nineteen largest cities was 0.88 from 1918 to 1964.

If, however, we include the planned capital cities of Goiánia and Brasília in our analysis, the results change. The overall correlation declines to the low seventies, substantially below the earlier findings. These two cities did not exist in 1920, but were ranked eleventh and tenth respectively in 1970. If, in addition, we add two emerging noncapital cities (Santos and Campinas) to the top twenty in 1970, the correlation falls even further. Thus, Brazil presents a relatively stable rank order of cities (i.e., a hierarchically ordered city system) in the twentieth century only if we restrict the analysis to the change in the rank order of the twenty state capitals (and Rio de Janeiro). If we include new cities (Brasília and Goiánia) and smaller cities that grew to substantial size by 1970 (Santos and Campinas), then the Brazilian city system appears much less stable over time. This pattern has been conditioned more by the growth of the frontier and of domestic markets for industrial products and commerce than through the spatial impact of foreign trade, with the influence of the latter on the pattern of urban growth declining after 1900.

Characteristics and Composition of Recent (1950–1970) Trends

The Data and Their Limitations

Data are more readily available for analysis of the spatial and size characteristics of Brazil's urban structure for the period after 1940. However, care must be taken in interpreting them to define exactly what is being measured, since definitional and compositional problems persist. The official definition of Brazil's urban population is based on administrative status (a county seat, *"sede de municipio,"* is an urban place) rather than a minimum population size. As seen in Table VIII–2, this results in a higher proportion reported as urban than would be obtained using a more conventional minimum-size criterion, such as the 20,000 and over base found in many United Nations publications (for example, United Nations 1969). Where possible we will follow the minimum size (20,000 and over) definition rather than the official administrative one. Since rural/urban breakdowns of data in Brazilian census publications follow the official definition, some tables (as indicated) will necessarily follow it.

With any definition of the urban population, urban growth can result both from increases in the population of places defined as urban at the beginning of the measurement interval and from additions of new cities that passed the urban threshold in the interval. For most analytical purposes, it is the first aspect of urban growth that is important, and this can be controlled by specifying the places classified as urban as of a particular census date. A similar problem arises in the analysis of urban growth by city-size class due to shifts of individual cities from one class to the next as their population increases. Again the analysis can be focused on increases in population for cities of specific size by specifying the size distribution as of one census date. We will focus our analysis on Brazilian cities of 20,000 and over in the size classes to which they belonged in 1970. Detailed decomposition of Brazilian urban growth between and within size categories can be found in Martine and Peláez (1971).

An additional aspect of the measurement of urban growth trends requiring careful refinement of published data is the increase in the size of particular cities through expansion into adjacent localities. In Brazil, this has become the major characteristic of growth trends in the larger cities, nine of which are now officially defined as metropolitan areas: São Paulo, Rio de Janeiro, Belo Horizonte, Recife, Salvador, Porto Alegre, Fortaleza, Belém, and Curitiba. The metropolitan areas consist of the central municipality of each metro area, plus a number of surrounding municipalities that have become absorbed in the metropolitan expansion. Data in census publications are still listed by municipality (so that Santo André, a suburb of São Paulo, appears as the eleventh largest Brazilian "city" in 1970), and recomposition of the data for such agglomerations is required to provide an accurate portrayal of the changing urban structure in recent decades. This becomes progressively more difficult (though statistically less significant) as one moves back in time, because of frequent changes in municipality boundaries. Fortunately for our purposes, the major task of sifting through municipality data to reconstruct the metropolitan areas and other important agglomerations from the 1950, 1960, and 1970 censuses has been performed by Robert W. Fox (1975), who recently recompiled data on the population of Brazilian cities of 20,000 or more.

The municipalities included in Fox's definitions of the major metropolitan areas differ slightly from the now official list, since he followed one initially proposed for consideration and that was amended by the time the metropolitan area legislation was enacted (Brazil, Secretaria de Planejamento, 1975). Fox also included other lesser-sized agglomerations that have not been adopted in official publications (see his Table 28). The definition of urban place in his data relates to the urban population in agglomerations of 20,000 or more in 1970. This definition includes in the list of urban places a number of municipalities that would not have qualified had they not been part of an agglomeration, which raised the total urban population as defined by the 20,000 or more limit above that which would result from treating the same municipalities as separate cities.[3]

Distribution of Urban Growth by City-Size Category

Tables VIII–3 and VIII–4 present data on Brazil's urban population according to city-size categories for 1950, 1960 and 1970. Table VIII–3 shows total population (in thousands) for each census date as well as average annual intercensal growth rates of population in each category. Table VIII–4 shows the percentage distribution of the urban (20,000 or more) and total population in each category. Six size categories are shown: (1) the "national" metropolitan areas, consisting of Rio de Janeiro and São Paulo, which are here subdivided into their central municipalities and peripheral municipalities; (2) the remaining metropolitan cities, officially called the "regional" metropolitan areas (Belo Horizonte, Recife, Salvador, Porto Alegre, Belém, Curitiba,

---

[3]Recent editions of the *Anuário Estatístico do Brasil* (Fundação, IBGE, 1977, for example) have been publishing population totals for the nine metropolitan areas. These totals include the entire (rural as well as urban) populations of all of the municipalities in each metropolitan area, figures that are somewhat larger than those reported in Fox's data, which exclude the rural population.

and Fortaleza), also divided into central and peripheral municipalities; (3) nine large nonmetropolitan cities (Brasilia, Santos, Campinas, Vitória, Manaus, Natal, João Pessoa, Pelotas, and Goiânia); (4) cities with population of 100,000 to 249,000 in 1970; (5) cities with a population of 50,000 to 99,000 in 1970; and (6) cities with a population of 20,000 to 49,000 in 1970. In all cases, the data refer to the urban rather than total populations of these municipalities. Also shown for reference is the remainder of the officially defined urban population, the official rural population, and the total population. As noted in Table VIII–3, the published 1960 data provide only the *população recenseada* for urban areas, which is an overstatement, since it counts nonresidents twice. Following Fox, the 1960 data have been adjusted on a pro-rata basis to facilitate comparisons with the resident population base available for 1950 and 1970.

The main features of the two decades of urban growth summarized in Table VIII–3 are as follows. In the 1950s, the rate of growth of population in officially defined urban areas was 5.4 percent per annum, compared to 1.4 percent for the rural population and 3 percent for the total population. Using a definition based on cities 20,000 or more in 1970, the urban growth rate was also 5.4 percent. In the 1960s, population growth rates declined in the case of total population, the officially defined urban population, and the rural population. In contrast, the growth rate for the urban population defined in terms of cities of 20,000 and over increased in the sixties. Small-town growth (officially defined urban areas with less than 20,000 inhabitants in 1970) declined substantially. This was part of a broad trend of declining growth rates in smaller cities (the 20,000 to 49,000 group and the 50,000 to 99,000 group) in the same period. In part, this has resulted from the way in which cities were grouped by size categories. A number of smaller localities that would have increased the growth rate in these categories were located in the peripheries of the metropolitan areas and have been counted in the metropolitan area categories shown here. The cities that remain in the 20,000 to 100,000 category are those located outside of the major agglomerations.

Turning to specific size categories, the average for the two national metropolitan areas masks some important differences between Rio de Janeiro and São Paulo. To show this, Table VIII–3 presents data for both cities. Rio de Janeiro's growth slowed from the 1950s to the 1960s, while São Paulo's increased, enabling it to overtake Rio de Janeiro as Brazil's largest city. In contrast to Rio de Janeiro, São Paulo's population growth increased in both the central and peripheral municipalities, with the latter revealing a striking 11.7 average annual percentage growth rate in the 1960s.

Among the remaining categories, the group with the highest average growth rate in both decades was the one that included larger nonmetropolitan cities in the 250,000 and over class. Cities belonging to this group include capital cities along the coast (Natal, João Pessoa, and Vitoria), Santos and Campinas in São Paulo, Pelotas in Rio Grande do Sul, and three rapidly growing interior

Table VIII-3. Growth of Brazilian Urban Population by Size Category, 1950-70

Size group	Population in thousand			Growth rates		No. of cities
	1950	1960	1970	1950/60	1960/70	
National metropolitan areas						
1. Rio de Janeiro						
a) Capital	2,378	3,262	4,252	3.2	2.7	
b) Periphery	666c	1,312c	2,595	7.0	7.1	
c) Total	3,044	4,574	6,847	4.2	4.1	
2. São Paulo						
a) Capital	2,052	3,300	5,870	4.9	5.9	
b) Periphery	284c	650c	1,968	8.6	11.7	
c) Total	2,336	3,950	7,738	5.4	7.0	
3. Total	5,380	8,524	14,685	4.7	5.6	(2)
Regional metropolitan areasa						
a) Capital	2,242	3,929	6,189	5.8	4.6	
b) Periphery	324c	526c	1,539	5.0	11.1	
c) Total	2,566	4,455	7,728	5.7	5.7	(7)
Remainingb cities of 250,000 or more (9n 1972)	925	1,717	3,286	6.4	6.7	(9)
Cities of 100,000 to 249,000 (in 1970)	1,467	2,610	4,422	5.9	5.4	(30)
Cities of 50,000 to 99,000 (in 1970)	1,020	1,810	2,954	5.9	5.0	(44)
Cities of 20,000 to 49,000 (in 1970)	1,623	2,903	4,706	6.0	5.0	(154)
Subtotal A	12,981	22,019d	37,781	5.4	5.5	(246)
Remainder of urban (official definition)	5,801	9,807	14,274	5.4	3.8	(3,588)
Subtotal B	18,782	31,826	52,085	5.4	5.0	(3,952)e
Rural (official definition)	33,162	38,293	41,054	1.4	0.7	
Total population	51,944	70,021	93,139	3.0	2.9	

aBelo Horizonte, Recife, Porto Alegre, Salvador, Curitiba, Belém, and Fortaleza.
bBrasilia, Santos, Vitória, João Pessoa, Natal, Campinas, Manaus, Pelotas (RS), Goiania;
cData on peripheries in 1950 and 1960 not supplied by Fox (1975). They were calculated by subtracting urban population of the central municipality from the total for each metropolitan area.
d1960 urban population total corrected to reflect *população residente*, as in 1950 and 1970.
eIncludes 118 municipalities located in peripheries of metropolitan areas.

Sources: Data compiled in Fox (1975: Tables 27 and 28); and Fundação IBGE, 1970 Population Census.

cities, Brasilia, Goiânia, and Manaus. The very high growth rates recorded for this group derive principally from the last three, suggesting that regional factors may be as important as size in the overall growth pattern.

The next most rapidly growing cities are the regional metropolitan areas, which recorded an average rate of 5.7 percent per annum in both decades. From the 1950s to the 1960s we observe a strong shift in the momentum of growth from the central municipalities to the peripheries in these metropolitan areas. While the central municipality average declined from 5.8 to 4.6 percent, the average rate for their peripheries increased from 5 to 11.1 percent.

Thus, the overall trend from the 1950s to the 1960s has been toward increasing growth of the larger cities (250,000 or more, including the metropolitan areas). As seen in Table VIII–4 (column a), this reverses a tendency toward decline in the weight of the larger cities in the urban population that occurred between 1950 and 1960. All three categories of cities in the 20,000 to 249,000 groups increased their share from 1950 to 1960, and then fell back in 1970. The bulk of the increase in the urban share in the total population has also shifted to the larger cities. Of the 6.4 percentage point increase in the share of population in cities of more than 20,000 in 1950–60, 3.9 (61 percent) went to larger cities. In 1960–70, 72 percent of the increase went to cities of over 250,000.

Regional Differentials in Urban Growth

The general pattern of Brazilian urban growth in the last two decades masks a number of important regional differences. Table VIII–5 shows that urban growth rates have been highest in the Central-West region where overall population increase has been inflated by recent migration to new settlement areas. This experience is paralleled to a more limited extent in the Northern region and in the South, in which Paraná is located. The cities in these regions, though few in number, have grown very rapidly since 1950.

The region with the lowest urban growth is the Northeast. The most significant change in this region is the rapidly increased growth in the 1960s of the peripheral areas of its three metropolitan areas: Fortaleza, Recife, and Salvador: 9.3 percent versus 5.7 percent in 1950–60. Growth rates for the remaining categories have been around 5 percent, with evidence of decline in rates for cities of less than 250,000.

Average rates for the Southeastern and Southern regions lie in between. Smaller (20,000 to 99,000) cities' growth rates declined from the fifties to the sixties, and the medium (100,000 to 249,000) also declined, especially in the Southeast. The larger cities in the Southeast (Santos, Campinas, and Vitória) all grew at about average rates (5.6 percent), whereas growth in Pelotas, in the South, was much slower.

Regional metropolitan areas in the South and Southeast (Belo Horizonte, Curitiba, Porto Alegre) all show a marked shift toward greater population increase in their peripheral municipalities in the 1960s, with a corresponding decline in the growth of the central municipality.

These regional differentials in growth patterns have led to a moderate regional redistribution of the urban population (Table VIII–6). The Southeast, with around 43 percent of the national population, accounts for about 63 percent of the urban (20,000 or more) population and nearly 70 percent of the large city (250,000 and over) population. The Northeast, in contrast, had about 35 percent of total population in 1950 (declining to 30 percent in 1970),

Table VIII–4. Percentage Distribution of Urban Population by City-Size Categories, 1950–70

	1950		1960		1970	
	Percentage of 20,000+ total		Percentage of 20,000+ total		Percentage of 20,000+ total	
	(a)	(b)	(a)	(b)	(a)	(b)
Rio de Janeiro and São Paulo						
a) Municípios of capitals	34.1	8.5	29.8	9.3	26.7	10.9
b) Periphery	7.3	1.8	8.9	2.8	12.1	4.9
c) Total	41.4	10.4	38.7	12.1	38.8	15.8
Regional metropolitan areas						
a) Municípios of capitals	17.3	4.3	17.8	5.6	16.4	6.6
b) Periphery	2.5	0.6	2.4	0.7	4.1	1.7
c) Total	19.8	4.9	20.3	6.3	20.5	8.3
Remaining cities of 250,000 or more (in 1970)	7.1	1.8	7.8	2.4	8.7	3.5
Cities of 100,000 to 249,000 (in 1970)	11.3	2.8	11.8	3.7	11.7	4.7
Cities of 50,000 to 99,000 (in 1970)	7.9	2.0	8.2	2.6	7.8	3.2
Cities of 20,000 to 49,000 (in 1970)	12.5	3.1	13.2	4.1	12.5	5.1
Subtotal A[a]	100.0	25.0	100.0	31.4	100.0	40.6
Remainder of urban (official definition)		11.2		14.0		15.3
Subtotal B		36.2		45.4		55.9
Rural (official definition)		63.8		54.6		44.1
Total population		100.0		100.0		100.0

[a]As indicated in the text, the proportion of the population reported as urban according to the 20,000 and over definition in this table slightly exceeds what is shown in Tables VIII–1 and VIII–2, because a number of peripheral municipalities in the metropolitan areas with 1970 population of less than 20,000 are included here, whereas Tables VIII–1 and VIII–2 show only those municipalities with populations of 20,000 or over.

less than 20 percent of the urban, and an even lower share in the large-city population. The dominance of the Southeast in urban population has been offset somewhat by the growth of cities in the new settlement areas of the Central-West (and Paraná in the South), but not enough to overcome the large imbalance between the Southeast and other regions in the ratio of urban to total population shares.

Rural-Urban Migration

Brazil's size, regional diversity, and lack of comparative vital registration data make it difficult to sort out the demographic components of recent urbanization trends. Added to large regional differentials in rates of fertility and mor-

Table VIII–5. Regional Differentials in Urban Growth Rates, 1950–70 (average annual percentage rate)

Region	(N)	1950/60	1960/70
NORTH			
a) Metropolitan-center-	(1)	4.5	4.9
periphery		7.1	4.1
b) 250,000+	(1)	5.3	6.4
c) 100–249,000	(0)	–	–
d) 20–99,000	(5)	7.8	7.4
e) Total	(7)	5.2	5.7
NORTHEAST			
a) Metropolitan-center-	(3)	5.2	4.3
periphery		5.7	9.3
b) 250,000+	(2)	4.6	5.1
c) 100–249,000	(9)	5.2	4.8
d) 20–99,000	(40)	5.4	5.1
e) Total	(54)	5.2	5.0
SOUTHEAST			
a) Metropolitan-center-[a]	(1)	6.9	6.4
periphery		5.4	9.2
b) 250,000+	(3)	5.6	5.6
c) 100–249,000	(14)	6.1	5.3
d) 20–99,000	(105)	5.9	4.6
e) Total[b]	(135)	5.2	5.5
SOUTH			
a) Metropolitan-center-	(2)	6.6	3.9
periphery		3.3	15.9
b) 250,000+	(1)	3.7	2.2
c) 100–249,000	(6)	7.3	6.8
d) 20–99,000	(39)	6.2	5.0
e) Total	(48)	6.1	5.6
CENTRAL-WEST			
a) Metropolitan	(0)	–	–
b) 250,000+	(2)	21.1	12.8
c) 100–249,000	(1)	7.2	7.4
d) 20–99,000	(9)	8.2	7.3
e) Total	(12)	12.7	10.4

[a]Excluding Rio de Janeiro and São Paulo.
[b]Including Rio de Janeiro and São Paulo.
Sources: Same as Table VIII–3.

tality for both urban and rural areas is a rather complex pattern of interregional and rural-urban migration flows. The usual demographic "balancing equation" approach to migration measurement (net migration = total increase − fertility + mortality), with "typical" magnitudes for rural and urban vital data to substitute the missing data, must be employed with great caution. Costa (1976a) has decomposed urban and rural population increases in 1960–70 into the shares contributed by migration and natural increase, using indirect measures of fertility and mortality derived from census data. His estimates of overall rural-urban migration in the decade is 9.36 million, which amounts to 46 percent of Brazil's 20.2 million increase in the urban population in the

Table VIII-6. Distribution of Urban Population between Regions by Size Category, 1950-70 (percentages)

	1950	1960	1970
Large cities (250,000+ and metropolitan)			
North	3.9	3.7	3.6
Northeast	17.0	17.1	16.0
Southeast	70.0	68.2	67.8
South	8.6	9.2	9.0
Central-West	0.5	1.8	3.5
Small and medium-sized cities (20,000 to 249,000)			
North	1.1	1.3	1.7
Northeast	25.9	24.3	23.8
Southeast	52.5	52.5	51.0
South	17.4	18.4	19.2
Central-West	2.9	3.5	4.3
Total city (20,000+)			
North	3.0	2.9	3.0
Northeast	19.8	19.5	18.5
Southeast	64.5	63.0	62.5
South	11.5	12.2	12.2
Central-West	1.2	2.4	3.8
Total population			
North	3.6	3.7	3.9
Northeast	34.6	31.5	30.2
Southeast	43.4	43.8	42.8
South	15.1	16.8	17.7
Central-West	3.3	4.2	5.4

Note: Percentages sum vertically to 100 in each category.
Sources: Same as Table VIII-3.

decade. At the state level, the contribution of migration is greater in such states as São Paulo (64 percent), where natural increase is lower. According to Costa's estimates, the Southeast accounted for nearly two-thirds of all net migration to urban areas in the decade. At the same time, the net out-migration from the region's rural areas amounted to 90 percent of the urban inflow. The balancing equation approach does not provide enough information to determine the extent to which these net gains and losses represent intraregional versus interregional migration flows. Other Brazilian statisticians have prepared estimates of the share of migration in total population growth for the nine metropolitan regions in 1960-70 (Brazil, Ministério do Interior, 1976).[4] Their estimates range from 34 percent for the migration share in Belém (which had low migration combined with higher natural increase) to 81 percent in

[4]Estimates of the relative contribution of migration to total metropolitan area population increase are: Belém 34.8 percent; Fortaleza 49.6 percent; Recife 62.6 percent; Salvador 45.0 percent; Belo Horizonte 66.9 percent; Rio de Janeiro 67 percent; São Paulo 68.5 percent; Curitiba 70.9 percent; and Porto Alegre 81.3 percent (Brazil, Ministério do Interior, 1976: 69).

Porto Alegre (a contrasting case of higher migration and low natural increase). The author's own estimates from survey data for Belo Horizonte yielded a migration share of 59 percent for 1960–70, compared with 67 percent reported above (Coelho and Merrick 1975). This difference occurs because intrametropolitan area migrants were included in the former estimates, but excluded in the latter. Additional evidence suggests that the migration share has been declining in Rio de Janeiro (Weller et al. 1971) and São Paulo (Shaefer and Spindel 1976).

In assessing these trends, it is important to note an indirect effect of migration on city growth, e.g., the effect of migrant natural increase. Migrants have added to the weight of higher fertility groups in urban populations, and the reproductive force of the migrants is an increasingly important factor in overall urban growth. When the indirect effect of migration was taken into account in the Belo Horizonte data, for example, the share of growth attributable to migration increased to 82 percent and is expected to rise to 85 percent in 1970–80.[5]

Recent censuses have included a number of questions aimed at specifying the direction and timing of interregional migration flows, as well as characteristics of migrants. The Brazilian census defines as a migrant anyone not residing in the municipality of his/her birth at the time of the census. Data have been tabulated both for individuals residing in places other than their native municipality and for those whose present residence is in a different state from the one in which the individual was born. Questions on length of residence at the present residence and (officially defined) rural or urban place of previous residence help to determine the nature and volume of more recent flows. However, there remains a fundamental difficulty with migration measures derived from these data in that return-migration and intervening steps in individual migration experience are overlooked. Over time those who appear as "migrants" in the data are, in fact, those who succeeded in assimilating to the destination environment, with those who failed having moved on or returned to their place of origin. Characteristics of migrants and migrant-native differentials will be discussed in the next chapter.

Here we will concentrate on the direction and timing of flows. Table VIII–7 summarizes some of the major dimensions of recent migration at the national level. The table shows the distribution of migrants by rural or urban place of

[5]Belo Horizonte's population increase in 1960–70 can be decomposed as follows:

	Absolute	Percent
1) Net migration	420,280	58.7
2) Natural increase of migrants	167,526	23.4
3) Natural increase of natives	127,534	17.9
4) Total	715,340	100.0

(Coelho and Merrick 1975: 217)

Table VIII-7. Distribution of Migrants by Origin-Destination and Duration and Residence, 1970 Brazilian Census Data

I

Distribution by previous/present residence	A. Interstate					B. Intermunicipality				
		(Duration of residence—years)					(Duration of residence—years)			
	Total	0–1	1–5	6–10	11+	Total	0–1	1–5	6–10	11+
Urban/urban	50.5	53.6	50.6	48.2	50.7	50.4	48.6	48.1	49.1	53.0
Rural/urban	17.4	16.5	15.4	16.3	18.8	17.9	15.6	16.3	18.0	19.7
Urban/rural	5.6	8.3	7.0	5.4	4.8	6.0	9.3	7.4	5.5	4.4
Rural/rural	26.5	21.6	27.0	30.1	25.7	25.7	26.5	28.2	27.4	22.9
Total	100.0	100.0	100.0	100.0	100.0	100.0	100.0	100.0	100.0	100.0

II

Distribution by previous/present residence	A. Interstate					B. Intermunicipality				
		(Duration of residence—years)					(Duration of residence—years)			
	Total	0–1	1–5	6–10	11+	Total	0–1	1–5	6–10	11+
Urban/urban	100.0	8.2	21.9	17.3	52.6	100.0	11.2	27.3	18.1	43.4
Rural/urban	100.0	7.3	19.4	16.9	56.4	100.0	10.1	26.0	18.6	45.3
Urban/rural	100.0	11.4	27.1	17.4	44.1	100.0	18.1	34.9	16.7	30.3
Rural/rural	100.0	6.3	22.2	20.6	50.9	100.0	12.0	31.4	19.8	36.7
Total	100.0	7.7	21.9	18.1	52.3	100.0	11.7	28.5	18.5	41.3

III

Ratio of Intermunicipality/Interstate

Urban/urban	Total	0–1	1–5	6–10	11+
Urban/urban	2.09	2.87	3.23	2.19	1.73
Rural/urban	2.16	2.99	2.90	2.38	1.73
Urban/rural	2.24	3.55	2.88	2.15	1.54
Rural/rural	2.03	3.88	2.87	1.96	1.47
Total	2.10	3.16	2.74	2.15	1.65

Source: Fundação IBGE, Censo Demográfico 1970, Tables 34 and 35.

most recent residence and place of current (1970) residence. Four categories (urban/urban, etc.) represent the four flows identifiable in the data. Migrants can be defined either as those residing in a different state from the one of birth (part A) or in a different municipality (part B). Of the 93 million total population in 1970, 14.4 million (15.5 percent) were residing in a different state, and 30.3 million (32.5 percent) in a different municipality. Migrants are also distributed by duration of present residence; less than one year, 1 to 5 years, 6 to 10 years, and 11 or more years. A separate category for migrants of less than one-year residence is given, because it is a relatively large group and probably represents a higher proportion of temporary and/or returning migrants.

The distribution of migrants is presented in two ways: a distribution of migrants in each duration group by flow category (I) and a distribution in each flow category by duration of residence (II). The ratio of intermunicipality migrants to interstate migrants in each group is also shown (III). This table permits us to make some rough comparisons of the composition of migration flows between the 1950s and the 1960s. Starting with the distribution of migrants by flow category in part I, we see that about one-half of both interstate and intermunicipality migrants are classed as "urban-urban." From this we can determine possible changes in composition over time. Setting aside the 0 to 1 year group because of temporary migrants, we find that there is no clear trend if we compare the 1- to 5- and 6- to 10-year classes to the 11 and more years of residence categories for the interstate migrants. However, there is a change in the case of intermunicipality migrants. For the "urban-urban" flow category the 11 years and over group is larger (53 percent) than the shorter duration groups (48 percent), suggesting that this type of migration was relatively less important in the 1960s than it was in the 1950s.

This appears to be related to the increase over time in the share of the "urban-rural" and "rural-rural" groups, since they weigh more heavily in shorter duration categories. The increase in the "urban-rural" flow over time also shows up at the state level, but not the "rural-rural." This raises a question as to the nature of these increased flows to rural destinations. Are they movements to new settlement regions, temporary migration of agricultural workers, resettlement of older areas, or part of the shift to the peripheral (but not yet urbanized) parts of the metropolitan regions?

State-by-state analysis of the destinations of urban-rural and rural-rural migrants suggests that a substantial part of it is either temporary or permanent migration to or within the new settlement areas (Goiás, Mato Grosso, Paraná, and the Northern region). In intermunicipality data, 41 percent of rural destinations for Brazil as a whole are in these areas. São Paulo and Minas Gerais account for another 22 percent. Resettlement and/or temporary migration may also be a factor in these states.

Less than 18 percent of migrants at either the state or municipality level are reported as "rural-urban," and the distributions suggest a declining trend at both levels. The most important explaining factor in this is that the "origin" is the place of *last* residence, which may well have been an urban *step* in an individual's rural-urban move. Brazil's broad administrative definition of an urban place, which would give added weight to smaller places in the step-migration process, contributes to this.

Examination of the distribution of migrants by duration of residence in part II of the table suggests caution in interpreting the time trend. The less-than-one-year group is quite large relative to the 1–5 category, suggesting that temporary migrants weigh heavily in the totals. The 6 to 10 group is relatively low in comparison with others. It is true that 1960–64 was a period of recession in Brazil (especially in such sectors as construction, which are important sources of migrant employment), but it is also possible that response errors in the duration questions are biased toward either recent (less than 5 years) or long-term (11+ years) residence categories at the expense of the 6–10 group.

Comparison of the time patterns in interstate and intermunicipality data suggests that migration flows since 1960 have been of shorter distance than those before, since the 11+ years category is lower in the intermunicipality data. A similar conclusion is drawn from the ratios of intermunicipality to interstate flows in part III of the table. The tendency is more accentuated with respect to rural destinations. Da Mata (1973) reached a similar conclusion with respect to *intra-* vs. *inter*regional flows in an analysis of the 1970 data. However, we must be cautious in this interpretation, because of the nature of the data. Both stage migration and temporary (and return-) migration could be of shorter distance, and the differential time pattern in the state vs. county results could be the result of the municipality data picking up a larger relative amount of these types of migrants in relation to the total flows recorded for them.

Data on the duration of residence of migrants in the nine metropolitan areas are provided in the Interior Ministry's national migration study report (Brazil, Ministério do Interior, 1976). Again the definition of migration in the census complicates interpretation of the data, since intermunicipality moves within the metropolitan region are included among migration totals reported there. Table VIII–8 presents a distribution of each metropolitan region's population into natives and nonnatives (remembering that the proportion includes those who moved within the metropolitan region), and the distribution of nonnatives by duration of residence. Also shown are the proportions of nonnatives residing in the periphery of each metropolitan region and an index showing how their proportion relates to the share of the periphery in overall populations. Nonnatives account for about one-half of the population of most metropolitan areas, with the proportion falling as low as 22 percent in Belém, and reaching 53 percent in São Paulo. The proportions of nonnatives in the adult (and therefore, working, population) are higher, since migrants generally arrive as adults and the children of migrants (born after arrival) count as natives.

Table VIII-8. Distribution of Migrants to Metropolitan Areas by Duration of Residence

| | Native | Nonnative | Total | Percentage distribution | | | | Periphery share | |
| | | | | Nonnative by duration of residence (yrs.) | | | | | |
				0–1	1–5	6–10	11+	%	Index[a]
Belém	78.2	21.8	100.0	11.2	28.8	17.3	42.7	5.9	1.7
Fortaleza	48.8	51.2	100.0	13.5	26.8	16.5	43.2	8.0	0.6
Recife	51.5	48.5	100.0	12.5	29.6	15.4	42.5	47.5	1.2
Salvador	70.5	29.5	100.0	12.1	26.9	16.2	44.8	11.4	0.9
Belo Horizonte	49.6	50.4	100.0	9.6	30.1	19.1	41.2	22.9	1.0
Rio de Janeiro	54.7	45.3	100.0	8.8	22.3	15.7	53.2	43.8	1.1
São Paulo	47.1	52.9	100.0	9.7	25.7	18.5	46.1	34.0	1.2
Curitiba	59.0	41.0	100.0	13.5	33.2	16.9	37.4	15.4	0.6
Porto Alegre	51.0	49.0	100.0	10.1	39.7	17.3	32.9	47.0	1.1

[a]Equal to one when peripheral share of nonnative is equal to peripheral share of population; more or less than one when peripheral share is more or less than population share.

Source: Brazil, Ministério do Interior (1976: 69).

The distribution of migrants by duration of residence shows Rio de Janeiro with the highest proportion (53 percent) of longer-term residents, followed by São Paulo. Porto Alegre and Curitiba have the highest proportions of more recent migrants, followed by Belo Horizonte and Recife. Very recent migrants (less-than-one-year residents) are lower in the three Southeastern metropolitan regions, however, the significance of this is difficult to determine. It is possible that the Southeast represents a more "final" destination, and that the temporary and/or stage-migration indicated by this duration category is lower in the Southeast.

There is considerable variation in the percentage of each metropolitan area's nonnatives who reside in their peripheral municipalities. In part, this reflects the number of municipalities included in the metropolitan area definition, which in turn reflects the degree to which each region has undergone the "metropolitanization" process (i.e., shifts of population, economic and other urban activities from the core municipality to outlying areas). Belém shows the lowest share of migrants in the periphery, and Recife, Rio de Janeiro, and Porto Alegre are highest. However, a better guide as to the extent to which a region's migration streams are becoming periphery-oriented is the ratio of the periphery migrant share to the periphery share in total population. Belém has a relatively small share of migrants in the periphery, but this well exceeds its peripheral population and suggests that migration is contributing substantially to the peripheral growth. This is also true of Recife and Rio de Janeiro, and much less so in Fortaleza and Curitiba. Thus, while there are a number of common growth patterns in the recent expansion of the metropolitan area populations, there are also a number of features that are specific to each metropolitan area case.

Balance between Industrial Employment and Urban Growth

Earlier in this chapter it was observed that Brazil's urban development, in constrast with other Latin American countries, has not been characterized by increased primacy in the distribution of population by city size. This is less true in relation to the growth of industrial activity, an important concomitant of urban population growth. The equilibrium between population growth and industrial employment has been a cause of increasing concern, because the capacity to support added population, directly through jobs as well as in providing the needed infrastructure from tax revenues, depends heavily on the industrial sector. Of further concern are the substantial regional imbalances in distribution of urban population and economic activity. The traditional dominance of the Southeast, especially São Paulo and Rio de Janeiro, has increased in this period and has created problems both for these areas and for regions like the Northeast, which have fallen behind in the expansion.

Patterns of Concentration in Industrial Employment

The tendency toward spatial concentration of industry in Brazil dates back to the earliest phases of industrialization at the beginning of this century. By 1950, 39 percent of all Brazilian industrial employment was located in the state of São Paulo.[6] The Rio de Janeiro-São Paulo axis accounted for 57 percent, and an additional 24 percent was located in three other states—Minas Gerais, Rio Grande do Sul, and Pernambuco—giving a six-state total of 81 percent. A recent study of trends in industrial concentration by Haddad (1975) reveals an increase in this concentration between 1950 and 1960. São Paulo alone accounted for 66.4 percent of new industrial employment in that decade, and the other five states listed above accounted for an additional 20 percent, thus leaving only 15 percent for the remaining 17 states. Haddad's data also show a leveling off of the concentration process in 1960–70. The 1970 share of the Rio de Janeiro-São Paulo axis was 61.6 percent, down just a little from its peak level of 62.2 percent in 1960.[7]

The bulk of the industrial activity reported for the state of São Paulo is located in the metropolitan area of the city of São Paulo. Unlike Rio de Janeiro, which was until recently a separate state, data for the São Paulo metropolitan area must be reconstructed from municipality data. Since this is a progressively more difficult task with each earlier census, because of municipality boundary changes, industrial census data for São Paulo, as well as other metropolitan areas and cities of 20,000 or more, could be reassembled only for 1960 and 1970. Table VIII–9 shows the distribution of industrial census data on employment, salaries, and value added for 1960 and 1970 by the city-size categories used in the previous section for all cities and agglomerations of 20,000 or more. Population distributions are also shown for comparative purposes.

To give some notion of the weight of the Rio de Janeiro and São Paulo metropolitan areas in the shares of total employment relative to the entire Rio-São Paulo axis (consisting of the states of Rio de Janeiro, Guanabara, and São Paulo), it is useful to compare the share of their metropolitan areas (46 percent) in total industrial employment to the share of the entire axis (62 percent), which suggests that the former represent about two-thirds of employment in the axis. Further, they accounted for 56 percent of industrial employment in cities of 20,000 or more. (Industrial employment in cities of

---

[6]According to economic census data for the industrial sector. As indicated in Chapter VI and discussed further in Chapter IX, economic censuses report a smaller number of workers than the population census, since they are based on reports of establishments rather than households. Since this section compares regional distribution of employment to salaries and value-added, which are also recorded on an establishment basis, the economic census is utilized.

[7]For a survey of recent work on regional inequality, see Andrade (1977).

Table VIII-9. Distribution of Industrial Sector Employment, Salaries, and Value-added by City Size, 1960–70

| | 1960 Percentage shares in | | | | 1970 Percentage shares in | | | |
| | Industrial sector | | | | Industrial sector | | | |
	Popula-tion	Employ-ment	Salaries	Value-added	Popula-tion	Employ-ment	Salaries	Value-added
Rio de Janeiro and São Paulo								
a) Center	29.8	43.6	49.3	45.5	26.7	38.2	43.2	40.9
b) Periphery	8.9	12.3	14.3	14.8	12.1	14.7	19.3	20.0
c) Total	38.7	55.9	63.6	60.3	38.8	52.9	62.5	60.9
Regional metropolitan areas								
a) Center	17.8	8.8	7.0	6.6	16.4	8.8	6.5	6.3
b) Periphery	2.4	4.4	3.5	3.6	4.1	5.5	4.6	5.0
c) Total	20.3	13.2	10.5	10.2	20.5	14.3	11.1	11.3
Remaining cities 250,000 and over, 1970	7.8	3.9	3.5	6.4	8.7	4.5	4.4	5.0
Medium cities 100,000 to 249,000, 1970	11.8	10.4	8.8	9.9	11.7	9.4	8.7	9.0
Small cities (a) 50,000 to 99,000, 1970	8.2	6.2	4.6	4.7	7.8	6.3	4.5	4.8
Small cities (b) 20,000 to 49,000, 1970	13.2	10.4	9.0	8.5	12.5	12.6	8.8	9.0
Total city population	100.0	100.0	100.0	100.0	100.0	100.0	100.0	100.0

Source: Industrial Censuses of 1960 and 1970, state volumes.

20,000+ was 82 percent of overall industrial employment in 1960 and 84 percent in 1970).

Table VIII–9 shows a slight decline (three percentage points) in the share of industrial employment in the metropolitan areas of Rio de Janeiro and São Paulo from 1960 to 1970. But their share in total salaries declined less (about one percentage point), value-added increased slightly, and their population shares remained virtually unchanged. The distribution of industrial activity within these metropolitan regions shifted from the central municipality to the peripheries, parallelling population trends, but at a slower pace.

Even with these declines, Rio de Janeiro and São Paulo still show nearly 40 percent greater shares in industrial employment than in population—indicating a much higher level of primacy in industrial activity than in population. Greater asymmetry is also observed in salaries and value-added, with the share of the latter being 57 percent greater than for population.

There is a corresponding deficit in the balance between industrial activity and population in other city-size categories. In 1960, employment was 35 percent lower than the population share in regional metropolitan areas and nearly 50 percent lower in other large cities. It should be noted that Brasilia, with relatively little industrial employment, weighs heavily in the latter class. The relative deficit was less in smaller cities. Salaries and value-added were even more unequally distributed, reflecting the added productivity advantage of Rio de Janeiro and São Paulo. The overall trend for 1960–70 appears to have been toward a slightly better balance between employment and population. The improvement is especially marked in smaller cities, and the 20,000 to 49,000 class achieved a one-to-one ratio in 1970.

Table VIII–10 reveals some important regional variation in these patterns. The percentage share of population and employment in each size category is given, by region for 1960 and 1970. Also shown in the ratio ($\times$ 100) of the share in employment to the share in population for each category. There is a clear break between the South and Southeast, with larger relative shares of employment relative to population and the North, Northeast, and Central-West, with lower ones. The regional concentration appears to have remained stable or increased slightly between 1960 and 1970, with relative shares for the Southeast declining from 124 to 120, and for the South rising from 97 to 121. This has occurred despite a decline in the very high concentration in the peripheral municipalities of the metropolitan areas of these regions and without substantial increases in the central municipalities of metropolitan area. Smaller cities (below 100,000) accounted for the gains in the South and Southeast. Middle-sized cities also gained in the South, but not in the Southeast.

The share of industrial employment in the Northeast declined even more than its share in population, resulting in a greater imbalance in relative shares in 1970 than in 1960. Smaller cities and the peripheral municipalities of the metropolitan areas suffered the greatest declines in relative shares. In con-

Table VIII-10. Distribution of Employment and Population by City Size and Region, 1960 and 1970

	1960 Percentage[a] of: Pop. (1)	Emplt. (2)	Ratio (x100) (2)/(1) (3)	1970 Percentage of: Pop. (4)	Emplt. (5)	Ratio (x100) (5)/(4) (6)
NORTH						
a) Metropolitan-center-	1.70	0.47	27	1.60	0.59	37
periphery	0.01	0.03	300	0.01	0.03	300
b) 250,000	0.73	0.27	37	0.79	0.39	49
c) 100,000	–	–	–	–	–	–
d) 20,000	0.44	0.22	50	0.54	0.19	35
e) Total	2.88	0.99	34	2.94	1.20	41
NORTHEAST						
a) Metropolitan-center-	8.62	3.29	38	7.68	3.24	42
periphery	1.23	1.11	90	1.74	1.29	74
b) 250,000	1.55	0.44	28	1.48	0.51	34
c) 100,000	4.23	1.57	37	3.94	1.28	33
d) 20,000	3.87	1.89	49	3.69	1.28	35
e) Total	19.50	8.30	43	18.53	7.59	41
SOUTHEAST						
a) Metropolitan-center-	3.01	1.33	44	3.25	1.42	44
periphery	0.52	1.33	256	.73	1.27	174
b) 250,000	3.34	2.28	68	3.35	2.59	77
c) 100,000	5.57	7.22	130	5.44	6.04	111
d) 20,000	11.87	10.33	87	10.88	11.32	104
e) Total[b]	63.02	78.40	124	62.52	75.33	120
SOUTH						
a) Metropolitan-center-	4.50	3.74	83	3.84	3.51	91
periphery	0.63	1.90	302	1.59	2.90	182
b) 250,000	0.95	0.86	91	0.69	0.57	83
c) 100,000	1.76	1.54	88	1.98	1.99	100
d) 20,000	4.36	3.82	88	4.15	5.79	140
e) Total	12.20	11.86	97	12.25	14.76	121
CENTRAL-WEST						
a) 250,000	1.23	0.08	6	2.38	0.45	19
b) 100,000	0.29	0.09	31	0.35	0.10	29
c) 20,000	0.88	0.28	32	1.03	0.36	35
d) Total	2.40	0.44	18	3.76	0.91	24

[a]Total urban (20,000 and over) equals 100 percent.
[b]Rio de Janeiro and São Paulo included total, but not in a.
Source: Same as for Table VIII-9.

trast, cities in the new settlement regions, the North and Central-West, show improved relative positions.

Except for cities on the frontier, which are relatively few in number, most of the deconcentration of industrial employment away from Rio de Janeiro and São Paulo proper thus appears to have been in the direction of the smaller cities in the South and Southeast. These cities may indeed be offering increasingly attractive cost advantages in comparison with Rio de Janeiro and São Paulo, because of their proximity and lower land values and labor costs.[8]

[8]An exploratory study of the relation between city size and the costs of production suggested that medium-sized cities (200,000–500,000) enjoyed such advantages (Boisier et al. 1973: 112).

Indeed, there is very little consistency between the main changes in the distribution of industrial employment by region and city size and population shifts. In the peripheral municipalities of the metropolitan areas, population shares increased more substantially than industrial employment, while in smaller cities of the Southeast there was a declining population share corresponding to small increase in the share of industrial employment. These trends suggest that migratory redistribution of population, insofar as it was responsive to differential employment opportunities, was clearly linked to employment outside of the more established industrial establishments that are represented in the industrial census data. The next chapter will examine the relation between these migration flows and urban employment in greater detail.

Implications for Demand and Supply of Urban Services

Imbalances between industrial employment and population have disturbing implications in regard to the provision of adequate urban services for the increased number of urban residents. In the Brazilian fiscal system the main source of tax revenues for local governments is a levy on value added in industrial production (Araújo 1974). Hence the gap between population growth and the growth of industrial employment and output has had a double effect. Urban population growth creates increased demand for services at the same time that the imbalance between population and industrial activity makes it increasingly difficult to generate the revenue needed to pay for them.

Table VIII–11 is a compilation of indices relating to the availability of urban services. Shown in the table are the average percentages of households reported in the 1970 census to have access to public water supply and electric power, as residing in what were classed as "durable" dwellings, and having a television set. The latter is included as an additional measure of modernization, in that is is closely related to the degree in which communities are exposed to a wider range of concerns and aware of goods available in national and even international markets. These averages are broken down by region and city-size class.

The highest proportions of households served by water and electricity are found in the larger cities in the South and Southeast. The noticeable exceptions are the peripheral municipalities of the metropolitan areas. The North and Northeast are lowest on these scales, with the small cities and peripheries of their metropolitan areas being the least served. The pattern is similar in housing durability and ownership of televisions, except that the small-city vs. large-city differential is somewhat more marked and the center city vs. periphery gap is less in the metropolitan areas. In terms of potential political tension, the juxtaposition of differential exposure to mass media with poor public services suggests that the atmosphere might be more explosive in the metropolitan area peripheries (especially in the Southeast) and less so in the

Table VIII-11. Percentages of Households with Water and Electricity Connections, Durable Dwellings, and TV, by Region and City Size, 1970

Region/city/group	Water connections	Electricity connections	Durability of dwellings	TV owners
NORTH				
a) Metropolitan-center-	55.8	77.6	69.0	36.3
periphery	5.9	29.6	88.6	8.6
b) 250,000	48.9	62.1	60.7	21.5
c) 100,000	—	—	—	—
d) 20,000	14.4	25.6	50.5	1.7
e) Total	22.8	37.2	58.9	9.4
NORTHEAST				
a) Metropolitan-center-	40.4	74.6	74.5	33.9
periphery	11.6	37.5	38.1	10.4
b) 250,000	49.3	38.6	74.8	15.3
c) 100,000	34.3	46.9	70.1	13.8
d) 20,000	18.9	33.0	67.5	5.2
e) Total	13.2	37.8	68.0	8.7
SOUTHEAST				
a) Metropolitan-center	65.0	91.8	91.9	64.4
periphery	43.5	74.8	88.5	41.8
b) 250,000	79.8	85.1	83.9	54.9
c) 100,000	64.5	78.9	98.8	44.0
d) 20,000	57.2	68.3	87.6	31.1
e) Total	58.4	70.5	88.0	34.1
SOUTH				
a) Metropolitan-center-	65.5	90.5	90.4	61.0
periphery	21.5	61.3	87.5	27.4
b) 250,000	67.3	65.2	85.2	30.9
c) 100,000	56.2	75.4	84.3	36.1
d) 20,000	33.5	54.5	79.9	19.4
e) Total	37.7	58.9	81.3	23.6
CENTRAL-WEST				
a) 250,000	54.3	75.6	78.1	45.1
b) 100,000	39.8	50.9	82.8	27.2
c) 20,000	31.8	36.4	64.2	10.3
d) Total	36.2	44.2	68.1	17.5
TOTAL	44.3	58.7	80.4	80.4

Source: Population censuses, 1960 and 1970.

small cities, relative to the comparative positions of these areas on service delivery alone.[9]

The relation between urban infrastructure and fiscal capacity is illustrated by the data in Table VIII-12 for the nine metropolitan areas, for which the indices reported in Table VIII-11 are given separately for central and peripheral municipalities, along with indices of industrial output per capita (average for all nine = 100) in 1950 and 1960. The table reveals considerable disparity between metropolitan areas as well as between central and peripheral municipalities within them. A further problem, not indicated by the table,

[9]Popular reaction to occasional breakdowns in public transportation and flooding in Rio de Janeiro and São Paulo, as well as the governments reaction to it, are illustrative. For more detail, see Gall (1976).

Table VIII-12. Water, Electricity, Durability, TV, and Industrial Indices for Metropolitan
Areas, 1970 (average for cities of 20,000 and over = 100)

	Water connections	Electricity connections	Durability of dwellings	TV owners	Value-added per capita	
					1960	1970
SOUTHEAST						
São Paulo						
a) center	64.2	95.7	94.6	72.0	149	161
b) periphery	44.3	86.5	88.9	57.1	260	264
Rio de Janeiro						
a) center	82.8	95.1	90.1	70.7	52	77
b) periphery	46.5	78.7	88.0	43.3	35	39
Belo Horizonte						
a) center	47.9	84.5	91.0	50.4	22	25
b) periphery	39.7	59.0	90.5	25.1	152	165
SOUTH						
Porto Alegre						
a) center	83.4	90.7	89.0	63.0	47	64
b) periphery	34.1	77.8	90.1	43.9	177	116
Curitiba						
a) center	47.6	90.2	91.8	59.1	35	49
b) periphery	8.6	44.8	84.8	19.9	64	100
NORTHEAST						
Recife						
a) center	53.1	85.6	74.0	37.1	31	33
b) periphery	22.5	57.2	65.8	15.6	34	32
Salvador						
a) center	54.7	79.2	76.3	37.6	16	18
b) periphery	6.1	35.9	62.4	10.9	450	329
Fortaleza						
a) center	13.4	58.9	73.3	27.1	8	19
b) periphery	6.4	19.5	45.9	4.7	8	31
NORTH						
Belém						
a) center	55.8	77.6	69.0	36.3	14	16
b) periphery	5.9	29.6	88.6	8.6	80	148

Sources: Same as Table VIII–11.

is imbalance among municipalities in the periphery. For example, within the
metropolitan region of São Paulo industrial activity is concentrated in a half
dozen municipalities that are very well off in terms of tax revenues and have
relatively adequate urban infrastructure, while the working population is
spread over the remaining thirty, which are much worse off.[10]

The problem differs in Rio de Janeiro, where industrial activity is more concentrated in the municipality of the capital, with almost all of the peripheral
areas worse off in terms of taxing power and urban infrastructure. The average
level of urban services in the peripheries of Rio de Janeiro and São Paulo do
not appear to be greatly different. However, value-added data show more
clearly that for São Paulo the problem is balance between municipalities

[10]For futher discussion, see Araújo (1974), who provides detailed breakdowns of the
population, infrastructure capacity, and tax structure of municipalities within the metropolitan
areas of Rio de Janeiro and São Paulo.

within the periphery, whereas for Rio de Janeiro it is a question of center-periphery balance. Belo Horizonte and Porto Alegre also contrast with Rio de Janeiro; their peripheral municipalities having higher value-added per capita. But the low level of urban services in their peripheries suggests imbalances between the location of industrial activity and worker residences. Salvador presents an extreme case of such an imbalance, the weight of which explains the unexpectedly high value-added ratio for the Northeast as a whole. Located in the Salvador metropolitan area is the Landulfo Alves oil refinery complex (in the municipality São Francisco do Conde). This is a highly capital-intensive activity and employs relatively few workers. Other municipalities in the environs of Salvador had little or no industrial value-added in 1969 nor levels of infrastructure to show for it.

Two points stand out in these comparisons of demographic and economic indices for the metropolitan areas and other city groups. One is that while some problems are common to all the groups and regions, there are also important aspects of these problems that are peculiar to each region and to each metropolitan area. Thus, the issue of center-periphery balance is more important, but different, for Rio de Janeiro and Belo Horizonte, whereas, balance among municipalities in the periphery is more an issue in São Paulo.

A second and final point is that institutional factors impinge heavily on capacities of municipalities and metropolitan areas to cope with the problems generated by their rapid population increase. It is not enough that São Paulo has the highest level of value-added per capita in urban Brazil. The way in which local government is organized and financed conditions the response to population pressures, even when resources are relatively abundant.[11]

---

[11]The National Urban Policy articulated in 1974 (Francisconi and Souza 1976) outlines the institutional changes that are being proposed to deal with this problem. The outcome will depend upon the extent to which competing interests within and outside of the existing institutional structure give way to concern for urban growth and its management.

IX Migration, Labor Absorption, and the Problem of Urban Poverty

One of the major concerns with the postwar industrial expansion in Brazil is that urban population has increased more rapidly than industrial employment. The main outline of the problem is familiar.[1] In the more dynamic branches of manufacturing, the ratio of increased employment to increased output has been low. Growing demand for durable goods, factor price policies favorable to capital, and the available technology combined to propagate a more capitalized and more productive industrial sector. This in turn generated a demand for quality, skilled workers rather than quantities of unskilled workers who migrated to the industrializing urban areas in the hope of obtaining a higher paying job. Even with limited industrial employment opportunities, larger cities remained attractive in comparison to small towns and rural areas because of their higher relative incomes, and migration has continued. Though a portion of the excess in urban labor force growth has been absorbed by the public sector and by more highly capitalized service establishments, substantial numbers sought employment and earnings in less productive activities. Profits and earnings accruing to new techniques, higher skills, and market advantages have contributed to concentration of incomes in favor of those in the capitalized sectors. The remainder, the urban working poor, appear to have gained much less from economic growth in terms of employment or earnings.

On the surface, at least, it would appear that such a characterization of postwar industrialization in Brazil is justified. While industrial production expanded at an average annual rate of nearly 8 percent during the period 1950–70, industrial employment grew at only half that rate. Using the broader population census definition, which includes construction and utilities, and which may also pick up more small-scale and traditional activities, industrial employment increased at a rate of 4.12 percent per annum between 1950 and 1970 (Table IX–1). In the more restricted (to larger establishments) industrial census data, the rate is 3.38 percent. Both measures show lower decadal rates of growth for 1950–60 compared to 1960–70, which is probably a reflec-

[1] For more detailed discussion, see Baer and Hervé (1966) and Tavares (1972).

Table IX-1. Growth of Output, Employment, and Urban Population, 1950-70 (percent)

	1950-60	1960-70	1950-70
Industrial product[a]	7.79	8.18	7.99
Industrial employment[b]			
1)	2.32	5.98	4.12
2)	2.96	3.77	3.38
Other nonagricultural product	6.75	7.90	7.35
Other nonagricultural employment	5.15	3.83	4.49
Urban population			
i) Official definition	5.42	5.05	5.23
ii) Cities of 20,000+ in 1970	5.43	5.55	5.49

[a]Data for 1949, 1959, 1970.
[b]1) Population census data (mining, manufacturing, construction, public utilities).
   2) Industrial Sector Census (manufacturing only).
   Data adjusted for census date changes.
Sources: Fundação Getúlio Vargas, *Sistema de Contas Nacionais*, Rio de Janeiro. Fundação Getúlio Vargas, 1974; Population censuses and industrial censuses, various dates.

tion of the labor-saving bias of the imported technology utilized in the import-substituting industrial expansion of that decade.[2] While both measures show an increase for 1960–70, the increase is much greater in the population census, suggesting that construction and the smaller and more traditional establishments not included in the industrial census contributed an important part of the increase. The 1950–60 pattern also contrasts with 1960–70 in that the overall rate of growth (in the population census) was lower than that in the industrial census in the 1950s and higher in the 1960s, a further indication of differences in the composition of industrial employment growth in the two decades.

Comparing industrial growth to the increase in urban population indicates that the latter was about 40 percent higher over the interval (depending on the definition of "urban" that is used in the comparison). Growth in other nonagricultural employment was closer (4.5 percent) to the increase in urban population, but not enough to compensate for the shortfall in industrial employment vis-à-vis urban growth. Thus, the overall trend was one in which employment in nonagricultural activities indeed failed to keep pace with the rapid growth of the urban population.

More and more, policy-makers are becoming concerned with, or confronted with, the equity dimension of these trends. One function of the

[2]As indicated in Chapter VII, caution is required in interpreting trends in employment by branch of activity, as reported in the population censuses, because of changes in classification schemes between censuses. As far as possible we have tried to maintain consistency between censuses by employing the corrections outlined in Chapter VII. The same caveat applies to employment reported in the sectoral economic censuses. Kahil (1965) is especially skeptical of the 1950–60 results for industry, because of a difference in the treatment of industrial workers in agricultural establishments, who were shifted from industry in 1950 to agriculture in 1960, and would have contributed to the slow growth of industry reported for 1950–60 in the industrial census data. However, the same pattern emerges in the population census data, which were not subject to this particular inconsistency, leading us to accept the differential between the two decades as a real occurrence.

migration process is that it has brought poverty from the remote countryside to the cities, where it is much more visible. But mere visibility does not offer a ready solution to the problem. Some economists caution against massive welfare schemes and "premature redistribution" on the grounds that the costs would bring growth to a halt and make matters even worse.[3] And although employment is seen as the means by which the poor should increase their share in the benefits of the growth process, there is doubt as to the feasibility of increasing employment in manufacturing and other more capitalized activities, either directly through the substitution of labor-using techniques or indirectly by redistribution of purchasing power to groups who tend to consume a larger share of the goods and services requiring labor-intensive production. The available technology limits direct labor-absorbing measures in much of manufacturing, and simulations testing the employment multiplier effect of income redistribution schemes have shown that even quite significant redistribution would have only a marginal impact.[4] Thus, the poor appear to be caught in a double bind. Direct redistribution of income is detrimental to overall economic growth, but opportunities for employment in the kinds of activities that would increase their income share are also limited by economic considerations.

The objective of this chapter is to bring the related issues of urban poverty and urban migration into sharper focus, particularly with regard to the role of migration in the larger problem of urban poverty. To what extent is migration a principal cause of urban poverty, or a complicating factor in the process of labor absorption and labor mobility? Our response puts greater emphasis on the structure of urban labor markets and policies that have affected that structure than on migration per se as the underlying causal factor in the urban poverty problem. We arrive at this conclusion by examining recent census and survey data on Brazil's urban labor force in the light of available analytical perspectives on the migration and labor-absorption processes.

Analytical Perspective on Migration and the Problem of Urban Poverty

In recent years the theoretical and empirical contributions to the understanding of the migration and urban problems in developing countries have increased considerably, and a full review, even for Latin America, would take us well beyond the scope of this study.[5] The range of opinion is also wide. Economists, in particular, have tended to take a more positive view of the contributions of the migration process, while sociologists and political scien-

---

[3] See, for example, Langoni (1973) and Simonsen (1972).

[4] See Cline (1972) for simulations on Brazil, and Morawetz (1974) for a general review of findings on this question.

[5] Morse (1965 and 1971) reviews the literature for Latin America. Another major source is the series, *Latin American Urban Research*, Sage Publications. See Rabinovitz and Trueblood (1971–76).

tists have concerned themselves more with the adverse aspects of migration. At the same time, there has been a definite tendency toward convergence in the two literatures as more empirical evidence is brought under scrutiny (Browning 1971, Cornelius 1971).

Until very recently, English-speaking economists have focused mainly on the determinants of migration. Not surprisingly, they have concluded that economic factors were dominant. Earnings differentials were seen as the main force generating migration from low-income to high-income areas. Migrant selectivity was viewed in a human-capital perspective arising from the larger lifetime earnings that accrued to younger and more educated migrants and that offset the direct and indirect costs of their migration (Sjaastad 1962, Herrick 1971).

Sociologists typically concerned themselves more with the effects than with the causes of migration. The discipline lends itself more neatly to this task by investigating such questions as social and occupational mobility, assimilation or integration into the receiving region's society, the institutional change in family, kinship and neighborhood organizations under the impact of migration, and, finally, the impact of migrants and migration on political institutions and their contribution in generating social anomie, alienation, and growing proletarianization of the labor force in the large urban centers of less developed countries. Latin American writers, in particular, have made important strides in linking sociological theory to economic history and in relating these trends to the broader structural problems that have their roots in previous periods of political and economic colonialism. Not surprisingly, many of these studies reflect a more pessimistic view of the alleged positive benefits of migration so common to economic analyses of the same phenomena. Frequently, their analyses focus on migrant/native-born socioeconomic differentials, which in many studies portray the migrant as an important contributor to the swelling rolls of the underemployed or marginalized urban labor force (Friedman and Sullivan 1974, Kowarick 1974, Hogan and Berlinck 1975). From this perspective the possibilities for significant upward and occupational mobility appear slim.

More recently, the economics literature has attempted to come to grips with the problems of migration and labor surplus in the cities of less developed countries. Wage differentials by themselves are not an adequate explanation of the problem. Starting with the important contribution of Todaro and Harris (1969, 1970), emphasis has shifted to the structure and functions of urban labor markets. Todaro first modified conventional economic models of migration responses to income differentials by substituting expected for actual urban earnings in the comparison, which had the effect of discounting the differential for the risk of unemployment. Further modifications of the Todaro–Harris model introduced a segmented urban labor market, in which workers who do not gain employment in the more capitalized establishment of the modern, formal sector are enabled to survive in the city by taking jobs in the informal labor market or urban traditional sector. In this model, migration is portrayed as a two-stage process. In the first stage, the migrant moves from the rural sector to the urban traditional sector and joins this pool of sporadically unemployed or underemployed labor. In the second stage, the migrant moves upward from the traditional to modern urban sector employment.

The relative length of time a migrant remains in the traditional or informal urban labor market (usually figured through the proxy of the changing relative size of this labor market vis-à-vis the modern or formal sector labor market) is taken as an indication of the dynamism of the urban labor market and the probability of successfully obtaining a job in modern sector employment. This, in combination with the expected (i.e., medium- to longer-run) income differential between rural and urban modern sector employment, determines the rate of migration. As modern sector jobs expand, expected rural-urban income differentials widen and employment in the traditional urban sector shrinks as these workers move into modern sector employment. Migration then "refills" the urban traditional sector, to replace those who have moved up to modern sector jobs. A decline in modern sector job openings reverses this process and induces a decline in rural-urban migration. This "equilibrium unemployment" model is a demand-oriented analysis incorporating a longer-run probabilistic permanent income differential common to standard economic theory. As such, it does add a broader conceptual framework to the earlier and simpler income differential and "selectivity" models in explaining the changing patterns of migration. In addition to broadening the more conventional two-sector model or rural-urban migration into a more realistic intersectoral mobility perspective within the urban labor market, it underscores the futility of concentrating public policy on wage and other benefits for the urban labor force alone. Policies raising urban employment or income without undertaking comparable reforms in the rural sector do not lessen the rural-urban expected income differential and thus do not reduce migration. On the contrary, they raise it. Without labor-absorbing changes in the rural areas the "urban unemployment equilibrium" remains a stable parameter.

Despite these conceptual gains, which have been amplified in the growing empirical literature on formal and informal urban labor markets in the less developed counties, the realism of these models is still questioned. Some have verified that this model consistently overestimates the true rate of stable unemployment (Fields 1972); others have shown that in the West African setting the patterns of urban migration do not conform to the probabilistic permanent income approach suggested by the model (Godfrey 1973). The inconsistencies are in part due to the very restricted assumption of labor homogeneity in the model, a necessary assumption to adopt a random upward job mobility mechanism from the informal to the formal urban sector. This ignores the well-known selectivity features of migrants and places too much emphasis on factor demand rather than factor supply as the exclusive determinant of vertical occupational mobility.

In addition, the labor homogeneity assumption characterizes the urban informal sector as an aggregate collection of underemployment, rather than recognizing the wide heterogeneity in the informal urban labor market and the possibilities for differentiated employment opportunities and mobility within this sector. In effect, an important determinant of migration may very well be the changing demand and the structural features within informal sector employment, rather than changes in the formal sector. Thus, more work is needed on the demand determinants for labor within the informal sector than has been done to date. Finally, most of the migration research building on the Todaro framework of analysis has a strong tendency to treat only one kind of developing country—the densely populated, less urbanized country in which a primate urban system stands out, separating the urban and rural labor markets. In this setting, the rural-urban dichotomy and rural-urban migration are key parameters in the analysis. Brazil, on the other hand, is a much more urbanized and industrialized society than that presumed in these models. Urban-urban migration is far more important and the formal labor market far more extensive than is found in African and Asian settings. Thus, it could be expected that the structural features of Brazilian urban labor markets would be different in some respects from the more homogenous milieu characterizing the assumptions in these models.

Migration and Urban Poverty

Before turning to the issue of urban labor markets in Brazil, it will be useful to review first the evidence on migrant assimilation and migrant mobility and the conclusions that can be drawn from this evidence regarding the contribution of migration to urban poverty.

Summary of Empirical Evidence on Migrant-Native Differentials

The earliest field work investigating migrant/native-born differentials is that undertaken by Bertram Hutchinson and associates, under the auspices of the Brazilian Center of Education Research in Rio de Janeiro and UNESCO. Sample surveys of the adult population of eight Brazilian cities were carried out in 1959 to study the process of urbanization and industrialization. The findings have been reported in a variety of later publications (Hutchinson 1962, 1963a, 1963b; Bock and Iutaka 1969). Some of the more commonly held beliefs about migration in Brazil were confirmed by these reports, such as: (1) the high percent of migrants among the adult population in these cities (75 percent); (2) the young average age of migrants (26 years); (3) the important component of rural migrants to smaller cities and the greater role of urban-origin migrants to the larger cities, such as Rio de Janeiro and São Paulo; (4) the importance of step-migration from rural to small towns and then to the larger city; and (5) the high component of female migrants to the larger cities.

In addition to these findings, Hutchinson and his colleagues concluded that migrants as a whole experienced significant upward occupational mobility after their arrival in their city of destination. Occupation mobility was inter-generational (i.e., measured by comparing the son's occupation to the father's occupation). Moreover, this pattern of occupational mobility was extremely important for the blue-collar working class and depended, to a large extent, on the expansion of new industrial jobs in the decade of the 1950s (which Hutchinson refers to as "structural mobility") rather than improved employment gained through taking over the positions of others ("exchange mobility"). Hutchinson's work basically reflects an optimistic perspective on the process of migration assimilation in Brazil, a view that was to prevail in much of the work on migrant/native-born differentials throughout the decade.

Two later studies by economists tended to reinforce this optimistic perspective. Yap, drawing upon a small sample of the then unpublished 1960 population census, investigated important socioeconomic differences between migrants and the native-born on a national and broad macroregional scale (Yap 1972, 1976). Among other findings, she reports: (1) migrants present the same educational profile as the native-born in the urban areas; (2) migrants do not have higher levels of underemployment than the urban native-born; (3) migrant worker incomes, on the average, are higher than the native-born workers from their areas of origin; and (4) when corrected for sex, age, and education, migrant worker income is roughly the same as native-born worker income in the cities of migrant destination.

Milton da Mata et al. (1974), drawing upon preliminary 1970 population census data, in general, replicated Yap's findings for the period ten years later. The economic position of migrants (in the country as a whole) was generally equal and perhaps slightly better than that of nonmigrants. Migrants also had higher educational levels, registered higher rates of labor force participation and lower rates of open unemployment and underemployment than non-migrants.

While the conclusions of these studies run counter to the more pessimistic perspective on rural-urban migration found in the traditional marginalist literature, caution is required because of some important limitations in their scope and methodology. A central issue in any discussion of migrant/non-migrant differentials is how migrant status is determined. The Brazilian census classifies as a migrant anyone who is residing in a municipality other than the one in which he was born. In 1970, this was supplemented by data on the duration of the then current residence. Adverse (to migrants) migrant/nonmigrant differentials, if they occur, tend generally to be accentuated when the duration of residence is shorter, and differences in conclusions about these differentials can often be attributed to differences in the determination of migrant status.

Timing is also an important factor in consideration of the success or failure of the migrant assimilation process. Hutchinson's work on occupational mobility came at the peak of the high-growth period in the Center-South at the end of the fifties. It is also not clear whether his intergenerational occupational comparisons catch fathers and sons at the same stage in their occupational life cycles. Moreover, there is some question whether one son's job is representative of the occupational status of all children in the family. Finally, Hutchinson's occupational hierarchy compresses all jobs into six categories. Clearly, there could be substantial wage and income differentials between migrants and nonmigrants within these strata.

Yap's work also investigates the migrant/native differential at the height of the import-substitution growth cycle. Conceivably, results could have been different during the ensuing cyclical decline in the economy in the mid-sixties. More importantly, her 1960 census sample of some 4,600 labor force participants, while perhaps representative of the country as a whole, was probably far too small to be representative of specific regions or cities within the country. Da Mata's results from the 1970 census came from a larger sample; however, his regional breakdown was still in very large units. The net result of all these findings is that within a "national" frame of reference, there are few substantial differences between migrants and the native-born (i.e., nonmigrants) or even a slightly more favorable socioeconomic position recorded for migrants. But what may be happening is that the superior socioeconomic position of the nonmigrants in the higher-income regions of the country (vis-à-vis the migrants into these regions) is offset, or more than offset, by the poverty levels of the other nonmigrants who remained in low-income regions and thus compare unfavorably to the migrants who left these areas for higher-income regions. In short, the broad, national analyses discussed above are too aggregate in scope to address the questions associated with possible migrant-oriented urban poverty within specific metropolitan areas and it is this latter perspective that is more pertinent for constructive insight into the issue of migration and urban poverty.

Migration and Urban Poverty

Recently, three major studies drawing on special tabulations of the entire 1970 census sample (Brazil, Ministerio do Interior, 1975; Costa 1975; Martine and Peliano 1977) have investigated the role of migration in the major metropolitan areas of Brazil. These studies have answered many additional questions concerning migration, urban poverty, and urban labor markets. The remainder of this section reviews these findings, primarily focusing on the last of these studies (Martine and Peliano 1977), and discusses the remaining questions growing out of these and related works.

The Martine and Peliano study derived detailed tables on migrants and nonmigrants in the urban labor force of the nine metropolitan areas of the country. Migrants in these centers (the authors follow the official IBGE definition) represented 36 percent of all the migrants recorded in the 1970 census and 62 percent of the total labor force in these nine metropolitan centers.

Most of Martine and Peliano's major findings are illustrated in data on the male labor force in three major urban centers in the Center-South (São Paulo, Rio de Janeiro, Belo Horizonte) and the three largest centers in the Northeast (Salvador, Recife, Fortaleza). Table IX–2 presents these regionalized results for selected labor force characteristics. The findings for the female labor force parallel the findings for men on these particular socioeconomic characteristics. First, it is clear that migrants comprise a substantial majority of the male labor force in the Center-South metropolises, but less so in the Northeastern region. In the Center-South they range from 60 to 70 percent and in the Northeast around 45 percent of the labor force. This is as expected, since the large urban centers in the South are the highest income urban centers in the country and draw from a national network of interregional migrants as well as from intraregional sources, whereas Northeastern centers are more dependent on intraregional migratory sources.

Second, migrants record consistently higher labor force participation rates than nonmigrants in all the metropolitan areas in Table IX–2. Moreover, these differences are substantial. Panels C and D throw additional light on this phenomenon. The sharpest cohort-specific labor force participation differentials occur in the adolescent ages, and these are shown in panel C. The overall participation differentials are largely influenced by this 15–19 cohort differential. Panel D shows that the major factor explaining the adolescent participation-rate contrasts lies in the differential access to schooling. Nonmigrant adolescents attend schools at a higher rate (of their total age cohort) than migrants. As in previous measures, this contrast stands out much more in the urban areas of the Center-South than in the Northeast. Finally, panel E points out that the native-born or nonmigrant are, on the whole, better educated than migrants (a smaller percent illiterate or with incomplete primary education). These results were also standardized for a national age distribution, thereby eliminating different age distributions as a factor in the educational differentials. Again, Martine and Peliano report that the differentials stand out more sharply in the higher-income urban centers of the Center-South. In the Northeast, these educational differentials are less signficant.

In assessing these findings, it is important to recognize that migrants are a major and, in some cases, an overwhelming component of the work force in these urban areas. Second, their higher participation rates, lower schooling and lesser educational credentials suggest that they enter the labor force at an earlier age with less credentials and probably receive initially less income than

Table IX-2. Selected Socioeconomic Differences between Migrant and Nonmigrant Labor Force for the Six Largest Metropolitan Areas in Brazil, 1970 (Census Data)

	Metropolitan areas					
Characteristics	São Paulo	Rio de Janeiro	Belo Horizonte	Salvador	Recife	Fortaleza
	(1)	(2)	(3)	(4)	(5)	(6)
A. *Total labor force*						
1. Migrants (%)	69	61	68	44	47	45
2. Nonmigrants (%)	31	39	32	56	53	55
Total number	2,214,913	1,693,848	353,883	243,941	349,048	210,639
B. *Total participation rates*						
1. Migrants	79	73	71	77	69	70
2. Nonmigrants	61	55	53	58	53	58
C. *Participation rates (15–19 yrs.)*[a]						
1. Migrants	69	50	54	51	44	43
2. Nonmigrants	56	34	44	38	34	37
D. *School attendance (15–19 yrs.)*[a]						
1. Migrants	33	37	33	40	39	47
2. Nonmigrants	37	53	42	51	45	49
E. *% illiterate & primary incomplete*[a]						
1. Migrants	39	47	36	58	60	55
2. Nonmigrants	22	35	28	53	64	51

[a]For standardized age cohorts.
Source: Martine and Peliano (1977).

nonmigrants. This latter conclusion, however, is highly conditioned by the regional variation in these differentials. Where these differentials are more marked (i.e., in the higher-income Southern cities), the likelihood of an income differential favoring nonmigrants is greatest. Conversely, in those regions where these differentials are minor (the low-income Northeast), the less likely that the native-born would enjoy any marked advantage over the migrant work force. It is precisely these income and poverty issues that are set forth in Tables IX-3 and IX-4.

The first point that emerges from Table IX-3 is the high level of urban poverty registered in most of these urban centers, when urban poverty is defined as the proportion of the work force earning less than the regional minimum wage. Between 40 to 50 percent of the male labor force in the Northeastern metropolises fall into this category. As expected, the Southern urban centers record a lower proportion, between 20 and 35 percent.

Second, the urban poverty levels for the female work force are far higher than for the males, reflecting the lower paying job characteristics of women workers in Brazil and elsewhere. About 70 percent of the female work force falls below the minimum wage in the Northeastern centers. This proportion declines somewhat in Rio de Janeiro and São Paulo . Much of this is explained by the high proportion of females employed as low-paid domestic servants, especially recent migrants. The poverty incidence here is somewhat overstated, since the census income data ignore income in kind (free lodging, food, some clothing, etc.) received by domestics.

Third, relative poverty differentials between male migrant and native-born workers are not significant either in the Northeast or the South (columns 2 and 3), when migrants are considered without regard to duration of residence. Thus, there is not a greater "relative" proportion of poverty among migrant men (as compared to nonmigrant men) in the urban areas, as marginality literature generally implies. However, there is a significant poverty differential between male nonmigrants and "recent" male migrants (columns 1 and 3), as one would expect. Further, this differential stands out much more clearly in the Southern metropolises than in the Northeastern cities. The disappearance or narrowing of this differential in many cities as we move from recent to total migrants suggests a gradual improvement in migrant income with the aging and acquisition of experience that accompanies longer residence in the city.

Finally, in contrast to male migrants, relative poverty does appear to be more common among female migrant workers than among female nonmigrant workers, both for total migrants as well as for recent migrants. Again, this differential stands out much more clearly in Rio de Janeiro and São Paulo than in the other metropolitan areas. At least in contrast with male migrants, female migrants compare less favorably to their female nonmigrant counterparts. Martine and Peliano report that control for age does not substantially change these results for either male or female migrants.

Table IX–3. Relative Distribution of Urban Poverty by Sex and Migrant Status for Selected Metropolitan Areas in Brazil, 1970 (Census Data)

	Urban poverty (percent of labor force earning less than regional minimum wage)		
	Migrants		
Metro area	0–2 years residence	Total	Nonmigrants
	(1)	(2)	(3)
A. *Men*			
1. São Paulo	31	20	19
2. Rio de Janeiro	38	27	25
3. Belo Horizonte	45	36	37
4. Salvador	47	40	40
5. Recife	40	40	42
6. Fortaleza	52	47	42
B. *Women*			
1. São Paulo	68	54	42
2. Rio de Janeiro	78	63	45
3. Belo Horizonte	81	71	68
4. Salvador	84	74	66
5. Recife	83	74	69
6. Fortaleza	86	77	76

Source: Same as Table IX–2.

Table IX–4 presents the interaction between migration and poverty from the perspective of the "absolute" contribution of migrants to the total number of workers earning less than the minimum wage. The results show a significant proportion of migrants earning less than the minimum wage in the three Southern cities and half, or slightly less than half, doing so in the Northeastern cities. Of importance here is to relate this finding to their overall participation in the labor force, as is done in panel C. In this perspective, it can be seen that, with the exception of female migrants in Rio de Janeiro and São Paulo, neither male nor female migrants make up a signficantly greater proportion of poverty-level workers than their share in the total labor force itself. Still the large percent of migrant labor among these poverty-level workers in the Southern metropolises no doubt goes far to explain the common image that migrants in these centers are poor or underemployed.

Finally, it is useful to contrast patterns of income distribution among migrants and nonmigrants. The major findings for all centers can be summarized by looking at the income profile in the two largest national urban centers in the Center-South and the two major metropolitan centers in the Northeast, in Table IX–5. Male migrants, in terms of income level, are clearly at a disadvantage vis-à-vis nonmigrants in São Pauló. In Rio de Janeiro, only recent male migrants would appear to be seriously disadvantaged with respect to nonmigrants. Migrants as a whole reflect a similar income profile to that of nonmigrants. The Northeastern urban centers, in contrast, present a striking picture of a migrant advantage over nonmigrants. In Recife, this even reaches a

Table IX-4. Contribution of Migrant and Nonmigrant Labor Force to Total Urban Poverty by Sex for Selected Metropolitan Areas in Brazil, 1970 (Census Data)

Sex & migrant status	Metropolitan areas					
	São Paulo	Rio de Janeiro	Belo Horizonte	Salvador	Recife	Fortaleza
A. *Male labor force*[a]	(1)	(2)	(3)	(4)	(5)	(6)
1. Migrants	70	63	68	43	46	48
2. Nonmigrants	30	37	32	56	54	52
B. *Female labor force*[a]						
1. Migrants	72	69	72	53	54	50
2. Nonmigrants	28	31	28	47	47	50
C. *Poverty%/labor force%*						
1. Male migrant workers	1.01	1.03	1.00	.98	.98	1.07
2. Female migrant workers	1.09	1.13	1.01	1.06	1.04	1.00

[a]Distributions (which sum vertically) of the poverty groups between migrants and nonmigrants.
Source: Same as Table IX-2.

point at which recent migrants (usually the most disadvantaged) enjoy an income advantage over nonmigrants. Correcting for age, Martine and Peliano report that the income differentials in favor of the native-born or nonmigrants in São Paulo and Rio de Janeiro widen slightly, while the migrant income advantage in the Northeastern centers is reduced but not eliminated.

Turning our attention to the female work force, it is clear that the conventional wisdom concerning the relatively more disadvantaged status for migrant workers is borne out in fact in all urban areas. The greater proportion of migrant workers in the lower-income brackets and, conversely, the larger proportion of nonmigrant women workers in the higher brackets is clear in all cities. These differentials are particularly sharp in the Southern cities, but also significant in the Northeast.

In summarizing these findings, several conclusions stand out and additional questions are raised. (1) Regional variations in migrant/nonmigrant differentials are sharp and clear, with the higher-income urban areas in the Center-South recording a relatively more disadvantageous socioeconomic status for migrants than the lower-income Northeastern cities and a lower incidence of urban poverty. (2) Sex differentials are likewise sharp and clear, with female migrants conforming in a more uniform fashion to the conventional wisdom that migrants are disadvantaged with respect to nonmigrants, but male migrants much less so. (3) Male migrants are in a relatively inferior income position to nonmigrants in São Paulo and, to a lesser extent, in Rio de Janeiro. In other urban centers, this differential either disappears or actually turns in favor of migrants. (4) Finally, the fact that recent migrants are invariably in a more disadvantageous income position than migrants as a whole suggests that migrants do experience some degree of social and occupational mobility after their arrival in these urban centers.

These regional contrasts conform to the expectation that the native-born in high-income urban centers like São Paulo and Rio de Janeiro have benefited from a more developed social infrastructure (especially education), informational networks, and kinship contacts than migrants coming from lesser

Table IX-5. Percentage Distribution of Income by Sex and Migrant Status for Selected Metropolitan Areas in Brazil, 1970

Income levels	São Paulo			Rio de Janeiro			Salvador			Recife		
	Recent migrants	Total migrants	Non-migrants	Recent migrants	Total migrants	Non-migrants	Recent migrants	Total migrants	Non-migrants	Recent migrants	Total migrants	Non-migrants
Male labor force												
0–200	43	27	27	47	33	34	58	48	54	58	54	64
201–500	41	43	37	36	40	38	24	30	29	26	28	25
501–1000	10	19	21	10	16	16	8	11	10	8	9	7
1000+	6	11	15	7	11	12	9	11	7	8	8	4
	100	100	100	100	100	100	100	100	100	100	100	100
Female labor force												
0–200	78	61	50	83	67	50	91	80	74	90	81	79
201–500	17	28	35	13	23	35	7	14	19	9	14	16
501–1,000	4	8	12	3	7	11	2	4	5	1	4	4
1,000+	1	3	3	1	3	4	0	2	2	0	1	1
	100	100	100	100	100	100	100	100	100	100	100	100

Source: Same as Table IX-2.

developed urban or rural areas. Social infrastructure, such as public education, is much less developed in the lower-income urban areas, thereby reducing
an important advantage for the native-born.

Similarly, selectivity differentials between migrants and nonmigrants in the
developed South would clearly be wider than within the Northeastern setting.
For example, "direct" migrants (i.e., using place of previous residence instead
of place of birth) from the considerably lower-income Northeastern region
comprised 48 percent of all the migrants in the metropolitan center of São
Paulo in 1970 and 31 percent in Rio de Janeiro. Such a large contingent from
the Northeast is bound to affect migrant/nonmigrant income differentials in
these centers. However, the intraregional migratory component of male
migrants into Recife, Salvador, and Fortaleza would be much less disadvantaged with respect to workers born in those cities.

An additional explanation for the favorable position of male migrants in the
Northeastern cities could be that the most ambitious and adept native-born
males may have moved to the higher-income urban areas in the South rather
than remain behind to compete for work in their cities of origin. This, of course,
would leave a residual of less capable native-born in these urban areas. This
argument takes on significance when one notes the extremely large numbers of
Northeastern migrants in the industrial labor markets of such large cities as
São Paulo.

Occupational Mobility of Migrants

The fact that migrants, on the whole, compare favorably to nonmigrants, and
that the differentials that do appear diminish as duration of residence
increases, suggests that migrants have been comparatively successful in the
Brazilian urban environment, despite the high level of poverty confronting
them on arrival. These results also conform to findings in survey data that are
reported below on mobility between the informal and formal sector. To what
extent do the national data support a more positive view of mobility? This final
section seeks to probe the assimilation issue somewhat further.

Published census tabulations on employment by occupation and branch of
activity are, for the most part, too aggregated to distinguish between skill levels
of migrants and nonmigrants. This is why most existing studies find few differences in the sectoral distribution of migrants and nonmigrants that cannot
be explained by age. For example, there is no difference between the share of
male migrants (either recent or older resident migrants) and the native-born in
industry. The only sharp and clear contrast is in the civil construction sector,
where recent migrants (uncontrolled for age) are relatively far more numerous
than either older migrants or nonmigrants, while native-born workers hold a
slight relative edge in commerce and sophisticated service occupations. For
women, recent migrants are far more common in personal domestic services

than older migrants or nonmigrants. The latter, in turn, hold a slight edge in social service activities and formal government employment. But beyond this, differences in the sectoral distribution of migrants and nonmigrants are minor or relatively insignificant. More useful in such comparisons are special occupational data on the population prepared by the IBGE, in which 259 occupations are grouped into 28 categories according to an occupational scale combining educational and income characteristics (Silva 1973). Within this hierarchical breakdown, it is possible to identify a set of occupations that provide a working definition of informal sector employment (Abreu 1976). Included (Table IX–6) are construction workers (except foremen), handicraft and apprentice jobs, domestic servants, janitors, doormen, watchmen, street vendors, primary sector (agricultural) activites, and ill-defined ocupations.

To facilitate analysis, Table IX–6 focuses only on the male labor force and, in addition, controls for age by concentrating on the prime-age cohorts of 20 to 29 and 30 to 39 years. In effect, there is control for sex, age, and a combined education-income variable (through our choice of these occupations to represent informal employment). Table IX–6 thus permits more meaningful migrant/nonmigrant contrasts and a static profile of mobility in allowing a check on the percent employed in the informal sector by duration of residence. We have chosen to focus on Rio de Janeiro and São Paulo, since these are the urban areas in which migrants are at their greatest disadvantage relative to nomigrants and, thus, the areas in which the process of mobility from recent to later migrants would presumably be greatest.

With respect to migrant/nonmigrant contrasts, the following stand out: (1) nonmigrant laborers show lower percentages in informal sector occupations than recent- or medium-resident migrants (0 to 5 years residence) in all locations except the periphery of Rio de Janeiro; (2) longer-resident male migrants (six years or more, but of the same age cohort), however, experience approximately equal proportions of informal sector employment, except for the central municipality of São Paulo. With these human capital corrections (age, sex, education) native-born males still register an advantage over recent male migrants in these major national metropolises, but this advantage disappears altogether, or becomes relatively insignificant, for longer-resident migrants of the same age cohort.

Turning now to the mobility features of migrants in Table IX–6 we can conclude the following. (1) There is a substantial decline in informal sector participation for longer-term migrants of the same age and sex. Close to 50 percent of recent migrants in prime-age cohorts are found in informal sector occupations. This percent drops to 40 percent for those resident three to five years, and even less for those resident longer, especially in São Paulo. (2) The changes are stronger in São Paulo than in Rio de Janeiro and, in addition, more so in the central municipalities than in the lower-income peripheral areas. (3) The periphery of Rio de Janeiro registers practically no migrant shift out of these informal occupations over time, while the periphery of São Paulo

Table IX-6. Percent of Male Labor Force in the Informal Sector in São Paulo and Rio de Janeiro by Age and Migrant Status, 1970

	0–2	3–5	6–10	11 years +	Native-born
São Paulo (center)					
1. 20–29 years	52.2	41.6	35.7	30.4	26.4
2. 30–39 years	48.5	41.7	37.9	29.7	23.4
Sao Paulo (periphery)					
1. 20–29 years	50.5	42.8	39.6	34.4	39.6
2. 30–39 years	47.6	44.8	39.8	34.3	41.6
Rio de Janeiro (center)					
1. 20–29 years	59.3	50.8	44.7	39.9	38.0
2. 30–39 years	52.7	47.0	43.9	36.6	29.9
Rio de Janeiro (periphery)					
1. 20–29 years	53.1	50.5	49.5	45.1	49.2
2. 30–39 years	48.6	46.1	46.2	41.9	45.5

Source: Special tabulations from the 1970 census. Informal sector occupations were derived from classifications established by Silva (1973). Occupations chosen for informal sector comprise occupations 20–24, 26–28 in classification by Silva (see discussion in text).

records a sharp decline, suggesting greater mobility in São Paulo's industrial suburbs.

At first glance, these results suggest a substantial degree of migrant mobility in the major national metropolises, where the migrant/nonmigrant differentials were initially the widest in Brazil. Substantial numbers of recent migrants appear to move out of informal sector occupations with longer periods of residence. In addition, the results were controlled so that sex and age differentials do not explain this different profile through time. However, the static nature of these profiles requires that they be interpreted with much greater caution. They could be measuring three distinct effects. One is mobility. The second is a differential selectivity effect in which migrants from an earlier time period could have had a different set of skills or other characteristics compared with those of a more recent period. This could be a result of the changing migrant supply characteristics from the areas of origin, but more likely it would be stimulated through the changing demand for a skill-mix of labor in the area of destination. A third and major qualification is the failure of these data to detect the depletion of labor force drop-outs. It is quite possible that this depletion effect is particularly high among low-income, low-skilled, recent migrants who cannot compete in the urban labor market, leaving only the more successful to be counted as longer-term residents who have moved to formal sector employment. This would be the complete opposite of the mobility effect. No mobility would have occurred at all, merely a reduction of the base population of recent migrants through the drop-out of unskilled migrants.

Martine and Peliano are especially concerned with this possibility and have attempted to measure depletion deriving from mortality and return-migration (see their Chapter VIII). While finding it very difficult to reach firm conclusions on its magnitude, they are convinced that the drop-out effect is significant. Since the issue is central to the question of migrant mobility, it is important to get a good fix on the limitations of their approach. To estimate the combined effects of mortality and continued or return-migration, they employ a survival-ratio technique similar to that used in measuring intercensal migration rates. The basis of the comparisons are rates of in-migration into various urban areas in the three years immediately preceding the 1970 census. From these they estimate the annual average for the years 1964–67 and 1959–64 (i.e., for migrants still residing in a given urban area 3 to 5 years and 6 to 10 years). These latter annual averages are increased by 10 and 25 percent, respectively, to correct for the larger base population at the end of the 1960s, compared to the smaller base earlier in the decade. The *theoretical* number of migrants who should have survived to 1970 from 1959–64 and 1964–67 migrant cohorts are then compared to the actual number recorded for these groups. The resulting "gap" represents depletion which, for the nine major metropolitan areas, ranged between 30 and 35 percent. In general, the gap or loss in the Northeastern cities was larger than in the Center-South.

While these figures are indeed significant, some major questions need to be asked about the very imaginative technique by which they were determined. Foremost here is to recognize the cyclical pattern of economic growth in Brazil in the 1960s. The years 1962–67 were among the most stagnant years of economic growth recorded in the last thirty years. By the same token, the period 1967–70 represents a period of rapid recovery that was to project Brazil into its economic "miracle." These highly contrasting cyclical phases neatly coincide with the migrant residency time cohorts used in the method. Thus, it is very possible that migration rates for 1964–67 and 1959–64 were considerably lower than in 1967–70, and that this, rather than depletion, could account for the reduced number of "survivors" of these migrant cohorts recorded in the 1970 census. It is impossible to reach any firm conclusions about the significance of depletion of these cohorts without knowing the effect of adverse economic conditions on migration rates in the early and mid-1960s and in the ensuing boom period (1968–70). Thus, the migration data of the 1970 census, though the only data available, appears to be particularly inappropriate for such a task. The Martine–Peliano exercise is very useful in providing a plausible upper limit for the depletion effect, but consideration of possible swings in migration rates leads us to be much more conservative about this.

The "selectivity" effect outlined earlier could also have affected the profiles during this period. The larger migrant cohorts in recent years undoubtedly included a relatively larger number of lower-skilled migrants than earlier migrant cohorts. This is due not only to the decline in migrant selectivity during high-growth or peak-inflow phases but also to the rapid growth of civil construction jobs in the late sixties in Brazil, as the BNH housing and public works programs took effect. Thus, we would expect that there would be a relatively large number of unskilled migrants in the recent (0- to 2-years residence) cohort than would have been characteristic of the 0- to 2-year, recent-migrant resident cohorts that entered these urban areas in the mid-sixties when the construction industry, in particular, was depressed. On balance, one would expect this selectivity differential effect to be more important than the drop-out effect, given the overall growth and labor demand features of the Brazilian economy during this period.

Clearly, the profile of implicit mobility portrayed earlier in Rio de Janeiro and São Paulo must be qualified for selectivity and drop-out effects. Unfortunately, there is no satisfactory way to identify them with census data, and survey data for specific destination areas are subject to the same problems, in that they too include only the migrants who have remained.

Despite the doubts about these mobility conclusions, other evidence lends support to at least a qualified positive view. Studies of the wage drift in the Brazilian economy since the mid-sixties point to the rising number of workers earning more than the minimum wage in Brazil. Thus, as the index of the real value of the minimum wage in Rio de Janeiro was declining in the middle to late sixties under the impact of stabilization policies, the number of workers in the manufacturing sector in Brazil earning less than the minimum wage fell from 43 percent in 1965 to roughly 30 percent in 1971. The decline in Rio de Janeiro was from 43 percent to 17 percent (Macedo 1977, Bacha et al. 1972). This fact, combined with evidence of very high turnover rates of employment in the manufacturing and service sectors, again suggests fairly signficant mobility patterns in the major labor markets of Brazil during the recent cycle of rapid economic growth.

However, these results also require caution in interpretation. Declines in shares of urban workers earning less than the minimum were paralleled by declines in the real value of the minimum wage. And while labor turnover may indicate vertical mobility, it has often been a sign of attempts by employers to avoid payment of legally required fringe benefits to workers that have been on the job for the required qualification period, in which case, mobility might also be lateral or downward.

In conclusion, the changing occupational profile for migrants in different residence cohorts in Table IX–6 would appear to be reflecting a mixture of mobility and selectivity differential effects and, to a lesser extent, some depletion effects. The most important point is that the degree of mobility in Brazilian labor markets is not specifically a migrant issue. Migrants as well as natives appear to have achieved some success, and at the same time both groups have encountered serious obstacles. The large absolute share of migrants in urban labor markets tends to make it appear a migrant problem, but in fact the experience of migrants is not atypical of that of workers in general. Two lessons are clear here: first, census data are too static in character to properly measure dynamic mobility; and second, the whole issue of occupational mobility is the next important step deserving study to complement the extensive comparative statistics of contemporary income distribution studies in Brazil. To study the welfare implications of the current growth process, we need to know not only the changing absolute and relative income distribution patterns but also the mobility flow through the income deciles over time. These two sets of information can then offer an unambiguous insight into the changing economic welfare of the labor force.

Evidence on Urban Labor Absorption and Unemployment

The evidence presented in the previous section suggests that the answer to the question whether migration is a "cause" of urban poverty is a double one. First, the urban poor do not consist entirely of unsuccessful migrants. In fact, migrants succeed rather well in adapting to the urban environment. Even if this assessment neglects those unsuccessful migrants who gave up and moved on or went home, it still means that they did not stay around in large numbers to become the urban poor. At the same time, we must recognize that the migration process has generated substantial growth in urban labor supply, growth that has exceeded the expansion of jobs in the manufacturing sector. Even if migrants are not poor, their members have certainly created pressures on urban labor markets. It is to these markets, and their capacity to absorb migration-fed increases in labor supply, that we now turn.

To what extent has migration created a stable equilibrium level of urban unemployment, as suggested by the Todaro-Harris model? There is little direct evidence to suggest that migration has increased urban unemployment in Brazil. Reported open unemployment rates for the nonagricultural labor force in the 1970 census and recent PNAD surveys are very low (Table IX–7). The significance of these rates (2.1 percent in the census and 2.6 percent in PNAD) is questionable. Since compensation for unemployment is not available, the only way to maintain income in the event of losing a job is to find something else, even if the new "job" consists of occasional work, begging, or even stealing. Our review of labor force trends in Chapter VII also suggested that workers who encounter difficulty obtaining jobs, especially older people, are more likely to revert to "inactive" status, that is, they drop out of the labor force as discouraged workers. One indication of this that we observed in Chapter VII was that the participation rate for males ages 40 to 59 declined significantly between 1950 and 1970.

Data from the PNAD surveys also show that unemployment is higher among females and younger workers, especially in ages 15 to 19. For females, this contrasts with the census data, which show higher unemployment among males. In part, this difference reflects the differences in labor force definition between the census and PNAD indicated in Chapter VII; namely, that the more restrictive definition of labor force participation in the census vis-à-vis dual roles (affecting rates for women and younger people more) has led to the classification of unemployed persons as inactive. More than anything, the

Table IX-7. Measures[a] of Unemployment and Underemployment for the Nonagricultural Labor Force, 1970–73

Measure, base population (source)	Total	Male	Female
1. Unemployment, nonagricultural workers (1970 census)	2.1	2.6	1.1
2. Seeking work for the first time, nonagricultural workers (1970 census)	1.3	1.5	0.9
3. Unemployment, nonagricultural workers (1973 PNAD survey)	2.6	2.6	2.7
4. Seeking work for the first time, nonagricultural workers (1973 PNAD)	1.2	0.9	1.2
5. Unemployment, ages 15–19, urban workers, including those seeking work for the first time (1973 PNAD)	11.8	n.a.	n.a.
6. Part-time (less than 40 hours per week), nonagricultural workers (1970 census)	13.6	9.0	24.5
7. Part-time workers, nonagricultural workers (1973 PNAD)	16.3	9.5	28.9
8. Part-time workers who prefer full-time work, urban workers (1973 PNAD)	4.5	2.5	9.0
9. Prime-age (20–49) unpaid family workers, nonagricultural workers (1973 PNAD)	1.1	0.5	2.2
10. Earning less than 1 minimum salary per month, nonagricultural workers (1973 PNAD)	34.5	29.2	49.1

[a]Percentage of base population that would be considered "unemployed" or "underemployed" according to each measure.

Sources: 1970 Population Census, Brazil, Fundação IBGE, 1973a, and 1973 PNAD, Fundação IBGE, 1975e.

reported unemployment rates confirm the difficulty of applying a concept meant for highly industrialized economies with social insurance to a much more traditional setting. This point is made by O'Brien and Salm (1970) in their review of unemployment data reported in the PNAD surveys. Their analysis suggests also that many who would have been reported as unemployed under other circumstances have sought lower paying employment in petty services in order to maintain income and suggest that underemployment is the more typical situation of individuals who cannot get a regular job.

Assessing the impact of this type of adjustment process on underemployment is also difficult. The concept itself is necessarily relative, and measurement is elusive. A definition based on income, assuming that low earnings indicate low productivity, leads us into implying that the urban poor could improve their lot by putting out more effort, which may not be true. Identifying underemployment in terms of work in specific occupations or sectors, such as services, or by analyzing trends in product per worker in these sectors, can be misleading unless it is possible to distinguish specific subsectors whose behavior may run counter to the trend in the larger categories with which they are grouped. Broad sectoral categories such as services, which include professional as well as domestic workers, and commerce, which groups street vendors with sales people in large department stores, are very hard to judge.

Even more direct measures of underemployment, such as hours worked and job status, are difficult to evaluate unless one can take account of the degree to which shorter hours are involuntary or specific to certain occupations, such as school teaching.

Statistical evidence on underemployment in Brazilian cities is limited. Both the census and PNAD surveys collected information on status of employment and hours of work, but provide few cross tabulations that are useful in assessing underemployment. The 1973 PNAD survey asked whether part-time workers would work full-time if able. Whereas 16 percent of urban workers were employed for fewer than 40 hours per week, only 4.5 percent (about one-quarter of part-time employees) said that they preferred full-time employment. Part-time employment is substantially higher for women. This is also true when status of employment is used as an index of underemployment. Using unpaid family workers in the main working ages (20 to 49 years) as an index, the overall rate is 1.1 percent, 0.5 percent for males and 2.2 for females. Neither measure, hours worked nor status, suggests a very high level of under-employment, which runs counter to the expectation that low open unemployment rates disguise high underemployment.

It is only when we turn to earnings that recent data indicate that a larger proportion of nonagricultural workers might be underemployed. About one-third of all workers reported earnings lower than the legal minimum wage in their region, with the proportion reaching closer to 50 percent for females. Serious problems arise in the interpretation of these data, however. For females, a significant proportion of those earning less than the minimum wage (about 60 percent) are domestic workers, who receive room and board in addition to monetary remuneration. While working conditions may be exploitative, this alone does not justify categorizing the work as underemployment. Construction workers, who comprise about 20 percent of all nonagricultural male workers earning less than the minimum wage, present a similar problem since many receive room and board in "camps" located close to construction sites. To classify workers with low earnings as underemployed, one would also have to show that under existing factor market conditions they could be employed more productively in other jobs. Since a large proportion of these low-paying positions are occupied by recent migrants and younger people entering the urban labor market for the first time, a closer examination of this segment of the urban labor market is required before judgment on its role in urban underemployment can be passed.

The sectoral distribution of nonagricultural employment can also be viewed as an index of the manner in which urban labor absorption is utilizing the flow of workers leaving agriculture. There has been much concern that the failure of industrial expansion to generate sufficient employment would result in a flooding of the remainder of the urban economy, principally commerce and services, with unskilled migrants who come in anticipation of industrial employment but had to settle for whatever they could find because of the

Table IX–8. Trend in Sectoral Shares of Nonagricultural Employment and Sectoral
Output per Worker, 1940–70

	1940	1950	1960	1970
A. Sectoral shares of nonagricultural				
employment (percentage)	100.0	100.0	100.0	100.0
1. Manufacturing, mining, utilities	22.9	25.7	20.6	22.0
2. Construction	5.2	8.5	7.5	10.6
3. Commerce	14.9	14.0	14.2	13.9
4. Finance	0.9	1.7	2.0	2.9
5. Transport and communication	9.5	10.2	10.1	7.6
6. Government	8.1	7.4	6.8	7.1
7. Personal and domestic services	30.6	24.4	26.2	22.3
8. Social services	4.0	6.3	6.6	9.1
9. Other (liberal professions, poorly defined)	3.9	1.8	6.0	4.7
B. Index of relative sectoral income per worker in nonagricultural activities (average = 100)				
1. Industry total	100	114	148	130
2. Services, total	100	93	81	86
2a. Services, excluding finance	88	86	77	79
3. Commerce	195	146	146	162
4. Finance	834	355	234	249
5. Transport and communication	97	103	89	90
6. Government	122	146	176	167
7. Others (lines 7, 8, and 9 above)	43	41	36	26

Sources: Same as Table IX–7.

limited supply of industrial jobs. In Brazil, "tertiarization" appeared to be a serious threat when the 1960 census revealed a declining share for industry in total nonagricultural employment.

As can be seen in Table IX–8 (panel A), which presents trend data and sectoral shares in nonagricultural employment for the period 1940 to 1970, the share of manufacturing declined from 26 percent of nonagricultural employment in 1950 to 21 percent in 1960. As mentioned earlier, the 1950s were the period in which Brazil's capital-intensive, import-substituting industrialization strategy was most intensive. A further one percentage point decline in the share of construction led to a net decline in the industry sector (manufacturing, mining, utilities, and construction) of six percentage points (from 34 to 28 percent) between 1950 and 1960. This trend was partially reversed to 33 percent, but most of the "recovery" occurred in construction, whose share increased by three percentage points.

It is true that the "residual" shows up as an increased share in services, especially in the 1950–60 interval. However, the overall 1940–70 trend does not support a characterization of the urban employment trend as a flooding of the tertiary sector. Except for a slight increase in 1950–60, the trend in the shares of the two service subsectors where one might expect such a flooding (commerce and personal services) is downward, with increases appearing in finance and other services (social services, the professions, and poorly defined). As shown in the detailed analysis of sectoral and occupational employment trends at the close of Chapter VII, occupations in commerce and personal services continued to provide the greatest absolute number of jobs created between 1950 and 1970, because of their greater weight in the service sector total, but the occupations that contributed most to the relative increase in services were teachers, clerical and administrative workers, social service workers, and the like. These are not the low-skill occupations one would expect to find if a rise in the share of services were to represent an increase in unemployment or a flooding of the urban labor market with low productivity workers.

What has happened to productivity per worker in services as a result of these changes in the share of service workers in nonagricultural employment? Panel B of Table IX–8 presents indices of sectoral income per worker for industry and services between 1940 and 1970. The index shows each sector's income per worker relative to the overall average for nonagricultural activities ($=100$) at each census date. In rows 1 and 2, we observe that relative income per worker was about equal in industry and services in 1940, and that the index for industry rose to 148 by 1960, while that for services declined to a level of 81. This divergent trend appears to reverse itself for 1960–70, with industry declining to 130 and services climbing to 86. The same pattern appears if we exclude finance (row 2a) except that the 1960–70 upswing is less. Does this mean that the shift to service employment, which was especially pronounced in the 1950s, was indeed accompanied by increased underemployment in services and that this process changed in the 1960s?

This is a possible interpretation. But caution is again suggested by the compositional features of the trend in relative income in service subsectors that appear in rows 3 through 7 of the table. Underlying the aggregate trend are a number of contrasting patterns for these subgroups. Except for government, all show a net decline from 1940 to 1970. Government increased from 1940 to 1960, then decreased from 1960 to 1970, while commerce declined from 1940 to 1950 and then increased in 1960–70; finance declined from 1940 to 1960 and then increased. Because product accounts aggregate output in personal and domestic services with social services and professions in an "other" category, and the "other" category in population census employment data indicates some suspicious swings due to poorly defined activities, the declining output per worker trend in the "other" category in panel B needs to be interpreted cautiously. To the extent that it is picking up the effect of workers being marginalized by the industrial expansion process, it may indeed be an indication of increased underemployment. On the other hand, the diversity of activities that have been grouped in the category makes it difficult to draw really firm conclusions from the trend.

What do these various trends imply? Kuznets (1966) has suggested that higher relative-income indices observed in commerce, finance, and the professions at earlier stages of modernization reflect monopolistic market advantages that are eliminated as more people enter those sectors. This appears to be a plausible explanation for the high relative income in finance and commerce in 1940. While this explanation does not exclude the possibility of underemployment induced by excess labor supply in other service subsectors, the initial divergent pattern in indices for services and industry may also signal differences in the pace at which traditional production units were being replaced, or outweighed in terms of contribution to total output, by modern ones. With the implantation of imported labor-saving technologies in the import-substituting industrial expansion of the 1950s, the industrial sector became more capital-intensive relative to services, which did not experience a similar capitalization as soon. The decline in relative product per worker was most pronounced in all of the service subsectors except government in that decade. The tendency toward convergence of the trend in 1960–70 suggests that commerce and finance have also started the capitalization process, and that only "other" services continue to be dominated by traditional activities.

The Urban Informal Sector in Brazil

Where then have low-income workers found employment? As indicated in the discussion of recent developments in the theoretical and empirical literature on migrant labor absorption, the urban informal sector has played an important role in this. Where we would depart slightly from the framework described earlier is in emphasizing that the informal sector performs this function not only for migrants but for the native population as well.

As a "sector," informal employment encompasses segments of the urban economy—activities producing goods and services and the labor markets on which they draw—that are found at the least capitalized and least organized end of the urban economic spectrum.[6] Difference in the type of organization rather than the lack of organization is probably a more appropriate distinction, since, as Peattie (1976) has observed, one often finds a high degree of organization *within* subsegments of the informal sector, even though the sector as a whole may lack organization features that distinguish the formal sector. Employment arrangements in the informal sector are typified by loose and sometimes temporary agreements, lack of coverage by minimum wage laws, social security, and other types of government regulations, as well as union contracts when they exist. In some parts of the informal sector, entry is very easy and turnover high, though a number of informal arrangements turn out to be long lasting. Small-scale establishments, domestic and own-account workers make up a large part of its workers. As such, informal activities are not

---

[6]General discussion of the main characteristics of informal sector employment can be found in Sethuraman (1976) and ILO (1972). Specific reference to Latin American informal employment is found in Souza and Tokman (1976).

new to the urban economy; indeed, the organization of artisan manufacturing and most services before the postwar industrial expansion could be characterized as informal. However, postwar growth did not eliminate informal activities. Rather, the capitalization of industry was accompanied by more complex forms of economic organization in production and labor markets, creating a more sharply defined formal sector, while the informal sector remained an important element in the urban economic structure and continued to play a major role in the employment of low-income workers within this structure.

The Brazilian Experience: A Macroperspective

The inconclusive evidence on the relation between urban population increase, nonagricultural employment, and surplus labor in Brazil, together with the indication that recent trends also reflect important changes in the composition of employment between modern and more traditional segments of the urban economy, suggests that closer study of labor market structure is required for adequate interpretation of recent trends. As shown in the previous section, industrialization has created a more highly segmented urban economy, affecting both kinds of productive activities found there and the factor markets on which these activities draw. Dualistic interpretations of the division of the urban economy into modern and traditional sectors have been criticized because they stress the isolation of the two sectors, competition between them, and the implication that more efficient modern units will eventually drive out the more traditional ones.[7] The evidence does not support such a sharp division. It is true that the capitalization process that has occurred in much of manufacturing and in some service activities, with its attendant propensity toward oligopolistic organization of factor and product markets, has created an increasingly segmented urban economy. But the less capitalized, less organized segment has not disappeared in the process. Rather this "other" urban sector has continued to absorb a significant share of the urban labor force and has generated goods and services that are purchased by both the more and less capitalized production and consumption units.

The concept of an urban informal sector attempts to capture this "other" urban sector for analytical and policy purposes. Its focus is on the structure of employment arrangements in less capitalized, less organized activities. Part of the appeal of the informal sector concept may derive from dissatisfaction with other residual approaches to these working population groups. The service sector has indeed absorbed a significant proportion of the excess in urban growth, but not all services are characterized by low levels of capitalization.

[7]For Brazil, this interpretation has been criticized very strongly by Oliveira (1972).

Thus, "tertiarization" is a dimension of the urban employment problem, but does not really define a target group. Marginality theory, also prominent as an analytical approach to low-income populations, has come under criticism because it was essentially negative and failed to account for political and economic dynamism that was assumed to be lacking, but that a number of recent studies by political scientists and anthropologists have shown to be very much present among low-income workers.[8] The informal sector concept also recognizes the heterogeneous structure of the urban economy and stresses the complementarity in terms of trade and labor mobility between the different segments of that structure as a means of promoting adequate employment opportunities.

Like all attempts to deal directly with the "other" segment of the urban economy, the informal sector approach is confronted with problems of measurement. The very nature of informal sector activities makes them statistically elusive. The Brazilian census's definition of economic activity in terms of habitual occupation is probably biased against inclusion of many informal workers in the labor force. Labor and "product" markets are often indistinguishable in services and some artisan activities (the autonomous carpenter whose client supplies the materials, and often the tools); transactions may not be fully monetized, as with the room and board provided domestic servants.

Neither the census nor PNAD surveys include information on employment that would permit direct measurement of the distribution of the labor force by type of work arrangement. They provide more conventional indices, such as occupation, major industrial sector status, and earnings. These provide some useful proxies for informal employment, but are subject to the same limitations that were mentioned earlier with regard to their use in measuring underemployment.

It is possible to derive indirect estimates of the informal component in nonagricultural employment between 1940 and 1970 from a comparison of the number of workers reported by branch of activity in the sectoral economic censuses to the corresponding categories in the population census. Sectoral censuses report on an establishment basis and are likely to represent larger, formal sector activities. The population census is based on individuals' reporting of their own occupations. The difference between the two in any given year is proxy for informal employment. Table IX–9 summarizes the results for three sectors (manufacturing, commerce, and personal services) for which the comparison can be made. Panel A shows employment in the informal sector as a percentage of total employment in each sector (as reported in the population census), while panel B gives employment in each sector as a percentage of total nonagricultural employment. As we would expect, infor-

---

[8] See, for example, Perlman's (1976) study of *favela* residents in Rio de Janeiro and Nelson's (1969) work on political orientation of low-income workers.

Table IX-9. Estimate of Trends in Percentage of Urban-Informal Employment in Brazil by Sector, 1940–70[a]

	1940	1950	1960	1970
A. Informal sector employment represented by differences between workers reported in population and economic censuses as percent of employment in sector				
1. Manufacturing	25.8	16.6	9.1	20.0
2. Commerce	38.6	25.8	33.0	23.6
3. Personal services	82.5	76.8	80.2	75.6
B. Informal employment as percent of total nonagricultural employment by sector				
1. Manufacturing	5.6	3.8	1.7	4.1
2. Commerce	5.7	3.6	4.5	3.3
3. Personal services	25.2	18.7	20.3	17.0
4. Total	36.5	26.1	26.5	24.4
5. Total, including all employment in construction in addition to above	41.7	34.6	33.9	35.0

[a]Adjusted for differences in dates of censuses by geometric interpolation.
Sources: Population Censuses and Sectoral Censuses, 1940 to 1970.

mal employment is highest in personal services, around 80 percent. In 1940, informal employment also represented about one-fourth of manufacturing jobs and about one-third of commerce. From 1940 to 1960, there was a steady decline (to 9 percent by 1960) in the informal share in manufacturing, suggesting that traditional units were being displaced by larger establishments during the import-substitution push in the 1950s. But there is a reversal of this trend in 1960–70, with the informal share returning to 20 percent in 1970. Patterns in commerce and services support the displacement hypothesis for the 1950s. Both experiencd a decline in the proportion of informal employment from 1940–50, and then increased in 1960. The 1970 data show a return to about the level of 1950.

The overall trend in the proportion of informal employment in the nonagricultural labor force (in panel B, line 4) shows a decline in the share of informal employment in manufacturing, commerce, and services of about ten percentage points in the 1940s, and then relative stability as the swings in informal employment in manufacturing were offset by changes in the other two sectors. Of course, these three sectors do not represent all of the informal employment in the urban economy. Construction, whose informal employment cannot be measured in this manner, constitutes another major block of the informal sector. If we in include it in the 1940–70 trend, then the informal sector increases again in 1960–70. Depending on the definition, it appears to represent between one-quarter and one-third of the urban work force.

Microperspective: The Case of Belo Horizonte

While these indirect measurements of informal activities provide an indication of the importance of informal employment in the urban economy and of changes in its composition by broad sectoral breakdowns in recent decades, they do not tell us much about the demographic composition of the informal sector and its role in generating employment and earnings in the urban economy. In an earlier study, one of the authors attempted to measure the size and major demographic characteristics of the informal sector in Brazil's third largest city, Belo Horizonte.[9] A sample survey of this metropolitan area's labor force was conducted in November 1972, and special effort was put into the design of the questionnaire to insure that it would yield information on labor market structure and traditional employment. A limited occupational life history was taken for 2,445 heads of households, and detailed current employment information was sought for the remaining members of the work force in the sample. The survey data permit a more direct definition of informal employment. This approach classifies workers according to characteristics of employment that relate to the structure of urban labor markets (regulation, size and type of establishment, entry, and turnover, etc.) and allows us to by-pass the limitation imposed by census data.

Government regulation provides the main institutional variable for directly identifying informal work arrangements in Brazil, where trade union influence was, in 1972, very weak. Several indicators of the degree of regulation exist, though few apply equally to all groups in the working population. The *carteira de trabalho* is required by law in most activities, and its being signed by an employer is a legally recognized work contract. In the survey, more people had *carteiras*, or claimed to, than actually used them for contracting employment. To complicate matters further, employers often kept an employee's *carteira*, thus leaving respondents with an excuse for not having one to show at the time of an interview.

A better indicator of the degree of regulation in the survey data was a question on contributions to social security, which were shared by employers and employees, and which insured that the work arrangement was the one envisioned by the law on signed *carteiras*. Not all groups were included in this. Government employees had their own social security "institute," and coverage of domestic service did not imply the guarantees of job security implied by the signing of the *carteira* elsewhere.

The survey data were screened, using responses on contribution to social security, size and type of establishment, and occupational data to set up a

---

[9]Details on the Belo Horizonte study are found in Merrick (1976a), Brito and Merrick (1974), and Sant'Anna, Merrick, and Mazumdar (1976). This section presents a brief review of the findings reported there.

variable that is called "type of work arrangement." It has two classes, formal and informal arrangements. The informal group includes domestic workers and those who did not contribute to a social security institute, except for the liberal professions, government workers, and employers in firms with five or more employees.

Just over 31 percent of Belo Horizonte's active population worked in the informal sector in 1972, the active population being those who were employed at the time of the survey. Four important household groups were distinguished in analyzing the data: (1) household heads; (2) their spouses; (3) other household members; (4) domestic workers residing in the household. For males, the last three are combined in one group in Table IX–10, which shows the percentage employed (the participation rate) and, of those employed, percentages in the informal sector by age, sex, and position in the household.

For males, heads of households show a higher percentage employed in all age categories and a lower percentage in informal employment for ages 20 to 54. There is a negative correlation between percentage active and percentage informal, which suggests that the informal sector functions as a buffer area for groups, like the young and old, whose participation in the labor force depends upon whether they can find a job and who are willing to accept an informal job rather than go unemployed.

Labor force and informal sector participation differ more sharply by position in the households for females. Female heads are most active and have the highest percentage informal, although the informal share is again lowest when participation is highest. The situation for spouses and other members is complicated by the interaction of these classes with domestic servants, and this in turn is related to the socioeconomic status of the household. In lower-income households, a wife or other member may be a domestic servant in another household, whereas, in upper-income households, wives and other members are generally not engaged in domestic service outside their own household. By definition, all of the domestic servants in Table IX–10 are active and in the informal sector. The data on wives and other members shown in the table exclude domestic servants and thus overrepresent higher socioeconomic status families. The table indicates lower percentages in informal activities for wives and other members than would be the case had domestic servants been included with them. This is clear if we examine females age 20 to 29. Of the 553 active females, 164 were domestic servants. With domestic servants included, the informal activities are 45 percent, whereas without them the result is 22 percent, close to the percentage in informal activities one finds when considering only higher-income households.

The Belo Horizonte data show, in fact, that informal sector employment plays a more significant role in providing earning opportunities for members of lower-income families than for other families. Table IX–11 shows percentages working and percentages of employment in the informal sector for

Table IX–10. Employment Patterns in Belo Horizonte: Percentages Employed and Percentage of Those Employed Working in Informal Sector by Age, Sex, and Position in Household, 1972

Household groups	Age groups 14-19	20-29	30-39	40-49	50-54	65+	Total
Males							
1. Heads:							
Working	85.2	94.4	95.6	90.8	68.3	29.7	85.0
Informal	52.2	11.1	9.5	13.6	23.2	50.0	14.9
(N)	(27)	(354)	(571)	(487)	(417)	(116)	(1,972)
2. Others:							
Working	29.8	66.3	67.3	32.1	28.0	20.7	46.5
Informal	49.0	15.0	23.5	22.2	57.1	33.3	27.1
(N)	(821)	(694)	(101)	(28)	(50)	(29)	(1,723)
Females							
1. Heads:							
Working	0	83.6	81.2	73.7	47.1	20.0	64.0
Informal	0	53.7	46.2	47.1	62.5	70.0	47.3
(N)	(6)	(73)	(96)	(95)	(119)	(50)	(439)
2. Spouses:							
Working	0	16.2	21.6	15.4	4.9	0	15.4
Informal	0	18.5	41.7	34.0	90.0	0	36.2
(N)	(24)	(333)	(444)	(305)	(203)	(39)	(1,348)
3. Others:							
Working	8.6	43.1	34.5	23.9	10.2	2.7	22.5
Informal	28.6	19.0	25.4	37.8	66.7	0	24.5
(N)	(818)	(635)	(206)	(155)	(176)	(112)	(2,102)
4. Domestic servants: (N)	(134)	(164)	(55)	(33)	(34)	(5)	(425)

Source: Survey data, Merrick (1976*a*).

families classified into four groups (poor, low, middle, and high) according to household income per adult equivalent member.[10] Data are classed by sex and position as in Table IX–10. The percentages working are lower in the poor families for heads of both sexes and for spouses and other female members. Informal employment is higher among the poor and decreases for all household groups as economic status improves. Male servants account for the increase in informal workers in the high-income households.

Supplemental earnings in the informal sector, while low, represent an important element in the economic welfare, if not the survival, of lower-income families. To illustrate the importance of these earnings, we can compare the distribution of families by income with and without informal sector earnings. Households were again divided into four groups, on the basis of household in-

[10]The stratification is somewhat artificial. The cut-off, 100 *cruzeiros* per month per adult equivalent consumer, was adopted on the basis of what the Brazilian government considered to be an adequate income for an average family in determining the regional minimum wage, and the remaining divisions were designed to pick up the upper-income groups by population percentiles, with the middle equal to the 75–90 and the rich roughly equal to the top decile. The breaks are not exact because they have been made in relation to Belo Horizonte's 1972 minimum wage of Cr $268 per month (roughly equivalent to $45, so that the "poor" category had an average annual per capita income of about $200, in a place in which the cost of living was about equivalent to the average U.S. city).

Table IX-11. Percentages Employed and Percentages of Those Employed Working in
Informal Sector by Sex, Position in Household, and Household Income Groups
in Belo Horizonte, 1972

Household group	Household income groups[a]				
	Poor	Low	Middle	High	Total
Males					
1. Heads:					
Working	76.4	86.6	90.1	92.0	85.0
Informal	27.7	14.4	4.6	4.6	14.0
(N)	(529)	(940)	(242)	(261)	(1,972)
2. Others:					
Working	29.4	59.1	45.4	40.1	46.5
Informal	43.3	25.2	1.1	34.4[b]	27.1
(N)	(580)	(792)	(202)	(149)	(1,723)
Females					
1. Heads:					
Working	69.3	63.4	61.1	75.3	64.0
Informal	80.2	39.7	21.2	20.7	47.3
(N)	(189)	(191)	(54)	(38)	(472)[c]
2. Spouses:					
Working	5.2	11.5	29.3	32.0	15.4
Informal	95.0	53.4	24.4	7.7	36.2
(N)	(342)	(636)	(167)	(203)	(1,348)
3. Other:					
Working	6.9	29.7	31.6	25.0	22.5
Informal	58.3	22.0	16.9	17.4	24.5
(N)	(686)	(1,026)	(206)	(184)	(2,102)
4. Domestic servants: (N)	(98)	(84)	(62)	(148)	392[d]

[a]Household Income Groups (Monthly Income per adult equivalent [infants=0.1; ages
1-10=0.5; others=1.0] in *cruzeiros*): poor: up to 100; low: 100-368; middle: 368-727;
high: over 727.
[b]Includes male domestic servants and household employees.
[c]Includes 33 domestic servants who were heads of their own households.
[d]Excludes the domestic servants in [c].
Source: Survey data (Merrick 1976a).

come per adult equivalent, as in Table IX–11, but now excluding their
earnings from the informal sector. This is shown in Table IX–12. Without informal sector earnings, 166 low-income households (7 percent of the total)
drop down into the "poor" category. Eight families drop from "high" to
"middle" and thirteen from "middle" to "low." This suggests that while
informal employment may be a factor in the widening of differentials in the personal income distribution it nevertheless serves to ameliorate the effect of
this on the distribution of incomes between households. Restrictive wage
policies vis-à-vis workers at the lower end of the formal sector, as reflected in
adjustments in the minimum wage that fell behind price increases have required households at the lower end of the scale to seek every possible source of
earnings to compensate for their deteriorating position, and this has been facilitated by the availability of informal employment.[11]

[11]General discussions of post-1964 wage policies are found in Furtado (1972) and Tavares
(1972), with more specific comparisons of the growing gap between incomes and prices facing low-
income workers in São Paulo to be found in DIESSE (1973, 1974).

Table IX-12. Distribution of Households by Household Income per Adult Equivalent, with and without Informal Sector Earnings

Group (*cruzeiros* per person per month)	Informal earnings included		Informal earnings excluded	
	N	%	N	%
1. Poor (less than 100)	718	29.4	884	36.2
2. Low (101 to 368)	1131	46.3	978	40.0
3. Middle (369 to 728)	296	12.1	291	11.9
4. High (729 and over)	300	12.3	292	11.9
TOTAL	2,445	100.0	2,445	100.0

Source: Survey data.

Examination of other characteristics of individuals in the informal sector shows that important educational, occupational, and sectoral employment differences are also associated with informal activity. However, the high inter-correlation between these variables makes it difficult to determine the independent effect of any one of the variables on either employment or earnings in the informal sector. This is especially true of education and occupation. Proportions in informal activities are highest (more than 60 percent) for unskilled workers with no formal education. Informal participation declines substantially with rising occupational and educational status, so that about 20 percent are informal in nonmanual occupational groups or with completed primary education.

The relation between migrant status and informal sector employment is also of interest, because of the buffer role attributed to it by labor absorption models during the period of job search by newly arrived migrants. The presence of such a buffer explains why open employment is lower than would be expected, given labor supply in excess of industrial employment. Care is required in such migrant/nonmigrant comparisons, because nonmigrants make up such a large share in the overall population. In Belo Horizonte, close to three-quarters of the population are nonnative, so it is not surprising that migrants should make up a large share of the informal sector. They also constitute a large share of the formal sector. The reverse comparison of informal employment shares among migrants and natives shows just about equal proportion for both groups, though it does reveal a higher proportion of informal employment among recently arrived migrants, especially females, for whom domestic service is a principal "entry" occupation. Closer examination of migrant/native differences, with controls for variables described above, such as age, education, and position in the household, reveals that the latter may be as important as migrant status per se in signaling the entry or transition of informal sector employment.

Migrants who entered the urban labor market through Belo Horizonte's informal sector appear to have been reasonably successful in moving on to formal employment. In an analysis of intersectoral mobility patterns for migrant males who started their work experience in the informal sector, the survey data revealed that 60 percent were still in it 6 to 10 years after entry, if their ages were 19 or less, with the proportion dropping to around 10 percent during the prime working ages (20 to 49) and then rising to about one-third after age 50. Caution is required in interpreting these favorable mobility patterns in that the data, like all surveys at the point of migrants' destinations, fail to include individuals who moved on or returned home.

But while the transition function of informal employment is important both for migrants and for natives, it is not the only role that informal employment plays. The evidence also suggests that informal employment may be the preferred alternative for individuals at other stages of the working life cycle. This notion runs counter to the conventional view that all jobs in the informal sector are "bad" jobs, and that individuals would move to the formal sector if given the choice. This is especially evident when we review earnings differentials between formal and informal sector workers. The overall pattern of differentials suggests that informal workers probably do earn less on average than their formal sector counterparts. However, there are also instances of informal earnings that equal or exceed those in the formal sector. Table IX–13, shows earnings ratios adjusted for the effects of part-time work and payment in kind. The most striking case is younger males with intermediate levels of education, whose average earnings in the informal sector exceeds those in the formal sector by 75 percent. This case illustrates some of the advantages as well as the disadvantages of informal employment as a career path. At an earlier stage in the working life cycle, informal activities may offer flexibility and mobility potential not found at lower echelons of the formal sector, but if a person has not "made it" by, say, age forty, his relative position deteriorates, as formal sector earnings start to reach their peak in later stages in the working life cycle.

Again, it is important not to overgeneralize from the type of informal sector experience described in the previous paragraph to all informal workers. The differential earnings observed for females suggest other patterns. There is less interaction with age and education in the case of females, many more of whom enter the informal sector for secondary employment or as heads of households with family responsibilities that preclude formal sector work arrangements. This "welfare" function of informal employment is important for a number of groups, whose employment and earnings opportunities would be very limited in its absence. Beside female heads of household, it includes the young and old, disabled and less skilled workers, as well as anyone who simply cannot make it in the formal sector. Since there is no public assistance to provide for the welfare of such individuals, the informal sector is, in such circumstances, employer of last resort.

Global Policy Implications of Informal Employment Data

Though the evidence on informal sector employment in Brazil is still fragmentary, the overall picture is one in which informal employment is a

Table IX-13. Ratio of Informal to Formal Sector Earnings by Age, Sex, and Education

Age	Illiterate	Incomplete primary	Complete primary	Secondary	University
Males:					
15–19	(.667)	.594	.500	a	a
20–24	a	.735	1.057	1.753	1.087
25–34	.676	.584	.936	(1.170)	(.393)
35–49	.461	.789	.697	(.455)	(.149)
50 +	.354	.505	.409	(.602)	(.587)
Females:					
15–19	a	.426	.637	(.583)	a
20–24	(.793)	(.097)	.621	.732	a
25–34	(.742)	.463	.474	a	.850
35–49	.486	.629	.531	(.928)	(.355)
50 +	(.547)	.604	.392	.850	a

Note: Ratios shown in parentheses when fewer than five of either sector in cell; a—one cell had no cases for comparison.
Source: Survey data.

major factor in urban labor absorption in Brazil. The informal sector is not simply a product of the excess growth of the urban labor force over industrial employment in recent decades. The 1940 census data suggest that the informal sector represented an important share of urban employment at the start of the postwar expansion of industry, and, to the extent that it incorporated household and artisan activities in manufacturing, it was probably even more significant prior to 1940. What did not occur, however, was a gradual replacement of informal activities by modernized, formal sector industrial (and service sector) establishments. The informal employment share in manufacturing declined in the 1940s and 1950s, during the import-substitution expansion, which favored capital-intensive growth. However, informal employment in commerce and services absorbed a larger share in the 1950s, after declining in the 1940s. And in the 1960s informal employment in manufacturing increased again, so that the overall trend from 1950 to 1970 was a return to the level of 1940.

The informal sector now provides employment and earning opportunities for individuals who would be less likely to obtain them in the formal sector. In so doing, it has cushioned for these groups the impact of wage and price policies that have favored the formal sector. Lest we be deceived by the word "cushioning," however, it should quickly be pointed out that the average earnings in the informal sector are relatively low, and that the cushioning generally occurs when other members of a household obtain work in the informal sector, in order to maintain that household's standard of living in the face of declining real earnings by the head. Clearly, things would be better if the head's earnings were adequate. The point is that they would also be worse if informal employment opportunities were absent.

Recognizing the diversity of functions performed by informal employment in the urban economy, especially its role in the provision of employment and earning opportunities for lower income groups, what are the most appropriate measures to deal with it? The possibilities fall into three headings, which are not mutually exclusive, but do represent some possible alternatives in approach. They are (1) to increase employment and earnings through increased demand for informal sector output; (2) to increase earnings in the sector by raising efficiency and/or improving its bargaining position in factor and product markets; and (3) direct subsidies to the urban poor in the form of reducing the costs to them of housing, transportation, and other urban services.

On the demand side, the potential consumers of informal goods and services are the government, formal sector establishments, other informal activities, and final demand of households. Both the growth and distribution of income affect the demand for informal sector output. With the exception of personal and domestic services, most of the final demand for informal output derives from lower-income groups, so that a worsening of the income distribution would also have an adverse effect on the informal sector. Much of the attention on informal activities has been directed to demand from households and other informal activities, but an important potential for increased informal sector output may actually be with government and formal sector establishments. Very little is known of the extent of subcontracting and piecework arrangements between informal workers and these formal sector establishments, but scattered evidence suggests that it is considerable. A general policy of promoting such arrangements could be beneficial for employment, as well as reducing capital and imported material requirements. Relaxation of purchasing standards and work rules (for example, the building codes that inhibit artisan-type inputs, which have been adopted by many government agencies in compliance with international loan agreements) might be worth considering. Specific recommendations for increasing procurement from the informal sector require case studies aimed at identifying opportunities for this.

Undercapitalization is often mentioned as a reason for the relatively low productivity of informal activities. Informal workers and establishments are often hampered by their inaccessability to credit for working capital and for the purchase of equipment, and are thereby forced to limit themselves to what can be done with cash on hand or what can be obtained at very high interest rates through informal credit arrangement. Another dimension of the problem stems from the complexities of dealing with banks and credit agencies, who are wary of lending to small-scale operators and generally require more bureaucratic machinery for dealing with the paperwork involved in obtaining credit than the average informal operator is likely to have at his disposal.[12] Cooperative arrangements among informal production units might be a means of breaking this bottleneck.

[12]Similar problems in obtaining credit for small operators have been a major concern of agricultural economists working in developing areas.

Technology presents both challenges and opportunities. The available equipment is generally expensive and labor-saving. Brazilian planners, especially those interested in promoting exports of manufactured goods, are skeptical of recommendations to adopt labor-intensive techniques in the more capitalized formal sector for valid economic reasons. The available labor-intensive technology is generally older technology. While it uses more labor per unit of capital, it also produces less output per unit of capital—so that capital costs are higher.[13] The paradox of this is that while labor is abundant and capital scarce, it still makes sense to purchase the "latest" in equipment, because it economizes on capital by giving a lower capital-output ratio. There is little logic, however, in recommending this type of capitalization for the labor-intensive informal sector. What is lacking is a technology appropriate for that sector, e.g., one which is labor-intensive and inexpensive in capital-output terms. An illustration of the problem is provided by the relative lack of good quality, inexpensive hand tools.

Factor and product-pricing relationships are probably more prejudicial to earnings than to employment in the informal sector. The informal sector has to keep labor costs low in order to maintain its share in product and service markets. But it is often at a disadvantage with respect to other costs. Informal sector subcontractors are often obliged to buy their supplies and material at retail prices and sell them at wholesale in order to get formal sector business. Outlays for marketing, obtaining government licenses, and payment of unavoidable taxes further raise the indirect cost per unit of informal production, with the informal operators having to absorb the added margin out of earnings, rather than risk the loss of business by passing it along to buyers in higher prices. Here, too, cooperative arrangements between informal workers and establishments might provide scale economies that would enable them to procure materials, equipment, and production and distribution services at lower cost. Cooperation could also provide the training needed to deploy new equipment efficiently.

A great deal of caution and careful study is required before implementing schemes to improve the market position of informal activities by organizing them. If such schemes end up raising rather than lowering the price of informal sector output, or exposing it to increased governmental regulation and taxes, then the negative effect on employment might worsen the overall flow of income to the sector. It is understandable but regretable that the typical first reaction of labor ministries and social security agencies to the "news" about the informal sector is to view it as "more business," which ususaly implies increasing the implementation of labor legislation and broadening social security coverage (and taxes). All measures affecting the informal sector need to be applied with care so as not to tip what may be a very delicate balance between

---

[13] See Morawetz (1974).

the kind and degree of organization currently governing the sector and the employment-generating capacity that depends on this balance. Markets are very subtle mechanisms, and most measures that tamper with them end up setting in motion many more reactions than were initially intended.

Because of the unpredictable outcome of direct measures to increase the flow of income to the informal sector, many prefer the alternative approach of raising the consumption of the urban poor indirectly through subsidies for housing and access to other urban services. Ideally, such schemes should be designed with a maximum of informal sector employment-generating capacity. Low-income housing programs combining sites (with titles) and services with availability of low-cost building materials have been viewed as promising.

Approaches combining work and welfare components are required if such efforts are to be financially viable. But compensatory measures are needed, especially for segments of the informal labor force who are in more disadvantaged positions in the urban economic structure and for whom it plays mainly a welfare function. Older workers and female heads of households may have disabilities and family responsibilties that limit their earning capacities, especially in the formal sector. They turn to the informal sector for survival and cannot be expected to "work their way out" of poverty. While more capable individuals can utilize the looser organization of the informal market to their advantage, the relative lack of security in informal activities can be especially hard on those with disadvantages.

X   Fertility and Mortality
in the Postwar Period

Introduction

Industrialization and rapid urban growth in the postwar period have accelerated changes in the structure of Brazilian society. We now turn to an examination of the interrelations between these changes and the determinants of population increase: fertility and mortality. European industrialization was accompanied by a transition from high birth and death rates to low birth and death rates, with a period of accelerated population growth during the transition, as declining birth rates lagged behind declining death rates—a process that has come to be known as the demographic transition. Assessments of economic and demographic trends in developing countries, including Brazil, have raised many questions about the applicability of a transition model to them. Mortality declines, which were gradual and concomitant with economic growth in Europe, have been expedited by the importation of modern medical technology to developing countries, making mortality decline an exogenous factor in the development process (Arriaga and Davis 1969, Preston 1975). Birth rates, which declined in response to the social and economic pressures of industrialized urban life in Europe, are substantially higher in developing countries than they were in Europe on the eve of the Industrial Revolution. They have remained high for the bulk of developing country populations, which have only had limited participation in the modernization process. International migration, which was a major outlet for European population pressure in the last century, is more restricted today.

   The net effect in demographic terms has been population growth rates that are often double those experienced by European countries during their demographic transitions. Pessimistic neo-Malthusians see the demographic situation of the developing countries as a circular process in which slow economic growth prevents declines in the birth rate, while the resulting population increase inhibits economic growth. In this perspective, control of population growth is a necessary requirement for breaking the vicious circle. Others are more optimistic. True, population increase is more rapid in developing countries compared to Western Europe during the transition, but so are other aspects of socioeconomic change. Fertility declines lag behind such changes, but will occur with a concerted development effort. Policy discussions have (unfortunately) become polarized into "population control" and "developmentalist" positions regarding the complex interrelationships between population change and development, generally to the detriment of a better understanding of the problem. The issues revolve around two complex questions: (1) To what extent have fertility and mortality in developing countries been responsive to socioeconomic change? and (2) To what extent has rapid population growth been detrimental to the process of economic development? While closely related, both questions merit detailed discussion with regard to Brazil; therefore, this chapter will focus on the first question and the next will address itself to the second.

Demographers are uneasy with efforts to explain or predict the course of demographic events in developing countries on the basis of transition theory. European experience, on which the theory is based, is itself full of exceptions to its main generalizations. Most are familiar with the textbook version of the theory, which is patterned on the transition in England and Wales. Other countries (France and Sweden are good examples) experienced quite different patterns, either because of differences in the initiation of changes or in the pace of declines once they had started. In reviewing nearly two decades of research on patterns of marital fertility in Europe since the Industrial Revolution, Coale (1973) concluded that three firm generalizations could be drawn from the European experience. For a decline in marital fertility to occur, three preconditions must be met: (1) control of fertility must be a matter of conscious choice to individuals; (2) they must have access to the means of fertility control; and (3) they must perceive some advantage to themselves in using these means to reduce the number of births. The onset of decline in marital fertility is related more to the meeting of these conditions than to broader socioeconomic changes, like urbanization, even though the two are closely associated in many instances.

Concern with the applicability of the transition model is not limited to the decline of marital fertility. Davis (1963) and Friedlander (1969) have stressed a view of the transition process that encompasses a multiplicity of demographic responses to modernization. Any combination of responses could direct a particular country's path from high to low fertility and mortality. Such paths might indeed appear to be different from the one that is considered normal in a narrower definition of the transition.

In the case of Latin America, reviews of recent demographic trands in a number of countries, including Brazil, by Beaver (1975) and Oeschli and Kirk (1975) suggest that birth and death rates in the region are conforming more to the transition model than was previously thought. An implication of their findings is that doubts about the applicability of demographic transition theory to developing country experiences outlined above may be based on too narrow an interpretation of the theory. After deriving composite indices of modernization from data on different socioeconomic characteristics, Oeschli and Kirk found that birth and death rates corresponded quite closely to the level of development indicated for them by the modernization measures. Interestingly, one country that provided a relatively poor fit was Brazil, which actually had lower fertility and mortality than would be suggested by its level of overall modernization.[1]

Factors Affecting Fertility and Mortality in Brazil

Our review of long-term demographic trends in Chapter III revealed a number of features in Brazilian experience that must be weighed in assessing the transition concept for Brazil. Chief among these is the great regional diversity that has characterized Brazilian development. The tendency toward lower fertility and mortality appears to have been underway in Southern and Southeastern regions since before 1950, whereas fertility rates in the Northeast remained high, along with those in the regions of recent settlement. Immigration, which had a differential regional impact, contributed to the earlier onset of demographic changes in the South, in addition to having a more general impact on North-South socioeconomic differences. A second important feature of the recent demographic trend is that fertility declines, though predominantly an urban phenomenon, have also occurred in some rural areas.

Brazil's birth rate, like that of many developing countries, remained higher (above 40 per thousand) for a longer time than was typical of most "late starters" among presently industrialized areas once their mortality was declining. Natural increase has been in excess of 1.8 percent per annum since the 1890s, and closer to 3 percent per annum in the post-World War II period. The persistence of high birth rates in Brazil up to the late 1950s, even after substantial urbanization and industrialization had occurred, was a cause of concern (Gendell 1967), at least until the 1970 census results revealed an incipient decline in the birth rate. Beaver's (1975) analysis found a similar lag

[1]There are a number of possible reasons for Brazil's deviation from the model tested by Oeschli and Kirk (1975). As will be seen below, Brazil's great regional diversity is probably the most important. It may also be that the United Nations' estimates of the crude birth rate for Brazil, which was employed in their study, was, in fact, lower than it should have been; Oeschli and Kirk employed a rate of 37.8 for Brazil in 1960–70, whereas our estimates indicated that it may have been closer to 40–41 per thousand. In this case, Brazil may "fit" the model better than indicated. However, our view is that such a fit would be misleading in that the aggregate data mask so many important differences in fertility within Brazil.

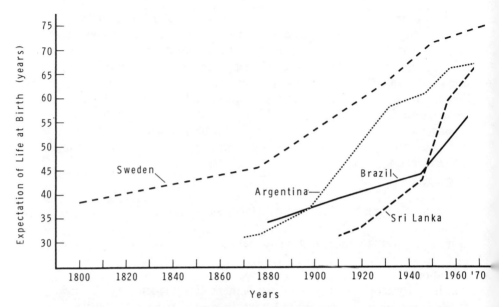

Figure X–1. Comparison of Trends in the Expectation of Life at Birth: Brazil, Sweden, Agentina, and Sri Lanka. *Sources:* Brazil, Table II–9; others, University of Pennsylvania, Graduate Group in Demography, *Report of Workshop in History of the Mortality Transition*, processed, May 1975.

in other Latin American countries, but also showed that fertility decline, once initiated, was more rapid than was the experience of European countries. While it is still too early to judge the strength of the Brazilian trend, it should be noted again that age structure effects accounted for a part of the decline in the crude birth rate, indicating that actual fertility decline was more limited.

Brazil's mortality decline, on the other hand, has not followed the pattern experienced in some Asian countries (Sri Lanka and Mauritius, for example), where precipitous increases in population growth occurred after introduction of modern medical techniques reduced their mortality in the space of a decade. Even though the pace of mortality decline in Brazil picked up after the adoption of many of these measures after 1930, its overall experience has been of that of a more gradual improvement in life expectancy (Figure X–1). Chapter III showed that a moderated mortality decline was under way by the end of the nineteenth century, and that it could have been related to immigration, public health campaigns or improved economic conditions, and probably a combination of all three. What then are the patterns of fertility and mortality change that have taken place in Brazil? It is useful to start with an overview of the main geographic differences: interregional, interstate, and rural-urban, around 1970.

Differences in Fertility and Mortality by Place of Residence

Patterns in the 1970 Census Data

Table X-1 presents estimates of total fertility rates and crude birth rates derived from the question in the 1970 census on births reported for the twelve months prior to the census interview. Costa (1976a) has employed the Brass technique to estimate these measures on a state-by-state basis; detailed discussion of the methodological issues is found in his work. In the table, estimates are broken down by state and rural urban residence; averages are also shown for the five macroregions and for Brazil.

Total fertility is 56 percent higher for rural areas than for urban areas at the national level. The rural/urban differential is greatest in states in which total fertility is at an intermediate level, and least in those whose fertility is very high. In the Northeast, for example, rural fertility is only 24 percent higher than urban fertility, while the rural/urban differential increases to 62 percent in the Southeast. Within the Southeast, though, the differential is larger in the states of Minas Gerais and Espirito Santo, where the total fertility rate is higher than in Rio de Janeiro and São Paulo, but lower than in the Northeast. Rural fertility is also comparatively high in states that have experienced considerable rural-to-rural migration in recent decades (Paraná, Mato Grosso, and Goiás). There rural fertility levels approach those observed in the Northeast, while urban levels are closer to those in the South and Southeast. High total fertility is also observed in the rural areas of the Northern region, in which the states Amazonas and Pará are located. Here, too, the pattern suggests that incipient rural-to-rural migration flows to these areas are affecting rural/urban differentials.

Lower urban fertility in the industrialized and more urbanized Southeastern region is the main factor in the large differential between total fertility in the Northeast and Southeast. Total fertility in the Northeast is 57 percent higher than in the Southeast for the entire population, but only 20 percent higher for the rural population. In contrast, the urban Northeast/Southeast differential is 59 percent. These differentials appear to confirm an earlier hypothesis that Brazil's incipient fertility decline, if it is occurring, is largely a phenomenon of the urban Southeast. There are some rural exceptions to this, for example, rural São Paulo and rural Rio Grande do Sul; still, the main thrust of the decline appears to be limited to the Southeastern urban centers.

A similar pattern of rural-urban and regional differences appears in the crude birth rates, shown in the last three columns of the table. Because of the age structure effects of interregional migration, crude birth rate differentials are somewhat less than those observed for total fertility. For example, while total fertility in the Northeast is 57 percent higher than in the Southeast, the

Table X-1. Regional and Interstate Differences in Fertility by Rural-Urban Residence, 1970 Census Data

Region-State	Total fertility rate[a]			Crude birth rate[b]		
	Rural	Urban	Total	Rural	Urban	Total
1. North	9.01	6.50	7.79	53.1	44.6	49.5
Amazonas	9.70	6.72	8.34	56.1	46.1	52.1
Pará	8.69	6.41	7.56	51.7	44.0	48.3
2. Northeast	8.15	6.57	7.53	51.4	47.7	50.0
Maranhão	7.06	7.00	7.03	47.5	49.1	47.9
Piauí	8.10	7.14	7.77	49.0	49.7	49.3
Ceará	7.63	6.65	7.71	51.5	48.5	50.4
Rio Grande do Norte	9.87	7.34	8.57	58.2	51.7	55.1
Paraíba	8.67	6.68	7.76	52.4	48.3	50.7
Pernambuco	8.62	6.26	7.23	53.0	46.9	49.7
Alagoas	8.35	6.49	7.55	53.1	47.5	50.9
Sergipe	7.03	6.69	7.87	55.0	46.4	51.0
Bahia	8.24	6.43	7.43	51.2	46.7	49.3
3. Southeast	6.76	4.12	4.79	43.6	32.0	34.9
Minas Gerais	7.70	5.23	6.28	46.8	37.8	42.0
Espírito Santo	7.85	5.24	6.54	45.9	37.7	42.1
Rio de Janeiro	6.98	4.60	5.03	41.5	35.0	36.4
Guanabara	–	2.90	2.90	–	24.6	24.6
São Paulo	4.99	3.70	4.02	39.0	29.8	31.4
4. South	6.97	4.28	5.59	42.5	33.8	38.3
Paraná	7.58	4.85	6.40	46.1	38.0	42.9
Santa Catarina	7.46	5.06	6.31	43.4	37.5	40.9
Rio Grande do Sul	5.87	3.57	4.43	37.0	29.3	32.3
5. Central-West	7.60	5.43	6.47	46.7	40.2	42.9
Mato Grosso	7.99	5.52	6.96	47.4	40.3	44.5
Goiás	7.38	5.38	6.21	46.2	40.1	42.0
Brazil[c]	7.66	4.92	5.83	47.2	36.1	40.8

[a]Births per woman.
[b]Births per thousand population.
[c]Includes territories and federal district, not included above.
Source: Costa (1976: 105–13).

crude birth rate is only 43 percent higher. Interregional migration from the Northeast to the Southeast has offset some of the effects of the total fertility differential on total births by increasing the proportion of population in age groups most likely to have children in the Southeast, while reducing it in the Northeast. Interactions between migration, population age structure, and fertility are quite complex and have been discussed in greater detail elsewhere (Merrick 1974).

Demographic as well as socioeconomic factors are important in understanding these regional and rural-urban differentials in fertility. The total fertility rate takes account of one of the main demographic influences—age. Another major demographic factor in fertility differentials is marriage. Both the average age at marriage and the proportion of the population ever marrying have an important influence on fertility by virtue of their effect on the number

Table X-2. Regional and Interstate Differences in Marriage Patterns by Rural-Urban
Residence, 1970 Census Data

Region-State	Singulate mean age at marriage (years)			Proportion single at age 50–54 (percent)		
	Rural	Urban	Total	Rural	Urban	Total
1. North	21.8	23.9	22.8	5.9	11.5	8.7
Amazonas	21.7	23.6	22.6	4.8	10.3	7.4
Para	21.8	24.3	23.0	6.9	12.7	10.0
2. Northeast	22.3	23.6	22.9	8.3	13.0	10.4
Maranhão	20.4	23.2	21.1	6.4	11.1	7.7
Piauí	22.0	23.5	22.5	7.6	11.9	9.1
Ceará	23.2	24.2	23.9	8.6	13.9	11.0
Rio Grande do Norte	23.0	24.3	23.7	8.1	11.4	9.7
Paraíba	23.6	24.3	23.9	10.0	12.0	10.8
Pernambuco	22.9	23.8	23.4	8.2	12.0	10.3
Alagoas	21.4	22.7	21.9	7.3	13.2	9.9
Sergipe	22.1	22.9	22.4	8.6	15.6	12.2
Bahia	22.5	23.5	23.0	10.0	16.2	12.7
3. Southeast	20.7	24.0	23.5	4.1	9.4	8.6
Minas Gerais	22.4	24.8	23.5	7.7	12.3	10.4
Espírito Santo	22.0	23.9	22.9	4.6	6.3	5.4
Rio de Janeiro	22.4	23.6	23.1	4.5	7.4	6.8
Guanabara	–	24.6	24.6	–	13.1	13.1
São Paulo	21.6	23.7	23.3	3.9	7.9	7.3
4. South	21.8	22.8	22.3	4.4	7.6	6.0
Paraná	20.6	22.5	21.4	2.9	6.0	4.2
Santa Catarina	22.0	22.8	22.4	4.2	6.5	5.2
Rio Grande do Sul	22.6	23.2	23.1	6.2	10.3	8.6
5. Central-West	20.5	23.0	21.7	4.5	6.9	5.7
Mato Grosso	20.7	23.1	21.8	3.4	7.1	5.3
Goiás	20.4	23.0	21.6	5.6	6.6	6.1
Brazil[a]	21.6	23.6	22.8	6.2	10.7	8.7

[a]Includes territories and federal district, not included above.
Source: Calculated from census data, using method of Hajnal (1953).

of years of exposure to the risk of child-bearing. In the European demographic
transition, a factor that accounted for the relatively low crude birth rates at the
beginning of the transition (when European countries are compared to currently developing countries) was their late average age of marriage and the
relatively high proportion of European women who never married.

Brazil is similar to other developing countries in that the age of marriage is
typically earlier, and that marriage is more universal, although, as Table X–2
shows, the average age at marriage is not as low (below 20 years of age) as is
common in some Asian societies. Table X–2 presents two measures that are
designed to show the effects of marriage on fertility in Brazil. These are the
singulate mean age of marriage and the proportion of women who are still
single at ages 50 to 54. Both are indirect measures, since Brazil does not pos-
sess comprehensive nuptiality data for the period around 1970. The singulate
mean age at marriage is a measure derived by John Hajnal (1953) from census

data on the proportions of women reported as single. It is useful to compare this measure to the proportion of women who are still single at ages 50 to 54, since the comparison gives some idea of the extent to which a particular population deviates from the European pattern of late average age at marriage and relatively high proportions of women who never marry. In Brazil, we observe an important rural/urban differential in the singulate mean age at marriage, with the average age of marriage in urban areas being two years higher than that in rural areas. The differential is lowest in the Northeast and highest in the frontier areas, with other regions showing intermediate differentials. The sex selectivity of migration explains the regional pattern. A higher proportion of males migrating out of both rural and urban areas of the Northeast have made it comparatively more difficult for Northeastern women who remain behind to find husbands. And the same male selectivity in in-migration to the frontier states has made it correspondingly difficult for males to find mates, thereby contributing to a reduction of the average age of marriage for females. Again the highest singulate mean age of marriage occurs in the urban Southeast, suggesting that delayed marriage related either to education or an increased number of years in the labor market by urban women contributes indirectly, through delays in marriage, to the lower rate of total fertility observed in the Southeast.

The comparatively late age of marriage in the Northeast is further evidence of the way in which migration dampens the effect of large regional differences in total fertility on the actual number of births that occur. The other measure shown in Table X–2, the proportion single at age fifty, serves mainly to confirm the point that marriage is still relatively universal in Brazil, although the comparatively high proportion of women remaining single in the urban Northeast is a further indication of the influence of male-oriented outmigration from that region over the past several decades.

Data limitations make it difficult to determine the extent to which changes in the mean age at marriage may have influenced fertility. It was possible to calculate the 1960 average for the national level only, and published data for 1950 do not include the required age breakdown. Between 1960 and 1970, the mean age of marriage increased from 22.2 to 22.6 years for the total population. All of this increase occurred in urban areas (23.0 to 23.6 years), since the rural level did not change. This suggests that increased involvement of women in activities other than child-bearing may have been a factor in declines in urban fertility. At this time, data to check on trends in the mean age of marriage at the state level are not available.

The other major demographic factor that could account for regional and rural–urban differentials in fertility is control of fertility within marriage. Again no comprehensive data on the use of contraceptives in Brazil are available, and it is necessary to turn to indirect measures in order to learn the extent to which fertility control may be prevalent. One useful indirect measure is the index of fertility control (m) developed by Coale and Trussel (1974). Their measure is

Table X-3. Index of Fertility Control by Region, State, and Rural-Urban Residence, 1970

Region-State	M^a	m^b, by age				
		25-29	30-34	35-39	40-44	45-49
1. North	1.296	.155	.193	.159	.106	-.544
Amazonas	1.294	.125	.144	.102	.086	-.612
Pará	1.298	.186	.241	.215	.125	-.477
2. Northeast	1.349	.216	.207	.212	.142	-.395
Maranhão	1.064	.104	.138	.196	.139	-.520
Piauí	1.267	.170	.151	.156	.066	-.312
Ceará	1.359	.145	.168	.151	.068	-.370
Rio Grande do Norte	1.510	.116	.174	.157	.088	-.381
Paraiba	1.436	.137	.152	.176	.090	-.355
Pernambuco	1.369	.276	.283	.268	.198	-.434
Alagoas	1.305	.304	.273	.290	.218	-.404
Sergipe	1.492	.536	.304	.299	.259	-.377
Bahia	1.344	.155	.220	.210	.156	-.406
3. Southeast	1.053	.779	.717	.599	.467	-.092
Minas Gerais	1.201	.434	.380	.298	.189	-.311
Espírito Santo	1.161	.556	.474	.329	.189	-.338
Rio de Janeiro	1.072	.880	.783	.605	.441	-.071
Guanabara	.893	1.097	1.076	1.003	.848	+.151
Sao Paulo	.937	.928	.873	.757	.667	+.110
4. South	1.008	.674	.570	.439	.297	-.183
Parana	1.022	.605	.491	.387	.235	-.270
Santa Catariná	1.076	.609	.515	.344	.237	-.240
Rio Grande do Sul	.927	.809	.704	.586	.420	-.039
5. Central-West	1.086	.497	.443	.366	.225	-.292
Mato Grosso	1.102	.446	.410	.337	.169	-.389
Goias	1.070	.547	.476	.394	.281	-.195
Brazil^c	1.200	.436	.401	.346	.246	-.297

^{a}Index of fertility level.
^{b}Index of fertility control.
^{c}Includes territories and federal district, not included above.

derived from the ratios of age-specific marital fertility rates to a standard representing natural fertility (therefore no fertility control). Marital fertility at ages 20 to 24 is first compared to the standard rate for that cohort, yielding an index of the level of fertility (M); then indices of fertility control (m) are determined for each of the remaining cohorts as a function of the degree to which they fall below the rates in the standard pattern (for further discussion of the computational aspects, see Knodel 1977).

Table X-3 presents average values of M and m derived from the 1970 census data by state and region. Values of m can range from zero (natural fertility) to nearly four. A value of one represents the average of 43 fertility schedules (for around the year 1965) employed by Coale and Trussel, with 0.2 representing very limited fertility control and 0.8 representing a moderate level. A value of one for M corresponds to fertility at ages 20 to 24 equal to that in the natural fertility standard. In the Brazilian data, M ranges from 0.9 to 1.5, with a national average of 1.2. On the surface, these data suggest that fertility in Brazil is above the natural fertility standard represented by the data assembled by Coale and Trussel. However, caution is required in interpreting M. The age-specific marital fertility rate on which M is based has been derived indirectly from census data, and then divided by the reported proportion married at ages 20 to 24 in the census data. Though the reported proportion of births occurring outside of marriage is quite low (about 0.5 percent), it is possible that errors in the census data are inflating M.

The index of fertility control (m) is based on the pattern of fertility by age, rather than the level of fertility, and therefore escapes this particular bias. The index for ages 25 to 29 ranges from 0.1 in Maranhão to 1.1 in Guanabara (Rio de Janeiro). Theoretically, there should be a fair degree of uniformity in the m values for different ages. This is not true of Brazilian data, in which the value of m declines substantially at ages above 40. Brazilian marital fertility at older ages, especially 45 to 49, is consistently higher than in the standard population. Page (1977) has pointed out that age differences in m could arise from deviation of a population in its composition by marital duration from the standard population used in computing the index. Differences in the singulate mean age of marriage in Table X–2 suggest that such differences occur within the Brazilian population, and indicate caution in interpretation of variation in m values at older ages. A possible explanation of the Brazilian pattern is that fertility control is more prevalent among younger married women, which if true would contrast Brazil to populations in which control begins more typically among older women. Richers and Almeida's (1975: 14–15) finding that the use of contraceptives obtained in the private market is concentrated among younger, lower parity women in higher socioeconomic groups would support this interpretation. The overall differences in the Brazilian data are large enough for us to conclude that deliberate control underlies differences between marital fertility rates in the Northeast and Southeast, and that the incipient fertility decline in the latter region is the result of conscious fertility control.

Turning finally to mortality, we find similar interregional differences but contrasting rural-urban patterns. Carvalho's (1977) estimates of state, regional, and rural-urban differentials in mortality are shown in Table X–4. Wide interstate and interregional differentials are observed, with life expectancy at birth in the Northeast (47.3) more than 20 percent lower than in the South (60.0), and the state of Rio Grande do Norte (40.6) more than one-third less than the state with the highest life expectancy, Rio Grande do Sul (63.8). Interestingly, rural-urban differences, which were a main factor in North-South fertility differentials, are much less in the case of mortality, and play a different role in regional patterns.

Expectation of life in urban areas is only 1.3 percent higher than in rural areas, and is 4.8 percent lower in the Northeast. Lower urban life expectancy is also observed in three Southeastern states and two of the three Southern states. Infant mortality rates, a major factor in life expectancy differentials,

Table X-4. Estimates of Life Expectancy and Infant Mortality by State, Region, and Rural-Urban Residence, 1960-70

Region-State	Life expectancy[a]			Infant mortality[b]		
	Rural	Urban	Total	Rural	Urban	Total
1. North	54.5	55.6	54.9	94.3	88.5	92.0
Amazonas	54.6	54.8	54.7	93.5	92.6	93.3
Pará	54.4	55.9	55.0	94.7	86.9	91.4
2. Northeast	47.7	45.4	47.3	137.8	153.2	141.5
Maranhão	50.4	49.5	50.5	117.0	122.5	117.9
Piauí	52.3	48.1	50.9	106.2	131.0	114.5
Ceará	47.3	42.9	45.5	137.5	169.3	150.1
Rio Grande do Norte	40.3	40.9	40.6	191.4	196.0	189.1
Paraíba	44.7	42.5	48.2	156.1	173.1	163.1
Pernambuco	43.0	44.4	43.8	168.7	157.8	163.0
Alagoas	45.0	45.2	45.1	153.5	152.3	153.0
Sergipe	46.8	46.8	46.8	141.0	140.5	140.7
Bahia	51.4	48.4	50.3	111.0	130.0	118.1
3. Southeast	56.4	57.5	57.2	82.9	79.4	81.2
Minas Gerais	55.2	54.4	54.8	85.7	94.3	90.2
Espírito Santo	58.8	56.8	58.4	73.2	82.6	84.9
Rio de Janeiro	57.0	56.2	56.4	81.5	85.5	84.5
Guanabara	–	59.2	59.2	–	71.5	71.5
São Paulo	57.7	59.1	58.8	78.6	72.0	73.4
4. South	60.0	60.0	60.0	67.2	68.5	67.3
Parana	56.9	57.4	57.0	82.1	79.8	81.4
Santa Catarina	61.0	58.8	60.0	64.2	73.2	68.3
Rio Grande do Sul	64.0	62.3	63.8	47.3	58.6	51.9
5. Central-West	58.4	58.3	58.3	74.7	75.6	74.8
Mato Grosso	56.7	58.1	57.3	83.0	76.3	80.1
Goias	59.2	58.4	58.8	71.6	75.2	73.4
Brazil[c]	53.3	54.0	53.7	100.9	96.7	98.7

[a]Years of life expectancy at births.
[b]Deaths at ages 0 to 1 per 1,000 live births.
[c]Includes territories and federal district, not included above.
Source: Carvalho (1977).

mirror this pattern, but the differences are more accentuated. In the Northeast, infant mortality is 11 percent higher in urban areas, and the differential reaches 10 percent even in the Southeastern state of Minas Gerais. Before attempting to interpret these differences, it will be useful also to examine data on changes in the pattern of regional differences over time.

Regional Trends in Fertility and Mortality

Available regional data for intervals earlier than 1960–70 are less extensive. The question on births in the year prior to the census, which is needed for calculating total fertility, is not found in the earlier census. Indirect estimates of total fertility and crude birth in a ten-way regional breakdown are available for 1940–50 and are shown in Table X–5. This regionalization delineates large states (e.g., São Paulo) and important subregions of the Northeast (Maranhão-Piauí and Bahia-Sergipe), thus preserving most of the distinctive features to be found in an interstate comparison.

It is clear that the differentials discussed in the previous section existed also in 1940–50. Two points stand out in comparing 1960–70 to 1940–50: (1) that regional differences in the crude birth rate widened in the two decade interval, with greater declines in the Southeast (Minas Gerais, Rio de Janeiro, and São Paulo) and South (Santa Catarina, Rio Grande do Sul), more limited declines in the Northeast, and no change or actual increases in the frontier regions (Paraná, Central-West, Amazónia); and (2) that migration and its effect on age structure played an important role in this, since total fertility, which controls for age, declines more in comparison to changes in the crude birth rates in some regions and less in others. The most striking case is Rio de Janeiro-Guanabara, were total fertility was constant, but the crude birth rate declined.

Crude birth rates hovered close to 50 per thousand in the Northeastern regions, but approached the low 30s in Rio de Janeiro-Guanabara and São Paulo. These changes in crude rates for the first five regions (Amazonas through Minas Gerais–Espírito Santo) mask increases or small declines in total fertility, because migration and high fertility reduced the weight of women in child-bearing ages in the total population in these regions (Merrick 1974). Rio de Janeiro-Guanabara is especially affected because it combines Guanabara with the state of Rio de Janeiro and has experienced more complex *intra-* as well as *inter*regional migration movements.

While interregional differences in fertility increased between 1950 and 1970, differences in a number of socioeconomic variables that are closely associated with them (income per capita, urbanization, adult literacy, proportion of children in school) narrowed when these differences were compared using a coefficient of regional variation. Substantial interregional differences in the *level* of these variables persist and are clearly associated with the differential level of fertility and mortality observed here. However, the *increase* in interregional differentials, especially in fertility, between 1940–50 and 1960–70 is unexpected, in view of the narrowing of differentials in these socioeconomic variables.

As suggested above, the substantial interregional migration flows that have occurred in Brazil between 1940 and 1970 help to explain the divergence of regional fertility trends from changes in socioeconomic variables. In addition to the age structure effects mentioned earlier, migration is also selective of individuals with a higher propensity to assume new behavior patterns than the nonmigrant group. This selectivity could, in effect, transfer individuals who are more likely to lead a fertility decline or undertake better child-care practices leading to a reduction in mortality in an area of out-migration (the Northeast) to an area of in-migration in which fertility and mortality declines are already under way (the Southeast). A similar process could be occurring in

Table X-5. Regional Trends in Fertility Measures, 1940–50 to 1960–70

Region	Crude birth rate			Total fertility rate		
	1940–50	1960–70	Percentage Change	1940–50	1960–70	Percentage Change
Amazonas-Pará	45.9	46.2	+0.6	7.3	7.8	+6.8
Maranhão-Piauí	46.8	44.0	−6.0	7.0	7.3	+4.3
Northeast	52.1	49.6	−4.8	7.7	7.6	−1.3
Bahia-Sergipe	47.9	48.5	+1.3	7.3	7.5	+2.3
Minas Gerais-Espírito Santo	44.7	39.9	−10.7	6.8	6.3	−7.4
Rio de Janeiro-Guanabara	33.9	31.1	−8.3	4.0	4.0	0.0
São Paulo	37.9	33.0	−12.9	4.4	4.0	−11.1
Paraná	43.7	45.3	+3.7	5.9	6.4	+8.5
S. Catarina-Rio Grande do Sul	41.1	35.9	−12.7	5.5	5.0	−9.1
Central-West	43.8	43.6	−0.5	6.4	6.5	+1.6
Brazil	43.5	40.5	−7.7	6.3	5.8	−7.9

Sources: Crude birth rate, Merrick (1974); total fertility rate, Carvalho (1973), Costa (1976*a*).

Table X-6. Regional Trends in the Expectation of Life at Birth, 1940–50 to 1960–70

Region	Life expectancy at birth (years)		Percent change 1940–50 to 1960–70
	1940–50	1960–70	
Amazonas-Pará	42.7	54.9	28.6
Maranhão-Piauí	43.7	50.6	15.8
Northeast	34.0	44.8	31.8
Bahia-Sergipe	39.2	44.9	27.3
Minas Gerais-Espírito Santo	46.1	55.2	19.7
Rio de Janeiro-Guanabara	48.7	57.7	18.5
São Paulo	49.4	58.8	19.0
Paraná	45.9	57.0	24.2
Santa Catarina-Rio Grande do Sul	55.3	62.6	13.2
Central-West	49.8	58.3	17.1
Brazil	43.6	53.7	23.2

Source: Carvalho (1973, 1977).

rural-urban shifts both within and between regions. Unfortunately, the 1950 data do not permit a comparison by region for both rural and urban areas. It is also possible that the exclusion of family planning from regional development programs has resulted in a less widespread fertility decline than might have occurred had such services been included. Factors affecting rural fertility in a selected number of states for which special 1970 census tabulation are available will be discussed below.

Regional mortality differentials, shown in Table X–6, also persisted from 1940–50 to 1960–70 and remain large. Life expectancy in the Northeast in 1960–70 barely surpasses the 1940–50 national level. Carvalho, whose estimates of life expectancy are shown in Table X–6, did not think that the infant mortality estimates ($_1q_0$) derived in his 1940–50 life tables were reliable (1973: 66), and for this reason we omit the interdecadal comparison of infant mortality rates from Table X–6.

In contrast to the fertility pattern, interregional mortality differentials appear to narrow between 1940–50 and 1960–70. Regions with lower life expectancy in the earlier period (principally the Northeast and Bahia-Sergipe) show the most improvement, while Santa Catarina-Rio Grande do Sul, with the highest level in 1940–50, show the least. The contrasting regional patterns in fertility and mortality are confirmed when their coefficients of regional variation for the two decades are compared:

Measure	Coefficient of Variation (Percent)	
	1940–50	1960–70
Crude Birth Rate	11.2	14.7
Total Fertility	19.2	21.9
Life Expectancy	12.5	9.0

These indices show that interregional variation in life expectancy declined by more than 25 percent, while fertility differences increased by about 15 percent.

The regional differences in fertility and mortality that we have observed, the trends that underlie them, and the divergence between fertility and mortality patterns raise a number of questions about Brazil's demographic transition, of which three are of particular importance: (1) What are the main factors in the fertility decline occurring in urban areas, especially as they affect migrants? (2) Why are rural-urban mortality differentials so much narrower than those in fertility? (3) What explains the rural fertility decline which, though much more limited, are nonetheless occurring in parts of the South and Southeast?

Socioeconomic Correlates of Fertility and Mortality

Fertility and Urbanization in Brazil

Education, increased female employment opportunities, changing aspirations brought about by exposure to mass media, and access to the means of family planning are well-known factors that contribute to a reduction in the average size of the urban family—through delayed marriage and by decreased fertility within marriage. Of particular importance in Brazil is the impact of these influences not only on the native urban population but also in the migrants, who have been the major reason for increased urban population growth since 1940.

Several recent studies of migration and fertility in Brazilian and other Latin American cities have shown that the influence of the urban setting on migrant fertility depends as much on educational and other socioeconomic characteristics of migrants as on migration status per se (for a summary, see Macisco et al. 1969). These analyses of migrant fertility, which control for length of residence, show that migrants with longer-term residence succeeded in assimilating urban reproductive norms, though this was conditioned by socioeconomic status variables like age and residence at marriage, and age at which migration occurred.

Analysis of survey data for six Brazilian cities in the early 1960s by Iutaka, Bock, and Varnes (1971) confirms the effects on socioeconomic status and length of residence on migrant reproductive patterns in Brazil. Further it was found that status played a more important role in migrants' fertility than was the case for natives. Thus, despite initial differences between fertility rates for recent migrants and other urban residents, the migrants succeeded in absorbing urban fertility patterns after a decade or more of urban residence.

Additional evidence on the relation between migration and urban fertility is found in the 1970 census data. Special tabulations for the metropolitan area of

Belo Horizonte, whose migration and fertility levels fall between those of the more industrialized São Paulo and Rio de Janeiro and the remaining regional centers like Salvador and Recife, illustrate differences in age-specific fertility rates for natives and migrants of different duration-of-residence classes. These data are shown in Table X–7. Total fertility of migrants is 4.68, as compared to 4.23 for natives. However, the migrant rates are clearly inflated by the rates for migrants of 10 or fewer years of residence, whose total fertility exceeds 5, while the total fertility of longer-residence migrants (4.19) is actually less than that for natives. There is a clear pattern of migrant assimilation of the native urban fertility pattern as one looks across the length of residence classes for each age group. The main exception appears to be the older migrants of 6–10 years residence, whose rates are closer to the 0–5 group than are the younger members of this class. These women arrived in the metropolitan area at a later stage of their reproductive lives than the younger women, and it appears that their absorption of the native urban pattern was slower because of this.

Examination of the shares of natives and migrants classed by length of residence in the total number of child-bearing women and births in metropolitan Belo Horizonte in 1970 (the last two rows of Table X–7) further illustrates the importance of migrants' births to that city's natural increase. Migrant women constituted 66 percent of the poulation in ages 15–49, but contributed 71 percent of births. Recent (especially 0–5 years) migrants were primarily responsible for this, because of their higher age-specific fertility rates and because of the concentration of younger women in the peak child-bearing ages among recent migrants. The emphasis placed by several authors (Macisco et al. 1969, Iutaka et al. 1971) on the contribution of migrants' natural increase to urban population growth in coming decades is warranted if Belo Horizonte's experience is at all typical of other cities. According to a recent SERFHAU (Brazil, Ministério do Interior, 1976) study of migrant's overall fertility levels in several major metropolitan areas in 1970, the relative potential for migrants' contribution to natural increase is even greater in São Paulo, Rio de Janeiro, and Southern cities like Porto Alegre than in Belo Horizonte, but less in cities of the North and Northeast.

The rapidly changing structure of female educational and labor force participation in urban Brazil described earlier has undoubtedly reinforced the declining urban fertility trend. Increases in the proportion of women in the earlier child-bearing ages who are working is a clear indication of the rise in activities that are an alternative to child-bearing, and increases in the proportions in school have a similar effect. Special tabulations of 1970 census data on the fertility of women classed by educational level have proved difficult to interpret (principally because there are so few women in the upper educational levels who have children before their late twenties, thus making it impossible to apply the United Nations' techniques that rely on reported fertility of younger women for establishing the level of fertility at all ages).

Table X-7. Age-Specific Fertility Rates[a] for Native and Migrant Women by Duration of Residence, Metropolitan Belo Horizonte, 1970

Age	Migrants 0-5 years	6-10 years	11 or more	Total	Native	Total Population
15-19	45	39	32	40	25	29
20-24	201	179	146	180	144	166
25-29	263	259	237	252	218	241
30-34	235	234	199	217	195	211
35-39	170	188	140	156	164	158
40-44	85	75	64	70	74	71
45-49	19	28	20	21	26	21
Total fertility	5.09	5.01	4.19	4.68	4.23	4.49
Percent of women 15-49	24.0	13.0	28.8	65.8	34.2	100.0
Percent of births in 1969	28.3	15.7	27.9	70.9	29.1	100.0

[a]Births per 1,000 women in each age group.
Source: Coelho and Merrick (1975: 207).

Survey results for a number of cities (Iutaka et al 1971, Camargo 1974) have shown the key role that education has played in the determination of urban fertility levels.

Rosen and Simmons's study (1971) of industrialization, family formation, and fertility in five communities in the state of São Paulo also supports the hypothesis that industrialization has influenced fertility through shifts in the social status of women, both in their work and at home. They found that new education and work opportunities facilitated the emergence of a modern view of the role of women in society and egalitarian decision-making in the family. These attitudes and patterns of husband-wife interaction were shown to be related to smaller family size ideals and lower fertility. However, these results also suggest that the effect of the changing role of women on fertility is a more complex process than simply increased labor force participation.

Camargo's (1974) analysis of survey data for Belo Horizonte showed that both education and work opportunities for women were associated with lower fertility, and that widespread employment of domestic servants made child-bearing a lesser obstacle to labor force participation by middle- and upper-class females than it would be in countries where child-care facilities are lacking. The opposite may be the case for women in lower socioeconomic groups, though the presence of other adults makes it possible for mothers to work even in these groups. Domestic service is the principal point of entry into the city for young female migrants (accounting for three-fourths of those employed in the recent migrant group). It is also an important employer of lower-class native urban women. Since employers provide servants with room and board, as well as pay for health care, in order to compensate for (or justify) the low money wage that is paid, there is a strong bias against marriage and child-bearing for domestic servants. A domestic servant who becomes pregnant often conceals the fact as long as possible in order to avoid losing her job.

The increasingly widespread use of oral contraceptives has undoubtedly had a major impact on recent reproductive practices in urban Brazil. Unlike many developing countries, Brazil has avoided publicly supported family planning, and private (IPPF supported) family planning has reached only a limited segment of the urban population. However, a recent survey of the production, distribution, and sales of contraceptives through commercial channels by Richers and Almeida (1975) has shown a rapid and widespread increase in the dissemination of contraceptives (mainly condoms and pills) through the private sector. Production of the pill by Brazilian subsidiaries of the international drug companies has increased dramatically since the mid-1960s. In 1974, their Brazilian production (39 million cycles) accounted for about 10 percent of their world total. Use of the pill by Brazilian women within reach of the commercial distribution networks is approaching levels found in developed countries. The preliminary results of this study indicate that contraception among younger women of the middle and upper classes is widespread, and suggest that it would spread quickly to the lower classes if it were included in publicly supported distribution of medicines through Brazil's public health and social security medical systems.

Urban Mortality Patterns

A major puzzle in recent Brazilian mortality patterns is the relatively narrow rural-urban differential underlying the general decline in mortality. Life expectancy in urban areas is much closer to that of rural areas than was the case with fertility and is actually less (and infant mortality greater) in urban areas in a good many states, especially in the Northeast. Further, evidence on a number of major cities, including São Paulo and Belo Horizonte, indicate that infant mortality increased during the late 1960s, principally during the period when very restrictive wage policies were putting a severe strain on low-income urban households (Yunez and Ronachezel 1974, Carvalho and Wood 1977).

To what extent do these patterns and trends reflect the deterioration of living conditions among the urban poor and increased pressures on such urban services as water, sanitation, and housing caused by migration and rapid urban population increase? Research on the links between infant and child mortality in Brazil and important factors like nutrition and safe water is still sparse. Data limitations, especially the lack of comprehensive and reliable trend data on mortality, make interpretation particularly hazardous, especially since coverage has been improving over time, which creates the additional problem of determining what portion of recent changes might be attributable to changes in data quality.[2] This has restricted most of the work that has been done to vital registration data on particular localities and to various breakdowns and indirect estimates derived from sample survey and census data.

A recent study of infant and child mortality in Latin America, which included selected Brazilian areas, found that child survival was closely tied to economic and social conditions, as well as certain demographic characteristics (Puffer and Serrano 1975). Nutrition, water supply, the practice of breast feeding, and educational attainment of mothers were shown to have a strong influence on differential mortality. Among more specifically demographic characteristics, maternal age, birth order, and birth weight (itself closely related to nutrition) were also cited. The evidence on these relationships was drawn from special surveys in twelve Latin American cities.

Comprehensive evidence on the relation between nutrition and child survival in Brazil is not yet available, though the National Survey of Household Expenditure, ENDEF, taken in 1974–75 represents a major potential for research on this question (Fundação IBGE 1977). To date, only summary tables for the major regions and selected subregions (including metropolitan areas) have been published, and breakdowns by household income level are not available. But even these summary results suggest that the situation is indeed critical. For the metropolitan areas of São Paulo and Belo Horizonte, the survey reports average calorie levels of 2,090 (SP) and 2,041 (BH), which are only 85 percent of the minimum requirement utilized for Latin America by Reutlinger and Selowsky (1976) in their recent study of malnutrition and poverty. If the *average* consumption level is so low, clearly the extent of malnutrition among lower-income groups must be severe, given what is known about the large inequalities in purchasing power that exists in these cities. DIESSE, a research institution funded by labor unions in São Paulo, calculated how many hours of work would be required by a laborer earning the minimum salary to purchase the necessary food items for a family of four, assuming that two children consume the equivalent of one adult. Since 1965

---

[2]Several important statistical problems arise in assessing the validity of the widely reported increases in infant mortality rates in larger Brazilian cities in recent years. The basic problem is to distinguish improved reporting, which has occurred during this period, from an actual increase in the death rate. Supporters of the rising death rate hypothesis point out that improved reporting also affects the number of births (the base of the infant death rate), which is true; on the other hand, there is a differential bias related to the time of reporting between the two rates. Births tend to be reported when a birth certificate is needed, e.g., when a child enters school (Cassinelli 1972). Improved death reporting, when it comes, would occur much closer to the time of the actual event. Another problem with death reporting in large cities is registration of deaths of individuals who resided elsewhere but came to the city for treatment and died. These and related problems have been examined by a number of Brazilian authors, who have concluded that an increase in mortality has actually occurred (see especially Berquó and Gonçalves 1974 and Carvalho and Wood 1976). While lingering doubts about statistical problems lead us to be cautious as to the extent to which there was an actual increase in infant mortality, it appears to be certain that an assumption of steadily declining infant mortality is not warranted in the Brazilian case.

the time necessary to provide basic food necessities at that salary level has nearly doubled, so that by 1975 it required nearly a full work week just to account for this one component of the monthly household budget, without adding the additional burden of increased expenses for housing, transport, education and health (DIESSE 1975:5).

Yunes and Ronchezel (1974: 27) compared infant mortality trends in major cities to real wage patterns in the cities and found a strikingly close association. While caution regarding the statistical significance of the mortality data is required, at the very least, this evidence suggests that conventional wisdom regarding "automatic" improvements in life expectancy following on growth of aggregate income is suspect. Closer study of the links between child survival and living conditions among Brazil's low-income groups, especially the urban poor, is much needed.

The extent of life-expectancy differentials among higher- and lower-income groups is revealed in a recent analysis of special tabulations of child survival data from the 1970 census by Carvalho and Wood (1977). Their data (represented in Table X–8) provide a breakdown of life expectancy by region for four income classes, including the very lowest group, whose family income averaged less than 150 *cruzeiros* per month in 1970. The breakdowns reveal a difference in life expectancy of 12 years (24 percent) between the lowest- and highest-income categories (49.9 versus 62 years). While the average for the lowest group is strongly affected by the comparatively large number of poor in the Northeast (where their life expectancy averages less than 43 years), large differentials are observable in other regions as well: 8 years in Rio de Janeiro-Guanabara and 9 years in São Paulo.

But income level differentials reflect more than just the higher concentration of low-income population residing in the Northeast. Further breakdowns of the data by rural-urban residence can be found in the Carvalho–Wood report. They show that the *urban* poor are actually worse off than the rural poor in all regions. In the Northeast, life expectancy for the urban poor is 40 years, compared to 44.3 years for the same income class in rural areas. In the state of São Paulo, the pattern is similar: 56.4 for the lowest rural group compared to 51.9 for the corresponding urban category. Thus, while average urban life expectancy in São Paulo is higher than in rural areas, this reflects an advantage that accrues only to upper-income groups, offsetting the disadvantaged position of lower-income residents on the average. Because the weight of urban poor is higher in the Northeast and their disadvantage vis-à-vis the rural poor greater, the urban average actually turns out to be lower than the rural, as was seen earlier.

As Carvalho and Wood point out, disaggregation of life espectancy estimates derived from census data by income level is tricky because of the effects of compositional factors on the estimating technique. Even if taken with caution, the results provide a very plausible explanation to the puzzling pattern of rural-urban differentials observed in the aggregate data and provide

Table X-8. Estimates of Life Expectancy by Household Income Level by Region, 1970

Region	Average monthly income in *cruzeiros*				
	1-150 (1)	151-300 (2)	301-500 (3)	501+ (4)	4/1 (5)
Amazonas-Pará	53.4	53.9	54.8	58.2	1.09
Maranhão-Píaui	50.0	50.8	52.7	55.7	1.11
Northeast	42.8	46.1	50.3	54.4	1.27
Bahia-Sergipe	48.9	50.3	51.9	54.9	1.12
Minas Gerais– Espírito Santo	53.8	55.4	55.6	62.3	1.16
Rio de Janeiro– Guanabara	54.1	54.8	57.6	62.1	1.15
São Paulo	54.7	56.1	58.7	63.9	1.17
Paraná	54.8	56.5	59.3	63.7	1.16
Santa Catarina– Rio Grande do Sul	60.5	61.2	63.4	66.9	1.11
Central-West	56.5	57.1	58.2	63.3	1.12
Brazil	49.9	54.5	57.6	62.0	1.24

Source: Carvalho and Wood (1977:11).

further statistical support for the view that deterioration of living conditions among the urban poor is having an effect on infant and child mortality. Clearly, much remains to be done in terms of both research and policy measures on this question.

Rural Fertility Patterns[3]

Four out of every ten Brazilians still resided in a rural area in the mid-1970s, and the proportion is higher if account is taken of Brazil's generous definition of an urban place. The path of Brazilian population growth is very much in-fluenceed by rural demographic patterns, more so to the extent that urban natural increase is declining, and rural growth is transmitted to urban areas via migration. While interstate and interregional fertility differentials were less for the rural population in 1970, rural fertility did appear to be declining in cer-tain states of the South and Southeast, especially São Paulo and Rio Grande do Sul. A particularly striking feature of the rural fertility patterns is the increase in crude birth rates observed in states in which rural settlement has occurred in recent decades (e.g., Paraná, Goiás, and Mato Grosso). These states were still predominantly (about 60 percent) rural in 1970, and were the principal destination of rural-rural migrants.

The combination of declining fertility in more settled rural areas like São Paulo and Rio Grande do Sul with increasing fertility in new settlement areas

[3]This section summarizes a more extensive analysis of the relation between frontier settlement and patterns of marriage and fertility in Southern Brazil, which have been reported in Merrick (1978).

raises interesting parallels with the experience of the United States in the nineteenth century. In a series of recent papers, Easterlin (1974, 1976) has argued that the decline in birth rates in rural areas of the United States during the nineteenth century was related to frontier settlement. Building on earlier findings of Tien (1957), Yasuba (1962), and Forster and Tucker (1972), he sought to explain why rural fertility was highest on the frontier and declining in older more settled regions. He proposed a bequest theory, in which inheritance was the important link between land availability and the fertility of American farm families. For their time American farmers owned a substantial share of the nation's wealth and were interested in preserving it, increasing it, and transmitting it to the next generation. One of their main aspirations was establishing their children with a proper start in life, preferably with a farm, or in proprietary rather than employee status in nonfarm occupations. Easterlin has shown that realization of this goal became increasingly difficult as one moved from newer to older, more settled regions of the United States in 1860. He attributed the decline in U.S. rural fertility to differences in land availability between these regions.

Land scarcity and its affect on fertility decline in more settled areas rather than fertility-raising influences on the frontier is the point of main interest. Historically, increased rural population density and continued fragmentation of rural land holdings led European populations to make demographic adjustments that included migration, delayed marriage, and reduced fertility (Davis 1963).

Anthropoligical studies of Brazil's more settled rural areas in the South suggest a similar influence of increasing land scarcity on demographic processes. Margolis (1973) has shown the negative effects of decreasing land availability on household formation in Northern Paraná as that state became more densely settled. Shirley (1971) documented the struggle for the limited lands in an older, more settled region of the state of São Paulo, where land tenure tended toward middle-sized holdings, as smaller tracts became uneconomical due to changing market conditions, and the Brazilian system of multigeniture inheritance led to the break-up of large farms. Seyferth (1973) observed a similar pattern of behavior in a study of an area colonized by German peasants in Rio Grande do Sul.

Merrick (1978) has analyzed differential rural fertility in six states in Brazil's Southern, Southeastern, and Central-Western macroregions (which will be referred to as the Center-South for brevity and to distinguish them from the remaining Northern and Northeastern macroregions, which were not included in the study). The states were chosen to represent a cross-section of more settled areas that have experienced rural exodus, as well as less settled areas that have been settled or resettled in recent decades. The effects of such socioeconomic factors as child mortality, literacy, and land-tenure patterns were also studied. Of particular relevance to policy is the question of prospects for rural fertility decline given (1) that quality agricultural land is becoming increasingly scarce (and rising in cost), and (2) that large segments of the rural population have very limited opportunity for ever owning land and thus being exposed to the economic forces that decreasing land supply might bring to bear on rural reproductive behavior.

For purposes of identifying frontier regions and comparing them to older, more settled areas, concepts such as land availability and the degree of settlement are highly relative. Frontier regions are typically characterized by a relative abundance of inexpensive land that could be incorporated into agricultural production, along with immigration of rural population seeking to take advantage of this situation. Land in highly settled regions is more scarce, resulting in greater intensity of land use, rising land prices, and out-migration of the rural population in response to these economic pressures. The scarcity or abundance of land relates not only to the actual amount that is available but also to such qualitative features as soil fertility, climate, the suitability of terrain for agricultrual purposes, and to competing patterns of land use for different agricultural (grazing versus crops, and various crop mixes) and nonagricultural purposes (e.g., urban settlements, water and forest resources, roads. See Schuh 1970: 124–28). For this reason, the amount of land utilized for agriculture may be comparatively low in relation to the total area in a "more settled" region at the same time that the region's capacity for additional agricultural expansion is very limited.

To measure land availability on the American frontier, Easterlin compared the amount of land used for agriculture in each of the counties included in his 1860 study to the maximum amount of improved land ever reported for each county. Many of the qualitative considerations mentioned above are thus built into his measure. Since expansion of agricultural land is still occurring in Brazil, this approach cannot be used. Different aspects of the relative scarcity or abundance of land in Brazil can be measured by such indicators as the ratio of land used for agriculture to total area, land value differentials, man/land ratios, migration patterns, and specific characteristics relating to terrain and location of cities. But no single measure will fully capture a particular region's potential for extension of agricultural land use.

The data analyzed were taken from published volumes of the 1970 Census of Agriculture (Fundação IBGE 1975) and special tabulations of the 1970 Population Census. In order to achieve some degree of disaggregation, the analysis was carried out at the level of homogeneous microregions as defined by the Brazilian Census Bureau (Fundação IBGE 1970). Microregions are groupings of municipalities (roughly equivalent to counties) with similar economic and social characteristics; they fall between states and municipalities in terms of aggregation. There were 155 such microregions in the six states included in the study.

Table X–9 shows important demographic characteristics of microregions, cross-tabulated by state and by the ratio of land utilized in agriculture in each region to its total area. This land-use ratio is a rough measure of land

Table X-9. Demographic Characteristics of Microregions by State and Land-use Ratio, 1970

	Land in farms/Total area (quintiles)					
	I	II	III	IV	V	Total
A. Migration (percentage of rural males age 25–29 with five or fewer years of residence):						
Minas Gerais	9	10	13	13	10	7
São Paulo	14	31	30	34	30	31
Rio Grande do Sul	–	16	9	9	11	11
Paraná	11	39	76	53	62	41
Mato Grosso	50	40	36	42	–	45
Goiás	33	31	32	–	–	32
Total	26	25	24	26	23	25
B. Marriage (percentage of rural females age 20–24 reported as married):						
Minas Gerais	50	52	60	59	55	55
São Paulo	61	59	60	60	60	60
Rio Grande do Sul	–	56	49	52	53	52
Paraná	58	70	75	68	72	68
Mato Grosso	67	66	66	65	–	66
Goiás	62	72	70	–	–	66
Total	59	61	60	59	58	59
C. Fertility (number of births in 1969 per thousand married rural women age 20–24):						
Minas Gerais	415	410	386	388	375	397
São Paulo	380	358	366	363	345	356
Rio Grande do Sul	–	325	333	360	351	344
Paraná	379	382	385	394	276	383
Mato Grosso	405	352	396	376	–	388
Goiás	418	391	395	–	–	407
TOTAL	408	381	371	372	356	378

Note: Dashes in this and subsequent tables indicate that there were no microregions in the category.
Source: Special Tabulations of 1970 Population Census.

availability, but serves as an approximation. To reduce distortion caused by the inclusion of areas with predominantly urban land use or mountain terrain largely unsuited to agriculture, eleven microregions (including the metropolitan areas of São Paulo, Belo Horizonte, Curitiba, and Porto Alegre) have been omitted. Rio de Janeiro and Brazilia were excluded by virtue of their having been separate states in the 1970 census tabulation. The land-use ratio is broken down into five categories (quintiles), ranging from the lowest (group 1) to the highest (group V) rate of land utilization.

The complexities of determining the degree of settlement are revealed by migration ratios (panel A), which show the proportion of rural males age 25 to 29 years who have resided for five or fewer years in their current (1970) municipality. The relations between migration and the land utilization index in the aggregated data is not strong, though state-by-state breakdowns suggest that migration is high in frontier regions. The rates are comparatively high in Group I–II regions of Mato Grosso and Goiás. However, the highest rates for Paraná and São Paulo are found in the upper quintiles (III–V), indicating that while resettlement is continuing in these states, it is no longer a frontier-type process. Also, regions in some lower land utilization categories appear to have been by-passed in the settlement process, because they were less suitable for agriculture: for example, migration ratios are comparatively low in Minas Gerais and Rio Grande do Sul, and the low ratios for their Group I–II land utilization regions indicates that these are areas that may have been by-passed.

An important demographic effect of frontier migration appears in marriage rate differentials, which are measured as the percentage of rural women age 20–24 years reported as married (including consensual unions, panel B). These differentials derive from the high proportion of males moving to the frontier and the resulting relative scarcity of females in the marriageable ages. The differentials are specific to the frontier regions. Marriage ratios are high in Paraná, Mato Grosso, and Goiás, but not as high in São Paulo, which does have comparatively high rural migration. The low ratios in Minas Gerais and Rio Grande do Sul are associated with their low migration rates.

To illustrate differences in fertility between more and less settled regions, fertility rates for married women age 20–24 are given in panel C. The 1970 population census provides data on children ever born and children born in the year prior to the census. In a closed population, the memory and reference period errors to which these measures are subject can be corrected (United Nations 1967). A further problem arose in the data on children ever born because of differences in the age at marriage and the effect of this on cumulative fertility, which could cause additional bias when migration has occurred. To avoid introducing this bias through the correction factors, the reported numbers of children born in the year prior to the census per 1,000 married women in each five-year age category between the ages of 15 and 49 were used as the fertility measure.

The data reveal a negative correlation between fertility levels and the level of land utilization. The highest fertility rates are recorded in the lowest quintiles of the three frontier states, suggesting that land availability does have a positive influence on fertility. However, caution is required in this interpretation, because comparatively high fertility levels also appear in the low quintiles for Minas Gerais, which clearly does not qualify as a frontier area if we consider its migration rates.

The detailed statistical analysis of relations between fertility and land availability is reported in Merrick (1978). A more refined measure of land availability was developed, and controls for differences in access to land and rural socioeconomic structure were introduced. The analysis revealed that differentials in land availability played a significant, though not exclusive, role in rural fertility differentials in Brazil's Center-South. While consistent with Easterlin's study of the United States, the findings also revealed important differences in the role of other factors. Neither child survival nor female literacy varied greatly between the frontier and more settled areas in the

United States, so that their influence relative to land availability was limited. Further, there were no major differences in rural socioeconomic structure that might have affected such variations (slave states were excluded from the Easterlin study). Brazilian data showed that the rural environment and demographic reponses to it are much more varied. Opportunities for Brazilian frontier settlers are constrained by land tenure structure and by the shifting of rural workers to employee status. This combination of institutional factors on the frontier with rapid urbanization and the persistence of traditional subsistence farming in the more settled regions implies that the ability of most rural Brazilians to transmit the fruits of their labors to their offspring through the acquisition of land is more limited than that of their American pioneer counterparts.

While the data support the hypothesis that land availability has been conducive to higher fertility in new settlement areas and contributed to its decline in older regions, they do not permit us to conclude that its effect is independent of other aspects of socioeconomic structure and the influence of these factors on literacy and child survival. Because of this the " population pressure" and "economic opportunities" characteristics of older and newer settlement regions are much more complex. Further, the increased mediation of literacy and child-survival differentials for younger women indicates that the role of other factors vis-à-vis the influence of land availability may be even more important in the future. The prospects for further decline in rural fertility in Brazil may well depend more on the course of public policy affecting access of the rural population to land than on its actual scarcity or abundance.

Recent Fertility and Mortality Trends: Conclusions

While reexamination of the applicability of demographic transition theory to Latin America has indicated, as reported earlier in this chapter, that recent experience may be conforming more to the theory than expected, the foregoing also suggests that considerable caution is required in the case of Brazil. There is strong evidence that important demographic changes are occurring. At the same time important regional and rural-urban differences in demographic variables have rendered the Brazilian response to change in socioeconomic structure even more complex than some of the "exceptions" to the European standard case as discussed by Davis (1963) and Friedlander (1969). Population pressures in the backward Northeast have had an impact on the industrial Southeast and the frontier Central-West, directly through migration itself, as well as indirectly through fertility and mortality characteristics brought by migrants to their destinations. Migration has also brought changes in population age and sex structure in both origin and destination regions, and this has altered the number of births and deaths through changes in the proportion married and in the share of population in the peak child-bearing ages and ages subject to risk of mortality.

Though the initial impact of migration in urban areas has been to dampen fertility decline, as migrants with higher initial fertility rates assimilate urban reproductive patterns, strong forces have been at work to reduce urban fertility rates: increased opportunities for alternatives to child-bearing, like education and employment (either a chosen alternative as in the case of working wives or a forced alternative as in the case of domestic servants), as well as growing accessibility to the means of fertility control. The one doubtful feature of the effect of urbanization on fertility as well as mortality is the distributional dimension. Growing evidence suggests that the inaccessbility of the urban poor to adequate health and sanitation services has had a detrimental effect on infant and child mortality. Given the strong association between fertility and infant mortality, a further result is that such poverty is a deterrent to fertility declines among poorer socioeconomic groups in cities. Another result of their inaccessibility to health services is that they have probably not participated in the rising use of contraceptives through the private market, which has been an important co-determinant of the fertility decline in Brazilian cities.

Demographic changes have not been limited to the urban sector, however. Important interregional differences in both fertility and mortality are observable in rural areas of the country, and there is growing evidence of declining fertility and mortality in the rural South. Comparison of regions of recent settlement in the South and Central-West with older, more established areas there showed that fertility is declining in regions where availability of land is more limited. Studies of rural fertility decline elsewhere (principally in the United States) have suggested that farm families respond to changing opportunities for establishing their children in life by decreasing fertility within marriage, as well as by delaying marriage and/or migrating. Brazil's more varied rural social structure requires that the land scarcity-fertility decline hypothesis be qualified to take into account the differences in the degree to which land ownership (a principal characteristic of the American farm family on which the model is based) is available to Brazilian farm families, and differences in the level of infant and child mortality in rural areas. Both sets of factors proved to be important determinants of fertility differentials. Rural fertility in the backward Northeast is substantially higher—along with a rural social structure that is different enough from the South to require separate analysis prior to incorporating it in a national model.

XI   Population, Development, and Planning in Brazil

Brazil's economic growth in the period 1968–73 was so spectacular that it has been characterized as the *"milagre brasileiro,"* or Brazilian miracle, of economic development. With gross national product multiplying at 10 percent per annum, population growth was hardly a matter of concern—though at 2.8 percent per annum it was among the highest in the world. Brazilian economists traditionally have been bullish about their nation's population increase, even when the economy was not performing very well and when they have been willing to admit that other parts of the world do have population problems. In part, this derives from recognition of Brazil's privileged endowment of land and natural resources. In part, it reflects the conviction that the path of Brazilian economic and demographic development is somehow different from that of other nations.

Brazilians have long been attracted to the idea of large size, whether it be territorial, economic, political, or demographic; one finds frequent reference to the concept in official and popular expressions of national consciousness (e.g., *"Brasil maior, você, melhor"*; see Balán 1974). Inhabiting the scarcely settled regions has been an aspiration since colonial times, and rapid population growth has generally been viewed as a positive factor in the accomplishment of this objective (Brazil, Secretaria de Planejamento, 1974: 58).

In many respects, Brazil indeed *is* different from the typical developing country envisaged by neo-Malthusian models of population and economic growth (Demeny 1965, Robinson and Horlacher 1971). Mortality did not decline abruptly after World War II; industrialization was well under way prior to the war; and fertility decline was apparently settling in, despite the government's refusal to support family planning. Population density is still quite low in Brazil by international standards: 12 persons per square kilometer, compared to a world average of 26, and densities that run over 300 per square kilometer in many European countries. Anyone seeking to diagnose population growth as the source of Brazil's problems would first have to come to terms with the fact that during 1950–70, when Brazil was experiencing one of the highest population growth rates in the world, the country also enjoyed considerable economic growth. Have Brazilians succeeded then in trading off the adverse effects of rapid population increase for its benefits? Is the formula that population growth retards development efforts disproved, at least for Brazil? This chapter summarizes Brazilian policies on population growth and reviews the evidence on positive and negative effects of population growth in Brazil.

Population in Brazilian Development Planning

One of the most significant features of Brazilian industrialization has been the important and increasing participation of the public sector in the economy. This has been accompanied by a succession of economic plans, starting with some uncompleted efforts during President Getulio Vargas' first administration (1930–45) and the sectoral plan of President Eurico Dutra's government (1946–51). The most recent is the *II Plano Nacional de Desenvolvimento,* the Second National Development Plan (Brazil, Secretaria de Planejamento, 1974).

Brazilian plans have traditionally been instruments for the design rather than the execution of developmental policy. Plan documents have consisted of analyses of important sectors, identification of bottlenecks, and statements of objectives. But while Brazilian planning has not been an instrument of direct control, as in centrally planned economies, the planning experience in Brazil has created, as an important byproduct, a cadre of economists and technocrats on whom recent military presidential administrations have relied very heavily for direction of the economy. Documents like the *II Plano Nacional de Desenvolvimento* appear as occasional formal expressions of the ongoing dialogue between technocrats and the administration on policies and goals, rather than as predetermined courses of action for direction of the economy.

In view of Brazil's long-standing public opposition to population control, it is hardly surprising that the topic of population has been treated rather gingerly in official planning documents. This is not to say that Brazilian planners have completely ignored the demographic aspect of development planning. Detailed population projections have been employed in a number of sector plans. For example, the analytical materials prepared under Roberto Campos for the plan submitted in 1966 included a volume entitled *Demografia* (Brazil, Escritório de Pesquisa Econômica Aplicada, 1966). That document discussed in some detail the implications of population growth for development and called attention to the dependency burden associated with Brazil's high rate of natural increase. It went so far as to conclude that a decline in the birth rate was not likely to occur spontaneously. Like most of the materials in the Campos plan, this volume received relatively little attention, since by the time it was published in 1966 a new government was coming in and had undertaken its own process of establishing objectives.

Discussion of population matters, especially relating to fertility control, became quite delicate in the later 1960s, when newspapers and some deputies charged that outside groups were pressuring Brazil to adopt some form of national family planning program.[1] Officially sanctioned discussion of population questions focused on population redistribution, migration and the labor force. Brazil took outspoken positions against control of population growth at the Stockholm Conference on the Environment in 1972 and in preparatory meetings for the 1974 World Population Conference that were held in Geneva in 1973.

Despite the monolithic appearance of the official stance on these occasions, there is evidence of considerable variance of opinion at the level of the technocrats directing the economy. A few public officials have expressed concern over the adverse effects of population growth on Brazilian development, the most notable being Rubens Vaz da Costa (1973) when he was president of the Bank of the Northeast of Brazil and later of the National Housing Bank, and Mário Henrique Simonsen (1969, 1972), formerly president of MOBRAL (the national literacy program) and finance minister, and recently named as secretary of planning.

Lengthy discussions of population issues were carried on at the technical level in preparation for Brazil's participation in the 1974 World Population Conference in Bucharest. The Brazilian Census Bureau (Fundação IBGE) sponsored a conference on Brazilian population that drew attention to the increasing volume of professional study of population questions. One important byproduct of the increased level of population research was a growing recognition of the demographic momentum inherent in the age structure of Brazil's population and realization that a slower rate of growth still implied substantial increase in total population size.

A commission made up of representatives and experts from various government ministries carried out the official preparations for Brazil's participation in the World Conference, and the document presented to the conference by Brazilian Ambassador Miguel Ozório de Almeida (1974) reflects the range of views they held.[2] The main text of his presentation is strongly pronatalist. It denounces population control as a solution to Third World problems and criticizes foreign interference in matters relating to population.[3] How

---

[1] A useful summary of this incident is found in Rodrigues (1968); further discussion can be found in Sanders (1970a) and, in Portuguese, by José Carlos Brandi Aleixo (1973).

[2] See Sanders (1973) and Machado (1974) for interpretations of the Brazilian position at the conference.

[3] See "Statement by the Brazilian Representative, III World Population Conference," General Debate, Plenary Session, Bucharest, 26 August 1974. The Ambassador's speech is a compromise between the strongly pronatalist position he had taken at the preparatory meetings in Geneva and the more moderate views held by other members of the Brazilian delegation. An English translation of the Geneva speech is found in *Brazil, Path to Paradise or Way to Dusty*

ever, the last paragraph of the speech contains a surprisingly positive (in view of what came before) statement of the rights of individuals to have access to family planning and the responsibility of the state to provide it: "Being able to resort to birth control measures should not be a privilege reserved for families that are well off, and therefore it is the responsibility of the State to provide the information and the means that may be required by families of limited income."

The Bucharest conference coincided with the period in which the *II Plano Nacional de Desenvolvimento* was being drafted. The new plan adopted the moderate position found at the close of the Bucharest statement. It is significant in that it is the first explicit articulation of national population policy to appear in the national planning context in Brazil. The chapter of the plan devoted to population begins with recognition of the potentially adverse effect of rapid growth in the developing world, but places Brazil at the underpopulated end of the world spectrum. According to the plan, Brazil could contribute to increasing the supplies of food and other resources needed to alleviate population pressures elsewhere, if the sparsely settled Amazon and Central-West regions were settled. The pressures of Brazil's own rapid population increase on per capita income growth and on the provision of social services are mentioned, but viewed in terms of the trade-off for benefits deriving from expanded markets and adequate labor supplies:

It is important, however, to realize that population affects growth both as a production factor and as a factor of consumption, by expanding production and enlarging the scale of the market . . . . The reconciliation of these two different angles is being achieved successfully. From the point of view of absolute global population Brazil still has room for considerable expansion. The critical problem which deserves the attention of demographic policy must be the examination of the rate of growth of the population. The rate considered capable of reconciling the two points of view must be related to the effective capacity of the country to expand employment (Brazil, Secretaria de Planejamento, 1974: 59).

Thus, the major emphasis of the document is on increasing employment and earnings opportunities in order to effectively utilize the human resource po-

---

Death? (Wadebridge, England: The Ecological Foundation and Wadebridge Ecological Center, 1974). The following excerpt gives a sense of his position:

. . . Power, be it political, economic or military does have, as one of its *necessary* ingredients—even though not a sufficient one—a large or a relatively large population. Other elements are obviously necessary, but, even though a large population is not a guarantee of power, there are no Great Powers without a large population. The advice being given to underpopulated, underdeveloped countries to stop breeding is, probably, in many instances, an honest appraisal by well-intentioned advisors. But it is obvious that these advisors have as a goal the minimization of the problem of raising per capita incomes and seem to forget everything else that presides over the life and behavior of a State in the community of nations. It is an assumption of my Delegation that all countries do aim at as high a level of independence from external pressures as can be reached. Even though in absolute terms this might be a utopia, it is only natural that States strive for a progressive approximation of this *desideratum*.

tential represented by population growth and to insure a more adequate distribution of income among population groups.

This assessment of Brazil's demographic situation is followed by a restatement of the population policy enunciated at the Bucharest conference. It is basically a laissez faire policy with respect to overall population growth:

> It is hoped that by allowing each family to make its own decision, taking into consideration their moral conscience and socioeconomic conditions, Brazil will achieve a population growth rate that will reconcile the various needs and demands.

> It is hoped that during this decade the population growth rate will decline, with the average between 1970 and 1980 being 2.7–2.8 percent. In the following decades, the decline should become more rapid.

> The demographic policy must closely follow the evolution of the population growth rate, in order to evaluate the trends, and if necessary, take into account factors which could change the present favorable outlook.

At the same time, it leaves the door open to publicly supported family planning on the grounds of providing each family with the means to choose the family size they desire, concluding with a statement that Brazil's population policy is "to respect the right of each family to decide how many children they want, and to offer information which will allow them to examine the question fully. Families have complete freedom to choose the number of children they desire."

As with the documents of previous plans, the *II Plano Nacional de Desenvolvimento* was a summary of policy discussions rather than a specific plan of action. Progress toward implementation of a national program to provide needy couples with the necessary information to make family-size decisions has been slow, suggesting that resistance to the idea of government-sponsored family planning still exists. However, the years since the new policy was announced have brought some important initiatives, mainly at the state level in cooperation with the private sector. BEMFAM, the Brazilian IPPF affiliate, has been contracted by several state governments (especially in the Northeast) to develop community-based programs (Rodriguez 1977). As the support for these programs is enlarged, they may prove to be the model for a broader distribution network.

The first step toward implementation of the policy at the federal government level was announced in mid-1977, when a new national health plan that included provision of contraceptives to prevent "high-risk" pregnancies was unveiled (Brazil, Ministério de Saúde, 1977). The proposed program is very modest (about 2 percent of the budget being earmarked for family planning), but it is significant in that it represents the first such effort financed with federal funds and in its being integrated into the existing national health care program.

At least one reason for the failure to implement the plan's family planning proposals may be that these, like many of the overall objectives, have become unrealizable in the face of the severe strains put on the Brazilian economy by rising costs of imported petroleum, on which Brazil is so dependent. In any event, the plan served an important role in legitimizing open official discussion of interrelationships between demographic factors and Brazilian development.

Population and Economic Development: An Assessment of the Brazilian Position

As was recognized in the *II Plano Nacional de Desenvolvimento*, theories on the effect of population increase on economic growth stress the dependency burden that a young and rapidly increasing population associated with high fertility puts on developmental budgets.[4] Beyond reducing the proportion of workers in the population, high dependency and rapid overall growth bring difficulties in increasing provision of such social services as education, health, and housing, and in overcoming unequal income distribution. Against these disadvantages are weighed the beneficial effects of a rapid renewal of the work force, investments and innovations stimulated by population pressure, and the expansion of internal markets, though these advantages depend as much on the quality of the population as on numerical increase.

Economists outside Brazil have analyzed these interactions systematically by constructing models of economic-demographic relations at the macro level. In their most basic form, these models consist of a demographic subsystem, which generates projections of the population by age and sex according to variant assumptions about fertility and mortality trends, and an economic subsystem, in which an economic growth model incorporating investment, labor force growth, and technological change generates output projections over several time periods. The two subsystems are linked, first by equations representing the effects of the different age structures in the population projections on investment and labor force growth, and second by equations representing the effect of population growth and size on per capita output, usually employed as the indicator of economic performance. More sophisticated models include effects of population composition on public expenditures in such areas as education, health services, and housing. The models are used to explore the conflict between expenditures to maintain and improve these services in the face of rapid population increase and the direct investment required to maintain growth in product per capita. Considerable attention has

[4]The "classic" in this field is the work of Coale and Hoover (1958). For a review of subsequent developments, see Robinson and Horlacher (1971: 9–17).

been given to the effects of different fertility assumptions, since high fertility in developing countries is responsible for both high dependency ratios and rapid population increase.

More than two decades ago, Coale and Hoover applied such a model to India and Mexico and showed that reducing fertility by about 50 percent in a 25-year period would increase per capita income by about 40 percent for the lower fertility projection. They tested the sensitivity of their results to a number of variations in the model's parameters, with little change in the basic outcome. The core of the argument is quite simple: two of the three basic resources required by an economy—resources and labor—do not change when fertility is reduced. The lag between birth and labor force entry accounts for the latter. Accumulation of capital, on the other hand, is at least potentially larger, because reduced fertility should make it easier to divert a large part of current output from consumption (or government expenditures related to population) to investment.

Critics of the Coale–Hoover model, and subsequent work inspired by it, have argued that the models miss much of the true complexity of the developmental process.[5] In particular, per capita income measures only one demension of the developmental process and is insensitive to the question of income distribution, the importance of which has been emphasized at several points in this study. Another major argument of the models, that capital accumulation will increase if fertility is reduced, has been challenged on the grounds that public sector and foreign sources play the lead role in determining the path of capital expansion (through new investment as well as reinvested profits) and that savings are in a sense "forced" because of the institutional structures that have evolved. The latter point is not unrelated to the income distribution issue, since consumers were not really given the option of increasing or decreasing consumption in response to the dependency burden, and governments tended simply to neglect population-related service expenditures rather than divert resources from publicly financed investment projects.

These considerations, particularly the second one, have not escaped the attention of Brazilian planners and explain much of their lack of interest in attempts to show the adverse effects of population growth on macroeconomic growth objectives. Since the beginning of the projection period in Coale and Hoover's model (1956), Brazil's economy has experienced cycles of both slow growth (3.7 percent 1962–67) and rapid growth (8.3 percent in 1957–61 and more than 10 percent in 1968–73), none of which can be linked very convincingly to demographic events.[6] Supposing that Coale and Hoover's model had depicted Brazil rather than Mexico, the 40 percent per capita income differential implied by the model represents less than five years of growth at the

---

[5]A useful critique of very recent developments in this field is found in Arthur and McNicholl (1975).

[6]Interpretations of the recent Brazilian growth experience were discussed in Chapter II.

rate at which the Brazilian economy expanded with its actual *high* fertility rate. This kind of back-of-the-envelope calculation prompted Brazil's former finance minister, Delfim Netto (an outspoken opponent of population control and architect of the *"milagre brasileiro"*) to observe that the economic and political costs of any attempt to lower Brazilian fertility would have far out-weighed the benefits (Netto 1973). He maintained that the best way to in-crease total product was through policies to maintain a high rate of growth in total product. He was surely more accurate on the political than the economic dimension of the costs of fertility control, but his reaction is illustrative of the thinking of growth-oriented Brazilian policy-makers.

Would slower population growth have made a difference for Brazil in terms other than the macroeconomic considerations offered above? Again, Mexico is illustrative. Twenty years after publication of his original work, Coale (1978) took a second look at the Mexican experience. In the interim, Mexico's population had followed the Coale–Hoover high fertility projection quite closely; indeed, the accuracy of projections made two decades ago is remark-able. On the other hand, Mexico's aggregative economic growth over the last two decades was, until 1973, among the highest in Latin America. Rapid pop-ulation growth did not deter economic growth, nor did it prevent some major improvements in the expansion of such social services as education.

Coale does not see this as a contradiction to his original argument. Despite the achievements in proportions of the population being educated, the absolute numbers of those not served has increased. With a more moderate rate of pop-ulation growth, he argues, the number of children who would have grown up during this period without achieving basic education would have been reduced, and the record of rising literacy would have been substantially better. Further, according to Coale:

> ... the most acute disadvantages that we can now see resulting from the failure of fertility to fall in Mexico during the last 20 years are the built-in difficulties that the past continuation of high fertility makes inevitable in the development of the Mexi-can population during the next 20 years. Since the persons who will be over 15 fifteen years from now are already born, and since any reduction in fertility is likely to occur gradually, we can foresee the size of the population over 15 in 1995 with some confidence. Mortality rates are already quite low and further declines in mortality will have only the modest effect of slightly accelerating the increase in the population above age 15. We can foresee then, with little margin of uncertainty, that there will be more than twice as many persons over 15 twenty years from now as today. (1978: 426–27).

This prospect was a key consideration in Mexico's decision to seek a slower rate of population growth after firmly resisting such a policy for most of the period that Coale and Hoover had studied.

While it is understandable that the Brazilian leadership also resisted macroeconomic arguments for the benefits of population control in Brazil and has registered irritation when such arguments have been put forward by outsiders in support of Brazilian acceptance of family planning, it is regrettable that this reaction may have drawn attention away from such important "micro" dimensions of economic-demographic relations. It is encouraging that the *II Plano* focused its discussion of population issues in Brazil on the questions of employment and income distribution, and on development and utilization of the country's human resource potential. And it is also noteworthy that Delfim's successor as finance minister, Mário Henrique Simonsen, has stressed the microeconomic dimension of the problems (family size and structure do affect the economic welfare of a poor family) and the aggravating effect of population growth on unequal income distribution in Brazil (1972: 65–74).

Population Growth, Employment, and Education

Brazil's high birth rate, coupled with its declining mortality in the 1940s and 1950s, resulted in a near doubling of the population in the labor force "entry" ages (10 to 24) between 1950 and 1970. Such growth represents a major challenge in the years ahead. Brazil has made important gains in education and creation of employment for these groups as they approached working ages. Nor should one neglect the advantages accruing from rapid renewal of the labor force—faster introduction of new skills and a larger proportion of individuals who are more likely to be adaptable and less costly to employ because they are at an earlier stage in their lifetime age-earnings cycle.

Brazil's population censuses of 1950 and 1970 provide limited but useful information on the interaction between population growth and the creation and utilization of human capital resources between 1950 and 1970. Changes in activities of the population age 10 to 24 years between 1950 and 1970 are presented in a three-way breakdown of the status of persons in the early working age groups in Table XI–1. The most striking features of the overall pattern of activity are (1) the decline in the proportion working and the increase in the proportion in school among males and (2) the increase in both proportions among females age 15 and older at the expense of the residual category.[7] For

[7] As indicated in Table XI–1, the summary data being presented here were compiled from various tables in the 1950 and 1970 census volumes. The published data are neither complete nor fully comparable in regard to the accounting of activities undertaken here. In 1970, there are separate tabulations for school attendance (Table 11) and economic activity (Table 12) by age and sex. Simply subtracting these from the total number of individuals in each age-sex category would lead to understatement of the residual because there are individuals, particularly ages 15 to 25, who belong to both groups by virtue of their being workers and going to school. Here we should note again that Brazil's restrictive labor force definition (which excludes individuals for whom work was not a principal activity) would class most of them as students. Data on educational attainment for different categories of earners in Table 25 were utilized to identify worker-students and permitted us to assign individuals who belonged to both categories only to the working group and to assign individuals who belonged to neither to the residual. The 1950 census provided a joint tabulation of economic activity and school attendance by age and sex (Table 22). A number

Table XI-1. Activities of Brazilian Population Age 10–24 by Sex, 1950 and 1970
(Percent Distribution)

Age and activity	Males		Females	
	1950	1970	1950	1970
10–14				
Working	31.0	18.6	8.6	6.2
Studying	38.2	70.4	37.5	68.7
Residual	30.8	11.0	53.9	25.1
Total				
Percent	100.0	100.0	100.0	100.0
Number (000)	3,165	5,923	3,144	5,926
15–19				
Working	80.6	60.1	23.4	23.8
Studying	10.8	37.9	9.6	35.1
Residual	8.6	2.0	67.0	41.1
Total				
Percent	100.0	100.0	100.0	100.0
Number (000)	2,645	5,014	2,858	5,306
20–24				
Working	93.4	86.5	16.7	28.0
Studying	2.5	10.2	1.9	13.5
Residual	4.1	3.3	81.4	58.5
Total				
Percent	100.0	100.0	100.0	100.0
Number (000)	2,384	4,089	2,607	4,309

Sources: 1950, Fundação IBGE, *Censo Demográfico,* 1950, Table 22.
1970, Fundação IBGE, *Censo Demográfico,* 1970, Tables, 11, 21, and 25.

males age 10 to 14 the school group increased from 38 percent to 70 percent and for those age 15 to 19 the increase was from 11 to 38 percent, more than offsetting the declines in the activity rates for those ages. For females, the increases in the school proportion are almost as great; however, the increases come almost entirely from the residual category. For ages 20 to 24, this increase, combined with the increase in economic activity, has resulted in over 40 percent of the cohort being engaged in activities outside the home (either education or work) in 1970, as compared with less than 20 percent in 1950. Migration and urbanization have surely contributed to this rise, and the combination of those working and studying represents a significant actual and potential contribution to the overall productivity of the Brazilian economy.

The decline in the residual category suggests that most of the increment in these early working age cohorts is either being utilized directly in production or being enhanced as a productive resource through education. Of course, school attendance rates and activity rates are very rough measures of human capital

of "residual unpaid family workers" (e.g., those who could not be assigned to specific industrial sectors) were grouped with students. Males in this category were considered students, and females were pro-rated on the basis of male-female proportions in these categories in 1970.

288   POPULATION, DEVELOPMENT, AND PLANNING

formation and utilization. They do not show the extent of unemployment and underemployment among the active, or the extent to which education consists of little more than repetition of the same grade among those attending school.

Younger workers constitute an important part of the Brazilian labor force: males ages 15 to 24 account for one-third of all male workers, and females in these ages represent half of all female employment. Unpaid family workers in agriculture contribute a major portion of the employment in ages 10 to 14, but even when they are discounted the 10- to 24-year age groups represent 29 percent of male and 46 percent of female workers. The census does not tabulate unemployment data by age, though the overall level reported was a low 1.2 percent. The PNAD survey data discussed in Chapter VII indicated somewhat higher unemployment rates among young adults. In addition to open unemployment, it is commonly supposed that there is substantial under-employment for younger workers. Indirect measurement of underemployment is generally based on such characteristics as job status, earnings, and hours worked. These measures of underemployment are more meaningful for non-agricultural occupations, and, when possible, the comparisons presented here will be limited to them. Tabulations of 1970 census data by age and sex are available for status and earnings but not hours. Table XI–2 shows the pro-portion of unpaid family workers and own-account workers for each of the younger age-sex categories. The share of these two job status groups is gen-erally regarded as a barometer of underemployment. Table XI–2 also gives the percentage of workers earning less than 100 *cruzeiros* per month, another indicator.

While younger workers account for about 60 percent of all unpaid family workers outside of agriculture (Table XI–2, panel B), these workers still re-present only 4 percent of those employed at ages 10 to 19 and less than 2 per-cent over age 20. If underemployment is concentrated in this status group, it is not very widespread. The proportion of younger workers in the own-account category is even smaller; employment shares for this status category increase with age, so that the representation of younger workers is much lower (13 per-cent for males and 18 percent for females) than their respective shares in the non-agricultural labor force as a whole (29 percent and 46 percent).

Income tells a different story. If we take the proportion of earners whose average monthly earnings fall in the two lowest categories (Cr$100 per month or less, excluding those with no earnings) as a measure of potential under-employment, then over 90 percent of the 10 to 14 age group and 60 to 70 percent of those ages 15 to 19 qualify. However, reported monthly earnings do not include remuneration in food and lodging, which are an important factor in jobs like domestic service. In such circumstances, reported earnings under-state the true productive contribution of these workers.

Another telling indicator is the proportion with low earnings for ages 20 to 24. These ages do as well (for males) or better (for females) than the older age groups, which one would not expect if younger workers were being locked into

Table XI-2. Characteristics of Younger Workers

| Sex/Age | 1. Employment status of nonagricultural workers | | 2. Monthly earnings (excluding unpaid family workers) |
	Unpaid family workers	Own-account workers	Workers earning less than Cr$100 per month
Males	A. Percentage of workers in age group with these characteristics:		
10–14	3.9	1.3	92.6
15–19	3.8	2.6	58.4
20–24	1.5	5.8	32.0
All ages (10–64)	1.5	9.8	33.7
Females			
10–14	2.7	2.7	94.2
15–19	2.0	2.7	69.1
20–24	0.8	7.0	41.6
All ages (10–64)	1.4	11.6	51.3
	B. Younger workers as a percentage of all workers with characteristic:		
Males	61.8	13.4	27.7
Females	62.2	18.8	44.2

Source: Brazil, Fundação IBGE, 1973a, Tables 21 and 25.

low productivity jobs as they entered the labor force. However, caution is required in interpreting this convergence, because the composition of the labor force changes with age. The most important change relates to educational attainment. Workers who start young forego additional schooling, whereas, those who stay in school delay entry into the labor force until they are older. As can be seen in Table XI–3, the highest level of educational attainment among Brazilian workers in 1970 was in the 15- to 19-year age cohort. About one-third of these workers had completed five or more years of schooling, approximately the equivalent of a completed primary education.

Table XI–3 also illustrates the interaction between improvements in educational attainment and labor force participation. It shows activity rates by level of educational attainment. For males it suggests that attainment of five or more years of education leads to a delay of about five years in the entry of this group into the labor force. For females it reveals sharply contrasting patterns of participation in the labor force by age. Females with four or fewer years of schooling reach a peak level of labor force participation at ages 15 to 19, whereas females with higher attainment have a later and higher peak rate at ages 20 to 24. Since female labor force participation in Brazil is concentrated in the younger age categories and is followed by departure from the labor force for purposes of marriage and child-bearing, higher educational attainment results in later entry and exit and may thus contribute to delay of marriage or initiaton of child-bearing within marriage, or both. Theories relating reproductive behavior to household economic behavior place important emphasis on the alternative roles provided for women through education and labor force

Table XI-3. Distribution of Young Adults by Education Attainment, Age, Sex, and Labor Force Participation, 1970

| | Educational Attainment (years completed) | | | | Activity rate by educational level | |
| | Total | | Active | | | |
	4 or less	5 or more	4 or less	5 or more	4 or less	5 or more
Males						
10–14	81.4	18.6	94.5	5.5	22.4	3.5
15–19	65.8	34.2	84.0	16.0	76.7	28.4
20–24	73.6	26.4	76.6	23.4	90.3	76.6
25–64	79.5	20.5	80.0	20.0	93.9	90.7
Females						
10–14	79.2	20.8	94.3	5.7	7.4	1.7
15–19	66.3	33.7	71.8	23.2	27.6	16.4
20–24	75.1	24.9	59.0	41.0	22.0	46.1
25–64	80.9	19.1	62.0	38.0	15.3	39.6

Source: Brazil, Fundação IBGE, 1973a, Table 22.

participation in the reduction of fertility. Work outside the home at earnings, levels that have been enhanced by education raise the opportunity costs of time devoted to care of children at home. This, combined with increased educational attainment of females ages 15 to 19 relative to those ages 20 to 24 in 1970, suggests that recent investment in education have the potential for yielding even greater declines in Brazil's birth rate.

As promising as these data appear, they also indicate that Brazil has a substantial way to go before exhausting the potential returns from improvements in its stock of human capital. Two-thirds of Brazilians are reaching adulthood without having completed primary education. While this is an improvement over the three-fourths figure for 1950, it is probable that if population growth rates in the 1940s and 1950s had been less, then more dramatic reduction in this residual would have been observed. The less educated have gone to work earlier and thus made an immediate contribution to growth in output, but their potential for a higher productive contribution is probably lost once they have passed out of the prime education years into the main working ages. Their earnings and productivity will not rise as much with age as those of individuals for whom educational opportunities existed. To the extent that this occurs, the opportunities represented by population growth turn into an aggravation of the problems of effective utilization of one of Brazil's main resources, its youth.

Population Growth and Income Distribution

Disparities in human resource endowments are also reflected in Brazil's income distribution, and attention has been drawn to the role of demographic

Table XI-4. Summary of Recent Changes in Brazilian Personal Income Distribution

Earning quintile	Shares in income (percentage)		1960 to 1970	
	1960	1970	Change in share (percentage)	Growth rate (percentage)
Lowest	3.49	3.16	−9.5	24.4
Second	8.07	6.85	−15.1	16.4
Third	13.07	10.81	−21.7	7.9
Fourth	20.26	16.94	−16.4	14.3
Lower four	45.63	37.76	−17.3	15.8
Upper	54.37	62.24	+14.5	50.8

Source: Kogut and Langoni (1975): Table 3.5.

factors in the growing income inequality that has been observed in Brazilian census data (Fishlow 1972, Langoni 1973). Table XI-4 summarizes the shifts that occurred between 1960 and 1970. Income per worker in the upper quintile increased by 50.8 percent in that decade, while the growth of the lower four quintiles was only 15.8 percent. This resulted in a 17 percent decline in the share of the latter in total income. However, the decline was not concentrated in the lowest-income group: the middle group (third quintile) showed the greatest decline, nearly 22 percent. Per capita income in this group increased by only 7.9 percent over the decade, as compared with 24 percent for the lowest quintile. The middle group consists mainly of the urban working classes, since the agricultural worker makes up most of the lowest groups.

Demographic factors enter into these changes in a number of ways. Langoni (1973) has demonstrated the effects of the changing age-sex structure of the working population on the income distribution. Although activity rates for young workers have been declining in recent years, the share of individuals in these age groups reporting earnings has been rising as a result of declines in the proportion of unpaid family workers. This increased proportion of younger earners (with lower average earnings) has tended to aggravate income inequality as measured by reported earnings. The rising share of female earners has had a similar effect, since increased female labor force participation has been concentrated in ages 15 to 24. In part, these findings reflect statistical problems relating to the adequate measurement of earnings in a changing economy. In part, they are a further reflection of the "gains" to the Brazilian economy in having a relatively young labor force, which is less costly to maintain.

A more fundamental question on the relation of demographic factors to the income distribution lies in the differential growth of population in upper- and lower-income groups. As in many developing countries, there is a strong negative correlation between fertility rates and income in Brazil. A rise in contraceptive use by upper-income groups is a factor in their lower fertility. The rise has occurred despite government eschewal of publicly supported family planning, because the upper-income groups have access to these services through the private sector (Richers and Almeida 1975). Although no published data are available on population growth by income level, it is almost certain that the poorer segment of the population is growing more rapidly just as its relative economic position is worsening.

The interaction between these two sets of factors is not simply a matter of an increasing denominator in the per capita income equation. Data on the distribution of income among earners (or families) understate the true dimensions of the differential. Poorer workers not only receive a lesser share of the national income, they must also support a larger number of consumers.

Since no national data on these realtionships are available, it is useful to turn again to the survey data for Belo Horizonte that were described earlier (Chapter X, Merrick 1976a; Sant'Anna, Merrick, and Mazumdar 1977). The 2,445 households in the survey were stratified by income level. Household structural characteristics are shown for each of the four income groups, ranging from the poorest to the richest, in Table XI–5. The poor households contain nearly 1.3 more members than the overall average (5.11 members) and over two persons more than middle- and high-income households. However, their earning capacity (in terms of the number of earners as well as for average earnings) is less, resulting in a substantially higher dependency burden and lower income per person. Poor households have only 1.41 earners on average, as compared with an overall average of 1.67 and 1.82 for households in the groups just above them. In addition to having a larger number of nonworking adults (1.81 versus the overall average of 1.37 and only 0.91 for the rich), the poor also have more children: an average of 3.15 members age 14 or less, as compared with 2.06 for all households and 1.26 for rich households. Household dependency ratios summarize the economic effects of these differences in household structure. Poor households have 4.51 consumers per earner, as compared with 2.34 for rich households and 3.06 for all households. A higher proportion of dependents in poor households are children, though these households outnumber others in both adult and child dependency.

The survey data were analyzed to determine whether household demographic structure had a direct effect on members' earning capacity. This could occur in two ways: through the influence of structural factors on the ability of members to obtain work, and on their earnings once working. Human capital theories of labor force participation and earnings differentials place major emphasis on the role of variables like age, sex, and education in these processes. Work status and earnings of individuals in the survey have been analyzed, utilizing these variables, and the results have been reported elsewhere (Merrick 1976a; Sant'Anna, Merrick, and Mazumdar 1977). Additional controls for household characteristics like the presence of young children and the age and sex of the principal earner were introduced in the analysis of work status, as were measures of labor market characteristics in the case of earnings. Using multiple regression techniques, estimates of labor force participa-

Table XI–5. Analysis of Household Earnings, Survey Data for Belo Horizonte, 1972

	Household income class[a]			
	Poor	Low	Middle	High
1. Family size, number of individuals	6.37	4.93	4.16	3.79
2. Number of adults	3.22	3.14	2.82	2.53
3. Number of children	3.15	1.79	1.34	1.26
4. Number of earners				
a) Actual number	1.41	1.82	1.76	1.62
b) Predicted number	1.51	1.62	1.62	1.59
5. Earnings (*cruzeiros* per month)				
a) Actual earnings	248	601	1.297	2,693
b) Predicted earnings	394	554	919	1,376
6. Number of equivalent consumers	5.24	4.26	3.65	3.32
7. Income[b] per equivalent consumer (*cruzeiros* per month)				
a) Actual income	50	144	393	1,080
b) Predicted income	78	133	290	683
8. Number of households	718	1,116	299	312

[a]Households stratified on basis of monthly *cruzeiro* income per adult equivalent consumer: poor, less than 100; low, 100 to 368; middle, 368 to 728; high, over 728. In 1972, 1 *cruzeiro* = US$0.17.

[b]Includes income from sources other than earnings.

Source: Derived from data in Sant'Anna, Merrick and Mazumdar (1977: Appendix Table 2).

tion and earnings of individual households were then computed and tabulated by household income group. These were then compared with the observed averages for the same household groups. The results are also summarized in Table XI–5 (line 4). Despite a larger number of adults (potential earners), poor families actually have the lowest average number of earners per household group. Control for individual's age and education, as well as household structure variables in multiple regression analysis (predicted values), suggests that poor households should have more workers than reported. In all other groups, starting with the low category, households report as many or more workers than would be predicted on the basis of individual characteristics of adults. The same thing happens with individual earnings, as seen (line 5 of Table XI–5) in the reported and predicted earnings component of household income. Poor households' workers do worse than even their already lower endowment of human capital would lead us to suspect.

Since economic and demographic factors like age, education, and household structure explain part but far from all of the differential earnings capacity of poorer urban households, additional explaining factors were sought. It was difficult to measure health, nutrition, housing and sanitary conditions, and other factors that might explain differences in the amount of effort an individual might be able to expend either in seeking work or on the job. Indicators that were available proved difficult to interpret, because they indicated as much the effects as the cause of poverty. However, analysis of residuals between actual and predicted earnings in the Belo Horizonte, using such indicators (access to health services, sanitation, water), showed that they were indeed an important element in the employment and earnings differences that were observed. This analysis revealed the circularity of poverty: the poor in Belo Horizonte had lower earnings capacity because they lacked basic necessities like health and sanitation services in addition to their lower level of education, and because of their lower earnings they were not able to obtain these necessities.

What these figures mean is that the adverse effect of the unequal income distribution on poor households is a double one: first the lower earning power of its members, and then the fact that these members' earnings must be spread further. The interaction between demographic and other factors in the poverty cycle is illustrated further in the relation between dependency and the age of heads of households in the different income groups, as shown in Figure XI-1. Because of limited education and the other factors just mentioned, earnings of heads of poorer households do not increase as much with age as those of upper-income groups. The full impact of this flatter age-earnings profile is felt as the main dependency burden falls in the prime working age portion of the life cycle. While upper income families have higher incomes to cushion rising consumption needs, poor families have fewer resources with which to provide for their larger numbers. Thus, an unequal income distribution combines with demographic structure to increase the pressure on poor households.

Clearly, the demographic characteristics of households have been an important factor in the widening gap between rich and poor. Yet it is difficult to isolate simple causal relations and be able to say that if public action could somehow reduce the fertility of poor families, the cycle would be broken. The problem is really more complex. The solution would no doubt be eased by reducing the dependency burden, but it also requires that deficiencies in education, health, nutrition, and public services be remedied.

Implications for Policy

Brazil has resisted macroeconomic arguments for population control on the grounds that development, not population increase, is the root problem. In reviewing the evidence, we have not found that three decades of rapid population increase have been detrimental to the growth of the aggregate Brazilian national product. Furthermore, the data show that Brazil has succeeded in the last two decades in making substantial gains in human resource investment and in utilization of this investment in productive activity. But population growth has had its social costs. Brazil's broad-based age distribution has made it harder to alleviate deficits in social services, like housing, health, and education, and the growing working-age population has placed pressures on the economy to create productive activities to use the increased flow effectively. Clearly, much remains to be done, and it is possible that more might have been achieved had population increases been less. Yet the assessment of what

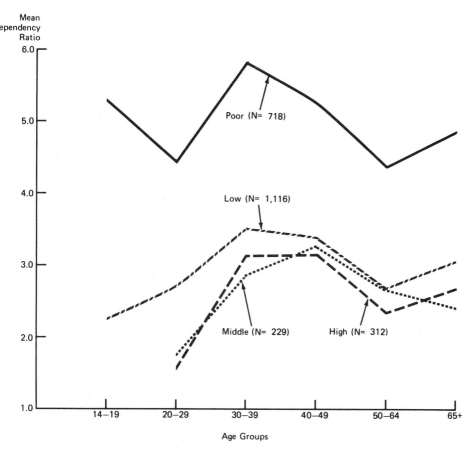

Mean
Dependency
Ratio

Poor (N= 718)

Low (N= 1,116)

Middle (N= 229)   High (N= 312)

Age Groups

Note: Age groups representing less than 5% of the income class are not shown.

Figure XI–1. Mean Dependency Ratio (Nonearners/Earners) of Households in Belo Horizonte by Age of Household Head and Household Income Class, 1972. *Source:* Santa'Anna, Merrick and Mazumdar (1977).

"might have been" requires careful balancing of these hypothetical cost savings against actual gains to the economy that might have been lost had the growth and structure of the labor force been altered. The structure of the Brazilian economy would have been different with a different rate of population growth, but it is most difficult to demonstrate how much better or worse it would have been.

At the micro level the economic-demographic relationships are clearer. A cause of increasing concern is the distribution of income. Because of the large differential in birth rates between different income groups, demographic factors are recognized as an important element in the dynamics of poverty. Analysis of the employment and earning capacities of poor households reveals complex and circular causal relationships between family structure, human resource endowments, and variables, like health and access to public services, which are as much the effects as the causes of poverty. The policy implication of these findings is that remedies must cut across all of the critical elements in the poverty cycle—living conditions, health, nutrition, family planning and child care, and education, as well as adequate employment and earnings opportunities.

Given the magnitude of the poverty that remains in Brazil, the resources required for this task are substantial, especially when viewed in the light of demands from other areas of the economy. In the past, allocation of resources has favored economic growth more than income distribution. The rationale has been that available resources could not support both, and recent planners have not contemplated any major social change that might place a damper on economic development. Since only growth would provide additional resources, it was better to redistribute later. Growing consciousness of the distribution problem has challenged this view, and a shifting of priorities is occurring. But, coming at a time when the changing international economy has put additional strains on the Brazilian balance of payments, the resource allocation dilemma to be faced in implementing a policy of "growth with distribution" is even more profound. The Brazilian government is moving toward provision of family planning methods and information as a social measure— and one that will surely benefit the poor segment of the population. Whether the formulation of such a policy will also be shaped by considerations of its potential redistributional effects and potential easing of the pressure in the provision of social and economic services at the macro level remains uncertain.

XII The Future
of Brazilian Population Growth

Introduction

Late in 1972 Brazilian census authorities announced that the country's population had passed the 100 million mark. A postage stamp was issued to commemorate the event. It is quite accurate to say that increase in population size in Brazil is a matter of national concern. Indeed, there is fear in some quarters that the recently observed decline in the birth rate will lead to an end of population increase before a large enough total population size is achieved. Supporters of family planning in Brazil have been accused of being unpatriotic on this account (Alves 1973), which leads us to ask what Brazil's population growth prospects really are, and to the question of how recently observed demographic events are likely to affect them.

Demographic theory tells us that, in the absence of substantial immigration, population growth is determined by the combined action of vital rates and age distribution. Two populations with similar age-specific fertility and mortality rates will have markedly different growth prospects if one of them is a comparatively young population, characterized by a broad-based age pyramid and the other is older, on average, with population distributed more evenly among all age categories. This is true because it is the birth or "entry" cohorts that will eventually determine population size. In any population, mortality reduces the size of the birth cohort as the population ages. However, as population growth approaches stability, the total population will just equal the number in the birth cohort times the expectation of life at birth, which is the average number of years that an individual will live. Populations with a broad base will eventually be larger than evenly distributed ones. This growth potential, or momentum, that results from the interaction of vital rates and age structure is an important consideration as population growth rates decline and eventually reach zero.

Brazil provides a striking illustration of the notion of demographic momentum. In 1950, with a population of 51 million and a birth rate of about 43 per thousand, Brazil had a birth cohort of about 2.2 million. In 1976, with a

297

population of about 110 million and a birth rate of about 35–36 per thousand, the cohort increases in size to about 4 million. Though the birth rate has declined, the size of the birth cohort has increased because the base population has also increased. Evidence presented in the previous chapter indicates that Brazil may have started the process that will lead eventually to low fertility and mortality and eventual population stabilization. What may not be clear to those concerned that declining fertility is leading to a premature end to Brazilian population growth is the momentum inherent in Brazil's current age structure. When the population does reach stability, Brazilians will probably be experiencing fertility and mortality levels typical in other countries that have completed the transition process. At birth, the average Brazilian will have an expectation of life of around 75 years. The total size of the stable population will depend on the size of the birth cohort. If its size stabilizes at the current level of around 4 million, then the stable total population will be 280–300 million; however, if it grows by 50 percent, then the stable total will be 420–450 million; and if it increases by 100 percent, then the total will be 560–600 million. This is a wide range, depending almost entirely upon the path of fertility as it declines over the next several decades.

It is possible that a very dramatic decline in the birth rate would actually reduce the size of future birth cohorts, but this is unlikely. Just to maintain the size of the birth cohort at the 4 million level the rate would have to decline in proportion with the increasing base population: to 27 per thousand as the population passes 150 million, to 23 per thousand as the population passes 175 million, to 20 per thousand as the population reaches 200 million, and so on. A 5 per thousand delay in the decline of the birth rate at the 200 million population level would add another 1 million to the size of the birth cohort and another 70–75 million to the eventual total stable population size. Thus, in examining population projections, it is important to pay attention to what different projections indicate about this birth cohort.

The wide range in stable population totals that we have just observed indicates how sensitive the population projection process is to small changes in the assumptions that underlie them. These assumptions are related to changes in human behavior that it is very difficult to predict. On the other hand, projections do have an inherent stability that derives from the interaction of age composition and vital rates. If behavior leads to rate x, then the projection result has to be y. Population projections are made for various purposes, time periods, and levels of aggregation. Projections of a decade or less are generally quite accurate, because only a small portion of the total population is affected by vital events in this interval. The longer the projection, the greater the risk of being wrong about behavioral assumptions; shocks like the depression of the 1930s and World War II led to significant shifts in behavior and large errors in projections, as is illustrated by forecasts of the population of the United States on the basis of patterns that were current in the early 1930s.

Despite the hazards, projections are an extremely useful tool for the planning and management of economic development. Besides indicating the path, or a range for the path of growth in the total population, projections also provide useful insights into future population composition. This is a fundamental requirement for planning to meet demands on the economy and society that derive from important population subgroups, like the school-age population, the labor force, the urban population, and formation of new households through marriage. Even with a margin of error, projections dramatize the need for advance planning to meet the needs that are inherent in population momentum. We do not know for certain whether Brazil's stable population will be 300 million or 600 million, but it is clear that it will be several times the present total and that planning for the task of educating, employing, housing— not to mention feeding—these two or three "other Brazils" is urgently needed.

Population Projections for Brazil

National level population projections prepared by the Brazilian Census Bureau (Fundação IBGE 1974a) soon after the publication of the 1970 census are the ones used most consistently by Brazilian authorities in planning matters that relate to population, as well as for annual national and state level population estimates. The IBGE made two sets of projections using the component method, one with relatively slow fertility decline, which yielded a total population of 222 million in the year 2000, and another with faster decline that gave 201 million in 2000. Mortality assumptions did not differ in the two projections. Another set of projections prepared by CEDIP (Santos 1974) assumes an even more rapid fertility decline and is useful for comparative purposes. Since mortality assumptions are almost identical in the different projections, most of the variation between them derives from differences in assumptions about the decline in fertility. The CEDIP "low" projection is based on a decline in the birth rate by about 40 percent between 1970 and 2000, whereas the IBGE "high" projection assumes that the decline will be only 15 percent. Mortality decline dampens the effect of these fertility declines on natural increase in all of the projections. This is due to continued improvements in life expectancy and to age structure effects of fertility changes.

The CEDIP "high" projection and IBGE's "low" variant are almost identical and indicate that Brazil will attain its second hundred million by the end of this century. Neither projection suggests that Brazil's population is likely to stop growing at that point. Both assume a birth rate of about 27 per thousand in the late 1990s and an expectation of life at birth that approaches 75 years. If Brazil eventually reaches a stable population, incorporating the population structure implied by these projections, then the stable total will be close to 400 million. This is double the total projected for the year 2000 and over four times the 1970 population.

That such an increase would occur even when there is as significant a decline in the birth rate as is incorporated in the projections is an indication of the strong demographic momentum of Brazil's population structure. Frejka has investigated the question of demographic momentum for Brazil, and a number of other countries, in his *Future of Population Growth* (1973). In this study, Frejka examines the effect of variation in the path that a population follows in approaching zero population growth on the size of the eventual stable population total. The demographic behavior pattern that is required in order to obtain zero population growth is one in which the combined effect of fertility and mortality result in the reproduction of succeeding generations at the "replacement level," e.g., generations are equal in size. This is the level at which each couple will have two children *on average* (therefore some will have 3 to 4, others none). It takes several decades for the population to stabilize, even when individual couples are having two children, again, because it is the size of the *birth* cohort rather than the number of parents that determines the final population total (see also, Frejka 1968). In a rapidly growing population like Brazil's, the birth cohort is relatively large in comparison with the population in reproductive age groups, and the time lag is needed for the difference to work its way through the age distribution.

Frejka has prepared population projections for Brazil that differ from those of IBGE and CEDIP, in that his projections plot the path of Brazilian population growth from the time that the population starts to reproduce itself at the replacement level to the time that total population size is finally stabilized. Variation in these projections results from differences in the date at which replacement behavior is initiated. Four of Frejka's projections are shown in Table XII–1. In the first (I), replacement starts immediately (1970–75), whereas, the second (II) starts in the years 2000–2005, the third (III) in 2020–25, and the last (IV) in 2040–45. Variant I is useful in demonstrating momentum inherent in the *present* structure of Brazil's population. Since the population is currently reproducing itself at more than twice the replacement rate, there is no chance (short of massive effort to control fertility or a major calamity that would increase mortality) that population would stabilize at the level indicated in Variant I. Still, it shows that even if population had started replacement behavior, the total would have increased by 80 percent before population growth ended. Even Variant II is optimistic in regard to fertility decline. The path for population growth indicated by it is lower than the "low" projection by CEDIP, which is the lowest medium-term projection made by Brazilians. Comparing the remaining Frejka projections to other CEDIP and IBGE projections, we observe that III, with replacement in 2020–25, corresponds very closely to the path indicated by the "consensus" projection (CEDIP high–IBGE low) in Table XII–1. On the other hand, Frejka's IV and IBGE "high" are quite similar. Neither CEDIP nor IBGE ran their projec-

Table XII-1. Projections of Brazilian Population (millions)

	CEDIP		IBGE		Frejka			
	Low	High	Low	High	I	II	III	IV
1970	93.5	93.5	93.0	93.0	94.0	94.0	94.0	94.0
1980	121.2	122.2	122.2	124.2	105.6	122.1	123.8	124.7
1990	154.1	158.5	159.0	166.9	121.4	152.7	159.9	163.3
2000	188.3	199.6	201.2	222.1	136.7	180.9	200.1	209.3
2050	n.a.	n.a.	n.a.	n.a.	165.7	265.9	357.9	459.3
Stable	327.6a	395.2a	413.5a	546.4a	168.4	274.4	389.3	554.7

Note: n.a. = not ascertained.

aNeither Santos nor the IBGE present stable population totals implied by their projections. These totals have been calculated here by using the birth cohort implied by their projections for the year 2000 and a life expectancy of 75 years. This assumes that the size of the birth cohort will remain at about its year 2000 level as stability is approached.

Sources: Santos (1974), IBGE (1974a), Frejka (1973).

tions beyond the year 2000; however, we can make a rough estimate of the probable stable population that would result from a continuation of these projections by using their birth cohorts as an indicator of the average size of all cohorts in the stable population. These stable equivalents are shown in Table XII–1, which shows that the above mentioned "consensus" projections and Frejka III all lead to a total stable population for Brazil of about 400 million. The assumption is that reproductive behavior will approach the replacement level sometime around 2020–25 and that there will not be significant fluctuations in fertility and mortality rates in the interim. Our knowledge of the sensitivity of population projections to such fluctuation should lead us to caution in treating these results as predictions of the future population of Brazil; on the other hand, as projections, they appear to represent the demographic consequences of interaction between existing population structure and informed opinion as to the future path of vital rates.

One caveat regarding the assumptions underlying projections relates to mortality. The IBGE projections have followed the traditional United Nations' practice of incorporating an improvement of about 2.5 years in the expectation of life for every 5 calendar years, so that the average life expectancy (for both sexes) increases from 61 years in 1970–75 to 73 years in 1995–2000, roughly a 20 percent improvement over the three decades.

While this rule of thumb was probably warranted during periods in the past, when consistent gains in life expectancy were being achieved through public health measures to control infectious, respiratory, and parasitic diseases, there are good reasons for doubting the validity of such a practice in future years, when mortality is much more likely to be determined by social and economic conditions. Because of this, improvement may occur more slowly. Chapter X provided evidence that Brazil has already experienced a slowing of mortality decline. Even if we take a very cautious attitude about reports that infant mortality in larger cities increased up to the early 1970s, it is hardly likely that the kind of improvements in life expectancy implied in the United Nations' recommendation could have been occurring in Brazil at the same time.

It is revealing indeed to examine the infant mortality rates implied in the life expectancy improvements assumed in the IBGE projections. The United Nations' model life table corresponding to a life expectancy of 73 years has an infant mortality rate of 24 per thousand live births. While it is conceivable that such a level might be obtainable in the more advanced states of the Southeast by the year 2000, the likelihood of such an improvement taking place in the Northeast is remote. Elsewhere (World Bank 1978) we have experimented with regionalized component projections that attempt to take account of regional differences in fertility and mortality, and to feedbacks that might result from changes in social policy affecting child survival. Brazil has embarked upon an ambitious program of extending water and sanitation to localities not previously served, which could have a significant impact on child survival. If the program goals can be met, and if the program impact on infant mortality is as great as expected, then there is more likelihood that the Northeast will have a lower mortality rate by the end of the century. As suggested in Chapter X, a key question is nutrition. Major efforts in the nutrition area are also being considered, but it is much too early to map out their impact. If conditions do not change, or if achievements are less than targeted goals, then continuation of the regional differentials in mortality (and fertility) are the more likely prospect.

Experiments with projections incorporating various policy alternatives are described in the World Bank Report cited above. Because of feedbacks between mortality and fertility, the effects of alternative policy strategies tend to cancel each other out: lower mortality and lower fertility are mutually reinforcing. As a consequence, total population at the end of the century is relatively invariant. The experiments suggest that a 200 million population figure for around 2000 is reasonably firm, though on the low rather than the high side of the range of estimates. To the extent that program efforts emphasize mortality reduction and exclude direct intervention on fertility, increased child survival raises total population in regions (like the Northeast) where there is most room for improvement. The feedback mechanisms are obviously complex, and uncertainties as to responsiveness of mortality and fertility to program interventions suggest the need for caution in interpreting results. The future path of regional as opposed to national demographic patterns remains one of Brazil's major research frontiers.

Implications of Trends in Size and Age Composition

The most important way in which changes and differentials in the demographic components of growth are transmitted to economic and social processes is through the age structure of the population. Economic-demographic models that have been prepared to aid planners in integrating population into development planning incorporate age composition in several ways, as indicated in the discussion of the previous chapter. Brazilian experience suggests that the more important effects may be the indirect ones that influence resource requirements in areas like education, health, and housing, resulting from increases in the size of specific age cohorts.

The review in Chapter XI of the impact of population on Brazilian development in recent decades indicates substantial progress in areas like education, despite a near doubling in the population in major educational age categories and the substantial deficit in educational opportunities that existed in 1950. Complexities in the flow of different age groups through the Brazilian educational system make exact comparison of the structure of the system over the last two decades difficult, especially since one of the major changes in the system was a reduction in grade repetition, a factor that led to the relatively large share of older children at the primary level. We can circumvent some of these complexities and still get a good view of the relation between age structure and educational needs by reviewing the experience of the school-age population, as was done in Chapter XI.

Because of high birth rates, Brazil has had a relatively young population over the entire twentieth century. As Table XII–2 shows, the share of population under age 10 has held constant at just about 29 percent since 1890. The slight decline from 1950 to 1970 could be a result of the incipient fertility decline of the 1960s, just as the slight increase in the proportion in ages 10 to 14 reflects the high birth rates of the 1950s.

Chapter XI shows that despite a near doubling of absolute numbers in key school age (10–14) and labor force entry (15–24) cohorts between 1950 and 1970, Brazil still had made substantial progress in investing in and utilizing human resources. For ages 10 to 14, the number in school increased more than three times, cutting the relative deficit in half (from 60 to 30 percent). However, the absolute declined by only 8 percent (from 3.9 million for this age category to 3.6 million), because of the increased base population. If we use the population ages 10 to 14 in IBGE's "low" projections (and the Frejka stable projection that corresponds most closely to it) as a guide, it is possible to estimate future demands on the education system deriving from populaton growth. Between 1970 and 2000 the size of this cohort will again double, though the doubling time will slow from the recent two-decade rate to three decades, because of the slower population increase assumed in the projections. If we consider the educational needs of this cohort, the 1970 data indicate that 8.2 of its 11.8 million children were in school and 3.6 million were not in school. To make up the deficit completely *and* take care of population increase between 1970 and 2000, an additional 14.4 million 10 to 14 year olds will have to be accommodated. Comparing this to the 1950–70 experience, the required relative increase is actually about 25 percent less, though the absolute increase is greater because of increased population. These figures refer only to the population ages 10 to 14 and do not take account of needed improvements in the quality of education. However, they do suggest that the effort required to expand educational capacity in the next three decade will be very similar to what has been accomplished in the last two decades. A large investment is required, but the data do not show that the Brazilian educational system is going to be swamped by a student-age population, if the present pace in educational expansion can be maintained. The slightly slower rate of increase in school-age population that is projected should also allow for further reduction in the current deficit.

The age-specific projections are also useful in relating near term (1970–2000) planning strategy with needs that will emerge in the longer run (2000 and after). The path toward stability in population size indicated by the IBGE "low" projection suggests that most of the increase in school-age population (as represented by ages 10 to 14) will occur in the next two to three decades. If

Table XII-2. Trend and Projections of Population by Major Age Category

Age	1890	1950	1970	2000[a]	Stable
A. Total (thousands)					
0–9	4,191	15,386	27,271	48,775	49,053
10–14	1,710	6.309	11,859	22,619	24,526
15–19	1,400	5,502	10,253	20,873	24,526
20–39	4,336	15,410	25,544	61,466	97,325
40–59	1,967	7,016	13,311	33,594	94,989
60+	673	2,205	4,716	13,835	98,882
Unknown	59	117	184	–	–
Total	14,336	51,944	93,139	201,162	389,300
B. Percentages					
0–9	29.3	29.7	29.3	24.2	12.6
10–14	12.2	12.2	12.8	11.2	6.3
15–19	9.8	10.6	11.0	10.4	6.3
20–39	30.4	29.7	27.5	30.6	25.0
40–59	13.8	13.5	14.3	16.7	24.4
60+	4.7	4.3	5.1	6.9	25.4
Total[b]	100.0	100.0	100.0	100.0	100.0

[a]IBGE low.
[b]Excludes age unknown.
Sources: IBGE (1974a, 1975a).

the major investments required to provide educational opportunities for this group can be made sooner rather than later, a number of important benefits would result. Since very little expansion of the relative size of the school-age cohort is indicated by the projections for after the year 2000, investment between 1975 and 2000 could be a "once and for all" effort to build up the educational system in terms of adequate coverage. The system's requirements after the year 2000 would shift to maintenance and improvements in quality, because the inflow of new students will be nearly stable. There is every indication that this indeed is the strategy of the Brazilian government. The II PND (Brazil, Secretaria de Planejamento, 1974) has set a goal of enrolling 90 percent of 7 to 14 year olds by the end of the 1975–79 planning period.

A strategy that emphasizes near-term expansion in the quantity of basic education would have other benefits that are indicated by the projections. As emphasized earlier, increased education and labor force participation of women are important factors in Brazil's recent fertility decline, through changes in attitudes about having children and possibly also delays in the age of marriage. Continued expansion of education would contribute to this directly, through changing attitudes that are associated with education, as well as indirectly, by involving many more young people in activity outside the home (teaching) during early reproductive years.

A further benefit of pushing educational expansion in the near term relates to the quality of the labor force and distribution of income in the long run. The age groups that will experience the greatest absolute increase in size between 1970 and 2000 are the so-called "prime working ages" (20 to 39 years old).

In 1970, three-fourths of the members of this group were entering the labor force without having completed primary education, an important factor in their low earnings and in Brazil's unequal income distribution. With low education levels, lifetime earnings expectations are limited—especially since Brazilian economic expansion is based on a strategy that pays a very high return to human capital investment and often penalizes the lack of it through restrictive wage policies for low-skill groups, on the grounds that their productivity is low. Future income distribution is likely to depend very heavily on more equal distribution of earning capacity, with education being an important component. Hence, there is further urgency in the need to expand educational opportunities. The longer the delay, the larger in both relative and absolute terms will be the low education/low earnings component of the 61 million population in ages 20 to 39 projected for the year 2000.

The stable population in Table XII–2 provides yet a further reason for improving the earnings capacity of prime-age workers. In the long run (after 2000), the age groups that will experience the greatest increase are the older-age cohorts (ages 60 and over). By the time Brazilian population stabilizes, the population age 60 and over will be larger (totaling nearly 100 million) than the total population of Brazil in 1970. Many of these older people will not have had the high level of earnings during their working lives required for them to save enough to maintain themselves in retirement. They will depend on the working age population for support—and the working age population will be able to provide this support, in addition to meeting their own needs, only if earnings capacity is increased substantially over the present average. Some intriguing intergenerational welfare issues are raised by this, and one of the important contributions of long-term population projections is that they provide the basis for analyzing alternative strategies in both the timing and distribution of investment in such areas of social need as education and social security.

Projections incorporating population composition and specific subpopulation estimates are also useful in determining needs and setting priorities in other social services: health and nutrition, housing and urban services, transport, etc. Health and nutritional needs vary by age, and the demand for housing can be judged by the growth and geographic distribution of population as it passes through the peak years of household formation (ages of marriage and child-bearing). Projections draw attention to differences in the time at which these needs reach their peak: e.g., because of age specificity, the peak in demand for child health and nutrition will come some years before that in education, which in its turn will come in advance of those needs associated with labor force entry and household formation. Geographic redistribution of the population (especially migration to urban areas) accelerates the rise in demand for housing and urban services as well as education, and attention must be given to both the age and geographic composition of populations in estimating resource needs. When resource constraints require that priorities be set, these differences in timing and distribution can be useful in evaluating trade-offs. Demographic factors are obviously not the only consideration. Interdependencies, like the relation between effective education and adequate health, nutrition, and housing for school children, must be recognized. Resource limitations may constrain the effort to achieve all social objectives at the same time, and consideration should be given to phasing of major efforts in specific fields in step with demands related to demographic structure. In the case of housing, for example, a delay in initiating a major push in order to funnel more resources into nutrition, health, and education might lead not only to improved human resource capacity but also to greater earnings capacity and productivity, which would in turn yield additional resources for the housing effort when peak demand is generated by these cohorts as they pass through the household-formation years.

Geographic Distribution of Population

Geographic distribution is another important dimension of future population growth in Brazil. The overall increase of population in recent decades has been accompanied by important shifts in the distribution of population between regions and between rural and urban areas, and these trends are likely to continue. Chapters VI and VIII have presented systematic reviews of these changes, and it will be useful here to examine possible future trends.

Because of the important role of migration in population redistribution and the difficulty of projecting migration over even a very short period, long-range projections incorporating geographic population distribution are very problematic. The technique most often used in projecting population by age and sex, the component method, requires age- and sex-specific migration rate assumptions, when population distribution is added. Past experience provides useful guidance only for very short-term projections, and for periods beyond a decade the detail they give can often be misleading. Methods requiring less complex assumptions are preferable, at least insofar as the limitations affecting them are made more explicit. One such technique is the ratio-trend method, which makes projections on the basis of redistribution that has occurred in the decades just prior to the projection period. Weighted averages of previous trend data are utilized, with the most recent period receiving the largest weight (Pittinger 1976: 94).

Projections of the urban population for Brazil and other Latin American countries have been prepared by a number of United Nations' agencies (Fox 1975, United Nations Population Division 1976, Herrera and Pecht 1976). Since we have utilized Fox's data on city growth in Brazil as the basis of discussions in Chapter VIII, it will be useful to consider his projections of urban growth also. Fox employed the ratio-trend method in a two-step process. He first estimated the distribution of population by states and then the distribution of city population within each state. The projections of Brazil's city population presented here depart slightly from Fox's results in that they employ *regional* rather than state-by-state population distribution as the intermediate step. This was done because it was felt that state population growth gives a misleading indication of the growth of cities as a result of differences in the size of states and location of the cities within them. Recent Brazilian migration flows (especially for the metropolitan areas) are related more to regional population trends than to the growth of the particular state in which they are located. For example, Minas Gerais is a large state (in area) that has lost population through migration to São Paulo and Rio de Janeiro; however, Belo Horizonte, its major city, has shared in the dynamics of the urban metropolitan area population growth of the Southeast, exceeding both Rio de Janeiro and São Paulo in its recent growth rate. Similarly, Recife, in the Northeast, has drawn heavily from neighboring Alagoas and Paraiba, in part because of the geography of the Northeast, where states run in narrow strips from the Atlantic coast.

Because the projections are basically a dampened extrapolation of recent (1950–70) patterns of redistribution, they are meaningful only in the context of a decade or two. Projections have been made for 1970 to 1990. Total population growth follows closely on the estimates in IBGE's "low" projection. The total population growth rate has been rounded here to 2.7 percent per annum in 1970–80 and to 2.6 percent in 1980–90 for use in the ratio-trend technique. The totals are still very close to those of IBGE. Regional projections are shown in Table XII–3. New settlement areas (the North, Paraná in the South, and Mato Grosso, Goiás, and Brasilia in the Central-West) show increasing shares. The coastal regions, while continuing to be the largest in absolute size, show declining relative shares. The decline is sharpest in the Northeast, where the relatively high rate of natural increase has been offset by out-migration. Since these projections reflect the migration trend, they could be in error to the extent that migration of Northeasterners shifts even more from interregional to intraregional flows, as indicated by comparison of the 1960–70 pattern to that of 1950–60.

Projections of the city population for 1970 to 1990 are presented in Table XII–4. The definition of the city population is the same as the one in Chapter VIII (localities and agglomerations of 20,000 or more in 1970) and differs from the official administration described there. In 1970, the officially defined urban share was 56 percent, whereas, the population in cities of 20,000 and over was 40.6 percent. The projections in Table XII–4 show the population of these cities increasing at a rate of 4.4 percent per annum in 1970–80 and 3.9 percent in 1980–90, which increases their share in the total population to 48 percent in 1980 and 54 percent in 1990.

Because the city population is defined in terms of 1970 population size, the projection understates the probable growth of cities over the next two decades to the extent that it excludes new cities that will cross the 20,000 population

Table XII–3. Projections of Population by Macroregion, 1970–90

Region	1970	1980	1990
A. Number (in thousands)			
North	3,604	4,884	6,496
Northeast	28,112	34,508	42,325
Southeast	39,853	51,355	65,831
South	16,497	22,835	31,385
Central-West	5,073	7.930	11,621
Total	93,139	121,512	157,658
B. Percentage distribution			
North	3.9	4.0	4.1
Northeast	30.2	28.4	26.1
Southeast	42.8	42.3	41.8
South	17.7	18.8	19.9
Central-West	5.4	6.5	7.4
Total	100.0	100.0	100.0

Source: IBGE (1974*a*).

size threshold in the projection interval. Between 1960 and 1970, 106 of the 225 cities reported in 1970 (7.4 percent of the 1970 city population) did so. If we assume a similar pattern for 1970–80 and 1980–90, then the city shares would be 51 percent in 1980 and 58 percent in 1990.

As in the presentation of city data in Chapter VIII, the projections of city population in Table XII–4 are broken down by size category and function. Center cities and peripheral municipalities of the two main metropolitan areas, Rio de Janeiro and São Paulo, are given separately in category 1, as are the central and peripheral municipalities of the regional metropolitan areas in category 2. Remaining cities are grouped according to their size in 1970. Because of the ratio-trend technique, which dampens past growth trends, the projections are conservative with respect to future city growth. Growth rates for all categories decline from their 1960–70 levels in 1970–80, and continue to decline in 1980–90. The overall distribution among size-functional categories projected for 1980 and 1990 is basically the same as in 1970. Within the metropolitan areas, the peripheral municipalities continue to grow in relative importance, and there is a very modest shift in the weight of Rio de Janeiro-São Paulo relative to the other metropolitan areas and medium and larger cities. The share of smaller cities (20,000 to 100,000) is stable in the projection.

An alternative approach to the projections would be to incorporate some of the goals regarding city-size distribution that have been articulated in Brazil's new national urban policy. During most of the postwar industrialization period, urban problems were given low priority relative to maintaining the overall level of economic expansion. The 1970s have brought growing recognition of the detrimental effects on the urban system of viewing urban policy and the preparation of the *II Plano Nacional de Desenvolvimento (II PND)*. The II PND presents specific objectives on the evolution of the Brazilian urban system and proposes mechanisms to design and execute an urban development

Table XII-4. Basic Urban Population Projections, 1970–90

Group	Population (thousands)			Growth rates			Implied Distribution	
	1970	1980	1990	1970/80	1980/90		1980	1990
Rio de Janeiro and São Paulo								
a) Municipios of capitals	10,122	14,005	18,822	3.3%	3.0%		24.1%	22.1%
b) Periphery	4,563	7,908	12,267	5.7	4.5		13.6	14.5
c) Total	14,685	21,913	31,089	4.1	3.6		37.7	36.6
Regional metropolitan areas								
a) Municipios of capitals	6,189	9,074	12,924	3.9	3.6		15.6	15.2
b) Periphery	1,539	2,992	5,063	6.9	5.4		5.2	5.9
c) Total	7,728	12,066	17,987	4.5	4.1		20.8	21.1
Remaining cities in 250,000 and over class as of 1970	3,286	5,548	8,784	5.4	4.7		9.6	10.3
Cities of 100,000 to 249,000 (in 1970)	4,422	6,823	10,082	4.4	4.0		11.8	11.9
Cities of 50,000 to 99,000 (in 1970)	2,954	4,505	6,601	4.3	3.9		7.8	7.8
Cities of 20,000 to 49,000 (in 1970)	4,706	7,162	10,481	4.3	3.9		12.3	12.3
Total 20,000+	37,781	58,017	85,024	4.4	3.9		100.0	100.0
Total population base	93,139	121,508	157,644	2.7	2.6			

Source: Base data from Table XII–3; projection method described in text.

strategy. In the II PND, the growth of the metropolitan areas is characterized as "premature" and small-city growth as "excessive." This evaluation has been made in reference to the growth of these areas relative to development of economic (especially employment) and urban service-delivery capacities. As a remedy for some of the current ills of the urban system, the plan recommends establishment of secondary nuclei that would divert some of the city growth away from the metropolitan areas. It would also promote urbanization in the new settlement regions in the Northern and Central-Western regions. While the new urban policy is still at a very formative stage, it is possible that forceful action could alter significantly the distribution of city population projected in Table XII–4. The distribution is already shifting in favor of new settlement regions and nonmetropolitan cities with a population of 100,000 and over, and the projections may well understate this trend if the deconcentration goal is pursued energetically.

The need for a national policy on city growth is demonstrated very dramatically if we consider the implications of the longer-tern stable population projections for geographic distribution. While about half of Brazil's present (1978) 115 million population reside in cities of 20,000 or more, it is likely that the proportion will be more than three-quarters by the time that population size stabilizes at the level indicated by the IBGE "low" projections that we have been using. Were the 1970 city-size distribution to hold, the combined populations of the metropolitan areas of Rio de Janeiro and São Paulo would be in the neighborhood of 110 million, more than three times their current level. While such population concentration is not impossible in demographic terms, the implications for urban services and employment creation are staggering. The alternative would be an urban distribution along the lines envisioned by the II PND, but this implies creation of hundreds of medium-sized cities, many times the 39 found in the 100,000 and over categories in 1970. The location and functions of such cities are matters of immediate concern. Since city building is a process that takes decades, it would be short-sighted indeed to ignore these concerns on the grounds that the population totals we have been talking about will be present only in the later decades of the next century.

Conclusion

Barring significant change in national policy on population growth, or a major catastrophe, the prospects for Brazilian population growth in the next several decades are for continued growth, but at a decreasing rate. If the trend toward declining fertility, which was first observed in the 1960s, continues, this will lead eventually to a final phase in the historical evolution of Brazil's population in which total population will stabilize with a zero or near zero growth rate. Because of the demographic momentum inherent in population structure, the current declining growth phase will still lead to a final stable population total that is several times the 1970 census level of 93 million.

The projections of Brazil's population examined in this chapter have important implications for the planning and management of social and economic development in Brazil. Projections are sometimes used to convince planners and decision-makers of the need to control population growth in order to avoid the detrimental effects of increased population size and the broad-based age structure characteristic of rapidly growing populations. Since fertility is the main demographic variable determining growth in the "high fertility-low mortality" phase of the demographic transition, the argument usually equates family planning with population control.

The Brazilian leadership has rejected this sort of population control in elaborating its recent population policy statement, as was shown in the previous chapter. The stance of current policy on population growth in Brazil is *laissez faire*. At the same time the policy states a willingness of the government to make family planning available as part of general social welfare programs. Even though the intent is *not* population control, we would expect such a policy to have an effect on the rate of growth, since it would extend family planning to population groups that do not have the access to it currently enjoyed by the middle- and upper-income classes.

In choosing among population projections currently available for Brazil, we have adopted the ones that incorporate assumptions of moderate fertility decline in the next several decades as being most likely to follow a path consonant with this *laissez faire* policy. In exploring short- and long-run implications of these projections, we have tried to avoid advocating control of population growth. There are two points about control that need to be made, however.

Should Brazil ever decide to adopt a policy *other* than *laissez faire*, the timing of the decision is very important vis-à-vis the long-term total population outcome of the path toward stability that is followed. The discussion of the momentum in Brazilian population increase demonstrated this. A difference of 5 per thousand in the birth rate, with the population of the late 1970s, implies an additonal 45 million in the stable total; the same 5 per thousand difference with the population projected by IBGE for the year 2000 becomes 75 million. Thus, the *lassez faire* position is not entirely neutral in regard to future population increase. It is a choice for substantial increase in population size.

A second point is that the projections dramatize very forcefully the need for a planned response to the effects of future population increase and its composition on social and economic development. Demographic factors will play a critical role in the achievement of development goals in areas like human resources, employment, urban structure, and public service capacity. Major time lags characterize both demographic processes on the demand side and investment strategies required to provide adequate education, employment, housing, etc. Financial resources are limited, and the pressures of population increase make it difficult to do everything at once. Careful assessment of trade-offs is needed. For this purpose, *laissez faire* is also an inadequate position, because the future is not going to take care of itself. Control of the effects of population growth and structure has to be part of Brazilian planning strategy, even if control of growth itself is not.

XIII Population and Development in Brazil: A Concluding Summary

Brazil's dissenting view regarding the adverse effects of population growth on development both in international forums and in their own domestic policies has stimulated much interest in the interrelations between her demographic and economic variables. This study has attempted to derive both an understanding and an assessment of the Brazilian position by examining population trends in the broader context of economic history, on the grounds that current policy, as well as the economic-demographic experience in which it is rooted, have historical bases that run deeper than recent neo-Malthusian concern about the adverse effect of population on economic growth. While this alone is not enough to validate the Brazilian position, it does, when combined with the recent dynamism of the Brazilian economy, warrant reappraisal of the proposition that population growth is detrimental to economic development in low-income countries. For Brazil, our principal conclusion is that the proposition applies less in terms of macroeconomic growth objectives (increases in total and per capita product) than when development is defined as growth with distribution, i.e., broad participation in the social, economic, and political benefits of the process. To say this does not imply that rapid population growth among lower-income groups is the cause of that inequality that has characterized recent Brazilian economic expansion, but rather that the relatively greater demographic increase of these groups is both an effect of inequality and likely to cause greater difficulty in measures to alleviate it and, further, that the adverse effects of growth without distribution are likely to be worse because of the demographic factor.

Our attempt to understand the issues underlying the relation between population and development in these terms led to a series of questions on which this study is focused: (1) how slavery and immigration altered both the demographic and socioeconomic structure of Brazil during the export expansion and early industrialization of the nineteenth and early twentieth centuries and the way in which they contributed to the regional imbalances that became such major concerns after World War II; (2) the extent to which large streams of internal migrants, which have accounted both for rural resettlement and for very rapid urban growth in recent decades, represent an adjustment mechanism for regional imbalances or have merely aggravated problems by increasing urban poverty and unemployment; (3) Brazil's transition from high birth and death rates to low birth and death rates and the relation of population increase to economic growth; (4) the impact of all three of these economic-demographic interactions—the structural legacy of slavery and immigration, the imbalanced urban-regional and labor force shifts that have accompanied industrialization, and the unevenness that marks recent changes in fertility and mortality—on the sticky problem of unequal participation in the benefits of the "Brazilian miracle." Are these problems natural growing pains in the transformation of a large, complex economy, or will persistent poverty, despite impressive aggregative gains, prove to be the Achilles' heel in Brazil's quest to become a major economic and political power?

It has not been our intention to argue that demographic factors lie at the root of all these problems, or to suggest a reductionism whereby all major issues are shown, in the final analysis, to be population problems. Indeed, the *purely* demographic nature of many of the processes and institutions whose demographic dimensions we have explored may be quite limited compared to other important social, cultural, and economic aspects. Still, to the extent that the growth, composition, and major characteristics of the population (and such important subpopulations as slaves, immigrants, and the work force) impinge upon the evolution of these processes and institutions, a specific focus on the role of population is required. Thus, we view our answers and interpretations for the questions posed above as partial but nonetheless important contributions to adequate understanding of the major questions facing Brazil.

Long-Term Population Growth Trends

The most prominent feature of the long-term population trend in Brazil is the very magnitude of its increase. Since the beginning of the nineteenth century, Brazil's population achieved a more than thirty-fold increase in size. Brazil's experience, like that of the United States, Canada, Australia, and (to some extent) Argentina, is one that is distinctive of "new lands," in that this increase in population started from a numerically insignificant indigenous population base. Excepting the United States, only Brazil has achieved a population of more than 100 million, thus also ranking it among the six most populous countries in the world.

Sources of information on the long-term trend in Brazilian population growth fell into three basic categories. Prior to the first national census in 1872, estimates of the size and growth of the population are based on reports and partial "censuses" by colonial and ecclesiastical authorities and, after independence, by a number of limited imperial censuses. More recently, demographers and historians have attempted to distill the basic parameters of early population change from these sources by using the archival techniques of historical demography and the consistency checks that are provided by modern demographic theory. Between 1872 and 1920 there were four national censuses (Brazil, Diretoria Geral de Estatistica, various dates), which, though uneven in quality, mark a significant advance in our knowledge of the Brazilian population and provide a second major data source. Four modern decadal censuses have been taken since 1940 (Brazil, Instituto Brasileiro de Geografia e Estatistica and Fundação IBGE, various dates) and these constitute the third building block for demographic study in Brazil. In these censuses, there is greater consistency and more complete coverage than before, though caution is still required because of deficiencies that remain.

The long-term trend in Brazil's population growth since 1800 can be broken down into five broad phases. Each of the phases accounts for roughly a doubling of the population, except, of course, the last, which is still not completed. Differing demographic composition distinguishes each of the growth phases. Brazil's population at the beginning of the nineteenth century was about 3.3 million: it grew to about 7.2 million by 1850, implying a growth rate of 1.56 percent per annum. Both slave imports and European immigration contributed to the moderate growth that occurred in this phase, but natural increase in the nonslave population, including ex-slaves freed through manumission, appears to have been the main demographic component of this growth.

Between 1850 and 1890 the population increased by another 7 million to 14.3 million, implying a 1.7 percent average annual growth rate, suggesting a gradual increase in the rate of population growth over the course of the nineteenth century. It is possible that the growth rate may have slowed just after 1850, because of the termination of slave imports, increase in mortality due to urban epidemics, and internal economic stagnation. But after 1870 increasing immigration was strong enough to offset these forces and the net increase for this second phase was greater than in the first. Immigration made its most substantial mark on the Brazilian population growth trend in the third phase, which ran from 1890 to around 1930. During this period the Brazilian population increased from 14.3 to 33.6 million, and the average annual growth rate exceeded 2 percent per annum (2.2 percent) for the first time. While immigration contributed to the rise in the rate of population growth in this period, natural increase still accounted for the largest part of overall growth. Mortara's estimates of the composition of total increase for this period show that the share of natural increase was still 70 percent, even in the peak immigration decade of 1890–1900.

Two world wars and the depression severely disrupted the flow of international immigrants and brought a gradual decline in the contribution of immigration to Brazil's overall population growth. But mortality decline after

1930 created a rise rather than a decline in the overall rate of growth. This occurred because the birth rate stayed relatively high, and natural increase rose from less than twenty to nearly thirty per thousand between the mid-1930s and the mid-1950s. Population doubled again in this three-decade period, which is the shortest phase and the one with the most rapid population increase in Brazilian demographic history.

The most recent phase appears to have started some time in the 1960s. Though it is still too early to judge the strength of Brazil'ls incipient decline in fertility, the 1960s were clearly a decade of slower growth than the 1950s. Since fertility is the only major demographic variable in which major future variation is likely, and since the only direction it can go is down, it appears that a new phase of declining growth has started. This phase differs from earlier ones in several important respects. It is the first to show a reversal in the growth trend from a previous phase. And though the trend in growth is downward, demographic momentum built up in the previous phase has given it growth potential that is likely to exceed those of previous phases by several times, in both absolute and relative terms. For the same reason, it is likely to last much longer than previous phases (perhaps a century rather than three to five decades) and thus have a more significant impact on the final composition of the Brazilian population than any previous one.

In a comparative perspective, Brazilian demographic expansion stands between the very rapid increase of the United States, which was fed both by high natural increase and by immigration, and most of the rest of Latin America. Within Latin America, only the Argentine population multiplied as much as Brazil's, whereas the ratio of Brazil's population to that of most of the rest of Latin America increased by several times. Today the population of Brazil accounts for one-third of Latin America and half of South America. That Brazil substantially increased its demographic weight in Latin America between 1800 and 1970 can be attributed to the fact that it is the only Latin American country to have participated in three major population increasing processes during this period: the importation of slaves, large intercontinental migration, and a sustained high rate of natural increase prior to fertility decline.

The only other country with a like experience is the United States, which is also the only new world country to which Brazil is comparable in population size. However, the path of Brazilian growth stands in sharp contrast to that of the United States. The United States recorded a 3 percent rate of growth throughout the nineteenth century, reflecting a high rate of natural increase in earlier decades and immigration in later ones. In the twentieth century, the U.S. growth rate has declined. In Brazil, the sequence was different, since the growth rate increased gradually over the nineteenth century, with immigration being the factor that first pushed the rate over the 2 percent level. High natural increase came after immigration, giving Brazilian population an increased momentum with which it will probably surpass the United States in population size sometime early in the next century. The difference between the United States and Brazil in the timing of high natural increase and immigration also means that the relative impact on economic and social structure will differ, and one of the main objectives of this study has been to understand this differential impact in Brazil.

The Structural Legacies of Slavery and Immigration

Slavery

The struggle to secure adequate supplies of low-cost labor for the production of export staples has been a recurrent theme in Brazilian economic history from colonial times through the early decades of this century. The Portuguese in Brazil were unable to exploit indigenous labor, which was both primitive and more sparsely settled than in the Spanish domains of Central and South America. Like the Southern United States and the Caribbean, Brazil turned in the beginning to the Atlantic slave traders for labor. In the course of three centuries, Brazil imported 3.6 million slaves, accounting for four out of every ten Africans brought to the Western Hemisphere. But slavery alone was not sufficient to meet Brazil's manpower needs. In the last quarter of the nineteenth century, after the abolition of the slave trade, manumission, and slave mortality combined with a changing regional economic balance to erode the demographic and economic base of slavery, Brazil turned to European immigration to meet the growing demand for labor in the São Paulo coffee production expansion. Between 1880 and 1930 nearly 4 million immigrants entered the country, with about 60 percent of them locating in São Paulo. In this way, populations of both African and European stock came to be major building blocks in Brazil's social and economic structure.

Brazil contrasts with the United States both in the stronger regional orientation of her European immigration and in the more national scope of the institution of slavery. Whereas slavery was regional and immigration national in scope in the United States, immigration was concentrated in São Paulo in Brazil, and slavery spread from the sugar plantation regions of Northeastern Brazil, where it first gained importance in the sixteenth century, to the mining regions of Minas Gerias in the seventeenth and eighteenth centuries, and finally to the coffee regions of Rio de Janeiro and São Paulo in the nineteenth century.

Slavery was the dominant form of labor organization in all of the major export cycles in colonial and imperial Brazil. Its durability and pervasiveness as an institution derived from its responsiveness to changing regional economic conditions, crops, and climate. Both the durability and national scope of slavery contributed to the large demographic weight that populations with African roots achieved in Brazil, both as slaves and in growing proportion as free people. By 1800, slaves comprised roughly half of the population, and if free colored are added, the figure is over 60 percent.

Another marked demographic feature of Brazilian slavery was its relatively large urban component, especially in the early nineteenth century. The growth of urban slavery was linked to declines in regional export economies at the end of the eighteenth century and to the absence of a European immigrant labor pool. Slaves occupied a large number of skilled and unskilled labor activities in coastal cities from Rio de Janeiro to Belém, and in some instances slaves accounted for as much as half of the urban labor force. There was also a significant transfer or sale of urban slaves back into rural cash crop activities in response to changing market conditions. This occurred in Rio de Janeiro in the 1840s, when expanded coffee production began to drain slave manpower from the cities to the plantations in that state.

Manumission and miscegenation were also important features of Brazilian slavery and provide another contrast with the United States. Manumission was a major factor in the decline of the slave population in Brazil during the nineteenth century. In 1800, the free colored population numbered about 12 percent of the total; by 1872 they comprised 45 percent (with the slave share declining from 48 to 15 percent). In contrast, the United States had less than 2 percent free Negroes in its population on the eve of the Civil War, whereas slaves were 13 percent. The increasing weight of the free colored population in Brazil also reflects a high level of miscegenation. The rapid rise in miscegenation throughout colonial and imperial Brazil has been attributed to the relative scarcity of European women among Portuguese colonizers. Less clear, however, are the social and economic reasons for manumission.

Demographic characteristics highlight some important dimensions of the manumission process. Females gained their freedom at about twice the rate of males, despite a preponderance of males in the slave trade. Brazilian-born slaves made up a substantial (70 percent) proportion of the manumitted reported in local sample data, and mulattoes were also favored; again, both groups were relatively less represented in the total slave population. Age was also a distinguishing factor, with children accounting for one-quarter to one-third of manumissions reported in the sample data mentioned above. These differentials were later reinforced by legislation such as the Rio Branco Law of 1871, which freed all children born of slave parents.

The other social and economic forces in manumissions are mixed and complex. Surrogate (and biological) paternity has been indicated as a reason for the freeing of slave mistresses and their offspring. Callous abandonment of older slaves was evident, but was a small proportion of total manumission. Female slaves were probably better placed in the urban environment to get jobs enabling them to buy their freedom than field hands, which was important, since a high proportion of manumission fees were paid by slaves themselves.

Owner resistance to manumission was apparently low. Slave owners employed former slaves in much the same tasks as slaves, especially in urban areas in the Southeast. Resistance was also less because as long as the slave trade continued, owners could replace manumitted slaves with new African imports. The latter were less familiar with the possibilities of self-purchase than natives, and since they also consisted mainly of younger males, they may actually have been the preferred alternative when the plantations' needs for field workers increased with a rise in export production.

This points to another important contrast between Brazil and the United States. In the United States, where slave imports were prohibited, owners attempted to maintain their stock of slaves by limiting manumissions and adopted what has been described as a "slave-breeding" strategy, e.g., encouragement of the natural increase of the slave population. Brazilian planters never resorted to breeding, as is evidenced in the high rate of manumissions and the very low natural increase of the Brazilian slave population.

It is difficult to determine the extent to which the high level of child as well as adult mortality among Brazilian slaves was cause and/or effect of the above differences. While the general level of mortality in Brazil was higher than in the United States, it is also true that differential mortality between the slave and free populations was greater. Estimation of slave mortality, even for the years after the 1872 census, is extremely difficult because of the lack of data required for indirect estimation and because manumission, which was depleting the slave stock just as the slave trade increased it, created a situation in which mortality was not the only factor responsible for slave population declines. A careful attempt by Mello (1975) to grapple with these problems has indicated that male slave life expectancy just prior to abolition was about 18.3 years, or 68 percent of the level for the total population (compared to a slave/total differential of 0.88 in the United States in 1850).

Low completed fertility also contributed to the failure of the Brazilian slave population to reproduce itself. The social conditions of Brazilian slavery had very adverse effects on family formation. Few slave marriages were recognized, and the toll in infant and child mortality rates for slave unions was very high. Actual slave fertility rates are also difficult to determine, owing to the lack of direct data and to the difficulties in applying indirect measures from the peculiar age-sex structure of slavery, manumissions, and high mortality in childhood. Direct estimates of marriage and child-woman ratios for the slave population reveal substantial differentials vis-à-vis the free-colored and white population. Indirect evidence for other slave populations (Eblen 1975, on Cuba) suggests that the number of births per slave woman may have been relatively high. But there is no direct way of adjusting for mortality and manumissions to determine how reported child-woman ratios would relate to more refined fertility measures.

Despite this basic demographic limitation, Brazilian slavery was able to adapt itself to a series of important changes in socioeconomic conditions and thus last longer as an institution than anywhere else in the Western Hemisphere. One of the principal mechanisms for achieving this after the abolition of the slave trade was the growing internal reallocation of slave labor. Major inter- and intraregional shifts occurred in the middle decades of the nineteenth century. The decline of sugar production in the Northeast and mining in Minas Gerais, combined with the rise of coffee production in Rio de Janeiro and São Paulo, contributed to a major regional redistribution of the slave population between 1823, when Rio de Janeiro and São Paulo had 15 percent of the slave population, and 1887, when their share had increased to 38 percent. Important intraregional shifts also took place. In the Northeast, a signficant proportion of the slave labor force shifted to urban occupations, while in the Southeast the shift favored coffee-production municipalities over urban activities (in Rio de Janeiro) and mining (in Minas Gerais.)

The last line of resistance to abolition was with the coffee planters, especially in the older coffee producing municipalities of Rio de Janeiro, where concern over the costs of obtaining free labor was more serious than in the more dynamic and expanding coffee-producing regions of São Paulo. A combination of the demographic events described above and a changing regional economic balance gradually eroded the institutional base of slavery to the point that abolition was merely a formality when it finally occurred. Abolition was a gradual process generated by four parliamentary acts, starting with the abolition of the slave trade in 1851, continuing with laws freeing children and older slaves in 1871 and 1886, and leading to final abolition in 1888. Abolition occurred without indemnification, as in the United States, though in the United States this was the result of a bloody civil war.

Immigration

Brazilian abolition was facilitated by relatively dynamic economic conditions in the region that needed slave manpower the most, São Paulo; while the coffee-producing upswing there generated additional labor demands, it also generated the revenues needed to attract an alternative labor supply, European immigrants. Tax revenues on the growing proceeds of the coffee-production expansion were used to subsidize immigrants.

The period of transition from slave to wage labor in Brazil (roughly 1880 to 1900) represents a major watershed in Brazilian history. On one hand, it brought great changes in the political and economic structure of the country; on the other hand, much of the legacy of the colonial-plantation-slave system remained. This paradox is at the root of much of the diversity and inequality at both the regional and socioeconomic structural levels in Brazil today. One of the major issues underlying all of this is why the coffee planters turned to immigrant labor rather than domestic sources and what effects this had on subsequent socioeconomic change.

The focal point of these events was the dynamic coffee-producing frontier of São Paulo. It provided the stimulus that initiated the major flow of immigrants into Brazil and was also the catalyst by which the effect of immigration on the economy and society was to reach far beyond the supply and demand for agricultural labor.

In demographic terms, European immigration accounted for larger absolute increases in Brazil's population than did slavery. However, several important contrasts qualify this generalization. Coming at a later stage in Brazil's demographic history, immigration's relative share in total increase was less because of a larger total population base. On the other hand, it was more concentrated regionally than slave imports, and thus had a much greater impact on population distribution than on total population growth.

The major upsurge of immigration in the last quarter of the nineteenth century reached its peak rapidly, increasing from 176,000 in the 1870s to nearly 1.2 million in the 1890s, a figure representing about 8 percent of the 1890 population base. Seventy percent of immigration in the 1890s located in São Paulo, and this, in contrast, represented 60 percent of the state's 1890 population. The 1890–99 peak was one of four major cyclical upswings in immigration in Brazil, the other three occurring in 1910–13, the 1920s, and the 1950s. These upswings contrast with sharp declines just after the turn of the century, the depression of the 1930s, and during the two world wars.

The ethnic composition of immigration varied in each of these periods. Portuguese immigrants were in the majority in earlier immigration and accounted for nearly one-third of the 1870–79 total. However, Italian immigrants soon came to dominate Brazilian immigration, and by the 1890s they accounted for nearly 60 percent of the total. Following this period, Italian immigration declined in both absolute and relative terms. Portuguese immigration generally held steady at between 30 and 40 percent of the total during most of the decades of this century. Only in the 1930s did another ethnic group, the Japanese, reach a level commensurate with that of the Portuguese. The three Southern European groups (Portuguese, Italian, and Spanish) accounted for three-fourths of the total immigration to Brazil, and though Northern European immigration was important regionally in the South, it never reached major national proportions.

Underlying these broad differentials in the ethnic composition of Brazilian immigration were important regional and occupational differentials. Italians, closely associated with the coffee culture, dominated in the major coffee-producing states of São Paulo, Minas Gerais, and Espírito Santo. Portuguese immigration, on the other hand, accounted for only a minor proportion of immigrants in the coffee-producing states and was more prevalent in the coastal cities of the Northeast and in Rio de Janeiro. The contrast relates to timing and differences in economic activity. Portuguese immigration reflected a longer tradition of settling in the older commercial centers, whereas Italians were recruited for agricultural work during the expansion of coffee exports. Males also tended to dominate in Portuguese migration, as is evidenced in the strong predominance of men in the foreign-born population reported in the 1872 census. Once we move from the Portuguese to the Italian phase in the 1880s, the nature of the inflow changes abruptly, as immigration of whole family units was encouraged, or even required to gain government subsidies for work on the coffee plantations of Western São Paulo. Wives and children were commonly utilized as part of the work force in coffee-producing areas. The net result was that women began to form a large part of the foreign-born work force.

Ethnic differentials also relate to the interaction between swings in migration and the international business cycle, especially in the case of the increased flow of Italians after 1885. In the early 1880s, both the United States and Argentina drew more Italians than Brazil. The growing dynamism of the Paulista coffee-producing expansion in the late 1880s permitted the São Paulo state government to subsidize Italian immigration. The attractiveness of São Paulo was reinforced by adverse economic conditions in both Argentina and the United States from 1890 to 1895: coffee prices continued to rise, while the other two economies passed through a slack period. In addition, economic conditions in Italy were stagnant in this period, further stimulating the outflow. Brazil captured a comparatively larger share of immigrants that might otherwise have gone to Argentina or to the United States. For one thing, the United States drew more heavily from the South of Italy, whereas Argentina and Brazil drew from the North. The assertion of this "detour" effect should be qualified, however, by noting that migration at a particular moment was not necessarily permanent, and that continued and return migration was common for Italians vis-à-vis both Brazil and Argentina. Nevertheless, this fortuitous set of economic circumstances among the three countries presented Brazil with an unusual opportunity to compete for the growing pool of underemployed Italian labor.

Paulista planters were able to develop some very effective mechanisms for attracting Italian farm workers to meet their growing labor needs. Armed with growing coffee export revenues, they sought to stimulate migration through subsidies and by a gradual "sweetening" of the *colono* agricultural labor arrangement. Earlier experiments with exploitative wage labor relationships and sharecropping failed to satisfy immigrants and gradually gave way to the *colono* system. Its diversified forms of income payment freed it of many negative features of traditional tenant, sharecropping, and fixed wage systems. The *colono* received a fixed wage for the weeding and care of a given number of trees throughout the year. This was supplemented by harvest wages and gave *colonos* a share in the gains (and risks) of changing yield. Day labor in and around the plantation provided a third source of income, and a fourth, nonmonetary, source was rent-free housing and land on which the *colono* could grow crops and raise livestock to meet his own subsistence needs and sell in local markets.

Rent-free provision of housing and land was facilitated by the abundance of land in São Paulo, which allowed the plantation owners to keep the money-wage bill low and still attract laborers. These laborers were able to maintain near self-sufficiency in food production and economize on money expenses. This in turn created the opportunities for savings for the purpose of buying small parcels of land or for migration to urban areas, with enough to get started in a new setting.

These aspects of the *colono* system, in conjunction with the relatively dynamic economic conditions of the period and a cultural milieu in which Italians adapted easily, contributed to the significant level of mobility that migrants were able to achieve within São Paulo's social and economic structure. Immigrants were able to achieve landowner status in substantial numbers in a relatively short time span, so that by 1920 they controlled 27 percent of all properties and 13 percent of cultivated land area in São Paulo. Migrants, and especially migrants' children, played key roles in the early industrialization that accompanied the coffee export boom in São Paulo. Migrants compared favorably to natives on such human capital scales as literacy and educational status. Migrants quickly assumed entrepreneurial roles in the growing urban-industrial sector during this period. A recent (Pereira 1974) inquiry into the ethnic origins of the founders of industrial establishments in São Paulo revealed that first or second generation Italians constituted the largest single ethnic group, even in comparison to those whose grandfathers were native Brazilians. The contrast is striking between the success of European immigrants in moving rapidly to a prominent position in Brazil's socioeconomic structure and the vastly different socioeconomic legacy of the ex-slave turned share-cropper or urban servant class that immigrant labor surpassed rather than displaced.

Population Redistribution and Urbanization

The main feature of population distribution in Brazil is its concentration in two regions, the Northeast and Southeast, and mostly in the relatively narrow coastal portions of these regions. In colonial times, these regions accounted for nearly 90 percent of Brazil's population (compared to about 30 percent of the land area), and as late as 1970 their share was still more than 70 percent. Only in the agricultural frontier expansion of recent decades has the vast interior (with 65 percent of Brazil's land area) begun to attract an appreciable share of Brazil's total population (about 10 percent in 1970), and most of this is located in the more settled Southern portions that are closer to Brasília and São Paulo. Brazilian settlement patterns contrast sharply with those of the United States, where Westward settlement reduced the share of population in the Atlantic coastal region from 97 percent at the end of the eighteenth century to 40 percent by 1900.

Economic, political, and geographic factors have contributed to Brazil's concentrated population distribution pattern. Travel and transport to the interior was difficult, because of the rugged, mountainous terrain that separated the coast from the interior plain, and because river systems linking the two were limited. In the case of the one potentially useful link—the São Francisco—river transport and communication were discouraged by Portuguese colonial administrators, who found coastal shipping easier to control and who wanted to limit access to gold and diamond regions in Minas Gerais.

Most of the redistribution of population that has occurred in the last two centuries took place between the Northeast and Southeast. Until 1870, the regional distribution of population remained quite stable, with the sugar- and cotton-producing states accounting for nearly half of the population. The major shift in distribution from the Northeast to the Southeast occurred after 1870. The most important demographic factor in this population redistribution was not the internal migration that occurred between 1940 and 1970, but rather the differential rate of international migration between 1870 and 1900. In this period, São Paulo raised its share in the national population from 8 to 17 percent. During the period, the Northeastern states suffered from drought and the depression of traditional export markets, while São Paulo experienced its coffee-production boom. In contrast, the forty-year period from 1900–40 brought only slight changes in the regional distribution. Between 1940 and 1970, the Northeast and Southeast both declined relative to the other macro-regions, due mainly to frontier settlement in the Northern (Amazonian), Southern (Paraná), and Central-Western regions. Another feature of more recent redistribution patterns is that shifts at the interstate and intermunicipality levels have gained in comparative importance. Within the Southeast, Minas Gerais experienced significant declines in its population share. Similarly, Bahia underwent a decrease in the Northeast.

Demographically, population redistribution can result either from differential natural increase, internal migration, or differential international migration. Interactions between these processes are also important. In the case of Brazil, determination of which of the components was the more important at different points in time must be done by way of indirect estimates, since no data on registration of migration and vital events are available.

Most of what can be done to estimate the migration component of population redistribution from Brazilian censuses is based on the survival-ratio technique, which determines the number of net migrants in a region or state over an intercensal period by comparing the actual "survivors" in an age cohort to the number that would be expected to survive the risk of mortality between the two census dates. In the absence of region-specific mortality data, national age-specific survival ratios (the complement of mortality rates) were employed—but subjecting the estimates to possible bias deriving from interregional mortality differences.

Survival-ratio estimates of Brazilian interregional migration by Graham and Hollanda (1971) show that the rate of net internal migration (i.e., the number of net intercensal migrants relative to the base period population) increased from the end of the last century to the 1950s and then declined in the

1960s. Four related patterns emerge in this secular trend of increasing interregional migration: (1) the competitive role of foreign immigrants from 1890 to 1930 and their eventual substitution by internal migrants; (2) the unfolding of four distinctive "frontier" migration streams throughout this period; (3) a distinct pattern of rural and urban components within the interregional population transfers, especially in recent decades; and (4) alternating regional divergence and convergence of income per capita associated with migration patterns after 1940.

The large inflow of foreign immigrants from 1890 to 1930 largely preempted any important labor supply role for internal migrants in the South. In São Paulo, foreign immigration dominated between 1890 and 1920, and there may even have been slightly negative net internal migration from 1900 to 1920. On one hand, competition from foreign-born workers pushed the local labor supply in and around São Paulo into marginal employment; on the other, expansion of rubber production in the North and subsistence agriculture in the Northeast diverted potential migrants from the São Paulo market. The net effect was a very limited contribution of internal migration to population redistribution in São Paulo between 1890 and 1920.

Rural resettlement has also been an important component of Brazilian population redistribution. Four distinct phases in the expansion of the agricultural frontier are observable. The first was the expansion of coffee production in Western São Paulo, which drew on the immigrant labor mentioned above. This was followed in the 1940s and 1950s by the extension of the coffee frontier into the state of Paraná. Internal migration, most of it from states in the Southern and Southeastern regions, was the main demographic factor in this redistribution. This is also true of the third major rural settlement movement into the Central-Western states of Mato Grosso and Goiás in the 1950s and 1960s. Intercensal rates of net inmigration reached to nearly one-quarter of these states' base population in this period. This was also the first frontier movement in Brazil that was not oriented to an export crop. Rather it was stimulated by increased demand for staples in the rapidly expanding urban markets in Brazil's Southeast, for which geographic proximity and extensive transport links give distinct advantages. It also contrasts with earlier frontier patterns, in that the internal migration on which it has drawn has had a much higher proportion of it migrants originating in states in the Northeast and from Minas Gerais.

The most recent frontier pattern is the Amazonian colonization effort that was launched in the 1970s. Massive public investments in road links and other infrastructure are being made in an effort to provide an escape valve for population pressure in the rural Northeast. Initial results have shown that colonization is much more expensive than expected. Poor soil and long-distance transport cost have made production of staples for the South impractical, and the strategy has changed from settlement to mere occupation and exploitation.

Large corporate investments in capital-intensive livestock, mining, and extractive activities rather than labor transfers have been the result.

All four frontier expansions have followed the classic Brazilian practice of increasing agricultural output by extensive increases in cultivation rather than intensive increases in productivity. Increased output has become associated with larger average units of operation and more capital-intensive and mechanized forms of production. Recent colonization experience suggests that the capacity of still unincorporated regions for absorption of rural population increase is limited, and this, in combination with the already limited carrying capacity of older, more settled rural regions, means that most of the future increase in Brazil's population will occur in urban areas.

Growth of the Urban Population

Rapid urban growth is one of the most striking features of recent Brazilian economic and demographic history. Cities of 20,000 or more inhabitants, which accounted for less than one-quarter of total population in 1950, accounted for half of the increase in total population in the last two decades. This raised their total share to 40 percent of the total population in 1970. The officially defined administrative measure of the urban population passed the 50 percent mark in the 1960s (56 percent in 1970) and is predicted to be close to 70 percent by the 1980s.

Historical patterns of urbanization in Brazil contrast with those of Spanish-speaking Latin America in several respects. Urban settlement in the colonial period was limited to coastal settlements and military outposts; there was no indigenous network of cities and roads comparable to the Inca and Aztec civilizations conquered by the Spanish. The Portuguese showed little interest in the "interior" until the gold and diamond rush of the eighteenth century.

It was not until the coffee export boom of the late nineteenth century that an urban system began to emerge from the dominant rural landscape of the country. In 1872, only 8 percent of the population resided in cities of 20,000 or more, and only three cities (Rio de Janeiro, Salvador, and Recife) had populations of over 100,000. São Paulo was the major center to emerge in this period; in the single decade of the 1890s it increased in size from 65 thousand to 240 thousand. This period is also one in which many Latin American countries experienced an increased primacy (dominance of a single city) associated with the export cycle. In the case of Brazil, the emergence of São Paulo had a dampening effect on the primacy of Rio de Janeiro and created a bipolar primacy pattern. Even this was never as pronounced as in the cases of Argentina, Chile, and Cuba.

During the industrialization that occurred in the first five decades of this century, the urban system remained relatively stable in terms of urban population distribution. The tendency toward primacy that had characterized the earlier part of the export phase did not persist—at least in terms of total urban population. The combined shares of metropolitan Rio and São Paulo in the total city population had increased from 38 percent in 1872 to 61 percent in 1900, but declined to about half by 1950. This is not true of the distribution of industrial employment, however. From the earliest stages of industrial growth in Brazil there was a heavy concentration in the Southeast. By 1950, the Rio de Janeiro-São Paulo regions accounted for 57 percent of industrial employment, and during the 1950s this increased to over 60 percent.

In recent decades, this concentration has had a marked effect on the distribution of the urban population by city size and by region. The overall trend has been toward increasing growth of larger cities (250,000 and over), especially the recently designated metropolitan areas (São Paulo, Rio de Janeiro, Belo Horizonte, Recife, Salvador, Porto Alegre, Belém, Curitiba, and Fortaleza). Within the larger metropolitan areas, there has been an important shift in the momentum of growth from the central municipalities to the peripheral ones. Except for larger nonmetropolitan centers like Brasília and Campinas, urban growth rates in the small and medium-sized cities have, on average, been slowing down. The dominance of the Southeast in urban population has been offset somewhat by the growth of cities in the new settlement areas in the Central-West and Paraná, but not enough to overcome the large imbalance between the Southeast and other regions in the ratio of urban to total population shares. The region with the lowest average urban growth rates is the Northeast, except for the periphery of Recife—the region's largest metropolitan center. Imbalances between urban population growth and increases in industrial employment have become a major concern to planners, since the capacity to support added population, directly through jobs as well as in providing the needed urban infrastructure from tax revenues, depends heavily on the industrial sector, because of the structure of the Brazilian tax and fiscal incentive system.

Brazil's size, regional diversity, and the lack of data make is difficult to sort out the demographic components of recent urbanization trends. In addition to large regional differentials in rates of fertility and mortality for both urban and rural areas, there is a rather complex pattern of interregional and rural-urban migration flows. On the basis of available information relating to interstate migration flows, two sets of net gaining regions emerge: (1) the industrial-metropolitan Southeast (São Paulo and Rio de Janeiro); and (2) the new settlement areas (Paraná, Mato Grosso, Goiás, and possibly the Amazon). In the case of Rio de Janeiro and São Paulo, migration offset the lower rates of natural increase to give a higher than average rate of total population increase. In the new settlement areas, migration and high rates of natural increase contributed to even greater differential growth. Comprehensive data on the role of migration in the growth of the cities are not readily available. On the basis of scattered estimates, it appears that the share of migrants in total population of the larger cities has tended to decline. However, it is important to note the indirect effect of migrant natural increase. Migrants have added to the weight of higher fertility groups in large urban populations, and the reproductive force of the migrants is an increasingly important factor in overall urban growth.

Underlying these patterns of interregional and rural-urban migration flows is Brazil's persistent problem of large regional disparities in income per capita and product per worker. In theory, migration should function as an equilibrating mechanism by transferring labor from less to more productive activities. Analysis of changes in regional inequality in income suggests that migration did play an equilibrating role in recent decades, especially in the 1950s. However, the convergence of incomes was weaker in the 1960s than in the 1950s suggesting some caution regarding expectations of continuation in this trend.

Of major concern are changes in regional differentials in sectoral output per worker that underlie the aggregated picture. There is little evidence of convergence in the case of regional differentials in product per worker in the industrial sector. Similarly, differentials in relative product per worker in agriculture increased in the 1960s, largely as a result of swings in world market prices for Brazilian exports. Most of the convergences that did in fact occur came in the service sector, reducing the Southeast-Northeast differential. Thus, while migration did redistribute labor, it did not do so in a way that affected differentials in product per worker in the sector primarily responsible for them—industry. This raises a further set of issues regarding the nature of growth and structural change in the labor force and the effects of industrialization on urban labor absorption in recent decades.

The Labor Force, Employment, and Urban Poverty

Imbalances between urban population increase, employment opportunities, and capacity to provide needed urban services have become a major concern of Brazilian authorities. Recent Brazilian industrialization, based on a growing demand for consumer durables, factor pricing policies favorable to capital, and available technology, fostered a capital-intensive expansion in manufacturing, which in turn generated demand for skilled workers rather than the large numbers of unskilled workers that were most in supply. Even with this limitation on employment opportunities, the larger cities have remained attractive in comparison to small towns and rural areas, because of their higher relative incomes. Migrants continue to move in the expectation that they may obtain a higher paying job. Though a portion of the excess in urban labor force growth has been absorbed by the public sector and by more highly capitalized service establishments, substantial numbers have sought employment and earnings opportunities in the less capitalized, informal or urban traditional sector, in which earnings have been much lower. Low-skill activities in construction and domestic services have been major absorbers of migrant labor.

The extent to which low earnings in these activities represent hidden unemployment or social marginalization is still controversial. Whatever the position one takes on this, it is clear that informal activities are a mixed blessing. On the one hand, they represent a viable alternative to unemployment or return migration; on the other, they have also been an important factor in the worsening relative income position of individuals and families at the lowest end of the urban income distribution.

Though these problems are currently drawing a lot of attention, it should be recognized that their roots run back into the plantation-oriented economic structure that dominated Brazil until well into the present century. Looking at the labor force as a whole, its size increased from 5 million to 30 million workers between 1872 and 1970. In the process, the share of agriculture declined from over 70 percent to 45 percent, with a corresponding rise in nonagricultural activities. The fundamental demographic characteristics differentiating trends in both the growth and composition of the active population are age and sex. For males, the trend in total growth between 1872 and 1970 is comparatively steady, though we do observe a moderate increase in the ratio of active to total working age (10+) males between 1872 and 1900 and a similar decline between 1950 and 1970. We have questioned the earlier increase on the basis of doubts about the accuracy of age reporting in the 1900 census. The 1950–70 decline, however, appears to be real. It is related, on the one hand, to decreased participation among the school-age group and, on the other, to declines in activity among older males. In part, this can be attributed to increased retirement, but concern was also expressed regarding premature withdrawal from the work force because of older workers' disability and/or discouragement in competing with younger, more able labor force entrants.

The sectoral dominance of agriculture is more pronounced for males, with the agricultural share hovering around 70 percent until the 1940s, when it started a decline to just above 50 percent in 1970. It is extremely difficult to distinguish between services and industry in the 30 percent of male nonagricultural employment that was maintained prior to 1940, because of the basically artisan orientation of these activities. In 1940, the ratio of services to industry (including mining, manufacturing, construction, and public utilities) was about 2:1, which was maintained until 1970, when the industry share was increased. Part of this reflects a reclassification of construction workers, who had been grouped in services prior to 1970, but even after discounting for this, it is clear that the main increase in industry between 1960 and 1970 had come from construction.

Interpretation of data on female activities and their composition in earlier censuses is extremely difficult, because of the complexity of female employment. The basic distinction in modern labor force analysis between household and market activities was blurred, if not meaningless, in a predominantly agricultural economy, especially one rooted in slavery and the plantation system. Early Brazilian censuses were not consistent in the definition of female activity, nor in the distribution by branch of activity among those who were considered active. The most important examples are the clearly exaggerated reports of domestic servants in the 1900 census and the inconsistencies in reporting of females in agriculture for 1940 and 1950. A further complication arises from the comparatively rigorous norms that were set for measurement of female employment in 1920, which yield results in which it is impossible to distinguish between actual changes in the level and composition of employment, changes in definition, and changes in attitudes regarding female employment underlying these definitions. It is only by making some arbitrary but needed adjustments regarding domestic services reported in 1872 and 1900 according to 1920 norms that is becomes possible to trace the long-term contours of female employment.

The basic pattern that emerges is the U-shaped trend in female activity rates that has been observed cross-sectionally and in trend data for a number of countries. Actually, the U-shaped trend is only modified by rather than dependent upon adjustments of early census data. Reported female activity rates were quite high in early censuses, reflecting the higher level of domestic and artisan production characteristic of an agricultural society and the variety of roles that were concomitant with this. The main effect of the adjustments was to reduce the domestic service component, and hopefully count as "market" work a more likely proportion of services performed outside the home. With or without the adjustment, female participation declined substantially during the early decades of this century, from 51 percent of the female population age 10 and over in 1872 (71 percent in the unadjusted data) to around 14 percent between 1920 and 1950. The decline appears in both the agricultural and industry branches, reflecting both a sectoral shift in employment and a sharper distinction of female roles that accompanied urban growth and the shift of formerly artisan activities from household to factory, with attendant constraints on females performing both household and market-related functions as these shifts occurred. Only very recently has the trend toward increased female employment in services been strong enough to offset the relative decreases in agriculture and industry and lead to an increase in the overall female participation rate. The recent rise in Brazil still falls far short of the major return of females to the work force that has occurred in more industrialized regions, principally because Brazil has not experienced the significant increases among older married women that have characterized those areas. Still, recent increases in female participation are observable in a number of age categories other than the typically more active young adults, and it is quite possible that a major turning point for the role of women in the Brazilian economy is occurring.

Postwar industrialization has accelerated shifts in the structure of employment both for males and for females, principally in the move from agricultural to nonagricultural activities. It is precisely the composition of employment in the recent expansion of nonagricultural activities and their implications for income distribution that have generated the concern about imbalances between industrial expansion and employment mentioned earlier. Industrial output increased at about twice the rate of industrial employment between 1950 and 1970, and the latter was about 40 percent less than the rate of growth of the urban population in the same period. Growth in other nonagricultural employmen was closer to the increase in urban population, but not enough to compensate for the shortfall in industrial employment vis-à-vis the rapid pace of urban growth.

There is little direct evidence to suggest that the excess of urban population growth has resulted in increased open unemployment. Reported unemployment rates for the nonagricultural labor force in both the 1970 census and recent PNAD surveys are very low, 2 to 3 percent. The significance of these rates is open to question, since there is no institutionalized form of unemployment compensation, and the only way to maintain income in the event of losing a job is to seek alternative sources. The declining activity rates for older males also suggest that workers who encounter difficulties obtaining jobs, especially older people, may be more likely to drop out of the labor force as discouraged workers. Analysis of unemployment data in PNAD surveys by O'Brien and Salm (1970) indicates that many who would have been reported as unemployed in other circumstances have sought lower pay in petty services in order to maintain income, and suggests that underemployment is the more typical situation of individuals in such cases.

Statistical evidence on underemployment in Brazilian cities is limited and difficult to interpret. Measures such as hours of work and unpaid family worker status yield relatively low percentages—those working less than 40 hours and who would prefer full-time work represent only 4.5 percent of the urban work force, and only 1.1 percent of prime-age (20 to 49) males were unpaid family workers. It is only when earnings data are utilized that the recent figures suggest a higher proportion of underemployment among urban workers. About one-third of all workers reported earnings less than the legal minimum wage in their region, with the share being closer to 50 percent for females. However, interpretation of these results is difficult. About 60 percent of females earning less than the minimum wage are domestic servants. They receive nonmonetary remuneration in room and board, and though their employment may be exploitative, it is questionable whether they would be more productive in other activities given their skills and existing labor market conditions. A similar situation is encountered in the case of male construction workers, who account for about 20 percent of those earning less than the minimum wage. Again, exploitative conditions, where they exist, do not necessarily mean underemployment, in that this concept implies misallocation of labor. Since a large proportion of these low-paying positions are occupied by individuals with lower skills, including recent migrants and younger people entering the labor market for the first time, closer examination of this segment of the urban labor market is required before judgement on its role in urban underemployment is passed.

Recent research on urban labor absorption in developing countries has emphasized the role of labor market structure in the determination of employment and earnings for lower-income groups in the cities. The urban informal sector—referring to activities and employment arrangements at the least capitalized and least organized end of the urban economic spectrum–has drawn increased attention because it has accounted for so much of the increase in employment for the less-skilled, younger, and migrant groups mentioned above. Informal employment is not a "sector" in the conventional sense of branches of activity, but is focused rather on labor market structure and variation in employment arrangements. In theory, this permits analysis of labor absorption without having to dichotomize activities into modern or traditional solely on the basis of the type of product. In practice, data limitations often force indirect measurement of informal activities in a manner that is, in fact, based on such a dichotomization. Conceptually, employment arrangements in the informal sector are distinguished by loose agreements, lack of coverage by minimum wage legislation, social security, and unions when they exist. The scale of establishments employing informal workers is generally smaller, and domestic and own-account workers figure importantly in it. As such, informal employment is not new to the urban economy in Brazil. Much of artisan manufacturing and most services before the postwar expansion could be so characterized. However, postwar growth did not eliminate informal activities. Rather, the capitalization of industry was accompanied by complex forms of economic organization in production and labor markets, creating a more sharply defined formal sector, while the informal sector remained an important alternative in urban labor absorption.

Informal activities are, by their very nature, statistically elusive. Most available estimates of the volume of informal employment are indirect: for example, by comparing employment by branch of activity (manufacturing, commerce, etc.) as reported in population censuses, which are broader in scope and, in theory at least, include all workers, to data on employment as reported in sectoral economic censuses, which are collected on an establishment basis and whose scope is limited to larger, more organized firms. Data on manufacturing, commerce, and services from the last four decennial censuses (1940–70) suggests that the share of informal employment during the postwar industrialization process was relatively steady after an initial decline in the 1940s. If we extend the definition of informal employment to include construction as well as the differential between employment in each branch reported by the population and economic censuses, then the share declined from 42 percent in 1940 to 35 percent in 1950 and after. Underlying this aggregative trend is a steady decline in informal employment in manufacturing from 1940 to 1960, a period in which more capital-intensive import substitution probably led to displacement of traditional units. This was offset by increased shares of informal employment in commerce and services in the 1950s, after they too had experienced declines in the 1940s. The sectoral pattern is somewhat reversed in the 1960s, when the informal share in manufacturing increased again. While caution regarding data from the 1960 population census is required, the above suggests that informal employment still plays a major role in urban labor absorption.

A possible explanation for the contrasting intersectoral shifts in the 1950s and 1960s is offered by Ozório de Almeida (1976), who found a higher level of subcontracting in formal sector manufacturing establishments for their service sector needs to the informal sector in the 1960s than in the 1950s. Although data limitations restricted her comparisons, she was able to show that subcontracting by smaller-scale industrial sector firms may have increased in the 1960s, which is consistent with the trend observed here.

Additional insight into the demographic and social characteristics of informal sector workers was obtained from survey data for Belo Horizonte, which focus specifically on informal employment. There the informal sector clearly worked as a buffer between rapid growth in the supply of unskilled labor and the limited demand for this labor in the more capitalized activities of the formal sector. This was not limited to the absorption of recent migrants, even though they were the proximate cause of excess urban labor supply. Informal employment was important for a number of groups whose earnings opportunities would have been more limited in its absence. These include the young and the old, females, the less skilled and the less educated—as well as recent migrants. When migrant/native differences were controlled for other factors, migrant status appeared to be among the less important criteria for an individual's being in the informal sector. One of the most striking pieces of evidence on the way in which sector participation operated on the employment process was the inverse relation between proportions employed and proportions in the informal sector in particular subgroups of the population. Informal employment tended to broaden the fringe area between full employment (according to formal sector criteria) and inactivity.

The close association between informal employment and lower average earnings also suggests that the informal sector provides much of the employment and earnings opportunities available to the lowest socioeconomic strata. Informal employment is much more prevalent in low-income families, both for heads and for secondary earners in these units. For the other members, especially females, informal employment has meant long hours at low pay to supplement low earnings or no earnings for the household head.

The above illustrates the diversity of functions that informal employment serves in the urban economy. Besides being a transition or buffer for labor force entry groups, like recent migrants and young people, it also provides increased earnings opportunities for individuals who may lack the credentials for higher-paying formal sector jobs. In addition, informal sector employment often represents the only equivalent of unemployment compensation or welfare for individuals who lose or cannot obtain formal sector jobs, because of disability and other obstacles, such as child care in the case of female heads of households. For policy purposes, it is important to recognize this diversity and the need to target actions in relation to these specific functions within the sector. While such diversity has led some to question the usefulness of grouping employment in all noncapitalized activities into a single category, it is seen as a more useful focus than approaches such as marginality and underemployment, which emphasize the lack of social and economic dynamics among lower-income groups that closer study reveals to be, in fact, very much present.

A final criticism of the informal sector approach, especially the way in which it is generally operationalized, is that is is just another way of talking about "residual" employment in services and commerce. It is true that a large portion of recent growth in urban employment in Brazil has occurred in non-manufacturing activities, but the overall 1950–70 trend does not support a characterization of this trend as a "flooding" of the tertiary sector. Except for a slight increase in 1950–60, the trend in the two tertiary subbranches where one might expect such overflow (commerce and personal services) is downward. Detailed analysis of the occupational and sectoral compositions of employment between 1950 and 1970 shows that these sectors provided the greatest absolute increase in employment because of their larger weight in the total, but that the occupations that contributed most to the relative increase in services were teaching, clerical and administrative work, social service work, and the like. The fact that employment increases for females were concentrated in these higher-earning jobs and low-paying domestic service, with likely adverse income distribution effects, suggests that the structure of labor and product markets rather than employment in services per se is the more important dimension of the labor absorption/income distribution problem in Brazilian cities. This bimodal shifting in female employment was the result of declines in some of the traditional female employment occupations in the "industry" sector, including food and beverages, textiles, and clothing.

Occupational shifts for males have been broader in the last two decades than for females. Declining shares of farm workers were replaced by a range of increases in urban-oriented occupations. It is true that street vendors and domestic workers increased, however, their contribution to 1950–70 employment growth was less than that of managerial, clerical, technical, and transport jobs and a large number of subbranches of manufacturing. Important shifts also occur within manufacturing and are somewhat paradoxical in that more capital-intensive industries, such as metal and machinery, absorbed relatively more than such traditional mass-consumption categories as textiles. Negative occupational growth within these groups for both males and females may have resulted from the replacement of older, labor-intensive technology, that had been installed during earlier stages of industrialization, by labor-saving equipment of more recent vintage.

Special attention was given in the review of urban employment and income distribution to differences between migrants and natives. It is true that the demographic impact of migration flows over and above natural growth has augmented urban population increase substantially, and that this has resulted in pressures on urban services, job creation, and so on. However, examination of differentials between migrants and nonmigrants suggests that socioeconomic characteristics (particularly age and education) of migrants rather than migration status per se account for most of the observed differentials. Migrants make up a large share of the urban poor in the major metropolitan areas. But this occurs because migrants are a large share of the overall population in these cities. Their proportional representation among the poor is no larger than their share in the total population. Unemployment rates are also about equal for migrants and nonmigrants. Regional factors appear to play an important role in differentials in the rate of unemployment, with lower rates recorded in the South and the highest ones occurring in the Northeast. The regional variation in unemployment contrasts with the data on earnings, in which more recent migrants show a consistently higher proportion of workers earning less than the monthly regional minimum wage. Age is an important factor in this differential, since recent migrants tend to be younger and therefore representative of a lower portion of the lifetime age/earnings profile.

The findings lead us to be cautious in attributing problems of urban unemployment and income distribution specifically to migration. Migration is only the "cause" of urban poverty in the sense of its being one of the main factors in the rapid demographic increase of the urban population. But in this sense natural increase is also a "cause." Migration is certainly not a cause in the sense that the marginalized masses in the cities consist entirely of poor migrants who have swarmed in from the countryside and remain locked into urban poverty. It should be noted that migrant/native comparisons for particular cities give only a partial view of population redistribution and may, because of return migration, give an overly optimistic impression of upward migrant mobility. Still, the "drop-out" effect that was discussed in assessing the mobility evidence does not imply that less successful migrants have remained to swell the rolls of the urban poor.

Brazilian Policy on Population Growth and Economic Development: An Assessment

In terms of the effects of overall population increase on economic growth, Brazilian economists have remained skeptical of macroeconomic arguments stressing the adverse effects on per capita income growth of population growth and a broad-based age distribution resulting from high fertility. They have discounted conventional arguments about the effects of age structure and dependence on investment and emphasize the role of the balance of payments (including coffee prices, manufactured exports, and requirements for imports of capital goods), inflation, and domestic institutional crises in postwar swings in the Brazilian economy. Even those aware of the implications of Brazil's 3 percent per annum population growth on employment creation and for overcoming deficits in health, education, and housing recognized the political liabilities of making too much of it. Population was treated very gingerly in official planning documents, especially after the 1967 incident described in Chapter XI.

Preparations for Brazilian participation in the 1974 World Population Conference in Bucharest, which coincided with the drafting of the Second National Development Plan, provided an occasion for broader discussion of the population issue. Though there was never anything approaching public debate, discussions at the technical and interministerial level reflected a broadening range of opinion. Publication of the 1970 population census and the growing number of trained demographers and economists working on population-related topics within the government technocracy helped to wear down sentiment that mention of the subject of population automatically implied advocacy of birth control.

In retrospect, captivation with macroeconomic arguments probably dulled sensitivities to other social costs associated with rapid population increase, particularly those related to the widening gap between the rich and the poor. Brazil's broad-based age distribution has made it harder to alleviate deficits in social services like housing, health, and education, and the growing working-age population has placed pressures on the economy to create productive activities to use the increased flow effectively. Since 1950, the population in labor force entry ages (10 to 24) has nearly doubled. While significant progress was made in raising school enrollment and reducing residual activity categories (neither working nor attending school) in these ages, especially among females, it is well to remember that nearly two-thirds of Brazilians still reach adulthood without completing primary schooling. This is an improvement over the three-fourths figure of 1950, but it also indicates how much remains to be done. The implications of unrealized human resource potential are serious. Though the less educated go to work earlier and thus make a more immediate contribution to total output, their lifetime contribution will be substantially less, because earnings and productivity will not rise as much with age as those of individuals for whom educational opportunities were available.

The resulting losses in productivity and earnings are both societal and individual, but the adverse impact on individual welfare is greater because it occurs in combination with another fundamental dimension of the relation between demographic factors and income distribution, which is the large fertility differential between high- and low-income groups. Household survey data on the relation between dependency and life cycle earnings capacity in poor and low-income families show that the adverse effect of unequal distribution on a poor family is a double one: first, the low-earnings capacity of its members, and then the fact that these members' earnings must be spread further. The full impact of this flatter age-earnings profile is felt as the main dependency burden of these poorer households falls on the prime working age portion of the life cycle of the head. While upper-income households have higher incomes to cushion rising consumption needs, poor families have fewer resources to provide for their larger numbers. These complex and circular causal relationships between family structure, human resource endowments, and variables like health and access to public services are as much the effect as the cause of poverty. Demographic factors are clearly important in the dynamics of poverty, though not the root cause in the sense that public action to reduce fertility alone is the way to break the cycle. The solution would no doubt be eased by reducing the dependency burden, but it also requires remedying deficiencies in education, health, nutrition, and access to other services, as well as adequate employment and earnings opportunities.

The unevenness of recent socioeconomic as well as demographic changes in Brazil raises some questions as to the viability of the Brazilian policy of *laissez faire* with respect to a decline in its birth rate. This position is based on the expectation that modernization will eventually have an effect on reproductive behavior, leading couples to limit fertility in response to personal benefits that they perceive arising from this course of action. Changes in parents' aspirations, both for themselves and their children, and in the ability to realize these aspirations, play an important role in the demographic responsiveness to modernization. Recent data suggest that a decline in birth rates has started to occur in Brazil, but that it is taking place within specific regions and among certain income groups rather than being spread across the entire population. Evidence on distribution of contraceptives through private channels indicates that family planning is widespread among higher-income families in the industrial South and Southeast, and the recent declines in birth rates in these areas are certainly a reflection of this.

An unequal distribution of the onset of fertility decline is not unusual, especially in a country with such great economic, regional, and cultural diversity as Brazil, but several aspects of the unequal distribution of demographic changes and their relation to socioeconomic conditions suggest caution regarding the expectation that a general transition from high to low fertility has begun.

Regional diversity is one of the principal reasons why Brazil appeared to be an anomaly in a recent attempt to relate aggregative demographic trends to indices of modernization for a large number of Latin American countries (Oeschli and Kirk 1975). Important rural-urban and interregional differentials in fertility and mortality existed in Brazil in the 1940s, and the indirect evidence derived from census data suggests that interregional differences in fertility widened between the 1940s and 1960s, while there was little change in the case of mortality. Fertility also contrasts with indices of interregional differentials for other socioeconomic aspects of modernization, like literacy and income per capita, which narrowed in the interval.

In Brazil's *laissez faire* policy, it is also expected that rural–urban migration will lead to fertility decline to the extent that population is redistributed to the cities and subjected to the influences of urban life. Evidence on migrant-native differentials is supportive of this view, but there are additional considerations that need to be taken into account. There is no reason to expect an abatement of the rural and regional sources of migration-related urban population increase, and the growing inequality within city population raises equal doubts about the "natural" response of low-income urban populations to child-bearing alternatives to which they appear to have very limited access. One of the ironies of Brazil's *laissez faire* population policy is that it is coupled with a policy that has been basically *laissez faire* with respect to socioeconomic inequality, e.g., a rejection of major interventions to remedy problems of income distribution and access to urban services on the grounds that these *too* will be solved in good time by the normal process of economic development. To the observer viewing both problems—high fertility and inequality—as joint and related, *laissez faire* with regard to both seems to be inconsistent. An interventionist position on at least one would appear to be necessary, and given the political, social, and economic constraints on achieving extensive change on either front, intervention combining mutually enhancing aspects of both would be desirable.

The expectation of a rapid decline in Brazil's birth rate in response to development, as articulated in the recent plan document, hinges on a number of "ifs." While it is based on the well-established generalization that fertility rates do decline in the normal course of economic development, it does not take account of the very uneven distribution of recent Brazilian development and the depressing effect that this is likely to have on the modernization of reproductive behavior.

In the absence of social policy combining a broad range of improvements in the earnings opportunities, access to social services, and family planning for both the rural and urban poor, it is more likely that the poor population will continue to reproduce itself at a rapid rate, further extending the problem of poverty. One adverse effect of the lack of such programs that has already begun to alarm local officials is the apparent rise in rates of infant and child mortality among low-income groups in large cities. This is likely to have an even further depressing effect on changes in the reproductive behavior of the poor, since couples are unlikely to have fewer children and to invest in these childrens' future until the chances for their survival to adulthood are more sure. On the positive side, Brazilian authorities have begun a major push in the areas of water, sanitation, and nutrition. It is still too early to judge how rapidly these programs are actually overcoming deficits. However, they could, if successful, accelerate the decline in child mortality and indirectly contribute to fertility decline.

In all likelihood, further declines in Brazil's rate of population increase are more likely to occur gradually. Given the momentum of current increase, there are important implications for the future size and composition of the population. Long-term population projections are particularly hazardous, and in Brazil's case the pattern of future increase depends heavily on birth rate assumptions. Despite the large number of "ifs" in any projection, the combination of Brazil's existing socioeconomic structure (and the policies affecting it) with some of the inherent dynamics of population change make some outcomes much more likely than others. A key determinant of any outcome is the size of the birth cohort (the number of births in any given year); which in an eventual stable population will determine the size of the total population.

As life expectancy approaches some maximum (the current world norm is about 75 years) a stable population total will equal the number in the birth cohort times the expectation of life. Presently, the birth cohort in Brazil totals about 4 million. Because mortality, especially in childhood, now reduces the size of this cohort substantially by the adult years, Brazil's current population size is still far below the 240 million stable total implied by its present birth and death rates. However, as Brazil approaches stability in the next several decades, these variables will determine the final outcome. With an expectation of life of 75 years and the present birth cohort of 4 million, that total would be close to 300 million. And it is not likely that the birth cohort, which has increased at a rate of about 1.5 percent per year (a considerable reduction from the 3 percent of the 1950s), will stop growing immediately. In fact, its growth may well increase in the late 1970s and early 1980s as a result of "demographic echo" effect of the high birth rate of the 1950s, which is now sending an increased number of women into the early reproductive age cohorts.

Any increase in the size of the birth cohort thus adds substantially to the size of the final stable population total. Supposing that the size of the birth cohort levels off at 5 million, we are talking about a stable population of 375 million: more than three times the current (1978) total of about 115 million. What kind of future is in store for these two or three "other Brazils"? Size is itself an issue in terms of the effect on natural resources, as well as Brazil's weight in world power relationships. But compositional issues are equally important. It is highly likely, for example, that most of the increase will occur in the urban population. With an urban share of 90 percent, a 375 million stable population total implies over a sevenfold increase over the 52 million urban population recorded in the 1970 census. Location of these cities, development of urban infrastructure, and the creation of adequate employment opportunities for such growth is a staggering prospect for Brazilian urban planners in coming decades. There is a great need for research and experimentation with low-cost delivery systems to reach the larger numbers who will have to be served. Unless significant headway is made in the equalization of access to services and earnings opportunities, this growth is also likely to be very heavily weighted with the urban poor.

The implications for research and planning extend to strategies for coping with substantial population increase while budgetary resources are limited. It is unrealistic to suppose that even a very dynamic Brazilian economy will be able to generate a surplus sufficient to meet all of the demands arising from both redistribution of opportunities and simple increase in the number of potential recipients. In terms of research recommendations, there is a clear need for strategies to stage and select programs in employment, education, health, and housing, and careful assessment of how changes in population structure during the approach to a stable level might relate to a "second best" solution of these demands should be a high priority on the agenda of Brazilian planners.

Glossary of Abbreviations
and Acronyms in References

ANPEC	Associação Nacional dos Centros de Pós-Graduação em Economia
BNB	Banco do Nordeste do Brasil
BNH	Banco Nacional de Habitação
CBED	Centro Brasileiro de Estudos Demográficos
CEBRAP	Centro Brasileiro de Análises e Planejamento
CEDEPLAR	Centro de Desenvolvimento e Planejamento Regional
CEDOPE	Centro de Documentação e Pesquisa
CELADE	Centro Latino-Americano de Demografia
CICRED	Comité International de Coordination des Recherches
CLACSO	Consejo Latinoamericano de Ciencias Sociales
CNPU	Comissão Nacional de Regiões Metropolitanas e Política Urbana
DIEESE	Departamento Intersindical de Estatistica e Estudos Sócio-eno-nômicos
EPGE–FGV	Escola de Pós-Graduação de Economia da Fundação Getulio Vargas
ETENE	Departamento de Estudos Econômicos do Nordeste (BNB)
IBGE	Instituto Brasileiro de Geografia e Estatística
IBRD	International Bank for Reconstruction and Development (The World Bank)
IDB	Interamerican Development Bank
ILO/OIT	International Labour Organization/Organização Internacional do Trabalho
IPE/USP	Instituto de Pesquisas Econômicas da Universidade de São Paulo
IPEA/INPES	Instituto de Planejamento Econômico e Social/Instituto de Pesquisa
IPEA/IPLAN	Instituto de Planejamento Econômico e Social/Instituto de Planejamento
NBER	National Bureau of Economic Research
PISPAL	Programa de Investigaciones Sociales Sobre Problemas de Poblacion Relevantes para Politicas de Poblacion en America Latina
PNAD	Pesquisa Nacional por Amostra de Domicilios
PREALC	Programa Regional del Empleo para America Latina e el Caribe
SBPC	Sociedade Brasileira para o Progresso da Ciencia
UNESCO	United Nations Educational, Scientific and Cultural Organization

342

References

Abreu, Marcelo de Paiva. 1975. "A Divida Pública Externa do Brasil, 1931–1943." *Pesquisa e Planejamento Econômico* 5 (June): 37–88.

Abreu, Maurício. 1976. "Migration, Urban Labor Absorption and Occupational Mobility in Brazil." Ph.D. dissertation, Ohio State University.

Alden, Dauril. 1963. "The Population of Brazil in the Late Eighteenth Century: A Preliminary Study." *Hispanic American Historical Review* 43 (May): 173–205.

Aleixo, José Carlos Brandi. 1973. "Considerações sobre os Aspectos Políticos do Problema Demográfico no Brasil." CEDOPE, *Seminário de População,* pp. 90–116. São Leopoldo, Brasil.

Almeida, José. *Industrialização e Emprego no Brasil.* Rio de Janeiro: IPEA/INPES.

Almeida, Wanderley J. Manso de, 1974. *Serviços e Desenvolvimento Econômico no Brasil: Aspectos Setoriais e suas Implicações.* Rio de Janeiro: IPEA/INPES.

Almeida, Wanderley J. Manso de, and da Conceição Silva, Maria. 1973. *Dinâmica do Setor Serviços no Brasil: Emprego e Produto.* Rio de Janeiro: IPEA/INPES.

Alves, João. 1973. *Contrôle da Natalidade e Disseminação dos Entorpecentes no Brasil.* Brasilia, Centro de Documentação e Informação, Câmara dos Deputados.

Andrade, Manoel Correia de. 1964. *A Terra e o Homem no Nordeste.* São Paulo: Editora Brasiliense.

————. 1973. *Paisagens e Problemas do Brasil,* 4th ed. Rio de Janeiro: Editora Brasiliense.

————. 1975. "O Processo de Modernização e sua Repercussão sobre as Relações de Trabalho no Meio Rural Brasileiro." *Anais da História* 7: 48–65.

Andrade, Thompson Almeida. 1977. "Desigualdades Regionais no Brasil: Uma Seleção de Estudos Empíricos." *Pesquisa e Planejamento Econômico* 7: 205–26.

Araújo, Aloiso Barbosa de. 1974. *Aspectos Fiscais das Areas Metropolitanas.* Rio de Janeiro: IPEA/INPES.

Arriaga, Eduardo. 1968a "Components of City Growth in Selected Latin American Countries." *Milbank Memorial Fund Quarterly* 46 (April): 237–52.

————. 1968b. *New Life Tables for Latin American Population in the Nineteenth and Twentieth Centuries.* Berkeley: Institute for International Studies.

————. 1970a. *Mortality Decline and Its Demographic Effects in Latin America.* Berkeley: Institute for International Studies.

————. 1970b. "The Nature and Effects of Latin America's Non-Western Trend in Fertility." *Demography* 7 (November): 483–501.

343

_____. 1972. "Impact of Population Changes on Education Costs." *Demography* 9 (May): 275–94.

Arriaga, Eduardo, and Davis, Kingsley. 1969. "The Pattern of Mortality Change in Latin America." *Demography* 6 (August): 223–42.

Arthur, W. Brian, and McNicoll, Geoffrey. 1975. "Large-Scale Models in Population and Development: What Use to Planners?" *Population and Development Review* 1 (December): 251–66.

Aufhauser, R. Keith. 1974*a*. "Profitability of Slavery in the British Caribbean." *Journal of Interdisciplinary History* 5 (Summer): 45–68.

_____. 1974*b*. "Slavery and Technological Change." *Journal of Economic History* 34 (March): 36–50.

Ávila, Fernando Bastos de, S.J. 1954. *Economic Impacts of Immigration: The Brazilian Immigration Problem*. The Hague: M. Nyhoff.

Bacha, Edmar L. 1974. "Hierarquia e Remuneração Gerencial." *Estudos Econômicos* 4 (1): 143–75.

_____. 1976*a*. "On Some Contributions to the Brazilian Income Distribution Debate—I." Harvard Institute for International Development: Development Discussion Paper No.11.

_____. 1976*b*. *Os Mitos de Uma Década*. Rio de Janeiro: Paz e Terra.

_____. 1977. "Issues and Evidence on Recent Brazilian Economic Growth." *World Development* 5 (½): 47–67.

Bacha, Edmar L., da Mata, Milton, and Modenesi, Rui. 1972. *Encargos Trabalhistas e Absorção de Mão de Obra*. Rio de Janeiro: Instituto de Planejamento Econômico e Social.

Baer, Werner. 1965. *Industrialization and Economic Development in Brazil*. Homewood, Illinois: Richard D. Irwin.

_____. 1973. "The Brazilian Boom 1968–1972: An Explanation and Interpretation." *World Development* 1 (August): 1–16.

_____. 1975. *A Industrialização e o Desenvolvimento Econômico do Brasil*, 2nd ed. Rio de Janeiro: Fundação Getúlio Vargas.

_____. 1976. "The Brazilian Growth and Development Experience 1964–1975." In *Brazil in the Seventies,* Riordan Roett (ed.). Washington, D.C.: American Enterprise Institute.

Baer, Werner, and Hervé, Michel E.A. 1966. "Employment and Industrialization in Developing Countries." *Quarterly Journal of Economics* 80 (February): 88–107.

Baer, Werner, and Kerstenetzky, Isaac. 1972. "The Economy of Brazil." In *Brazil in the Sixties*, Riordan Roett (ed.). Nashville, Tennessee: Vanderbilt University Press.

Baer, Werner and Villela, Annibal. 1973. "Industrial Growth and Industrialization: Revisions in the Stages of Brazil's Economic Development." *Journal of Developing Areas* 7: (January) 217–234.

Baer, Werner; Geiger, Pedro Pinchas; and Haddad, Paulo Roberto. 1978. *Dimensões do Desenvolvimento Brasileiro*. Rio de Janeiro: Editora Campus Ltda.

Balán, Jorge. 1973. Migrações e Desenvolvimento Capitalista no Brasil. *Estudos CEBRAP* 5 (July–September): 7–79.

_____. 1974. *Centro e Periferia no Desenvolvimento Brasileiro*, editor's introduction. São Paulo: Difusão Européia do Livro.

Balán, Jorge; Browning, Harley; and Jelin, Elizabeth. 1973. *Men in a Developing Society: Geographic and Social Mobility in Monterrey*. Austin: University of Texas Press.

Baldwin, Robert. 1956. "Patterns of Development in Newly Settled Regions." *Manchester School of Economic and Social Studies* 24 (May): 161–79.

Barat, Joseph (ed.). 1976. *Politica de Desenvolvimento Urbano: Aspectos Metropolitanos e Locais*. Rio de Janeiro: IPEA/INPES.

Barros, José Roberto Mendonça de, and Graham, Douglas H. 1978. "The Brazilian Economic Miracle Revisited: Public and Private Sector Initiative in a Market Economy." *Latin American Research Review* 13(2): 5–38.

Battalio, Raymond C., and Kagel, John. 1970. "The Structure of Antebellum Southern Agriculture: South Carolina, A Case Study." *Agricultural History* 44 (January): 25–37.

Baum, Samuel, and Frank, Nancy B. 1976. "Projeções Ilustrativas da População do Brasil sob Diferentes Hipóteses de Fecundidade: Perspectivas a Longo Prazo." In Fundação IBGE: *Encontro*, pp. 536–42.

Beaver, Steven E. 1975. *Demographic Transition Theory Reinterpreted*. Lexington, Massachusetts: Heath Lexington Books.

Becker, Gary S. 1960. "An Economic Analysis of Fertility." In Universities–National Bureau, Committee for Economic Research, *Demographic and Economic Change in Developed Countries*. Princeton: Princeton University Press.

Beckford, George. 1972. *Persistent Poverty: Underdevelopment in the Plantation Economies of the Third World*. New York: Oxford University Press.

Beiguelman, Paula. 1966. *A Formação do Povo no Complexo Cafeeiro: Aspectos Políticos*. São Paulo: Livraria Pioneira Editora.

Bergsman, Joel. 1970. *Brazil: Industrialization and Trade Policies*. Paris-London: OECD and Oxford University Press.

Berlink, Manoel T. 1969. The Structure of the Brazilian Family in the City of São Paulo." Ph.D. dissertation, Cornell University.

———. 1975. *Marginalidade Social e Relações de Classes em São Paulo*. Petrópolis: Editora Vozes.

Berquó, Elza. 1975. "A Fecundidade Rural-Urbana dos Estados Brasileiros em 1970." Paper presented at Meeting of Sociedade Brasileira para o Progresso da Ciência, Belo Horizonte, July 12, 1975.

———. 1976a. "A Pesquisa Sobre Reprodução e Desenvolvimento (CLACSO), Mexico City, February 23–28, 1976.

———. 1976b. "Fecondité." In CICRED, *La Population du Brésil*, pp. 31–45.

Berquó, Elza, and Gonçalves, Mirna. 1974. "A Invasão de Óbitos no Municipio de São Paulo." *Cadernos CEBRAP* 19: 3–63.

Berry, Brian J. L. 1961. "City Size Distribution and Economic Development." *Economic Development and Cultural Change* 9(4), part 1: 573–88.

Berry, R. Albert. 1975. "Open Unemployment as a Social Problem in Urban Columbia: Myth and Reality." *Economic Development and Cultural Change* 23 (January): 276–91.

Best, Lloyd. 1968. "Outline of a Model of Pure Plantation Economy." *Social and Economic Studies* 17, 3 (September): 283–324.

Birdsall, Nancy. 1977. "Analytical Approaches to the Relationship of Population

Growth and Development." *Population and Development Review* 3 (March/June): 63–102.

Blake, J. 1968. "Are Babies Consumer Durables? Critique of the Economic Theory of Reproductive Motivation." *Population Studies* 22 (March): 5–25.

Bock, E. Wilber, and Iutaka, Sugiyama. 1969. "Rural Urban Migration and Social Mobility: The Controversy in Latin America." *Rural Sociology* 34, 3 (September): 343–55.

Boisier, Sergio; Smolka, Martin O.; and de Barros, Aluizio A. 1973. *Desenvolvimento Regional e Urbano*. Rio de Janeiro: IPEA/INPES.

Borges, T. Pompeu Accioly, and Loeb, Gustaaf E. 1957. "Desenvolvimento Econômico e Distribuição da Pouplação Ativa." In Fundação Getúlio Vargas, Instituto Brasileiro de Economia, *Contribuições à Análise do Desenvolvimento* Econômico pp. 27–40. Rio de Janeiro: Editora AGIR.

Boserup, Ester. 1965. *The Conditions of Agricultural Growth*. New York: Aldine.

Boxer, C. R. 1962. *The Golden Age of Brazil, 1695–1750*. Berkeley: University of California Press.

Boyer, Richard E., and Davies, Keith A. 1973. *Urbanization in Nineteenth Century Latin America: Statistics and Sources*. Los Angeles: University of California, Latin American Center.

Brazil, Diretoria Geral de Estatística. 1873–76. *Recenseamento da População do Império do Brasil a que se Procedeu no Dia 1° de Agosto de 1872*. Rio de Janeiro.

_____.1898. *Recenseamento Geral da República dos Estados Unidos do Brasil em 31 de Dezembro de 1890. Sexo, Raça e Estado Civil, Nacionalidade, Filiação, Culto e Analphabetismo da População Recenseada em 31 de Dezembro de 1890*. Rio de Janeiro: Officina de Estatística.

_____. 1900. *Recenseamento de 31 de Dezembro de 1900. Quadros do Trabalho Preliminar*. Rio de Janeiro: Officina de Estatística.

_____. 1905. *Synopse de Recenseamento de 31 de Dezembro de 1900*. Rio de Janeiro: Typographia da Estatística.

_____. 1922–30. *Recenseamento do Brasil Realizado em 1° de Setembro de 1920*. Rio de Janeiro: Typographia da Estatística. 5 volumes.

Brazil, Escritório de Pesquisa Econômica Aplicada. 1966. *Demografia: Diagnóstico Preliminar, Macroeconomia*. Rio de Janeiro.

Brazil, Fundação Getúlio Vargas. 1971. "Contas Nacionais do Brasil-Atualização." *Conjuntura Econômica* 25: 91–114.

Brazil, Fundação IBGE. Note: In 1967, the name of the Brazilian census bureau was changed from Instituto Brasileiro de Geografia e Estatística to Fundação IBGE. Brazilian census materials for 1940–60 will be found under that reference. The 1920 and earlier materials are found under Brazil, Diretoria Geral de Estatistica.

Brazil, Fundação IBGE. 1967–77. *Censo Demográfico de 1960*. (Brazil and state volumes). Rio de Janeiro: Fundação IBGE.

_____. 1969. *Alguns Aspectos da População do Brasil o Censo de 1960*. Rio de Janeiro: Fundação IBGE.

_____. 1970a. *Contribuições Para o Estudo da Demografia do Brasil*. 2a edição. Rio de Janeiro: Fundação IBGE.

_____. 1970b. *Divisão do Brasil em Micro-Regiões Homogêneas* 1968. Rio de Janeiro: Fundação IBGE.

_____. 1971a. *Sinopse Preliminar do Censo Demográfico, VII Recenseamento Geral, 1970.* Rio de Janeiro: Fundação IBGE.

_____. 1971b. *VII Recenseamento Geral, 1970, Tabulações Avançadas do Censo Demográfico.* Rio de Janeiro: Fundação IBGE.

_____. 1973a. *Censo Demográfico, 1970* (Brazil and state volumes). Rio de Janeiro: Fundação IBGE.

_____. 1973b. *Sinopse Preliminar do Censo Agropecuário.* Rio de Janeiro: Fundação IBGE.

_____. 1974a. Centro Brasileiro de Estudos Demográficos. "Projeção da População Brasileira por Idade e Sexo—Periodo 1970–2000." *Revista Brasileira de Estatística* 35–139 (July/September): 357–70.

_____. 1974b. *Censo Industrial, 1970* (Brazil and state volumes). Rio de Janeiro: Fundação IBGE.

_____. 1975a. *Anuário Estatístico do Brasil.* Various Years: 1936–1976. Rio de Janeiro: Fundação IBGE.

_____. 1975b. *Censo Agropecuário, 1970* (Brazil and state volumes). Rio de Janeiro: Fundação IBGE.

_____. 1975c. *Censo Comercial, 1970* (Brazil and state volumes). Rio de Janeiro: Fundação IBGE.

_____. 1975d. *Censo dos Serviços, 1970* (Brazil and state volumes). Rio de Janeiro: Fundação IBGE.

_____. 1975e. *Pesquisa Nacional por Amostra de Domicilios 4° Semestre de 1973,* 2a Triagem. Rio de Janeiro: Fundação IBGE.

_____. 1976a. "Alguns Problemas nos Levantamentos Censitários de População." In Fundação IBGE: *Encontro*, pp. 9–11.

_____. 1976b. *Encontro Brasileiro de Estudos Populacionais.* Rio de Janeiro: Fundação IBGE.

_____. 1977. *Geografia do Brasil,* 5 volumes. Rio de Janeiro: Fundação IBGE.

Brazil, Instituto Brasileiro de Geografia e Estatística. 1950a. *Recenseamento Geral do Brasil (1° de Setembro de 1940) Censo demográfico* (Brazil and state volumes). Rio de Janeiro: Serviço Gráfico do IBGE.

_____. 1950b. *Recenseamento Geral do Brasil (1° de Setembro de 1940) Censos Econômicos: Agricola, Industrial, Comercial e dos Serviços.* Rio de Janeiro: Serviço Gráfico do IBGE.

_____. 1956a. *VI Recenseamento Geral do Brasil—1950—Censo Agrícola* (Brazil and state volumes). Rio de Janeiro: IBGE.

_____. 1956b. *VI Recenseamento Geral do Brasil—1950—Censo Demográfico* (Brazil and state volumes). Rio de Janeiro: IBGE.

_____. 1957a. *VI Recenseamento Geral do Brasil—1950—Censo Comercial e dos Serviços* (Brazil and state volumes). Rio de Janeiro: IBGE.

_____. 1957b. *VI Recenseamento Geral do Brasil—1950—Censo Industrial* (Brazil and state volumes). Rio de Janeiro: IBGE.

_____. 1965. *VII Recenseamento Geral do Brasil—1960—Censo Demográfico, Resultados Preliminares.* Rio de Janeiro: IBGE.

_____. 1967a. *VII Recenseamento Geral do Brasil, Censo Agricola de 1960* (Brazil and state volumes). Rio de Janeiro: Serviço Gráfico do IBGE.

_____. 1967b. *VII Recenseamento Geral do Brasil, Censo Comercial e dos*

348   REFERENCES

Serviços de 1960 (Brazil and state volumes). Rio de Janeiro: Serviço Gráfico do IBGE.

———. 1967c. *VII Recenseamento Geral do Brasil, Censo Industrial de 1960* (Brazil and state volumes). Rio de Janeiro: Serviço Gráfico do IBGE.

Brazil, Instituto Histórico e Geográphico Brasileiro. 1895. (Reprint of anonymous article written about 1829). "Memória Estatística do Império do Brasil." *Revista do Instituto Histórico e Geográfico Brasileiro* 58: 93–99.

Brazil, Instituto de Planejamento Econômico e Social—IPEA. 1969. *Aspectos Econômicos e Demográficos da Mão-de-Obra no Brasil 1940/64.* Rio de Janeiro.

Brazil, Ministério do Interior, Secretaria Geral. 1976. *Mudanças na Composição do Emprego e na Distribuição da Renda: Efeitos Sobre as Migrações Internas.* Brasília: Organização Internacional do Trabalho—Banco Nacional da Habitação.

Brazil, Ministério da Saúde. 1977. *Saúde Materno-Infantil.* Brasília: Secretaria Nacional de Programas Especiais de Saúde.

Brazil, Secretaria de Planejamento. 1974. *II Plano Nacional de Desenvolvimento.* Brasília.

———. 1975a. *II National Development Plan (1975–1979).* Rio de Janeiro: Fundação IBGE.

———. 1975b. *Política Nacional de Desenvolvimento Urbano.* Brasília: Comissão Nacional de Regiões Metropolitanas e Política Urbana (CNPU).

Brennan, Ellen M. 1977. "National Experience in the Formation and Implementation of Population Policy." New York: United Nations, Population Division Working Paper.

Brito, Fausto A., and Merrick, Thomas. 1974. "Migração, Absorção de Mão-de-Obra e Distribuição de Renda." *Estudos Econômicos* 4: 75–122.

Browning, Harley. 1971. "Migrant Selectivity and the Growth of Large Cities in Developing Societies." In National Academy of Sciences, *Rapid Population Growth*, volume 2, pp. 273–314. Baltimore: The Johns Hopkins University Press.

———. 1972. "Primacy Variation in Latin America during the Twentieth Century." In *Urbanizactión y Progreso Social en América,* by R. P. Schaedel et al., pp. 55–77. Lima: Instituto de Estudios Peruanos.

Buarque de Holanda, Sergio. 1960. *História Geral da Civilização Brasileira.* São Paulo: Difusão Européia do Livro.

Buescu, Mircea. 1970. *História Econômica do Brasil: Pesquisas e Análises.* APEC, Rio de Janeiro.

Bush, Winston D. 1973. "Population and Mill's Peasant Proprietor Economy." *History of Political Economy* 5 (Spring): 110–20.

Calmon, Pedro. 1938. "A Abolição." *Revista do Arquivo Municipal* 47 (May), São Paulo, Ano IV.

Camargo, Cândido Procópio F. 1975. "Politique Démographique." In CICRED, *La Population du Brésil.* Paris: Comité International de Coordination des Recherches Nationales en Demographie.

Camargo, José Francisco de. 1952. *Crescimento da População no Estado de São Paulo e Seus Aspectos Econômicos.* São Paulo: Universidade de São Paulo, Faculdade de Filosofia.

———. 1966. *Êxodo Rural no Brasil.* Rio de Janeiro: Conquistas, Temas Brasileiros.

————. 1970. "A População Brasileira." In *Brasil: a Terra e o Homen*, Aroldo de Azevedo (ed.), pp. 61–126. São Paulo: Companhia Editora Nacional.

Camargo, Liscio Fábio. 1974. "Padrões de Fecundidade na Região Metropolitana de Belo Horizonte: Um Enfoque Sócio-Econômico." Belo Horizonte: CEDEPLAR.

Camisa, Zulia Carmen. 1965. "Effects of Migration on the Growth and Structure of Population in the Cities of Latin America."United Nations, *World Population Conference*, 4.

Cardoso, Fernando H. 1962. *Capitalismo e Escravidão no Brasil Meridional*. São Paulo: Difusão Européia do Livro.

————. 1961*a*. "Condições e Fatores Sociais da Industrialização de São Paulo." *Revista Brasileira de Estudos Políticos*, no. 11, Belo Horizonte.

————. 1961*b*. "Condições Sociais de Industrialização de São Paulo." *Revista Brasiliense*, no. 28. São Paulo.

————. 1974. "As Tradições do Desenvolvimento Associado." *Estudos CEBRAP* 8 (April–June): 43–75.

Carone, Edgard. 1970. *A República Velha: Instituições e Classes Socias*. São Paulo: Difusão Européia do Livro.

————. 1971. *A República Velha: Evolução Política*. São Paulo: Difusão Européia do Livro.

Carvalho, José Alberto M. de. 1973. "Analysis of Regional Trends in Fertility, Mortality and Migration in Brazil: 1950–1970." Ph.D. dissertation, London School of Economics.

————. 1974. "Regional Trends in Fertility and Mortality in Brazil." *Population Studies* 28 (December): 402–22.

————. 1976. "Diferenciais de Fecundidade no Brasil por Níveis de Renda Familiar." Paper presented at Simpósio Sobre o Progresso da Pesquisa Demográfica no Brasil. Rio de Janeiro, June 7.

————. 1977. "Fecundidade e Mortalidade no Brasil." Research Report submitted to Ford Foundation. Belo Horizonte: CEDEPLAR.

Carvalho, José Alberto M. de, and Wood, Charles. 1976. "Renda e Concentração de Mortalidade no Brasil." Paper Presented at Meetings of Brazilian Association of Graduate Centers of Economics. Guarujá, São Paulo: ANPEC.

Cassen, Robert H. 1976. "Population and Development: A Survey." *World Development* 4 (10–11): 785–830.

Cassinelli, Roberto R., et al. 1972. "Estatísticas de Nascimentos." *Revista Brasileira de Estatística* 33: (October-December): 715-22.

Castro, Antonio B. 1971. *Sete Ensaios de Economia*. São Paulo: Editora Forense.

Castro, Mary Garcia. 1977. "Experiências de Pesquisas sobre Migrações Internas através de Dados Secundários." In *Migrações Internas,* George Martine (ed.), pp. 15–34. Rio de Janeiro: Altiva Gráfica e Editora.

CELADE. 1972. *Fertility and Family Planning in Metropolitan Latin America*. Community and Family Study Center, University of Chicago.

Centro Brasileiro de Estudos Demográficos—CBED. 1974. "Projeção da População Brasileira por Idade e Sexo-Período 1970–2000." *Revista Brasileira de Estatística* 35 (July–September): 357–70.

CICRED. 1975. *La Population du Brésil*. Paris: Comité International de Coordination des Recherches Nationales en Demographie.

Cintra, José Thiago. 1971. *La Migración Japonesa en Brasil*. Mexico: El Colégio de Mexico, Centro de Estudios Orientales.

Clark, Colin. 1965. *Population Growth and Land Use*. New York: St. Martin's Press.

Cline, William R. 1972. *Potential Effects of Income Redistribution on Economic Growth: Latin American Cases*. New York: Praeger.

Coale, Ansley J. 1969. "The Decline of Fertility in Europe from the French Revolution to World War II." In *Fertility and Family Planning*, S. J. Behrman, Leslie Corsa, and Ronald Freedman (eds.), pp. 3–24. Ann Arbor: The University of Michigan Press.

———. 1973. "The Demographic Transition." In *International Population Conference*, pp. 53–72. Liège: International Union for the Scientific Study of Population.

———. 1978. "Population Growth and Economic Development: The Case of Mexico," *Foreign Affairs* 56 (January): 415–29.

Coale, Ansley J., and Hoover, E.M. 1958. *Population Growth and Economic Development in Low Income Countries*. Princeton: Princeton University Press.

Coale, Ansley J., and Trussell, T. James. 1974. "Model Fertility Schedules: Variaation in the Age Structure of Childbearing in Human Populations." *Population Index* 40:185–258 and Erratum, *Population Index* 41:572.

Cochrane, Susan H. 1975. "Children as By-Products, Investment Goods and Consumer Goods: A Review of Some Micro-economic Models of Fertility." *Population Studies* 29 (November): 373–90.

———. 1977. "Education and Fertility: What Do We Really Know?" Mimeo. Population and Human Resources Division, World Bank.

Coelho, Alzira Nunes, and Merrick, Thomas W. 1975. "Migração e Crescimento Demográfico na Grande Belo Horizonte." In *Estudos de Demografia Urbana*, Manoel Costa (ed.), pp. 197–220. Rio de Janeiro: IPEA/INPES.

Cohen, David, and Green, Jack P. (eds.) 1972. *Neither Slave Nor Free: The Freedmen of African Descent in the Slave Societies of the New World*. Baltimore: The Johns Hopkins University Press.

Cole, J. P. 1976. "População e Produção no Brasil 1970–2000." In Fundação IBGE: *Encontro*, pp. 465–72.

Collver, O. Andrew. 1965. *Birth Rates in Latin America*. Berkeley: University of California.

———. 1968. "Current Trends and Differentials in Fertility as Revealed by Official Data." *Milbank Memorial Fund Quarterly* 46 (July): 39–48.

Conde, Roberto Cortes. 1974. *The First Stages of Modernization in Spanish America*. New York: Harper and Row.

Coniff, Michael L. 1975. "Voluntary Associations in Rio 1870–1945: A New Approach to Urban Social Dynamics." *Journal of Interamerican Studies and World Affairs* 17, 1 (February): 64–81.

Coniff, Michael L.; Hendrix,Melvin; and Nohlgren, Stephen. 1971. "Brazil." In *The Urban Development of Latin America, 1750–1920*, Richard M. Morse (ed.), p. 37.

Conrad, Robert. 1972. *The Destruction of Brazilian Slavery, 1850–1880*. Berkeley: University of California Press.

Conroy, Michael. 1974. "Recent Research in Economic Demography Related to Latin America: A Critical Survey and an Agenda." *Latin American Research Review* 9 (Summer): 3–27.

Cooper, Donald B. 1975. "Brazil's Long Fight Against Epidemic Disease, 1849–1917." *Bulletin, New York Academy of Medicine* 51, 5 (May): 672–96.

Cornelius, Wayne A. 1971. "The Political Sociology of Cityward Migration in Latin America: Toward Empirical Theory." *Latin American Urban Research* 1: 95–147.

Cortes, Geraldo de Menezes. 1959. *Migração e Colonização no Brasil.* Rio de Janeiro: José Olympio Editora.

Costa, Emilia Viotti da. 1966. *Da Senzala à Colônia.* São Paulo: Difusão Européia do Livro.

————. 1969. "O Escravo na Grande Lavoura." *História Geral da Civilização Brasileira.* Sergio Buarque de Holanda (ed.) Tomo 2, vol. 3. São Paulo: Difusão Européia do Livro.

Costa, Manoel A. 1975. *Urbanização Urbana no Brasil,* Série Monográfica No. 21. Rio de Janeiro: IPEA/INPES.

————. 1976a. "Componentes do Crescimento Demográfico Urbano, Rural, e Total entre 1960–1970." In *Politica de Desenvolvimento Urbano,* Joseph Barat (ed.), pp. 87–120. Rio de Janeiro: IPEA/INPES, série monográfica no. 22.

————. 1976b. "Urbanization and Urban Migration." *Brazilian Economic Studies 2,* Rio de Janeiro: IPEA/INPES.

Cowell, Bainbridge. 1975. "Cityward Migration in the Nineteenth Century: The Case of Recife, Brazil." *Journal of Interamerican Studies and World Affairs* 17, 1 (February): 43–63.

Curtin, Philip D. 1969. *The Atlantic Slave Trade: A Census.* Madison: The University of Wisconsin Press.

Daland, Robert T. 1967. *Brazilian Planning.* Chapel Hill: The University of North Carolina Press.

Daly, Herman E. 1970. "The Population Question in Northeast Brazil: Its Economic and Ideological Dimension." *Economic Development and Cultural Change* 18 (July), Part 1: 536–74.

————. 1971. "A Marxian-Malthusian View of Poverty and Development." *Population Studies* 25 (March): 25–37.

Da Mata, Milton; Carvalho, Werneck de; and Castro e Silva, Maria Theresa de. 1972. *Migrações Internas no Brasil.* Rio de Janeiro: IPEA/INPES.

Da Mata, Milton, and Bacha, Edmar. 1973. "Emprego e Salários na Indústria de Transformação 1949/69. *Pesquisa e Planejamento Econômico 3(2): 303–40.*

David, Paul, and Temin, Peter. 1974. "Slavery: The Progressive Institution?" *Journal of Economic History* 34, 3 (September): 739–83.

————. 1975. "Capitalist Masters and Bourgeois Slaves." *Journal of Interdisciplinary History* 5, 3 (Winter): 445–58.

Davidson, Donald M. 1973. "How the Brazilian West Was Won." In *Colonial Roots of Modern Brasil,* Dauril Alden (ed.), pp. 61–106. Berkeley, Los Angeles; London: University of California Press.

Davis, Kingsley. 1963. "The Theory of Change and Response in Modern Demographic History." *Population Index* 29 (October): 345–66.

Davis, Kingsley, and Blake, Judith. 1956. "Social Structure and Fertility: An Analytic Framework." *Economic Development and Cultural Change* 4 (April): 211–35.

Dean, Warren. 1969. *The Industrialization of São Paulo, 1880–1945.* Austin: University of Texas Press.

_____. 1971. "Latifúndia and Land Policy in Nineteenth Century Brazil." *Hispanic American Historical Review* 51, 4 (November): 606–25.

_____. 1976. *Rio Claro: A Brazilian Plantation System 1820–1920*. Stanford: Stanford University Press.

De Canio, Stephen J. 1973. "Cotton 'Overporduction' in Late Nineteenth Century Southern Agriculture." *Journal of Economic History* 33, 3 (September): 608–33.

_____. 1974a. *Agriculture in the Postbellum South: The Economics of Production and Supply*. Cambridge, Massachusetts: M.I.T. Press.

_____. 1974b. "Productivity and Income Distribution in the Postbellum South." *Journal of Economic History* 34, 2 (June): 244–46.

Degler, Carl. 1971. *Neither Black Nor White: Slavery and Race Relations in Brazil and the United States*. New York: Macmillan.

Demeny, Paul. 1965. "Investment Allocation and Population Growth." *Demography* 2: 203–32.

Denslow, David, Jr. 1972. "Economic Considerations in the Treatment of Slaves in Brazil and Cuba." Paper Presented at the Mathematical Social Science Board Conference on Slavery, Rochester, New York.

_____. 1973. "As Origens da Desigualdade Regional no Brasil." *Estudos Econômicos* 3, 1 (April): 65–88.

_____. 1974. "Sugar Production in Northeastern Brazil and Cuba, 1858–1908." Ph.D. dissertation, Yale University.

_____. 1975. "The High Importation-to-Stock Ratio for Slaves in Northeastern Brazil: An Interpretation." Paper prepared for Southwestern Social Sciences Conference, San Antonio, Texas (March).

_____. 1978 "As Exportações e a Origem do Padrão de Industrialização Regional do Brasil." In *Dimensões do Desenvolvimento Brasileiro*, Werner Baer et al. (eds.). Rio de Janeiro:Editora Campus.

De Vany, Arthur, and Sanchez, Nicholas. 1975. "Property Rights, Uncertainty and Fertility: An Analysis of the Effect of Land Reform on Fertility in Rural Mexico." Mimeographed, Texas A. and M. University.

De Vanzo, Julie. 1971. *The Determinants of Family Formation in Chile: 1960*. R-830-AID. Santa Monica: The RAND Corporation.

Diaz Alejandro, C. 1970. *Essays on the Economic History of the Argentine Republic*. New Haven: Yale University Press.

DIEESE. 1973. "Nível Alimentar da População Trabalhadora da Cidade de São Paulo." *Estudos Sócio-Econômicos* 1:7 (July) São Paulo.

_____. 1974. "Família Assalariada: Padrão e Custo de Vida." *Estudos Sócio-Econômicos* 1: 2 (January). São Paulo.

_____. 1975. "Dez Anos de Política Salarial" *Estudos Sócio-Econômicos* 1:3 (August) São Paulo.

Duarte, J. C. 1971. *Aspectos da distribuição da renda no Brasil em 1970*. São Paulo: Universidade de São Paulo em Piracicaba.

Durand, John D. 1974. *Historical Estimates of World Population: An Evaluation*. University of Pennsylvania Population Studies Center.

_____. 1975. *The Labor Force in Economic Development*. Princeton: Princeton University Press.

Durand, John D., and Cezar Peláez. 1965. "Patterns of Urbanization in Latin America." *Milbank Memorial Fund Quarterly* 43, part 2 (October): 166–91.

Easterlin, Richard A. 1960. "Interregional Differences in Per Capita Income, Population, and Total Income, 1840–1950." In Universities—National Bureau, Committee for Economic Research, *Trends in the American Economy*. Studies in Income and Wealth, vol. 24. Princeton: Princeton University Press.

——. 1961. "Influences in European Overseas Emigration before World War I." *Economic Development and Cultural Change* 9 (April): 331–51.

——. 1972. "The American Population." In Davis, L.E. et al. (eds.),*American Economic Growth: An Economist's History,* pp. 120–80. New York: Harper and Row.

——. 1974. "Factors in the Decline of Farm Family Fertility in the American North: Some Preliminary Results." Paper presented at the Annual Meeting of American Historical Association, Chicago, December 29, 1974.

——. 1975. "An Economic Framework for Fertility Analysis." *Studies in Family Planning* 6 (March): 54–63.

——. 1976. "Population Change and Farm Settlement in the Northern United States." *Journal of Economic History* 36 (March): 45–75.

Eblen, Jack. 1975. "On the Natural Increase of Slave Populations: The Example of the Cuban Black Population, 1775–1900." In *Race and Slavery in the Western Hemisphere: Quantitative Studies*, Stanley L. Engerman and Eugene Genovese (eds.), pp. 211–47. Princeton: Princeton University Press.

Economic Commission for Latin America. 1975. "Population and Modernization in Latin America." In *The Population Debate: Dimensions and Perspective.* New York: The United Nations.

Eisenberg, Peter L. 1972. "Abolishing Slavery: The Process on Pernambuco's Sugar Plantations." *Hispanic American Historical Review* 52, 4 (November): 580–97.

——. 1975. *The Sugar Industry in Pernambuco, 1840–1910.* Berkeley: University of California Press.

Elizaga, Juan C. 1965. "Internal Migration in Latin America." *Milbank Memorial Fund Quarterly* 43, part 2, (October): 144–65.

——. 1970. *Migraciones a las areas metropolitanas de América Latina.* Santiago: CELADE.

Ellis, Howard A. (ed.) 1969. *The Economy of Brazil.* Berkeley: University of California Press.

Engerman, Stanley L. 1970. "The Antebellum South: What Probably Was and What Should Have Been." *Agricultural History* 44, 1 (January): 127–42.

——. 1971. "Some Economic Factors in Southern Backwardness in the Nineteenth Century." In *Essays in Regional Economics*, John F. Kain and John R. Meyer (eds.). Cambridge, Mass.: Harvard University Press.

——. 1973. "Some Considerations Relating to Property Rights in Man." *Journal of Economic History* 33, 1 (March): 43–65.

——. 1975. "Up or Out: Social and Geographic Mobility in the United States." *Journal of Interdisciplinary History* 5, 3 (Winter): 469–90.

Engerman, Stanley L. and Genovese, Eugene D. 1975. *Race and Slavery in the Western Hemisphere.* Princeton: Princeton University Press.

Enke, S. 1966. "The Economic Aspects of Slowing Population Growth." *Economic Journal* 76 (March): 44–56.

Evans, Robert, Jr. 1962. "Some Notes on Coerced Labor." *Journal of Economic History* 30, 4 (December): 861–66.

——. 1970. "The Economics of American Negro Slavery." In *Aspects of Labor*

Economics. A Conference of the Universities, National Bureau of Economic Research. Princeton: Princeton University Press.

Faissol, Speridião. 1973. *Migrações Internas no Brasil e Suas Repercussões no Crescimento Urbano e Desenvolvimento Econômico*. Rio de Janeiro: Fundação IBGE, Superintendência de Pesquisa e Desenvolvimento.

Faria, Vilmar E. 1976. "Occupational Marginality, Employment, and Poverty in Urban Brazil." Ph.D. dissertation, Harvand University.

Fausto, Boris (ed.). 1975. *O Brasil Republicano—Tomo III, 1° Volume, Estrutura de Poder e Economia (1889–1930)*. *História Geral da Civilização Brasileira*. São Paulo: Difusão Européia do Livro.

Fernandes, Florestan. 1965. *A Integração do Negro à Sociedade de Classe*. São Paulo: Dominus Editora e Editora da Universidade de São Paulo.

———. 1969. *The Negro in Brazilian Society*. New York: Columbia University Press.

Fields, Gary S. 1975. "Rural-Urban Migration, Urban Unemployment, and Job Search Activities in LDCs." *Journal of Development Economics* 2:165–87.

Fishlow, Albert. 1972a. "Brazilian Size Distribution of Income." *American Economic Review* 62 (May): 391–402.

———. 1972b. "Origins and Consequences of Import Substitution in Brazil." In *International Economics and Development*, Luis Eugenio DeMarco (ed.). New York: Academic Press.

———. 1973a. "Distribuição da Renda no Brasil: Um Novo Exame." *DADOS* 11: 10–80.

———. 1973b. "Reflections on Post-1964 Economic Policy in Brazil." In *Authoritarian Brazil*, Alfred Stepan (ed.). New Haven: Yale University Press.

———. 1974. "Indexing Brazilian Style: Inflation without Tears." *Brookings Papers on Economic Activity* 1. Washington, D.C.: Brookings Institution.

Foerster, Robert T. 1924. *The Italian Emigration of Our Times*. Cambridge, Mass.: Harvard University Press.

Fogel, Robert W., and Engerman, Stanley. 1974. *Time on the Cross*, 2 vols. Waltham, Massachusetts: Little, Brown and Company.

Foner, Laura, and Genovese, Eugene (eds.). 1969. *Slavery in the New World*. Englewood Cliffs, N.J.: Prentice-Hall.

Ford, A. G. 1971. "British Investment in Argentina and Long Swings 1880–1914." *Journal of Economic History* 31:3 (September).

Forman, Shepard. 1975. *The Brazilian Peasantry*. New York: Columbia University Press.

Forster, Colin, and Tucker, G. S. L. 1972. *Economic Opportunity and White American Fertility Ratios 1800–1860*. New Haven and London: Yale University Press.

Foust, James D. and Swan, Dale E. 1970. "Productivity and Profitability of Antebellum Slave Labor: A Micro Approach." *Agricultural History* 44, 1 (January): 39–62.

Fox, Robert W. 1975. *Urban Population Growth Trends in Latin America*. Washington: The Inter-American Development Bank.

Fraenkel, Leda Maria et al. 1975. "Employment Structure, Income Distribution and Internal Migration in Brazil." Geneva: ILO Population and Employment Working Paper #18: (May).

Francisconi, Jorge Guilherme, and Souza, Maris Adélia Aparecida de. 1976. *Politica Nacional de Desenvolvimento Urbano,* Brasília: IPEA/IPLAN.

Freedman, Ronald, 1961–62. "The Sociology of Human Fertility: A Trend Report and Annotated Bibliography." *Current Sociology* 10/11, 2: 35–121.

_____. 1975. *The Sociology of Human Fertility: An Annotated Bibliography.* New York: Irvington Publishers.

Frejka, Tomas. 1968. "Reflections on the Demographic Conditions Needed to Establish a U.S. Stationary Population Growth." *Population Studies* 22 (November): 379–97.

_____. 1973. *The Future of Population Growth,* II, "Reference Tables," pp. 794–803. New York: John Wiley and Sons.

Freyre, Gilberto. 1958. *Casa-Grande e Senzala.* 9th ed., Rio de Janeiro: Livraria José Olympio.

Frias, Luis Armando, and Leite, Valeria. 1976. "Estudo Comparativo entre os Padrões de Mortalidade Observados no Brasil e os Modelos Propostos pelas Nações Unidas." In Fundação IBGE: *Encontro,* pp. 27–48.

Friedlander, Dov. 1969. "Demographic Responses and Population Change." *Demography* 6 (November): 359–81.

Friedman, John and Sullivan, Flora. 1974. "The Absorption of Labor in the Urban Economy: The Case of Developing Economies." *Economic Development and Cultural Change* 22, 3 (April): 385–413.

Furtado, Celso. 1959. *Formação Econômica do Brasil.* Rio de Janeiro: Editora Fundo de Cultura.

_____. 1971. *The Economic Growth of Brazil.* Berkeley: University of California Press.

_____. 1972. *Análise do Modelo Brasileiro.* Rio de Janeiro: Editora Civilização Brasileira, S.A.

Gall, Norman. 1977. "The Rise of Brazil." *Commentary* 63 (January): 45–55.

Gallman, Robert E. 1970. "Self-Sufficiency in the Cotton Economy of the Antebellum South." *Agricultural History* 44, 1 (January): 5–23.

Gallo, Ezequiel. 1969. "Ocupación de Tierras y Colonización Agrícola en Santa Fe (1870–1895)." In *Tierras Nuevas,* Alvaro Jara (ed.). Mexico: El Colegio de Mexico.

_____. 1973. "Conflictos Sócio-Políticos en las Colonias Agrícolas de Santa Fe 1870–1880." Documento de Trabajo #87. (August). Instituto Torcuato Di Tella, Buenos Aires.

_____. 1974. "Boom Cerealero y Cambios en la Estructura Socio-Política de Santa Fe (1870–1895)." Documento de Trabajo #88, (March) Instituto Torcuato Di Tella, Buenos Aires.

Galloway, J. H. 1971. "The Last Years of Slavery on the Sugar Plantations of Northeast Brazil." *Hispanic American Historical Review* 51, 4 (November): 285–303.

Gauthier, Howard L., and Semple, Robert K. 1972. "Tendências nas Desigualdades Regionais da Economia Brasileira 1947–1966." *DADOS* (9).

Gendell, Murray. 1967. "Fertility and Development in Brazil." *Demography* 4:143–57.

Genovese, Eugene. 1971. *The World the Slaveholders Made.* New York: Vintage Books.

Germani, Gino. 1966. "Mass Immigration and Modernization in Argentina." *Studies in Comparative International Development* 2 (11):165–82.

Gerschenkron, Alexander. 1962. *Economic Backwardness in Historical Perspective.* Cambridge, Mass.: Belknap Press of Harvard University Press.

Glass, David. 1965. "Population Growth and Population Policy." In *Public Health and Population Change*, Mindel C. Sheps and Jeanne Clare Ridley (eds.), pp.3–24. Pittsburgh: University of Pittsburgh Press.

Godfrey, E. M. 1973. "Economic Variables and Rural-Urban Migration: Some Thoughts on the Todaro Hypothesis." *Journal of Development Studies* 10 (October): 66–78.

Goldin, Claudia. 1973. "The Economics of Emancipation." *Journal of Economic History* 33, 1 (March): 66–85.

Gonçalves, Mirna A. I. 1975a. "Age et Sexe." In CICRED, *La Population du Brésil*, pp. 71–88.

———. 1975b. "La Population Brésilienne de 1872 a 1970." In CICRED, *La Population du Brésil*, pp. 25–30.

Gonzales, Elbio N., and Bastos, Maria I. 1976. "Migração Rural e o Trabalho Volante na Agricultura Brasileira." In Fundação IBGE: *Encontro*, pp. 240–61.

Goodman, David E., and Cavalcanti de Albuquerque, Roberto. 1974. *Incentivos à Industrialização e Desenvolvimento do Nordeste.* Rio de Janeiro: IPEA/INPES.

Goodman, David E. 1974. "The Brazilian Economic Miracle and Urban Labor Markets: A Regional Perspective." (Mimeo.)

Goulart, Mauricio. 1949. *Escravidão Africana no Brasil das Origens à Extinção do Tráfico.* São Paulo: Editora Martins.

Gouveia, Maurilio de. 1955. *História da Escravidão.* Rio de Janeiro.

Graham, Douglas H. 1970. "Divergent and Convergent Regional Economic Growth and Internal Migration in Brazil 1940–1960." *Economic Development and Cultural Change* 18, 3 (April).

———. 1973. "Migração Estrangeira e a Questão da Oferta de Mão de Obra no Crescimento Econômico Brasileiro 1880-1930." *Estudos Econômicos* 3:7–64.

———. 1977. "Interstate Migration and the Industrial Labor Force in Center-South Brazil." *Journal of Developing Areas* 12, 1 (October): 31–46.

Graham, Douglas H., and Hollanda Filho, Sergio Buarque de. 1971. *Migration, Regional and Urban Growth and Development in Brazil: A Selective Analysis of the Historical Record, 1872–1970.* Vol. 1. São Paulo; IPE/USP.

Graham, Richard. 1966. "Causes for the Abolition of Negro Slavery in Brazil: An Interpretive Essay." *Hispanic American Historical Review* 46, 2 (May): 123–37.

———. 1968. *Britain and the Onset of Modernization in Brazil, 1850–1914.* London: Cambridge University Press.

———. 1970. "Brazilian Slavery Re-examined: A Review Article."*Journal of Social History* 3, 4 (Summer): 431–53.

Habakkuk, H. J. 1971. *Population Growth and Economic Development since 1750.* Leicester: Leicester University Press.

Haddad, Cláudio Luiz da Silva. 1974. "Crescimento do Produto Real Brasileiro 1900–1947." *Ensaios Econômicos da EPGE*, no. 14. Rio de Janeiro.

Haddad, Paulo R. 1975. "Padrões Regionais de Crescimento do Emprego Industrial de 1950 a 1970." In CEDEPLAR, *Textos Para Discussão* 6, Belo Horizonte.

———. (ed.). 1975. *Desequilibrios Regionais e Descentralização Industrial.* Rio de Janeiro: IPEA/INPES.

Haddad, Paulo R., and Andrade, Thompson. 1974. "Política Fiscal e Desequilíbrios Regionais." *Estudos Econômicos* 4(1): 9–54.

Hajnal, John. 1953. "Age at Marriage and Proportions Marrying," *Population Studies* 7:111–136.

———. 1965. "European Marriage Patterns in Perspective." In *Population in History,* D. V. Glass and D. E. C. Eversley (eds). Chicago: Aldine Publishing Company.

Hall, Michael. 1969. "The Origins of Mass Immigration in Brazil 1871–1914." Ph.D. dissertation, Columbia University.

Harberger, Arnold C. 1971. "On Measuring the Social Opportunity Cost of Labor." *International Labour Review* 103 (June).

Harman, A. J. 1970. *Fertility and Economic Behavior of Families in the Philippines.* RM-6385-AID, Santa Monica: The RAND Corporation.

Harris, John and Sabot, R. 1976. "Urban Unemployment in LDC's: Toward a More General Search Model." Washington, D.C.: The World Bank.

Harris, John R., and Todaro, Michael P. 1970. "Migration, Unemployment and Development: A Two Sector Model." *American Economic Review* 60 (March): 126–42.

Herrera, Ligia; Gatica, Fernando; and Jordan, Ricardo. 1975. "Consideraciones sobre el proceso de urbanización, la concentración y la dispersión de la población en America Latina: situaciones críticas." Documento de trabajo #6. Santiago: CELADE-PISPAL.

Herrera, Ligia, and Pecht, Waldomiro. 1976. *Crecimiento Urbano de America Latina.* Santiago: CELADE-IDB.

Herrick, Bruce. 1971. "Urbanization and Urban Migration in Latin America: An Economist's View." *Latin American Urban Research,* F. Ravinovitz and F. Trueblood (eds.). Beverly Hills, Calif.: Sage Publications.

Higgs, Robert. 1973. "Race Tenure and Resource Allocation in Southern Agriculture 1910." *Journal of Economic History* 33 (March): 149–69.

———. 1974. "Pattern of Farm Rental in the Georgia Cotton Belt." *Journal of Economic History* 34, 2 (June): 468–82.

Hill, Peter J. 1975. "Relative Skill and Income Levels of Native and Foreign Born Workers in the United States." *Explorations in Economic History* 12, 1 (January): 47–60.

Hirschman, Albert O. 1963. *Journeys Towards Progress.* New York: Twentieth Century Fund.

———. 1977. "A Generalized Linkage Approach to Development, with Special Reference to Staples." In *Essays on Economic Development and Cultural Change,* Manning Nash, (ed.). Chicago: The University of Chicago Press.

Hoffman, Helga. 1977. *Desemprego e Subemprego no Brasil.* São Paulo: Editora Atica.

Hoffman, R. 1975. "Tendências na distribuição da renda no Brasil e suas relações com o desenvolvimento econômico." In *A Controvérsia sobre distribuição da renda no Brasil,* R. Tolipan and A. C. Tinelli (eds.), pp. 105–23. Rio de Janeiro: Zahar.

Hogan, Daniel, and Berlinck, Manoel. 1973. "Occupation, Access to Information, and the Use of Urban Resources: A Study of Population Adaption in São Paulo, Brazil." Paper prepared for the 1973 General Conference of the International Union for the Scientific Study of Population, August 27–September 1, Liège, Belgium.

———. 1974. "Migration and Social Mobility in São Paulo: An Analysis of Declining Job Opportunities in Brazil's Industrial Capital in the 20th Century." Paper presented at the Annual Meeting of the American Sociological Association, Montreal, Canada (August).

――――. 1975. "Changing Patterns of Urban Migration in Brazil: 1930–1970." Paper presented at Annual Meeting of the Population Association of America, April 17–19, Seattle.

Holloway, Thomas H. 1972. "Condições do Mercado de Trabalho e Organização do Trabalho nas Plantações na Economia Cafeeira de São Paulo 1885–1915: Um Estudo Preliminar." *Estudos Econômicos* 2(6) (December): 145–80.

――――. 1974. "Migration and Mobility: Immigrants as Laborers and Landowners in the Coffee Zone of São Paulo, Brazil, 1886–1934." Ph.D. dissertation, University of Wisconsin.

――――. 1978. "Creating the Reserve Army? The Immigration Problem of São Paulo 1886–1930." *International Migration Review* 12, 2 (Summer): 187–209.

Hugon, Paul. 1973. *Demografia Brasileira.* São Paul: Atlas Editora.

Hutchinson, Bertram. 1958. "Structural and Exchange Mobility in the Assimilation of Immigrants to Brazil." *Population Studies* 12 (November): 111–120.

――――. 1962. "Social Mobility Rates in Buenos Aires, Montevideo, and São Paulo." *América Latina* 5(4): 3–19.

――――. 1963a. "The Migrant Population of Urban Brazil." *América Latina* 6(2): 47–71.

――――. 1963b. "Urban Social Mobility Rates in Brazil Related to Migration and Changing Occupational Structure." *América Latina* 6(3): 47–61.

Hutchinson, Edward P. 1956. *Immigrants and Their Children 1850–1950.* New York: John Wiley & Sons.

Hutter, Lucy Maffei. 1972. *Imigração Italiana em São Paulo 1880–1889: os Primeiros Contactos do Imigrante com o Brasil.* São Paulo: Instituto de Estudos Brasileiros.

Ianni, Octavio. 1962. *As Metamorfoses do Escravo.* São Paulo: Difusão Européia do Livro.

――――. 1969. "O Progresso Econômico e O Trabalhador Livre." *História Geral da Civilização Brasileira.* Sergio Buarque de Holanda (ed.), Tome II, vol. 3. São Paulo.

Instituto Interamericano de Estatística. 1971. *Programa del Censo de América de 1970—Clasificación Ocupacional.* Washington, D.C.: Organization of American States.

International Labour Office. 1972. *Employment, Incomes, and Equality.* Geneva: International Labour Office.

Irwin, Richard, and Lyra Madeira, João. 1972. "Dedução de Uma Tábua de Vida Através de Análise Demográfica Brasil, 1960/70." *Revista Brasileira de Estatística* 33 (October-December): 697–714.

Irwin, Richard, and Spielman, Evelyn. 1976. "Rede Censitária: 1940–1970." In Fundação IBGE: *Encontro,* pp. 504–18.

Italy, Commissariato Generale dell' Emigrazione. 1926. *Annuario Statistico dell' Emigrazione Italiana dal 1876 al 1925.* Rome: Commissariato Generale.

Italy, Istituto Centrale di Statistica. 1958. *Sommario di Statistiche Storiche Italiane 1861–1955.* Rome: Istituto Centrale di Statistica.

Iutaka, S.; Bock, E. W.; and Varnes, W. G. 1971. "Factors Affecting Fertility of Natives and Migrants in Urban Brazil." *Population Studies* 25 (March): 55–62.

Jelin, Elisabeth. 1974. "Formas de organização da atividade econômica e estrutura ocupacional: o caso de Salvador." Estudos CEBRAP 9:53–78.

_____. 1976. "O Trabalho Feminino na Bahia." DADOS (12).

Jerome, Harry. 1926. *Migration and Business Cycles*. New York: National Bureau of Economic Research.

Jones, William O. 1968. "Plantation" In *The International Encyclopedia of the Social Sciences*, David L. Sills (ed.). New York: MacMillan Company and Free Press.

Kahil, Raouf. 1965. "The Absorption of Manpower by the Urban and Rural Sectors of Brazil." *Bulletin, Oxford University Institute of Statistics* 21, 1 (February): 45–53.

Karasch, Mary. 1973. "Manumission in the City of Rio de Janeiro 1807–1831." Paper presented to the American Historical Association, San Francisco.

_____. 1975. "From Porterage to Proprietorship: African Occupations in Rio de Janeiro 1808–1850." In *Race and Slavery in the Western Hemisphere: Quantitative Studies*, Stanley L. Engerman and Eugene D. Genovese (eds.), pp. 369–93. Princeton: Princeton University Press.

Katzman, Martin T. 1974. "Urbanização e Concentração Industrial 1940–70." *Pesquisa e Planejamento Econômico* 4 (December): 475–532.

_____. 1975a. "Regional Development Policy in Brazil: The Development of Growth Poles and Highways in Goiás." *Economic Development and Cultural Change* 24 (October): 75–108.

_____. 1975b. "The Brazilian Frontier in Comparative Perspective." *Comparative Studies in Society and History* 17 (July): 266–85.

_____. 1976. "Paradoxes of Amazonian Development in a 'Resource Starved' World." *Journal of Developing Areas* 10 (July): 445–59.

_____. 1977a. *Cities and Frontiers in Brazil: Regional Dimensions of Economic Development*. Cambridge, Mass.: Harvard University Press.

_____. 1977b. "City and Hinterland: The Regional Systems of São Paulo." Paper presented at Conference on Manchester and São Paulo: The Crisis of Rapid Urban Development. Stanford University, April 21–23.

_____. 1977. "Social Relations of Production on the Brazilian Frontier." In *The Frontier: Comparative Studies*, D.H. Miller and J.O. Steffan (eds.). Norman, Okla.: The University of Oklahoma Press.

Keller, Elza, C. 1977. "Diferenciais entre Migrantes e Nativos na Região Sudeste," In *Migrações Internas,* George Martine (ed.), pp. 89–98. Rio de Janeiro: Altiva Gráfica e Editora.

Kessler, Arnold. 1973. "Bahian Manumission Practices in the Early Nineteenth Century." Paper presented to the American Historical Association, San Francisco.

King, Timothy. 1970. "Economic Aspects of Population and Labor Force Growth in Brazil." Economics Department Working Paper No. 88, IBRD. Washington, D.C., October 13.

Kiple, Kenneth F. 1976. *Blacks in Colonial Cuba, 1774–1899*. Gainesville: The University Presses of Florida.

Klein, Herbert S. 1969a "The Colored Freedman in Brazilian Slave Society." *Journal of Social History* 3, 1 (Fall): 30–52.

————. 1969*b*. "The Trade in African Slaves to Rio de Janeiro 1795–1811: Estimates of Mortality and Patterns of Voyages." *Journal of African History* 10, 4:533–50.

————. 1971. "The Internal Slave Trade in Nineteenth Century Brazil: A Study of Slave Importations into Rio de Janeiro in 1852." *Hispanic American Historical Review* 51, 4 (November): 567–85.

————. 1972. "The Portuguese Slave Trade from Angola in the Eighteenth Century." *Journal of Economic History* 32(December): 894–918.

Knodel, John. 1977. Family Limitation and the Fertility Transition: Evidence from the Age Patterns of Fertility in Europe and Asia. *Population Studies* 31:219–249.

Kogut, Edy Luiz. 1972. "The Economic Analysis of Demographic Phenomena." Ph.D. dissertation, University of Chicago.

Kogut, Edy Luiz, and Langoni, Carlos Geraldo. 1975. "Population Growth, Income Distribution, and Economic Development." *International Labour Review* 111: 321–33.

Kowarick, Lucio. 1974. "Capitalismo, Dependência e Marginalidade na América Latina: Uma Contribuição Teórica." *Estudos* CEBRAP 8 (April–June): 79–101.

Kuznets, Simon. 1957. "Quantitave Aspects of the Economic Growth of Nations: Industrial Distribution of National Product and Labor Force." *Economic Development and Cultural Change*, Supplement to volume 5, no. 4, part 2 (July).

————. 1966. *Modern Economic Growth*. New Haven: Yale University Press.

————. 1967. "Population and Economic Growth." *Proceedings of the American Philosophical Society,* 111 (June): 170–93.

————. 1971. "Notes on the Pattern of U.S. Economic Growth." In *The Reinterpretation of American Economic History*, Robert W. Fogel and Stanley L. Engerman (eds.). New York: Harper and Row.

————. 1973. *Population, Growth, and Capital*. New York: W. W. Norton.

Landes, David S. 1972. *The Unbound Prometheus*. Cambridge: Cambridge University Press.

Langoni, Carlos Geraldo. 1973. *Distribuição da Renda e Desenvolvimento Econômico do Brasil.* Rio de Janeiro: Editora Expressão e Cutura.

————. 1974. *As Causas do Crescimento Econômico do Brasil*. Rio de Janeiro: Editora APEC.

Lattes, Zulma Recchini, and Lattes, Alfredo E. 1975. *La Población de Argentina*. Buenos Aires: Talleres Gráficos Zlotopioro, for CICRED.

Laurenti, R. 1975. "Fontes de Erros na Mensuração da Mortalidade Infantil." *Revista de Saúde Pública* 9: 529–37.

Leeds, Anthony. 1973. "Political, Economic and Social Effects of Producer and Consumer Orientations Toward Housing in Brazil and Peru: A Systems Analysis." In *Latin American Urban Research*, vol. 3 Francine Rabinovitz and Felicity H. Trueblood (eds.): Beverly Hills, Calif.: Sage Publications.

Leff, Nathaniel H. 1969. "Long-Term Brazilian Economic Development." *Journal of Economic History* 29 (September): 473–93.

————. 1970. "Population Growth and the Economic Underdevelopment of Latin America: Some Historical Perspective." Paper presented to Conferencia Regional Latinoamericana de Población, Mexico (August).

————. 1972*a*. "A Technique for Estimating Income Trends from Currency Data and an Application to Nineteenth-Century Brazil." *Review of Income and Wealth* 18, 4 (December): 355–68.

————. 1972*b*. "Economic Development and Regional Inequality: Origins of the

Brazilian Case." *Quarterly Journal of Economics* 86 (May): 243–62.

_____. 1972c. "Economic Retardation in Nineteenth-Century Brazil." *Economic History Review* 25, 3 (August): 487–507.

_____. 1973. "Tropical Trade and Development in the Nineteenth Century: The Brazilian Experience." *Journal of Political Economy* 81 (May–June): 678–96.

_____. 1974. "Long-Term Viability of Slavery in a Backward, Closed Economy." *Journal of Interdisciplinary History* 5, 1 (Summer): 103–08.

_____. 1975. "Economic-Demographic Theory and Long-Term Population Growth in an Underdeveloped Economy: A Case Study of Nineteenth Century Brazil." Economic History Workshop, University of Pennsylvania, April 8.

Leff, Nathaniel H., and Klein, Herbert S. 1974. "O Crescimento da População não Européia Antes do Início do Desenvolvimento: O Brasil no Século XIX." *Anais da História* 6: 51–70.

Leibenstein, Harvey. 1954. *A Theory of Economic-Demographic Development.* Princeton: Princeton University Press.

_____. 1974. "An Interpretation of the Economic Theory of Fertility: Promising Path or Blind Alley." *Journal of Economic Literature* 12 (June): 457–79.

Leite, Valeria da Motta. 1975. "Estimativa da Fecundidade a Partir da Análise Combinada de Informação sobre os Filhos Nascidos Vivos Referentes a Mulheres em Idade Reprodutiva e Nascimentos Ocorridos no Ano Anterior ao Censo." Paper Presented at meeting of SBPC, Belo Horizonte, July 12.

Levy, Maria Stella Ferreira. 1974. "O Papel da Migração Internacional na Evolução da População Brasileira, 1872–1972." *Revista de Saúde Pública,* Suplemento (June): 49–90.

_____. 1975. "Les Migrations Internationales et La Population Brésilienne de 1872 a 1972." In CICRED, *La Population du Brésil,* pp. 65–70.

Lewin, Helena. 1976. "Qualificação Educacional da Força de Trabalho no Brasil." In Fundação IBGE: *Encontro,* pp. 473–93.

Lewis, W. Arthur. 1952. "World Production, Prices, and Trade 1870–1960." *The Manchester School* (May).

_____. 1969. *Aspects of Tropical Trade 1883–1965.* Stockholm.

_____. (ed.). 1970. *Tropical Development 1880–1913.* Evanston, Ill.: Northwestern University Press.

Lima, Lilia M., and Bogas, Lúcia. 1975. "A Familia em Santa Cruz do Sul." (Mimeograph) São Paulo: CEBRAP.

Lindstrom, Diane. 1970. "Southern Dependence Upon Interregional Grain Supplies: A Review of the Trade Flows, 1840–1860." *Agricultural History* 44, 1 (January): 101–13.

Lisante, Luis. 1962. *Le Brésil et l'Europe à la fin du XVIIIe siècle et au debut du XIXe.* São Paulo: University of São Paulo.

Livi Bacci, Massimo. 1971. *A Century of Portuguese Fertility.* Princeton: Princeton University Press.

Lobo, Eulalia M. de. 1975. "A História do Rio de Janeiro." Rio de Janeiro: Instituto Brasileiro de Mercados de Capitais, mimeographed.

Lopes, Juarez Rubens Brandão. 1964. *Sociedade Industrial no Brasil.* São Paulo: Difusão Européia do Livro.

_____. 1968. *Desenvolvimento e Mudança Social.* São Paulo: Companhia Nacional Editora.

_____. 1973. "Desenvolvimento e Migrações: Uma Abordagem Histórico—

362   REFERENCES

Estrutural." *Estudos CEBRAP* 6 (October–December).
_____. 1976. "Do Latifúndio à Empresa." *Cadernos CEBRAP* 26.
Loureiro, Maria Rita Garcia de. 1977. *Parceria e Capitalismo.* Rio de Janeiro: Zahar Editora.
Love, Joseph L. 1973. "External Financing and Domestic Politics: The Case of São Paulo, Brazil, 1889–1937." In *Latin American Modernization Problems,* Robert E. Scott (ed.). Urbana: University of Illinois Press.
Luz, Nicia Vilela. 1961. *A Luta pela Industrialização do Brasil, 1808 a 1930.* São Paulo: Difusão Européia do Livro.
Macedo, Roberto B. M. 1977. "A Critical Review of the Relation between the Post–1964 Wage Policy and the Worsening of Brazil's Size Income Distribution in the Sixties." *Explorations in Economic Research* 4, 1 (Winter): 117–40.
Machado, Wilson. 1974. "Brasil em Bucharest." *Jornal do Brasil Caderno Especial,* July 28.
Machado da Silva, L.A. 1971. "Mercados Metropolitanos de Trabalho Manual à Marginalidade." M.A. thesis, Universidade Federal do Rio de Janeiro, Programa de Pós–Graduação em Antropoligia Social.
Macisco, John; Weller, Robert H.; and Leon F. Bouvier. 1969. "Some General Considerations on Migration, Urbanization, and Fertility in Latin America." In *The Family of Transition,* pp. 285–97. Washington D.C.: U.S. Government Printing Office.
Madeira, Felicia. 1975. "La Population Active au Brésil de 1940 au 1970." In CICRED, *La Population du Brésil,* pp. 153–72.
Madeira, Felicia R., and Singer, Paul I. 1973. "Estrutura do Emprego e Trabalho Feminino no Brasil, 1920–1970." Cadernos CEBRAP 13.
Madeira, João Lyra. 1972. "O IBGE e os Estudos da Fecundidade no Brasil." *Revista Brasileira de Estatística* 33 (April/June): 211–39.
_____. 1973. "Dados Estatísticos para a Análise Demográfica da População Brasileira." *Revista Brasileira de Estatística* 34 (April/June): 231–51.
Madeira, João Lyra, and Cassinelli, Roberto Robichez. 1970. "Algunas tablas de mortalidad brasileña para los periodos de 1959–1961 y 1950–1960." *Actas.* Conferencia Regional Latinoamericana de Población, Mexico, vol. I: 73–79.
Makler, Harry. 1974. "Labor Problems of Native, Migrant, and Foreign Born Members of the Recife Industrial Elite." *Journal of Developing Areas* 9, 1 (October) : 27–52.
Malan, Pedro S., and Bonelli, Regis. 1977. "The Brazilian Economy in the Seventies: Old and New Developments." *World Development* 5 (½): 19–45.
Mandle, Jay. 1973. *The Plantation Economy: Population and Economic Change in Guyana, 1838–1960.* Philadelphia: Temple University Press.
_____. 1974. "The Plantation States as a Sub-Region of the Postbellum South." *Journal of Economic History* 34, 3 (September): 732–38.
Marcílio, Maria Luiza. 1968. *La Ville de São Paulo.* Rouen: Université de Rouen.
_____. 1973. "Crescimento populacional da população brasileira até 1872." Apresentado à XXV Reunião Anual da SBPC, Guanabara.
_____. 1975. "Evolution historique de la Population brésilienne jusqu'en 1872." In CICRED, *La Population du Brésil,* pp. 7–24.
Margolis, Maxine L. 1973. *The Moving Frontier.* Gainesville: The University of

Florida Press.

Martine, George. 1976. "Adaptação de Imigrantes ou Sobrevivência dos Mais Fortes." Relatório Técnico No. 30. Brasilia: United Nations Development Program, Human Resources Planning Project.

Martine, George, and Peliano, José Carlos. 1975. "Migração, Estrutura Ocupacional e Renda Nas Áreas Metropolitanas." In *Estudos de Demografica Urbana,* Manoel Costa (ed.), pp. 161–96. Rio de Janeiro: IPEA/INPES.

———. 1977. "Migrantes no Mercado de Trabalho Metropolitano." Relatório Técnico #32. Brasilia: Projeto de Planejamento de Recursos Humanos.

Mattos, General Carlos de Meira. 1975. *Brasil-Geopolitica e Destino.* Rio de Janeiro: Livraria José Olympio.

Mattoso, Kátia M. Queiroz. 1972. "A Propósito de Cartas de Alforria na Bahia 1779–1850." *Anais de História,* Ano IV (Assis) São Paulo.

Mazumdar, Dipak. 1976. "The Urban Informal Sector." *World Development* 4: 655–79.

McGreevey, William. 1974. "Urban Growth in Colombia." *Journal of Inter-American and World Affairs* 16, 4 (November): 387–408.

Mello, Pedro Carvalho de. 1974. "Estimating Slave Longevity in Nineteenth Century Brazil." Latin American Workshop Report 7475–21. University of Chicago, Department of Economics.

———. 1977. "The Economics of Labor in Brazilian Coffee Plantations, 1871–1888." Ph.D. dissertation, University of Chicago.

———. 1978. "Aspectos Econômicos da Organização do Trabalho da Economia Cafeeira do Rio de Janeiro 1850–1888." *Revista Brasileira de Economia* 32(1): 19–67.

Merrick, Thomas W. 1974. "Interregional Differences in Fertility in Brazil, 1950–1970." *Demography* 11 (August): 423–40.

———. 1976a. "Employment and Earnings in the Informal Sector in Brazil: The Case of Belo Horizonte." *Journal of Developing Areas* 10 (April): 337–54.

———. 1976b. "Population, Development, and Planning in Brazil." *Population and Development Review* 2 (June): 181–99.

———. 1978. "Fertility and Land Availability in Rural Brazil." *Demography* 15 (August): 321–36.

Mincer, Jacob. 1962. "Labor Force Participation of Married Women." In *Aspects of Labor Economics,* pp. 73–112. Universities-National Bureau of Economic Research Conference Series 14. Princeton: Princeton University Press for NBER.

Morawetz, David. 1974. "Employment Implications of Industrialization in Developing Countries: A Survey." *Economic Journal* 84 (September): 491–542.

Moreira, Morvan de Mello; da Silva, Lea Mello; and McLaughlin, Robert T. 1978. "Brazil." The Population Council, *Country Profiles.* New York: The Population Council, Inc.

Morley, Samuel, and Williamson, Jeffrey. 1975. "Growth, Wage Policy and Inequality: Brazil during the Sixties." Social Science Research Institute Workshop Series, No. 7519. University of Wisconsin–Madison (mimeo.)

Morse, Richard. 1965. "Recent Research on Latin American Urbanization: A Selective Survey with Commentary." *Latin American Research Review* 1(Fall): 35–74.

———. 1971a. "Trends and Issues in Latin American Urban Research, 1965–1970. *Latin American Research Review* 6, 1 (Part 1, Spring and Summer): 19–76.

——— (ed.). 1971 b. *The Urban Development of Latin America*. Stanford: Center for Latin American Studies.

———. 1974. "Trends and Patterns of Latin American Urbanization, 1750–1920." *Comparative Studies in Society and History* 16, 4 (September): 416–47.

———. 1975. "The Development of Urban Systems in the Americas in the Nineteenth Century." *Journal of Interamerican Studies and World Affairs* 17, 1 (February): 4–26.

Mortara, Giorgio. 1970. Note: Many of Mortara's papers have been collected in the volume, *Contribuições Para o Estudo de Demografia no Brasil*, Fundação IBGE.

———. 1941a. "Estudos sobre a Utilização do Censo Demográfico para a Reconstrução das Estatísticas do Movimento da População do Brasil. V. Retificação da Distribuição por Idade da População Natural do Brasil, Constante dos Censos, e Cálculo de Óbitos, dos Nascimentos e das Variações dessa População no Periodo 1870–1920." *Revista Brasileira de Estatistica* 2: 39–81.

———. 1941b. "Estudos sobre a Utilização do Censo Demográfico para a Reconstrução das Estatísticas do Movimento da População do Brasil. VI. Sinopse da Dinàmica da População do Brasil nos Últimos Cem Anos." *Revista Brasileira de Estatitica* 2: 267–76.

———. 1942. "Contribuição ao Estudo da Influência da Imigração sobre a Taxa de Natalidade." *Revista Brasileira de Estatistica* 3: 575–84.

———. 1947a. "Análise Comparativa dos Resultados dos Censos Brasileiros de 1900, 1920 e 1940 e Determinação da Mortalidade nos Periodos Intercensitários." In *Pesquisas sobre Populações Americanas*, pp. 101–14. Rio de Janeiro: Fundação Getúlio Vargas.

———. 1947b "Contribuição para o Estudo da Influência da Imigração sobre a Taxa de Mortalidade." In *Pequisas sobre Populações Americanas*, pp. 51–70. Rio de Janeiro: Fundação Getúlio Vargas.

———. 1947c. "Crescimento da População do Brasil entre 1872 e 1940." In *Pesquisas sobre Populações Americanas*, pp. 81–100. Rio de Janeiro: Fundação Getúlio Vargas.

———. 1947d. "Os Fatores Demográficos do Crescimento das Populações Americanas nos Ultimos Cem Anos." In *Pesquisas sobre Populações Americanas*, pp. 9–36. Rio de Janeiro: Fundação Getúlio Vargas.

———. 1948. "A Prolificidade das Mulheres Naturais do Exterior Conforme o Censo Demografico de 1° de setembro de 1940." *Revista Brasileira de Estatistica* 9(35): 475–81.

———. 1952. "Contribuições do Instituto Brasileiro de Geografia e Estatistica para os Estudos Demográficos (1936–1951)." *Revista Brasileira de Estatistica* 13 (January/March): 97–106.

———. 1953. "A Mortalidade de População Natural do Brasil (Ensaio de Determinação pela Comparacão entre os Censos de 40 e 50)." *Revista Brasileira de Estatistica* 15(56): 313–23.

———. 1954a. "The Brazilian Birth Rate: Its Economic and Social Factors." In *Culture and Human Fertility*, pp. 405–501. Lorimer, F. (ed.), New York: UNESCO.

———. 1954b. "The Development and Structure of Brazil's Population." *Population*

Studies (November) 8: 121–39. Also in Spengler and Duncan, 1956. *Demographic Analysis.* Glencoe: The Free Press.

Moura Hélio A.; Holder, Carmen S.; and Sampaio, Ardil. 1977. "Diferenciais de Renda entre Naturais e Migrantes no Nordeste Urbano." In *Migrações Internas,* George Martine (ed.), pp. 53–88. Rio de Janeiro: Altiva Gráfica e Editora.

Moura, Hélio, and Coelho, J. O. 1975. *Migrações para As Grandes Cidades do Nordeste: Intensidades e Caracteristicas Demográficas.* BNB, ETENE: Fortaleza.

Moura, Margarida M. 1973. *Os Sitiantes e a Herança.* Rio de Janeiro, Masters' thesis, Museu Nacional da Universidade Federal do Rio de Janeiro.

Namboodiri, N. K. 1972. "Some Observations on the Economic Framework for Fertility Analysis." *Population Studies* 26 (July): 185–206.

Neher, Philip. 1971. "Peasants, Procreation, and Pensions." *American Economic Review* 61 (June): 380–89.

Neiva, Artur H. 1965. "International Migrations Affecting Latin America." *Milbank Memorial Fund Quarterly* 43 (October), part 2: 119–35.

Nelson, Joan M. 1969. "Migrants, Urban Poverty, and Instability in Developing Nations." Occasional Papers in International Affairs, #22, Harvard University, Center for International Affairs (September).

Nelson, R. R. 1956. "A Theory of the Low-Level Equilibrium Trap in Underdeveloped Countries." *American Economic Review* 46, 5 (December): 894–908.

Netto, A. Delfim. 1973. Interview reported in *Jornal do Brasil,* January 1, Caderno Especial, p. 6.

Nicholls, William H. 1969. "The Agricultural Frontier in Modern Brazilian History: The State of Paraná, 1920–1965," In *Cultural Change in Brazil*, Merril Rippy (ed.). Muncie, Indiana: Ball State University.

Nicol, Robert N. V. C. 1974. "A Agricultura e a Industrialização no Brasil 1850–1930." Tese de doutorado do Departamento de Ciências Sociais da Faculdade de Filosofia, Letras e Ciências Humanas, Universidade de São Paulo.

O'Brien, F. S., and Salm, C. L. 1970. "Desemprego e Subemprego no Brasil." *Revista Brasileira de Economia* 24 (December): 93–138.

Oeschli, Frank W., and Kirk, Dudley. 1975. "Modernization and the Demographic Transition in Latin America and the Caribbean." *Economic Development and Cultural Change* 23 (April): 391–419.

Oliveira, Francisco. 1972. "A Economia Brasileira: Critica à Razão Dualista." Estudos CEBRAP 2 (October): 82.

Oliveira Vianna, Francisco José. 1922. "Resumo Histórico dos Inquéritos Censitários Realizados no Brasil." In Brazil, Diretoria Geral de Estatistica, *Recenseamento do Brasil, 1920, vol. 1, Introdução,* Rio de Janeiro.

Ozório de Almeida, Miguel. 1974. "Statement to Seventeenth Session of U.N. Population Commission." Published by the Ecological Foundation and Wadebridge Ecological Center.

Ozório de Almeida, Anna Luiza. 1976. "Labor Market Dualism and Industrial Subcontracting of Low-Skill Service Workers in Brazil." Ph.D. dissertation, Stanford University.

Pang, Eul-Soo. 1974. "Bahia's Planter Elite and Their Attempt to Modernize Agriculture 1842–1889." Paper presented at Conference on the Northeast of Brazil, the Johnson Foundation, Racine, Wisconsin, November.

Pang, Eul-Soo, and Seckinger, Ron L. 1972. "The Mandarins of Imperial Brazil." *Comparative Studies in Society and History* 14, 2 (March): 215–44.

Pastore, José; Haller, A.; and Gomez-Buéndia. 1975. "Wage Differentials in São Paulo's Labor Force." *Industrial Relations* 14:3.

Peattie, Lisa. 1975. *The Informal Sector*. Washington, D.C.: The World Bank.

Peláez, Carlos Manuel. 1969. "Acerca da Política Governamental da Grande Depressão e da Industrialização no Brasil." *Revista Brasileira de Economia* 23,3 (July/September): 77–88.

————. 1971. "As Consequências Econômicas da Ortodoxia Monetária Cambial e Fiscal no Brasil, 1889–1945." *Revista Brasileira de Economia* 25, 3 (July–September): 5–82.

————. 1972. *História da Industrialização Brasileira: Critica à Teoria Estruturalista no Brasil.* Rio de Janeiro: Editora Análise e Perspectiva Econômica.

————. 1976. "The Theory and the Reality of Imperialism in the Coffee Economy of Nineteenth Century Brazil." *The Economic History Review* 29 (May).

Peláez, Carlos Manuel, and Suzigan, Wilson. 1976. *História Monetária do Brasil: Análise da Política, Comportamento, e Instituições Monetárias,* Série Monográfica No. 23. Rio de Janeiro: IPEA/INPES.

Peliano, José Carlos, 1977. "Setor Informal ou Pobreza Urbana?" In *Migrações Internas,* George Martine (ed.), pp. 35–52. Rio de Janeiro: Altiva Gráfica e Editora.

Pereira, Luis Carlos Bresser. 1974. *Empresários e Administradores no Brasil.* São Paulo: Editora Brasiliense.

Perlman, Janice E. 1976. *The Myth of Marginality: Urban Poverty Politics in Rio de Janeiro.* Berkeley: University of California Press.

Perruci, Gadiel. 1974. "Estrutura e Conjuntura da Economia Açucareira no Nordeste do Brasil 1889–1930." Paper presented at Conference on the Northeast of Brazil, The Johnson Foundation, Racine, Wisconsin, November.

Pescatello, Ann. 1970. "Both Ends of the Journey: An Historical Study of Migration and Change in Brazil and Portugal 1889–1914." Ph.D. dissertation, University of California at Los Angeles.

———— (ed.). 1975. *The African in Latin America.* New York: Alfred Knopf.

Pitchford, J. D. 1974. *Population in Economic Growth.* Amsterdam and London: North Holland Publishing Co.

Pittinger, Donald B. 1976. *Projecting State and Local Populations.* Cambridge, Massachusetts: Ballinger Publishing Company.

Pope, Christie Farnham. 1970. "Southern Homesteads for Negroes." *Agricultural History* 44, 2 (April): 201–12.

Poppino, Rollie E. 1973. *Brazil, The Land and the People,* 2nd ed. New York: Oxford University Press.

Population Research Center, University of Texas. 1965. *International Population Census Bibliography, No. 1, Latin America and the Caribbean.* Austin: Bureau of Business Research, The University of Texas at Austin.

Prado, Jr., Caio. 1963. *Formação do Brasil Contemporâneo* (Colônia), 7th ed. São Paulo: Editora Brasiliense.

————. 1971. *História Econômica do Brasil,* 14th ed. São Paulo: Editora Brasiliense.

PREALC. 1976. *The Employment Problem in Latin America: Facts, Outlooks, and Policies.* Santiago: PREALC.

Preston, Samuel H. 1975. "The Changing Relation between Mortality and Level of Economic Development." *Population Studies* 29 (July): 231–48.

Puffer, Ruth R., and Serrano, Carlos V. 1975. *Patterns of Mortality in Childhood.* Washington, D.C.: Pan American Health Organization.

Rabinovitz, Francine, and Trueblood, Felicity. 1971–76. *Latin American Urban Research* (5 volumes). Beverly Hills, California: Sage Publications.

Ramos, Joseph. 1970. *Labor and Development in Latin America.* New York: Columbia University Press.

Ransom, Roger L., and Sutch, Richard. 1972. "Debt Peonage in the Cotton South After the Civil War." *Journal of Economic History* 32 (September): 641–69.

———. 1973. "The Ex-Slave in the Postbellum South: A Study of the Economic Impact of Racism in a Market Environment." *Journal of Economic History* 33, 1 (March): 131–48.

———. 1975. "The Impact of the Civil War and of Emancipation on Southern Agriculture." *Explorations in Economic History* 12, 1 (January): 1–28.

Rato, Helena. 1975. "Bachue-Brasil I." OIT-IBGE Working Paper #1, March 3.

Redwood, John, III. 1974. "Internal Migration in Brazil: Characteristics, Causes and Consequences and Policy Implications: A Review of Existing Studies and Suggestions for Further Research." Relatório do Ministério do Interior, December.

Reid, Joseph D. 1973. "Sharecropping as an Understandable Market Response—The Postbellum South." *Journal of Economic History* 33 (March): 106–30.

Reis, Jaime. 1972. "From Bangüê to Usina: Social Aspects of Growth and Modernization in the Sugar Industry of Pernambuco, 1850–1920." Presented at Symposium on Landlord and Peasant in Latin America and the Caribbean at Cambridge University, December.

———. 1974a. "The Realm of the Hoe: Plantation Agriculture in Pernambuco Before and After the Abolition of Slavery." Paper presented at Conference on the Northeast of Brazil, The Johnson Foundation, Racine, Wisconsin, November.

———. 1974b. "Abolition and the Economics of Slaveholding in Northeast Brazil." *Boletin de Estudios Latinoamericanos y del Caribe* 17 (December): 3–20.

———. 1975. "The Abolition of Slavery and its Aftermath in Pernambuco, 1880–1920." Ph.D. dissertation, Oxford University.

———. 1977. "The Impact of Abolitionism in Northeast Brazil: A Quantitative Approach." *Annals, New York Academy of Sciences* 292: 107–22.

Reutlinger, Shlomo, and Selowsky, Marcelo. 1976. *Malnutrition and Poverty: Magnitude and Policy Options.* Baltimore and London: The Johns Hopkins University Press.

Reynolds, Clark, and Carpenter, Robert. 1975. "Housing Finance in Brazil: Towards a New Distribution of Wealth." In *Urbanization and Inequality: The Political Economy of Urban and Rural Development in Latin America*, Wayne A. Cornelius and Felicity M. Trueblood, (eds.). Beverly Hills, California: Sage Publications.

Ribeiro, Airton Mauro Sepulveda. 1973. "Diferenças Sócio-Econômicas Entre Migrantes e Não-Migrantes no Município de São Paulo." Tese de Mestrado, IPE/USP, São Paulo.

Richers, Raimar, and Almeida, Eduardo Aususto Buarque de. 1975. "O Planejamento Familiar e o Mercado de Anteconcepcionais no Brasil." *Revista de Administração de Empresa* 15 (July/August): 7–21.

Rios, José Arthur. 1973. "O Café e a Mão de Obra Agricola." In *Ensaios Sobre Café e Desenvolvimento*. Rio de Janeiro: Instituto Brasileiro de Café.

Robinson, Warren C. (ed.). 1975. *Population and Development Planning*. New York: The Population Council.

Robinson, W. C., and Horlacher, D. 1971. "Population Growth and Economic Welfare." *Reports on Population/Family Planning* 6. New York: The Population Council.

Rodrigues, Felix Contreiras. 1935. *Traços da economia social e politica do Brasil colonial*. Rio de Janeiro: Ariel Editora.

Rodrigues, Walter. 1968. "Progress and Problems of Family Planning in Brazil." *Demography* 5:800–10.

———. 1977. "Brazil." In *Family Planning in the Developing World*, Walter B. Watson (ed.). New York: The Population Council.

Rodrigues, Walter, et al. 1975. *Law and Population in Brazil*. Law and Population Programme, Tufts University.

Roett, Riordan (ed.). 1972. *Brazil in the Sixties*. Nashville: Vanderbilt University Press.

———. 1976. *Brazil in the Seventies*. Washington. D.C.: American Enterprise Institute.

Rosen, Bernard C., and Simmons, Alan B. 1971. "Industrialization, Family and Fertility: A Structural-Psychological Analysis of the Brazilian Case." *Demography* 8 (February): 49–69.

Rosenzweig, Mark R., and Evensen, Robert. 1976. "Fertility, Schooling, and the Economic Contributions of Children in Rural India." Paper presented at Annual Meetings of the Population Association of America, Montreal, Canada, April 30.

Russel, Robert R. 1941. "The Effects of Slavery Upon Non-Slaveholders in the Antebellum South." *Agricultural History* 15, 2 (April): 112–26.

Russell-Wood, A. J. R. 1972. "Colonial Brazil." In *Neither Slave nor Free: The Freedmen of African Descent in the Slave Societies of the New World*, David W. Cohen and Jack P. Greene (eds.). Baltimore: The Johns Hopkins University Press.

Sahota, Gian S. 1968. "An Economic Analysis of Internal Migration in Brazil." *Journal of Political Economy* 76 (March–April): 218–45.

Saito, Hiroshi, 1961. *O Japonês no Brasil: Estudo de Mobilidade e Fixação*. São Paulo: Editora Sociologia e Política (Fundação da Escola de Sociologia e Politica de São Paulo).

Salm, Claudio. 1974. "Evolucão do Mercado de Trabalho 1969/1972." *Estudos CEBRAP* 8 (April-June): 103–19.

Sanchez-Albornoz, Nicholas. 1974. *The Population of Latin America: A History*. Berkeley: University of California Press.

Sanders, Thomas G. 1970a. "Population Review 1970: Brazil." *American Universities Field Staff Reports*, East Coast South America Series 14:6.

———. 1970b. "The Relationship between Population Planning and Belief Systems: The Catholic Church in Latin America." *American Universities Field Staff Reports*, West Coast South America Series 17:7.

———. 1973. "Development and Environment: Brazil and the Stockholm Conference." *American Universities Field Staff Reports*, East Coast South America Series 17:7 (June).

_____. 1974. "Latin Americans at Bucharest." *American Universities Field Staff Reports*, East Coast South America Series 18: 2.

Sant'Anna, Anna M.; Merrick, Thomas W.; and Mazumdar, Dipak. 1977. "Distribuição de Renda e a Economia da Família Urbana: O Caso de Belo Horizonte." *Pesquisa e Planejamento Econômico* 7: 1–68.

Santos, Jair L. F. 1974. "Projeção da População Brasileira." *Revista da Saúde Pública* 8, Suplemento (June): 91–102.

_____. 1975. "Projection démographique du Brésil: 1970–2000." In CICRED, *La Population du Brésil*, pp. 173–87.

Santos, Jair L. F.; Garcia, Ana Lúcia; Preziosi, Adarosa; Fernandes, Luiza Regina Branco; Taddei, Marie Ann Worms. 1976. "A Mortalidade no Brasil em 1970." Paper presented at Conferência sobre o Progresso da Pesquisa Demográfica no Brasil. Terezópolis, June.

Santos, Jair L. F., and Singer, Paul. 1971. *A Dinâmica Populational de Salvador, 1940–1968*. Salvador: Edição Universidade Federal da Bahia.

Saunders, John V. D. 1958. *Differential Fertility in Brazil*. Gainesville: University of Florida Press.

Sawyer, Diana Oya, and Sawyer, Donald R. 1975. "Estrutura Social e Formação de Família numa Frente de Expansão Agricola da Amazônia." (Mimeo.)

Schaefer, Kalmann, and Spindel, Cheywa R. 1976. *São Paulo: Urban Development and Employment*. Geneva: International Labour Office.

Schneider, Ronald M. 1971. *The Political System of Brazil*. New York: Columbia University Press.

Schuh, G. Edward. 1970. *The Agricultural Development of Brazil*. New York: Praeger Publishers.

Schultz, T. Paul. 1969. "An Economic Model of Family Planning and Fertility." *Journal of Political Economy* 77, 2 (March/April): 153–80.

_____. 1970. *Fertility Patterns and Their Determinants in the Arab Middle East*. RM-5978-FF. Santa Monica: The RAND Corporation.

_____. 1973. "Explanation of Birth Rate Changes over Space and Time: A Study of Taiwan." *Journal of Political Economy* 81 (March/April), part 2: 238–74.

Schultz, T. W. (ed.). 1973. *New Economic Approaches to Fertility*. Supplement to *Journal of Political Economy* 81 (March/April).

Schwartz, Stuart. 1974. "The Manumission of Slaves in Colonial Brazil: Bahia 1684–1745." *The Hispanic American Historical Review* 54, 4 (November): 603–35.

Serviço Federal de Habitação e Urbanismo (SERFHAU). 1975. *The Effects of Changes in Employment and Income Distribution on Internal Migration. Report No. 2.3 Employment Composition, Income Distribution and Internal Migration*. Rio de Janeiro.

Sethuraman, S. V. 1976. "The Urban Informal Sector: Concept, Measurement, and Policy." *International Labour Review* 114 (July/August): 69–81.

Seyferth, Geralda. 1973. "A Colonização Alemã no Vale do Itajai-Mirim." Masters' thesis, Museu Nacional da Universidade do Rio de Janeiro.

Shanin, Teodor. 1972. *The Awkward Class*. Oxford: Clarendon Press.

Shirley, Robert W. 1971. *The End of a Tradition*. New York and London: Columbia University Press.

Silva, Nelson do Valle. 1973. "Posição Social das Ocupações." Rio de Janeiro:

Centro de Informática, Fundação IBGE.

Silvers, Arthur L., and de M. Moreira, Morvan. 1974*a*. "A Absorção da Força de Trabalho Não Qualificado em Minas Gerais: Evidência em Favor da Hipótese de Todaro?" *Estudos Econômicos* 4(1): 55–74.

Silvers, Arthur L. and de M. Moreira, Morvan. 1974*b*. "Migração, Transição e Absorção em Vinte Cidades." *Pesquisa e Planejamento Econômico 4,* 1 (February): 83–109.

Silber, Simão. 1973. "Análise da Política Econômica e do Comportamento da Economia Brasileira Durante o Período 1929/1939." Tese de Mestrado, EPGE, Fundação Getúlio Vargas, Rio de Janeiro.

Simon, Julian L. 1976. "Population Growth May Be Good for LDC's in the Long-Run." *Economic Development and Cultural Change* 24 (January): 309–37.

Simonsen, Mário Henrique. 1969. *Brasil 2001.* Rio de Janeiro: APEC Editora.

———. 1972. *Brasil 2002.* Rio de Janeiro: APEC Editora.

Simonsen, Roberto C. 1969. *História Econômica do Brasil, 1500–1820,* 6th ed. São Paulo: Companhia Editora Nacional.

Singer, Paul I. 1968. *Desenvolvimento Econômico e Evolução Urbana.* São Paulo: Editora da Universidade.

———. 1970. *Dinâmica Populacional e Desenvolvimento.* São Paulo: Universidade de São Paulo.

———. 1971. *Força de Trabalho e Emprego no Brasil, 1920–1969.* São Paulo: Cadernos CEBRAP, #3.

———. 1972. "Migrações Internas: Considerações Teóricas para o Seu Estudo." CEBRAP (mimeo.)

———. 1975*a*. *Implicações Econômicas e Sociais da Dinâmica Populacional Brasileira.* São Paulo: Cadernos CEBRAP, #20: 5–16.

———. 1975*b*. "Implications Economiques et Sociales de l'Evolution de la Population Brésilienne et de la Politique Démographique." In CICRED, *La Population du Brésil,* pp. 188–203.

Sinha, J. N. 1965. "Dynamics of Female Participation in Economic Activity in a Developing Economy." United Nations, *World Population Conference,* Belgrade.

Sjaastad, Larry. 1962. "The Costs and Returns of Human Migration." *Journal of Political Economy* 70 (5), October Supplement.

Skidmore, Thomas E. 1967. *Politics in Brazil.* New York: Oxford University Press.

———. 1969. "The Death of Brazilian Slavery, 1866–1888." In *Latin-American History: Select Problems,* Frederick B. Pike (ed.). New York: Harcourt, Brace, and World.

———. 1974. *Black into White: Race and Nationality in Brazilian Thought.* New York: Oxford University Press.

Slenes, Robert W. 1975. "The Demography and Economics of Brazilian Slavery 1850–1888." Ph.D. dissertation, Stanford University.

Smith, Gordon W. 1969. "Brazilian Agricultural Policy, 1950–1967." In *The Economy of Brazil,* Howard S. Ellis (ed.).

Smith, T. Lynn. 1960. *Latin American Population Studies.* Gainesville: University of Florida Press, Monograph Series #8.

———. 1972. *Brazil: People and Institutions,* 4th ed. Baton Rouge: Louisiana State University Press.

Sousa e Silva, Joachim Norberto de. 1870. "Investigações sobre os recenseamentos da população geral do Império e de cada provincia de per si tentados desde os tempos coloniais até hoje." *Relatório do Ministério dos Negócios do Império, Anexo D*. Rio de Janeiro: Typographia Nacional.

Souza, Paulo R., and Tokman, Victor E. 1976. "The Informal Urban Sector in Latin America." *International Labour Review* 114 (December): 355–65.

Spielman, Evelyn, and Leite, Valeria da Motta. 1974. "Avaliação Critica da Estrutura por Sexo e Idade da População Brasileira, Segundo os Censos Demográficos." *Revista Brasileira de Estatistica* 35 (April–June): 203–26.

Stein, Stanley J. 1957a. *The Brazilian Cotton Manufacture 1850–1950*. Cambridge, Mass.: Harvard University Press.

———. 1957b. *Vassouras, a Brazilian Coffee County 1850–1900*. Cambridge, Mass.: Harvard University Press.

Stewart, F., and Streeten, Paul. 1971. "Conflicts between Output and Employment Objectives in Developing Economies." *Oxford Economic Papers* 23 (July): 145–68.

Stycos, J. M. et al. 1971. *Ideology, Faith and Family Planning in Latin America*. New York: The Population Council.

Suzigan, Wilson. 1971. "A Politica Cambial Brasileira. 1889–1946." *Revista Brasileira de Economia* 25, 3 (July/September): 93–111.

———. 1976. "Industrialization and Economic Policy in Historical Perspective." *Brazilian Economic Studies* (2), Rio de Janeiro: IPEA/INPES. A Portuguese version appeared in *Pesquisa e Planejamento Econômico*, April.

——— et al. 1972. *Financiamento de Projetos Industriais no Brasil.* Rio de Janeiro: IPEA/INPES.

Suzuki, Teiti. 1969. *The Japanese Immigrant in Brazil*. Tokyo: University of Tokyo Press.

Taunay, Affonso d'Escragnolle. 1945. *História do Café no Brasil*, 15 volumes. São Paulo: Departamento Nacional do Café.

Tavares, Maria da Conceição. 1972. *Da Substituição de Importações ao Capitalismo Financeiro*. Rio de Janeiro: Zahar Editores.

Tavares, Maria C., and Mello, João Manuel Cardoso de. n.d. "The Impact of External Forces on the National Economies of Latin America during 1880–1930: The Brazilian Case." (mimeo.)

Tavares, Maria de Conceição, and Serra, José J. 1973. "Beyond Stagnation: A Discussion on the Nature of Recent Development in Brazil." In *Latin America: From Dependence to Revolution*, James Petras (ed.). New York: Wiley Press.

Taylor, Kit Sims. 1970. "The Economics of Sugar and Slavery in Northeastern Brazil." *Agricultural History* 44, 3 (July): 267–80.

di Tella, Guido, and Zymelman, Manuel. 1967. *Las Etapas del Desarrollo Econômico Argentino*. Buenos Aires: Eudeba.

Thomas, Brinley. 1973. *Migration and Economic Growth: A Study of Great Britain and the Atlantic Economy*. Cambridge: Cambridge University Press.

Thomas, Robert N. (ed.). 1973. *Population Dynamics of Latin America: A Review and Bibliography*. East Lansing, Michigan: C.L.A.G. Publications.

Thomas, Robert P., and Bean, Richard N. 1974. "The Fishers of Men: The Profits of the Slave Trade." *Journal of Economic History* 34, 4 (December): 885–914.

Tien, H. Yuan. 1957. "A Demographic Aspect of Interstate Variations in American Fertility, 1880–1860." *Milbank Memorial Fund Quarterly* 37: 49–59.

Todaro, Michael P. 1969. "A Model of Labor Absorption and Urban Unemployment in Less Developed Countries." *American Economic Review* 59, 1 (March): 138–48.

Tolipan, Ricardo, and Tinelli, Arthur C. 1975. *A Controvérsia Sobre Distribuição de Renda e Desenvolvimento*. Rio de Janeiro: Zahar Editores.

Tolosa, Hamilton C. 1973. "Macroeconomia da Urbanização Brasileira." *Pesquisa e Planejamento Econômico* 3, 3 (October): 585–643.

———. 1975. "Dualismo no Mercado de Trabalho Urbano." *Pesquisa e Planejamento Econômico* 5, 1 (June): 1–36.

Toplin, Robert Brent. 1969. "Upheaval, Violence and the Abolition of Slavery in Brazil: The Case of São Paulo." *Hispanic American Historical Review* 49, 4 (November): 639–55.

———. 1972. *The Abolition of Slavery in Brazil*. New York: Atheneum.

Turnham, David. 1971. *The Employment Problem in Less Developed Countries*. Paris: OECD.

Tyler, William G. 1976. "A Industrialização e a Política Industrial no Brasil: Uma Visão Global." *Estudos Econômicos* 6:2.

United Nations. 1955. *Age and Sex Patterns of Mortality*. New York: United Nations.

———. 1956. *Manual III—Methods for Population Projection by Age and Sex*. New York: United Nations.

———. 1967a. *Manual IV—Methods of Estimating Basic Demographic Measures for Incomplete Data*. New York: United Nations.

———. 1967b. *Principles and Methods for the 1970 Population Census*. New York: United Nations.

———. 1968. *Methods of Analysing Census Data on Economic Activities of the Population*. New York: United Nations.

———. 1969. *Growth of the World's Urban and Rural Population, 1920–2000*. New York: United Nations.

———. 1973. *The Determinants and Consequences of Population Trends*, vol. 1. New York: United Nations.

———. 1976. "Trends and Prospects in the Population of Urban Agglomerations." New York: United Nations.

United States, Department of Commerce. 1975. *Statistical Abstract of the United States, 1975*. Washington, D.C.: U.S. Goverment Printing Office.

Van Delden Laerne, C. H. 1885. *Brazil and Java: Report on Coffee Culture in America, Asia, and Africa*. London.

Vásquez-Presedo, Vicente. 1971a. "The Role of Italian Migration in the Development of the Argentine Economy 1875–1914." *Economia Internazionale* 24 (August–November): 3–4.

———. 1971b. *El Caso Argentino: Migración de Factores: Comercio Exterior y Desarrollo 1875–1914*. Buenos Aires: Eudeba.

Vaughan, Denton. 1969. *Urbanization in Twentieth Century Latin America: A Working Bibliography*. Austin: University of Texas.

Vaz da Costa, Rubens. 1973. *A Explosão Demográfica no Mundo e no Brasil*. Rio de Janeiro: Banco Nacional da Habitação.

Velho. Otavio G. 1973. "Modes of Capitalist Development: Peasantry and the Moving Frontier." Ph.D. dissertation, University of Manchester.

Veloso, Hector. 1975. "O Sistema de Informação Sobre Força De Trabalho no Brasil." In Brazil, Instituto de Planejamento Econômico e Social, *Sistemas de Informação para Poliiticas de Emprego*, pp. 297–373.

Versiani, Flávio Rabelo. 1974. "Resenha Bibliográfica—História da Industrialização Brasileira por Carlos Manuel Peláez." *Pesquisa e Planejamento Econômico* 4, 1 (February): 181–88.

Versiani, Flávio Rabelo, and Barros, José Roberto Mendonca de (eds.) 1977. *A Formação Econômica do Brasil: A Experiência da Industrialização*. Série ANPEC. São Paulo: Edição Saraiva.

Versiani, Flávio Rabelo, and Versiani, Maria Tereza. 1977. "A Industrialização Brasileira antes de 1930: Uma Contribuição." In *A Formação Econômico do Brasil: A Experiência da Industrialização*, Flávio Rabelo Versiani and José M. Barros, (eds.). Série'ANPEC. São Paulo: Edição Saraiva.

Villela, Annibal Villanova, and Suzigan, Wilson. 1973. *Politica do Governo e Crescimento da Economia Brasileira, 1889-1945*, Série Monográfica No. 10. Rio de Janeiro: IPEA/INPES.

Vinovskis, Maris A. 1975. "The Demography of the Slave Population in Antebellum America." *Journal of Interdisciplinary History* 5, 3 (Winter): 459–68.

Von Doellinger, Carlos, et al. 1974. *A Politica Brasileira de Comércio Exteriore e Seus Efeitos 1967-1973*. Rio de Janeiro: IPEA/INPES.

Von Humboldt, Alexander. 1966a. *Personal Narrative of Travels to the Equinoctal Regions of the New Continent*, 1826 ed. New York: AMS Press.

———. 1966b. *Political Essay on the Kingdom of New Spain* (1811). New York: AMS Press.

Wachter, Michael L. 1974. "Primary and Secondary Labor Markets: A Critique of the Dual Approach." *Brookings Papers on Economic Activity* 3: 637–80.

Wagley, Charles. 1963. *An Introduction to Brazil*. New York and London: Columbia University Press.

Watkins, Melville H. 1963. "A Staple Theory of Economic Growth." *Canadian Journal of Economics and Political Science* 29 (May): 141–58.

Webb, Richard C. 1977. *Government Policy and the Distribution of Income in Peru*. Cambridge: Harvard University Press.

Weeks, John. 1975. "Policies for Expanding Employment in the Informal Urban Sector of Developing Economies." *International Labour Review* 111 (January): 1–14.

Weller, Robert H.; Macisco, John Jr,; and Martine, George R. 1971. "The Relative Importance of the Components of Urban Growth in Latin America." *Demography* 8 (May): 225–32.

Wells, John, 1974. "Distribution of Earnings, Growth, and the Structure of Demand in Brazil During the 1960's." *World Development* 2 (January): 9–24.

———. 1976. "Underconsumption, Market Size and Expenditure Patterns in Brazil." *Bulletin for the Society of Latin American Studies* (Univ. of Liverpool), no. 4: 23–58.

Willems, Emilio. 1940. "Assimilation of German Immigrants in Brazil." *Sociology and Social Research* 25, 2 (November/December): 125–32.

———. 1942. "Some Aspects of Cultural Conflict and Acculturation in Southern Rural Brazil."*Rural Sociology* 7, 4(December): 375–83.

———. 1951. "Immigrants and Their Assimilation in Brazil." In *Brazil: Portrait of*

Half a Continent, T. Lynn Smith and Alexander Marchant (eds.), New York: Dryden Press.

_____. 1953. "The Structure of the Brazilian Family." *Social Forces* 31, 4(May): 339–45.

_____. 1955. "Brazil." In *The Positive Contribution by Immigrants*. Paris: UNESCO.

_____. 1972. "The Rise of a Rural Middle Class in a Frontier Society." In *Brazil in the Sixties*, Riordan Roett (ed.) Nashville: Vanderbilt University Press.

Willems, Emilio, and Baldens, Herbert. 1942. "Cultural Change among Japanese Immigrants in Brazil." *Sociology and Social Research* 26, 6 (July/August): 525–37.

Williamson, Jeffrey. 1965. "Regional Inequalities and the Process of National Development." *Economic Development and Cultural Change* 13, 4, (July), part 2.

_____. 1974. "Migration to the New World: Long-Term Influences and Impact." *Explorations in Economic History* 2, 4 (Summer): 357–89.

World Bank. 1978. *Brazil: Human Resources Special Report. Annex I—Population.* (Processed.) Washington, D.C.: The World Bank.

Wright, Gavin. 1970. "Economic Democracy and the Concentration of Agricultural Wealth in the Cotton South 1850–1860." *Agricultural History* 44, 1 (January): 63–93.

_____. 1974. "Cotton Competition and the Postbellum Recovery of the American South." *Journal of Economic History* 34, 3 (September): 610–35.

Yap, Lorene. 1972. "Internal Migration and Economic Development in Brazil." Ph.D. dissertation, Harvard University.

_____. 1976. "Rural-Urban Migration and Urban Underemployment in Brazil." *Journal of Development Economics* 3: 227–43.

Yasuba, Yasukichi. 1962. *Birth Rates of the White Population in the United States, 1800–1860.* Baltimore: The Johns Hopkins University Press.

Yates, Paul Lamartine. 1959. *Forty Years of Foreign Trade,* London: Allen & Unwin, Ltd.

Yunes. João. 1975. "Mortalité." In CICRED, *La Population du Brésil,* pp. 46–64.

Yunes, João, and Ronchezel, Vera S. C. 1974. "Evoluçáo da Mortalidade Geral, Infantil e Proporcional no Brasil." *Revista de Saúde Pública* 8 (June Supplement): 3–48.

Index

382   INDEX

National Housing Bank. *See* Banco Nacional
  de Habitação
National Integration Program, 127
Nationalist sentiment, 1
National Survey of Household Expenditure,
  269
National urban policy, 212n
Natural increase, 29–30; differential patterns
  of, 5, 119, 197; high rate of, 1, 46, 48, 317–
  18; in the nineteenth century, 4; of non-
  slaves, 36; steady rate of, 39
Natural resources, 273; policies on, 22
Nelson, Joan M., 239n
Neo-Malthusianism, 1, 6, 251, 278, 314
Netto, A. Delfim, 1, 20, 81n, 285, 286
Nicholls, William H., 126
Nineteenth century, Brazil in the, 13–15
North (region of Brazil), definition of, 8
Northeast (region of Brazil), definition of, 8–
  9
Notorial registers, 52–53
Nutrition, 294, 330

O'Brien, F. S., 233, 332
Occupational structure, 5
Occupations: agricultural, 108; categories of
  for decomposition analysis, 183–84; clerical, 236; distribution of, 76; in the employ
  of the government, 228, 236, 242; industrial, 75–77, 110; mechanical, 74; non-
  agricultural, 74, 101, 108, 234–36, 288;
  nonmanufacturing, 101; rural, 51; service,
  227, 231; slave, 74. *See also specific occu-
  pations;* Labor force
Oeschli, Frank W., 252–53, 338
Ohio State University, xviii
Ohio State University, Department of Agricultural Economics and Rural Sociology,
  xviii
Oliveira, Francisco, 238n
Oliveira, Velloso de, 27
Oliveira Vianna, Francisco José, 25n, 26, 66
Output, growth of, 214
Ozório de Almeida, Anna Luiza, 177, 334
Ozório de Almeida, Miguel, 280

Paiva, Paulo, 167n, 182n
Paper industry, 17
Paraguay, 11
Paraguayan War, 15
Paraná river system, 8
Pastore, Affonso C., xviii
Paternity, surrogate, 53
Peattie, Lisa, 237
Pecht, Waldomiro, 307
Pedro I, 14
Pedro II, 15

Peláez, Carlos Manuel, 81n
Peláez, Cesar, 188, 191
Peliano, José Carlos, 220–23, 225, 229–30
Pereira, Luis Carlos Bresser, 115, 324
Perlman, Janice E., 239n
Peru, 45
Pescatello, Ann, 80n, 93n
Pesquisa e Planejamento Econômico, xviii
Pesquisa Nacional por Amostra de Domi-
  cílios (PNAD), 26, 165–68, 232–35, 239,
  288, 332
Petroleum, 20–22
Piece-rate arrangement, 114
Pill, contraceptive, 268
PIN. *See* National Integration Program
Pittinger, Donald B., 307
Planalto, 8
Plantation system, 2, 15, 51, 63, 68; labor
  needs of, 77; wages in, 82
Planters, Paulista, 60
PNAD. *See* Pesquisa Nacional por Amostra
  de Domicílios
Poppino, Rollie E., 8n, 11, 14–15, 17
População presente, 47n, 48n
População recensenda, 48n
População residente, 47n, 48n, 194
Population: "Brazilian model" of, 6; colored,
  50, 56, 64, 69; and development, 278–96;
  distribution of, 126, 196, 198; economically active, 150, 153, 158–59, 161; in
  1800, 26–30; estimates for 1770–1820,
  28; European, 29–30; foreign-born, 30,
  37, 93–94, 96, 109–15; free-colored, 52,
  59–60, 319; living conditions of rural, 82;
  males in, 104, 166; and migration, 280;
  projections for Brazil, 299–303, 311; redistribution of, 118–45, 280; regional differentials, 6, 326; size and composition,
  303–7; slave, 59; spatial distribution of, 4,
  118–21, 208, 278, 307–11; stable, 299,
  302, 312; rural-urban differentials, 6
Population, slave: in coffee regions, 67; distribution of, 66; reallocations of, 63–77
Population, urban, 9; growth of, 214; and
  industrial employment, 204–13; in Latin
  America and elsewhere, 186; limitations
  of data on, 191–92; trends in, 35, 191–204
Population and Development Review, xviii
Population control position, 252
Population growth: in Brazil and the United
  States, 31; by city size, 192–95; and education, 286–90; 1850–1970, 37; and employment, 286–90; by ethnic origin, 29;
  factors in various countries, 39; high rates
  of, 1, 15, 251, 278–79, 281; and immigration, 38; and income distribution, 282,
  290–94; nineteenth-century, 65; policy on,
  311; reduction of rate of, 2; slave, 50; total,